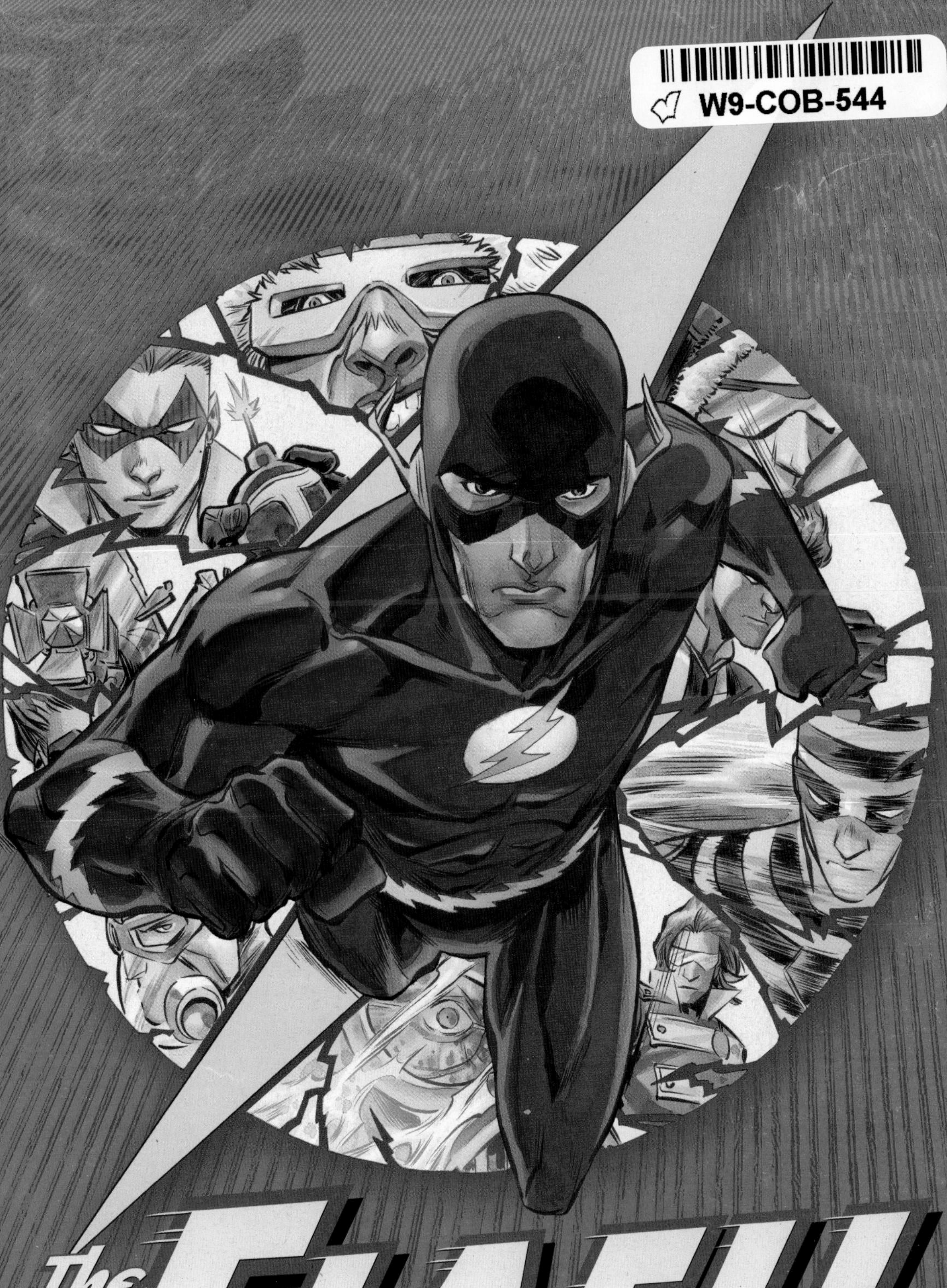

The FLASH

THE DASTARDLY DEATH OF THE ROGUES

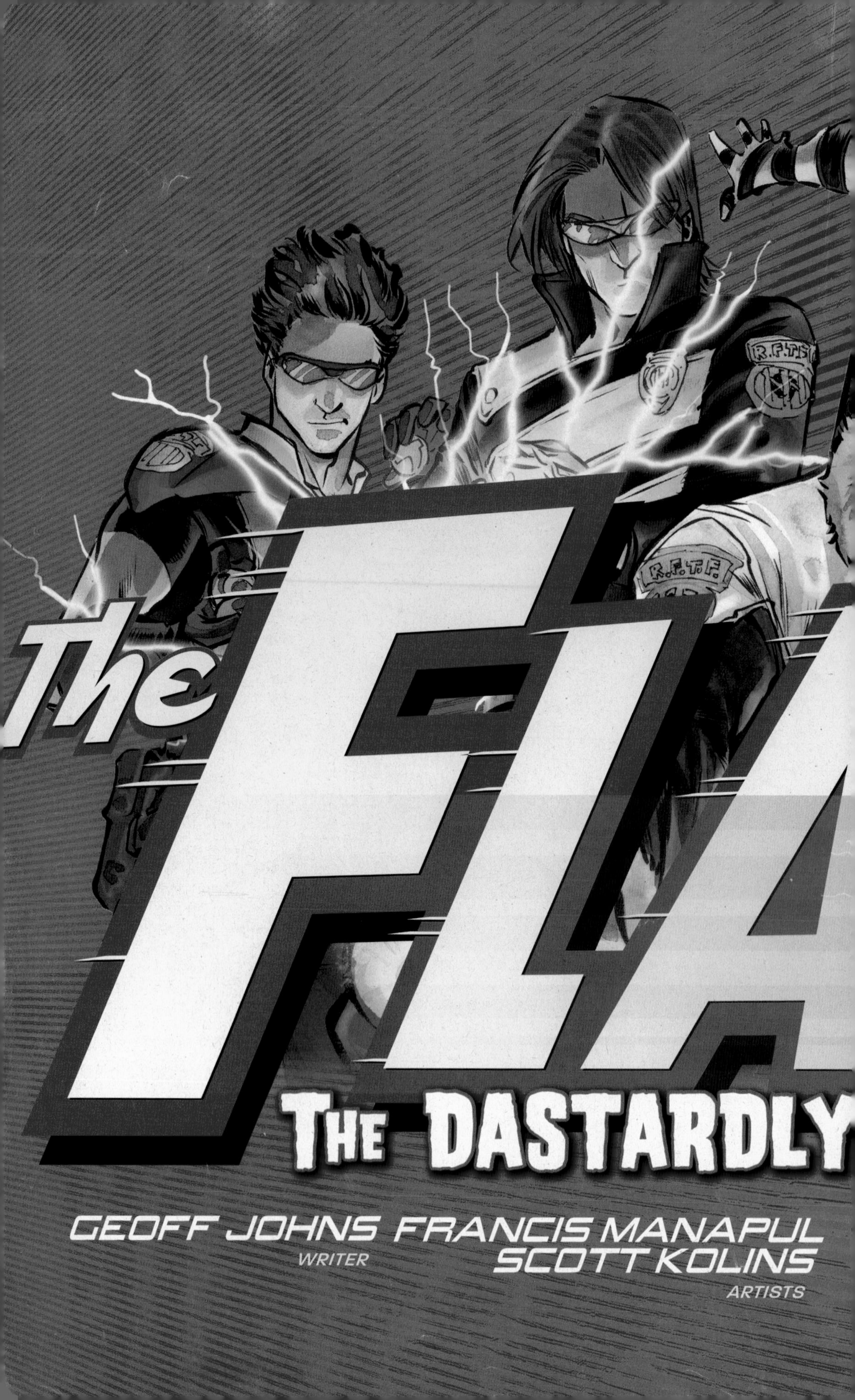
R.F.T.F.
R.F.T.F.
The
FLA
THE DASTARDLY
GEOFF JOHNS
WRITER
FRANCIS MANAPUL
SCOTT KOLINS
ARTISTS

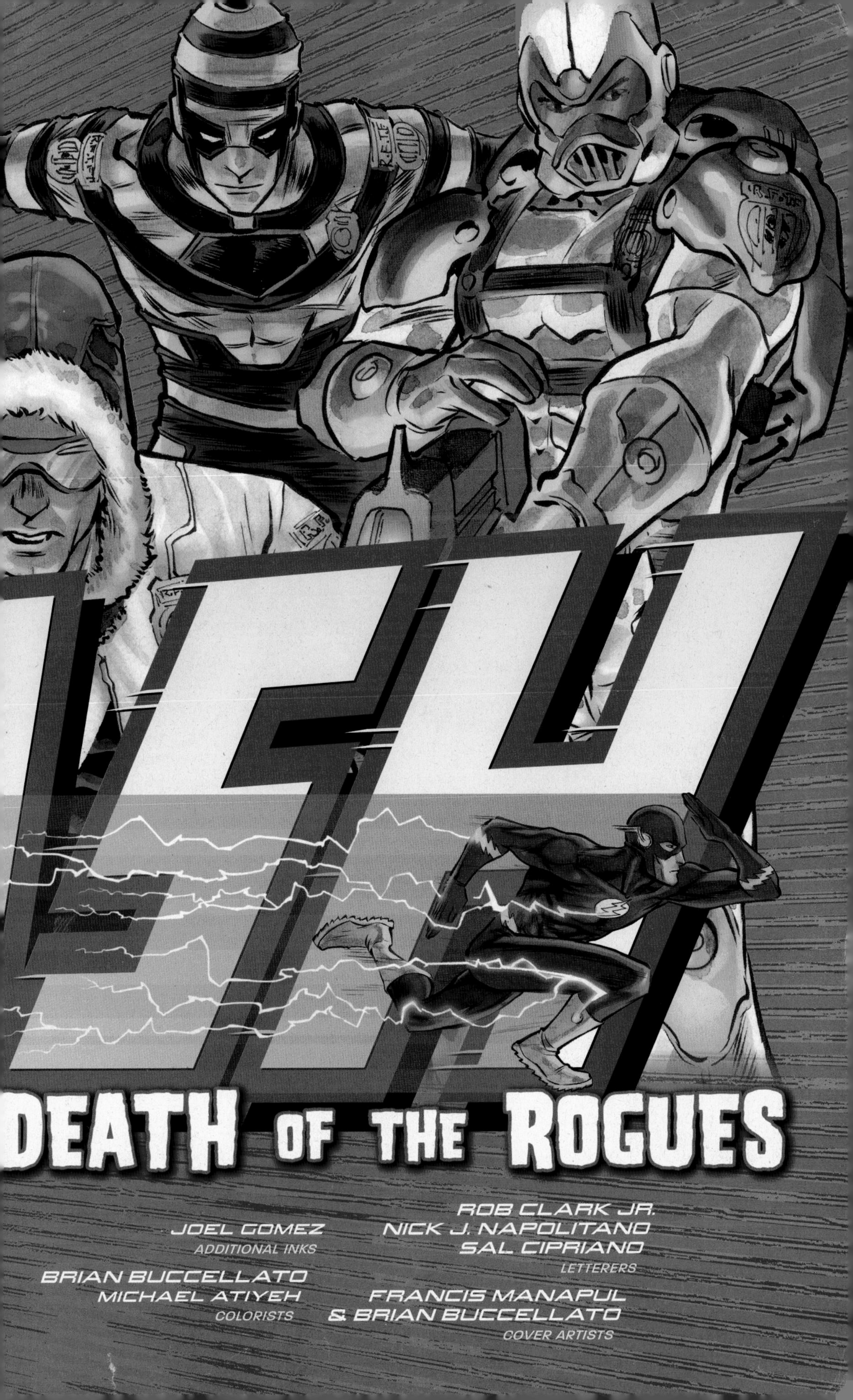

DEATH OF THE ROGUES

JOEL GOMEZ
ADDITIONAL INKS

BRIAN BUCCELLATO
MICHAEL ATIYEH
COLORISTS

ROB CLARK JR.
NICK J. NAPOLITANO
SAL CIPRIANO
LETTERERS

FRANCIS MANAPUL
& BRIAN BUCCELLATO
COVER ARTISTS

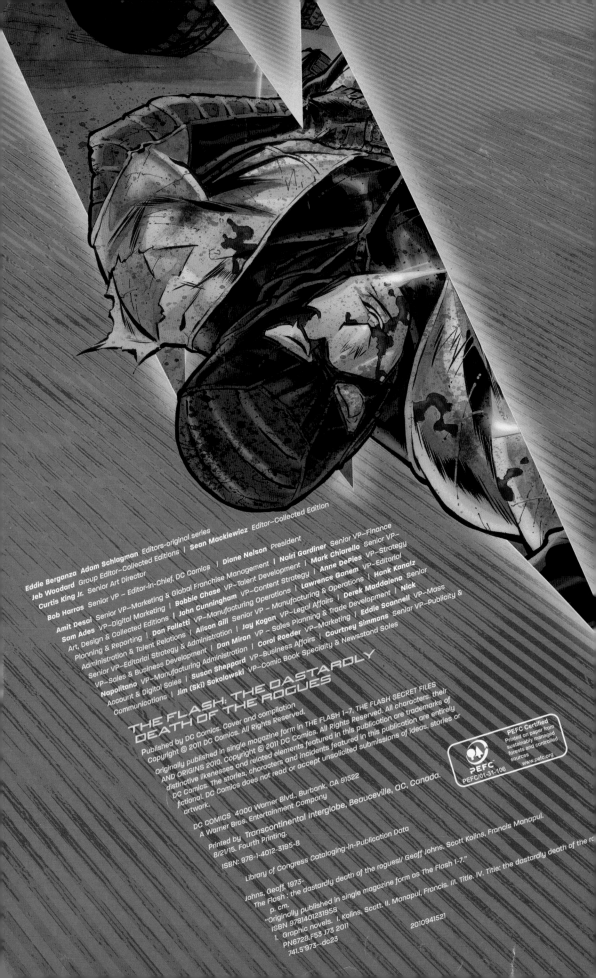

Eddie Berganza Adam Schlagman Editors-original series
Jeb Woodard Group Editor–Collected Editions | Sean Mackiewicz Editor–Collected Edition
Curtis King Jr. Senior Art Director
Bob Harras Senior VP – Editor-In-Chief, DC Comics | Diane Nelson President
Amit Desai Senior VP–Marketing & Global Franchise Management | Nairi Gardiner Senior VP–Finance
Sam Ades VP–Digital Marketing | Bobbie Chase VP–Talent Development | Mark Chiarello Senior VP–
Art, Design & Collected Editions | John Cunningham VP–Content Strategy | Anne DePies VP–Strategy
Planning & Reporting | Don Falletti VP–Manufacturing Operations | Lawrence Ganem VP–Editorial
Administration & Talent Relations | Alison Gill Senior VP – Manufacturing & Operations | Hank Kanalz Senior
VP–Editorial Strategy & Administration | Dan Miron VP – Sales Planning & Trade Development | Nick
Napolitano VP–Manufacturing Administration | Carol Roeder VP–Marketing | Eddie Scannell VP–Mass
Account & Digital Sales | Susan Sheppard VP–Business Affairs | Courtney Simmons Senior VP–Publicity &
Communications | Jim (Ski) Sokolowski VP–Comic Book Specialty & Newsstand Sales

THE FLASH: THE DASTAROLY
DEATH OF THE ROGUES

Published by DC Comics. Cover and compilation
Copyright © 2011 DC Comics. All Rights Reserved.

Originally published in single magazine form in THE FLASH 1–7, THE FLASH SECRET FILES
AND ORIGINS 2010. Copyright © 2011 DC Comics. All Rights Reserved. All characters, their
distinctive likenesses and related elements featured in this publication are trademarks of
DC Comics. The stories, characters and incidents featured in this publication are entirely
fictional. DC Comics does not read or accept unsolicited submissions of ideas, stories or
artwork.

DC COMICS 4000 Warner Blvd., Burbank, CA 91522
A Warner Bros. Entertainment Company
Printed by Transcontinental Interglobe, Beauceville, QC, Canada.
8/21/15. Fourth Printing.
ISBN: 978-1-4012-3195-8

Library of Congress Cataloging-in-Publication Data

Johns, Geoff, 1973-
  The Flash : the dastardly death of the rogues/ Geoff Johns, Scott Kolins, Francis Manapul.
    p. cm.
  "Originally published in single magazine form as The Flash 1-7."
  ISBN 9781401231958
  1. Graphic novels. I. Kolins, Scott. II. Manapul, Francis. III. Title. IV. Title: the dastardly death of the ro
PN6728.F53 J73 2011
741.5'973--dc23   2010941521

THE FLASH 1

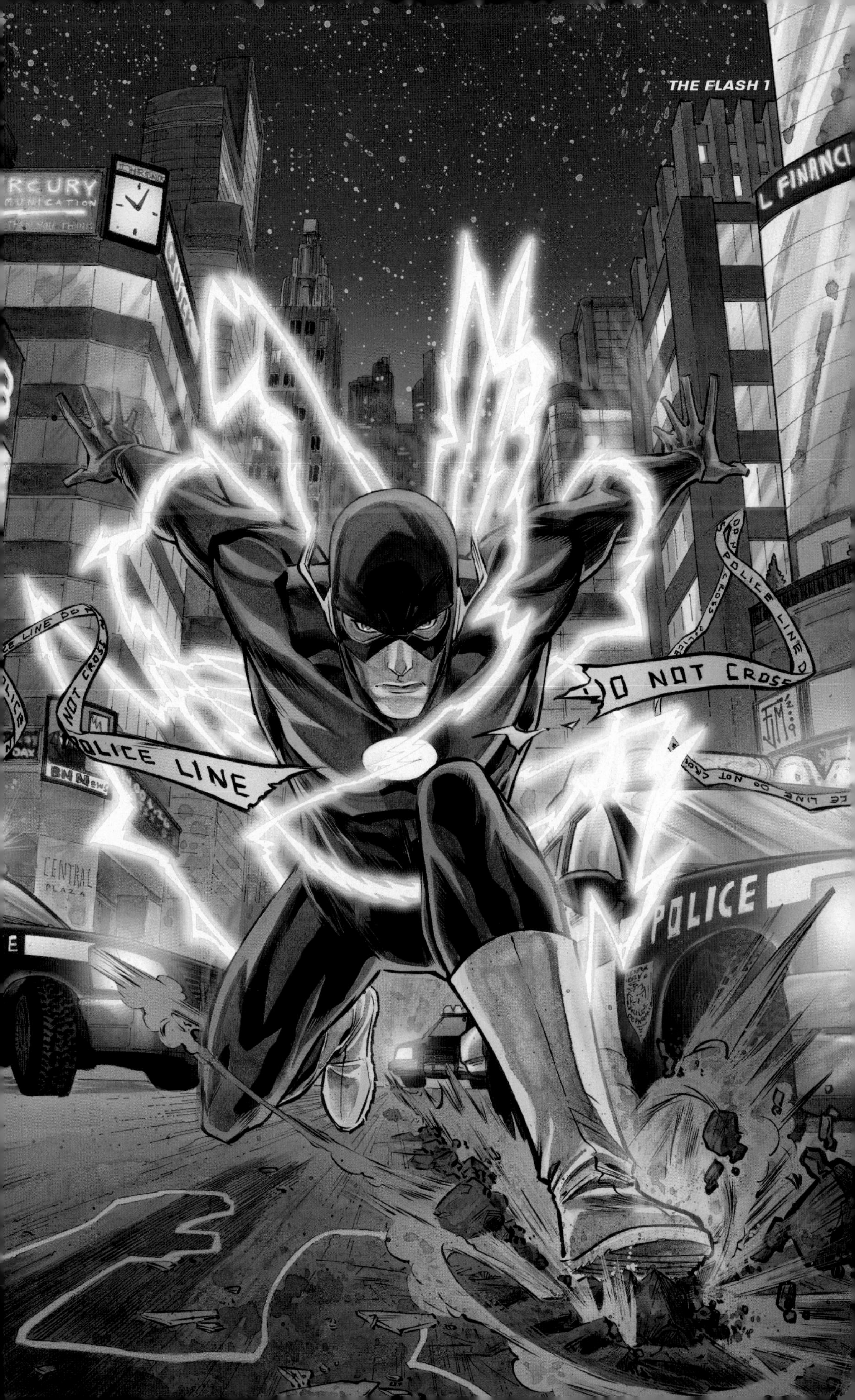
RCURY
MUNICATION
L FINANCI
POLICE LINE
DO NOT CROSS
POLICE LINE
DO NOT CROSS
CENTRAL
PLAZA
POLICE

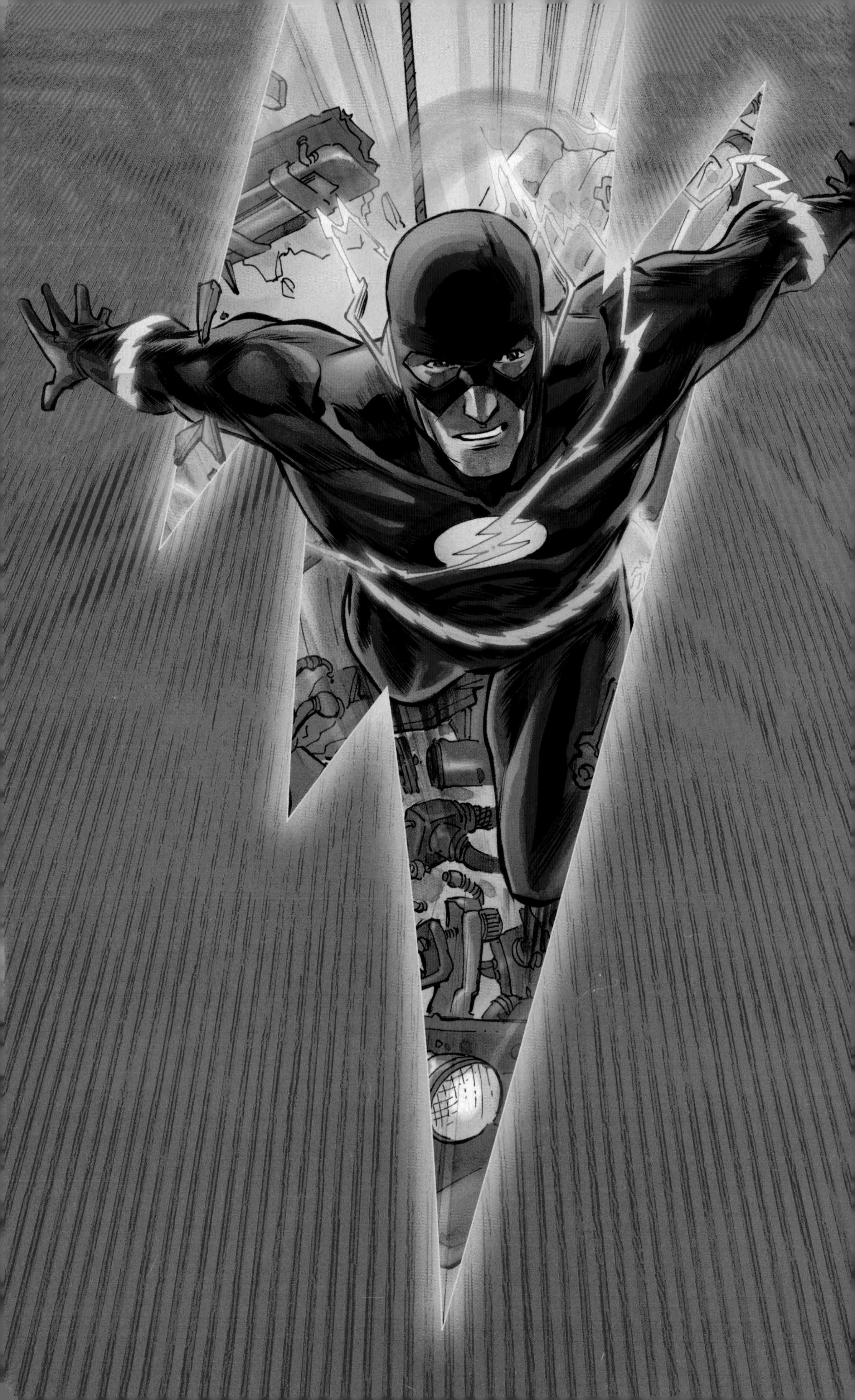

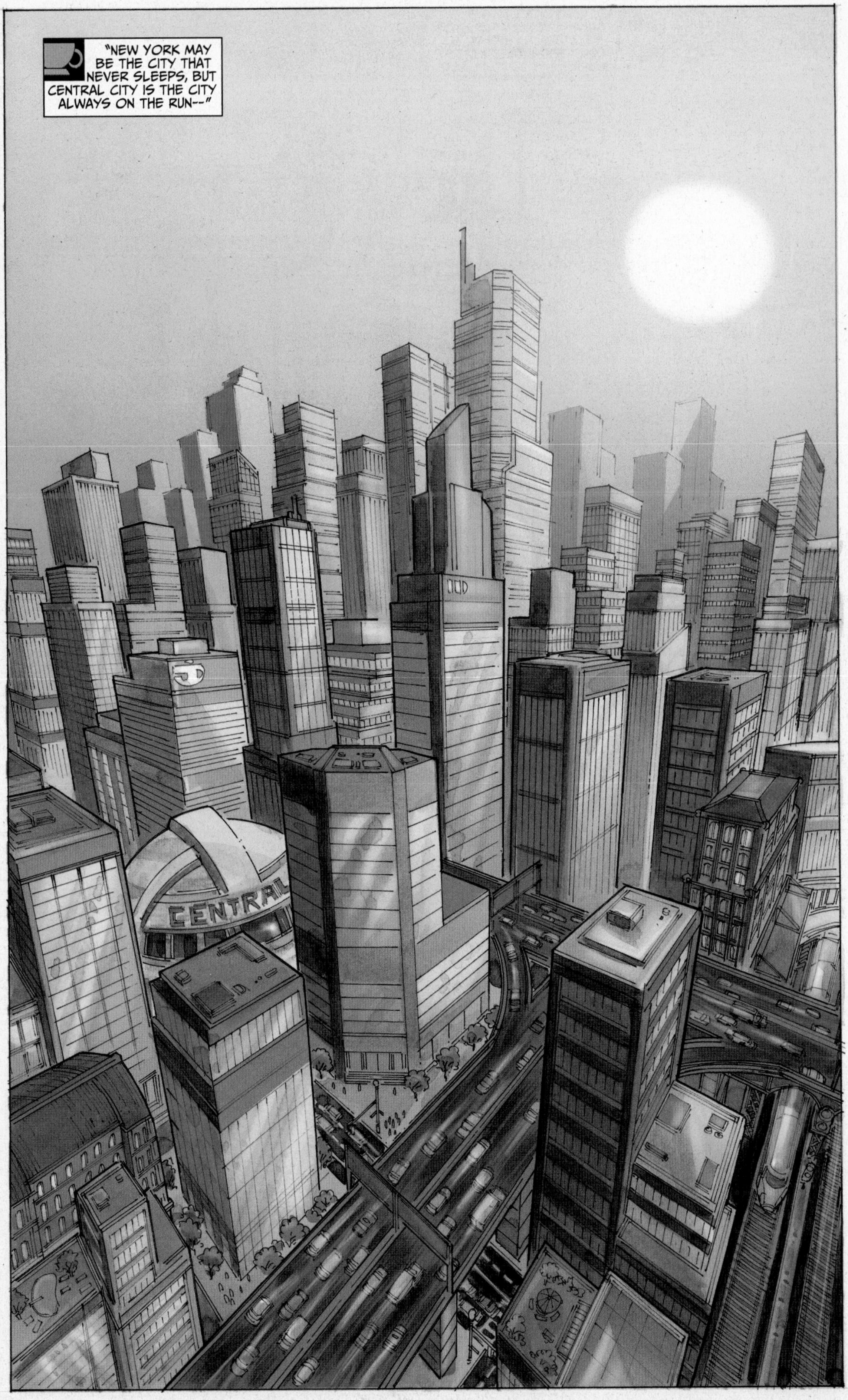
"NEW YORK MAY BE THE CITY THAT NEVER SLEEPS, BUT CENTRAL CITY IS THE CITY ALWAYS ON THE RUN--"
CENTRAL

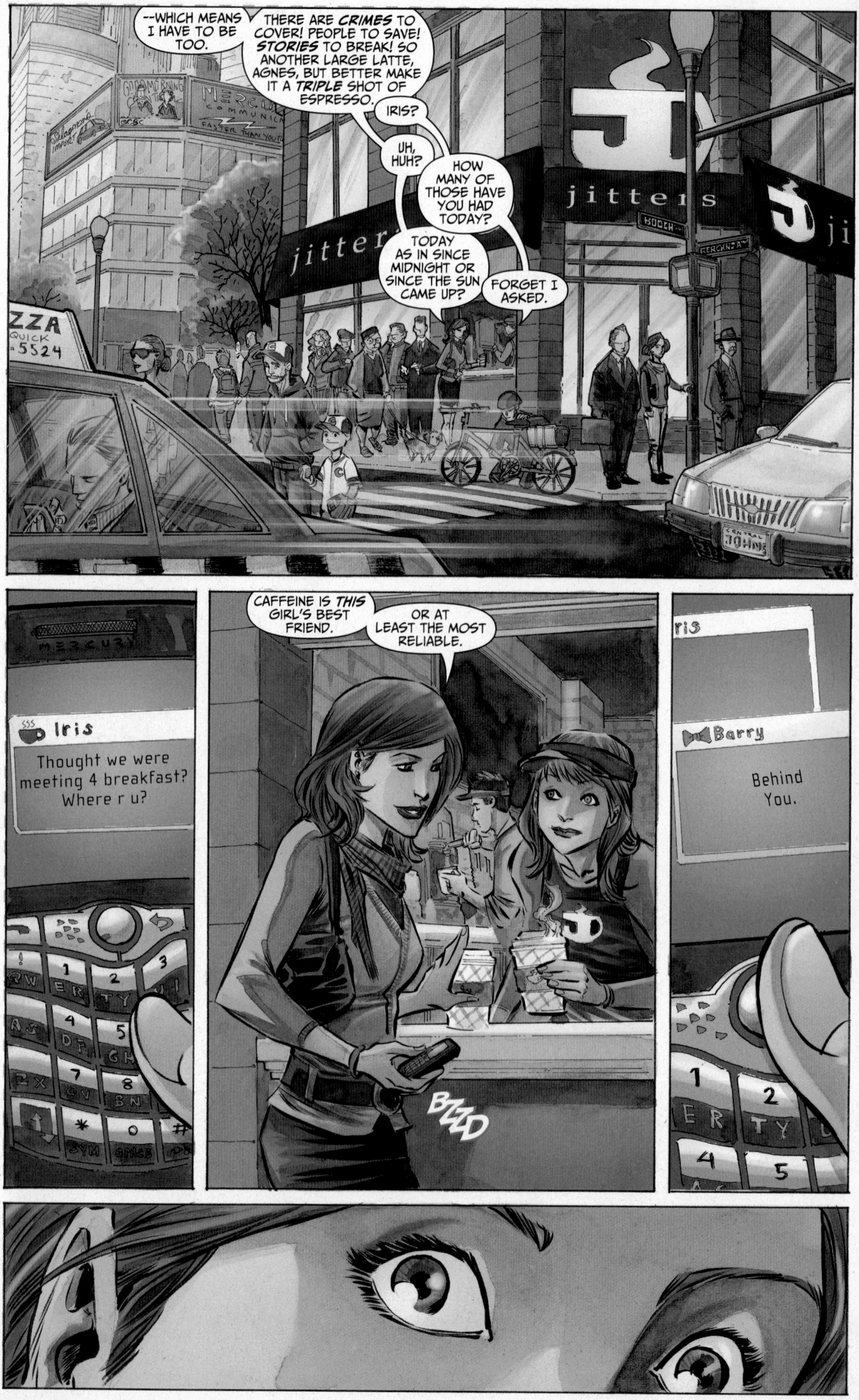

--WHICH MEANS I HAVE TO BE TOO.
THERE ARE CRIMES TO COVER! PEOPLE TO SAVE! STORIES TO BREAK! SO ANOTHER LARGE LATTE, AGNES, BUT BETTER MAKE IT A TRIPLE SHOT OF ESPRESSO.
IRIS?
UH, HUH?
HOW MANY OF THOSE HAVE YOU HAD TODAY?
TODAY AS IN SINCE MIDNIGHT OR SINCE THE SUN CAME UP?
FORGET I ASKED.
jitters
Iris
Thought we were meeting 4 breakfast? Where r u?
CAFFEINE IS THIS GIRL'S BEST FRIEND.
OR AT LEAST THE MOST RELIABLE.
BZZZD
Iris
Barry
Behind You.

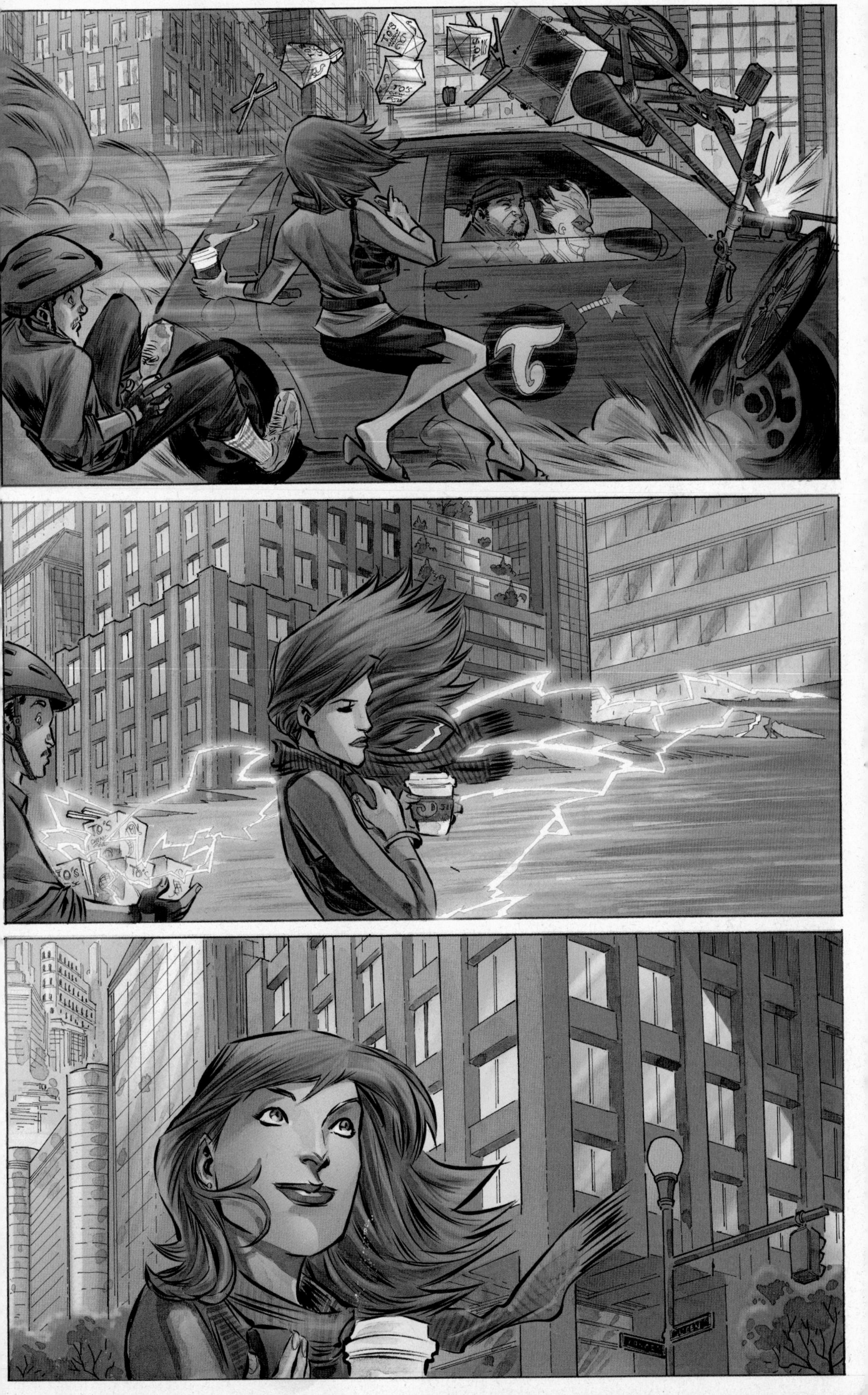

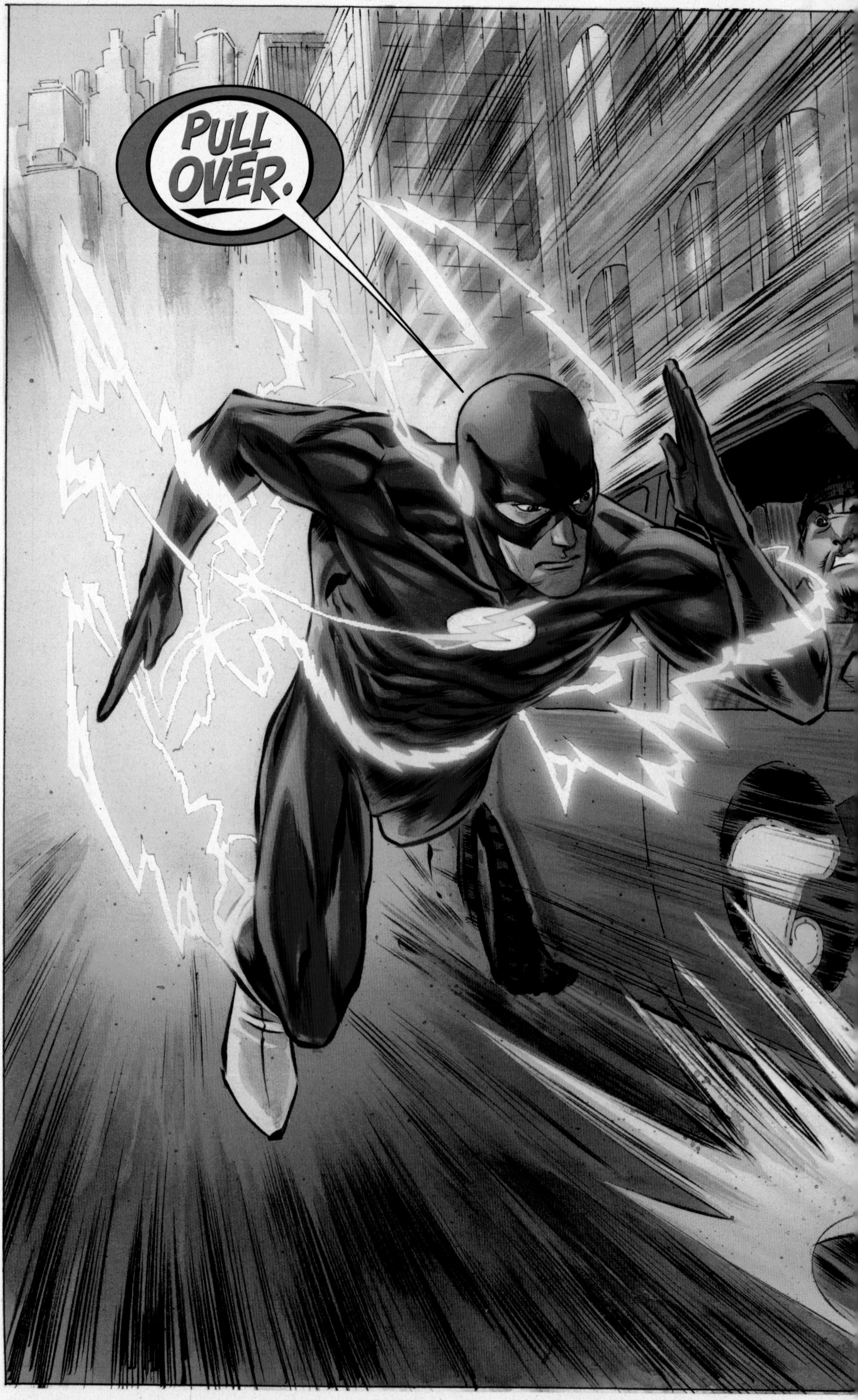
PULL OVER.

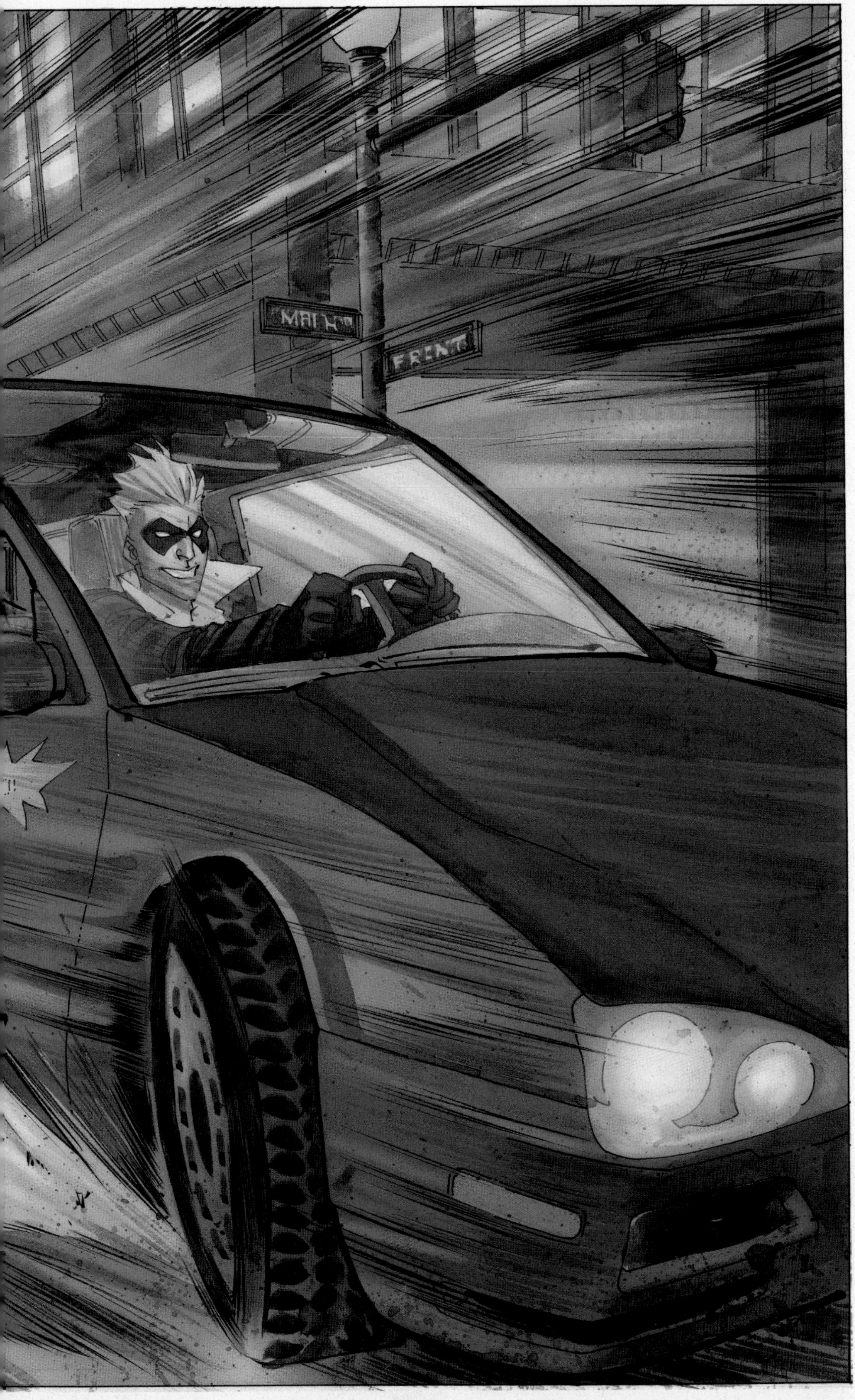
MAIN
FRONT

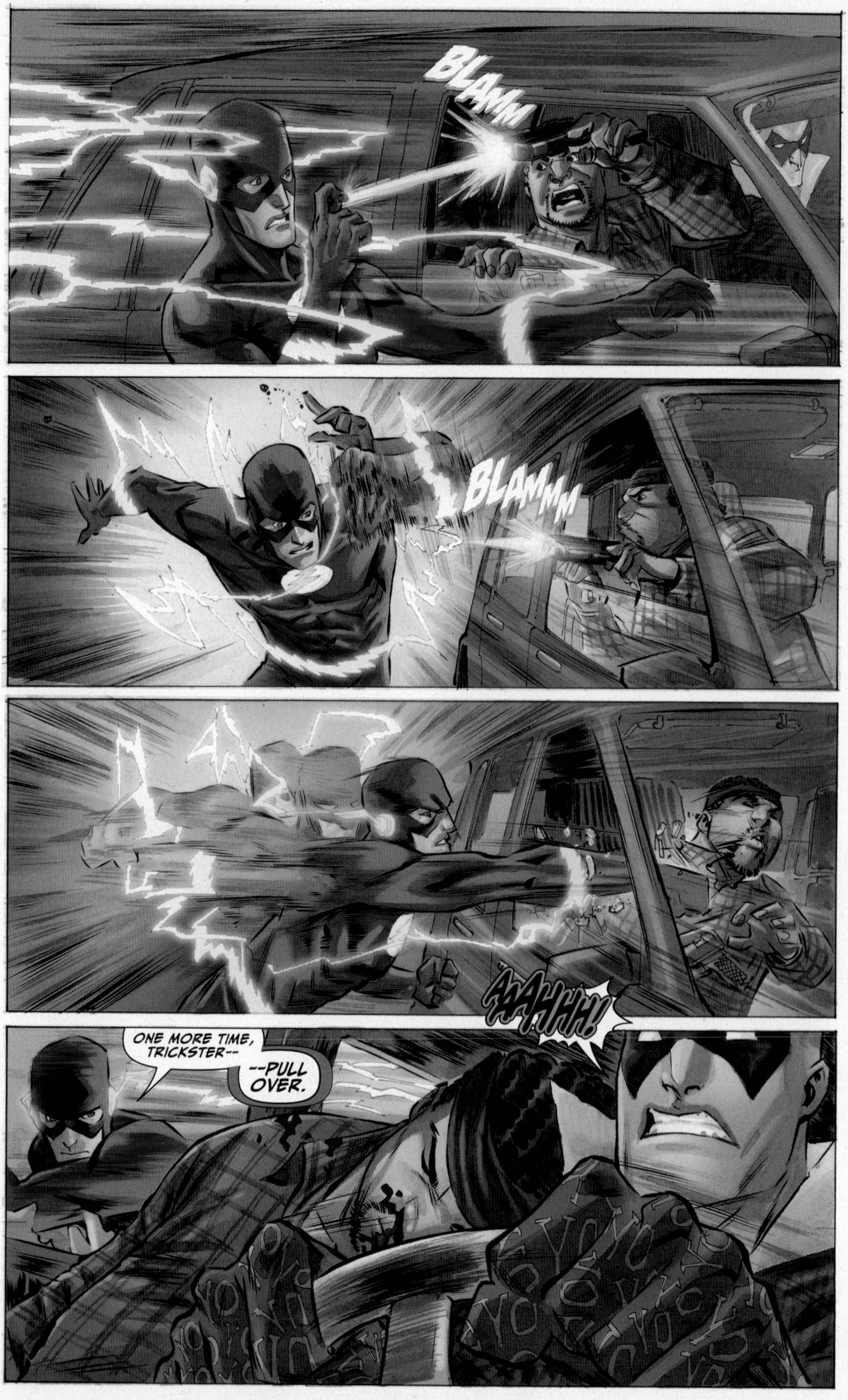
BLAMM
BLAMMM
AAAHHH!
ONE MORE TIME, TRICKSTER--
--PULL OVER.

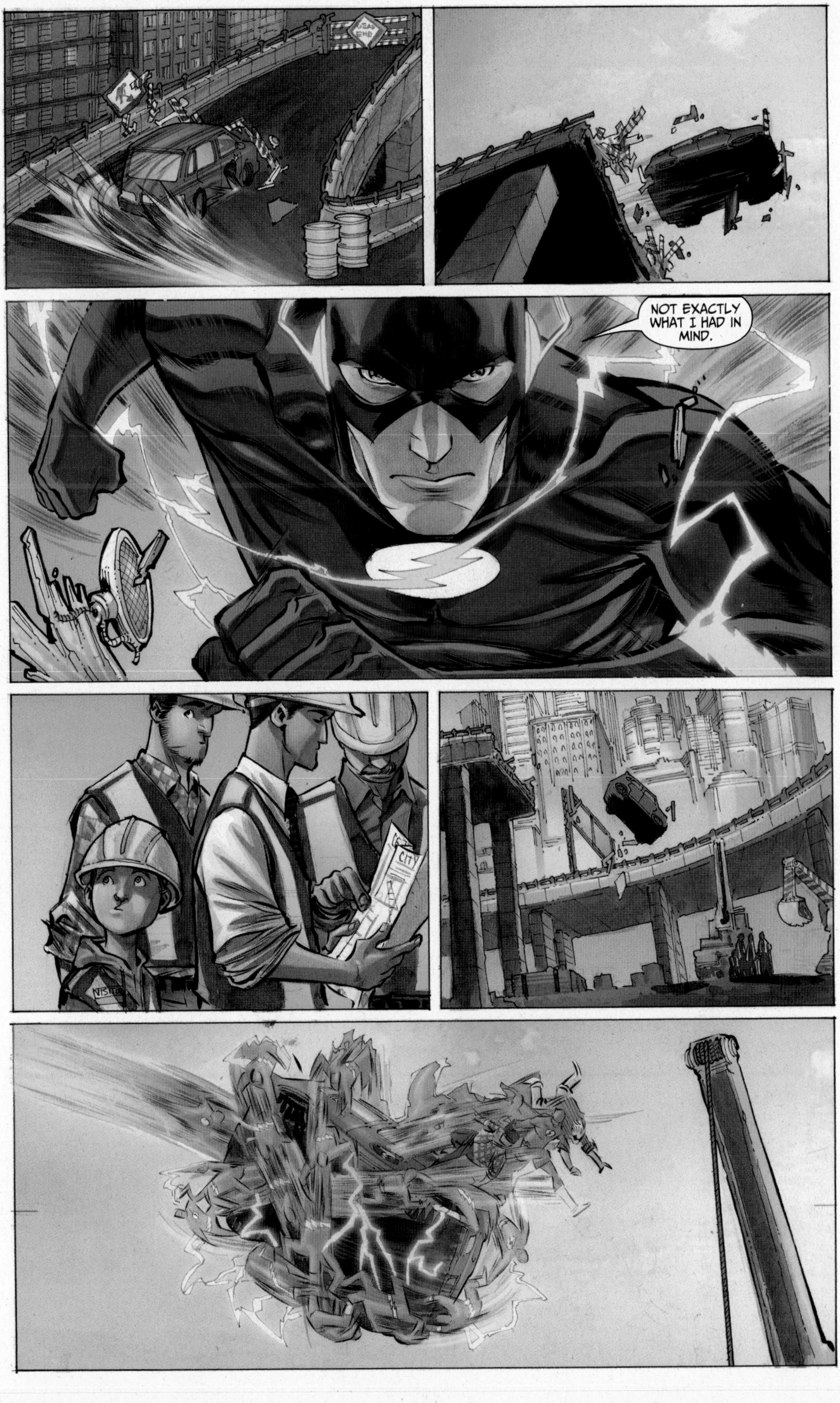
NOT EXACTLY WHAT I HAD IN MIND.

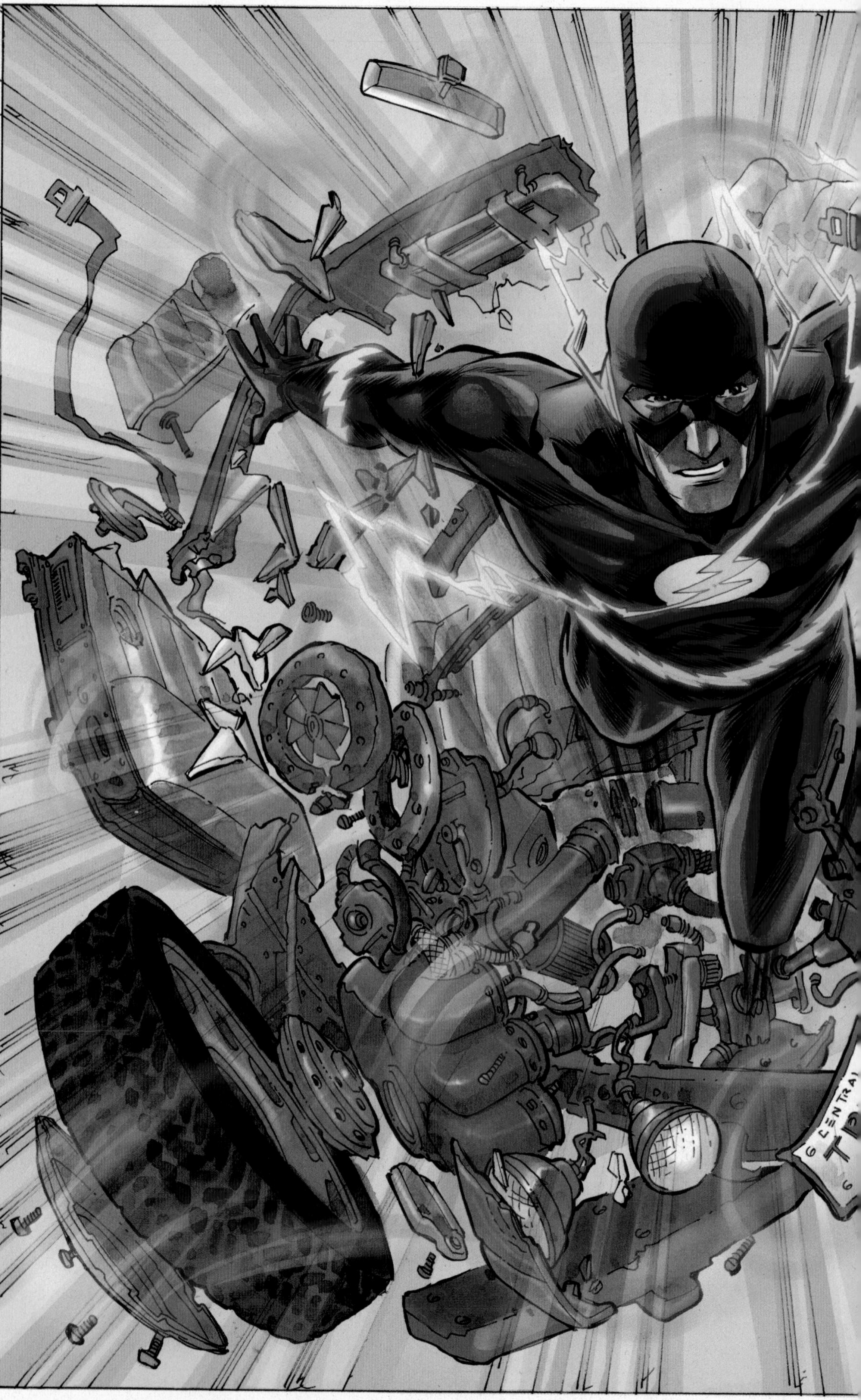

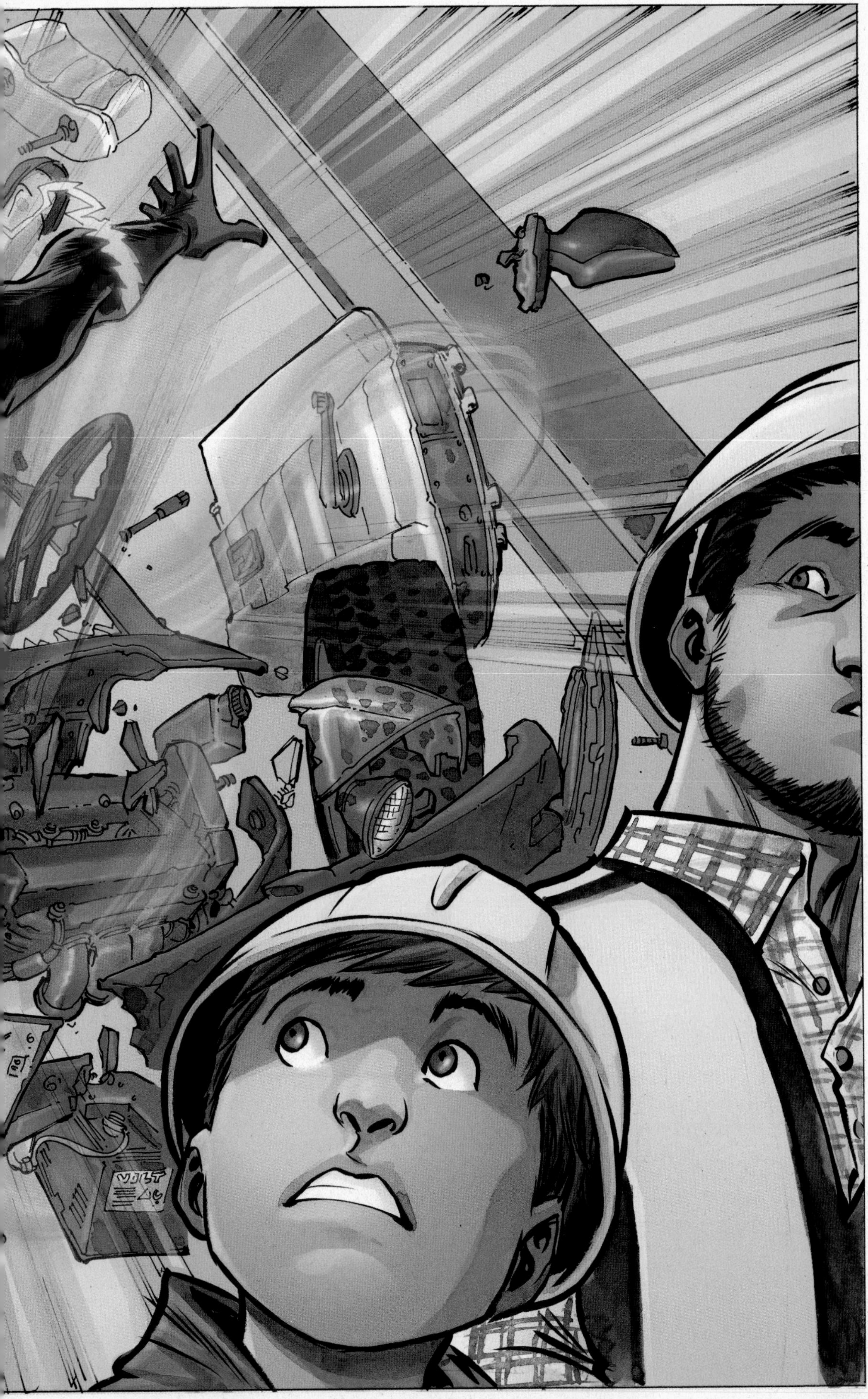

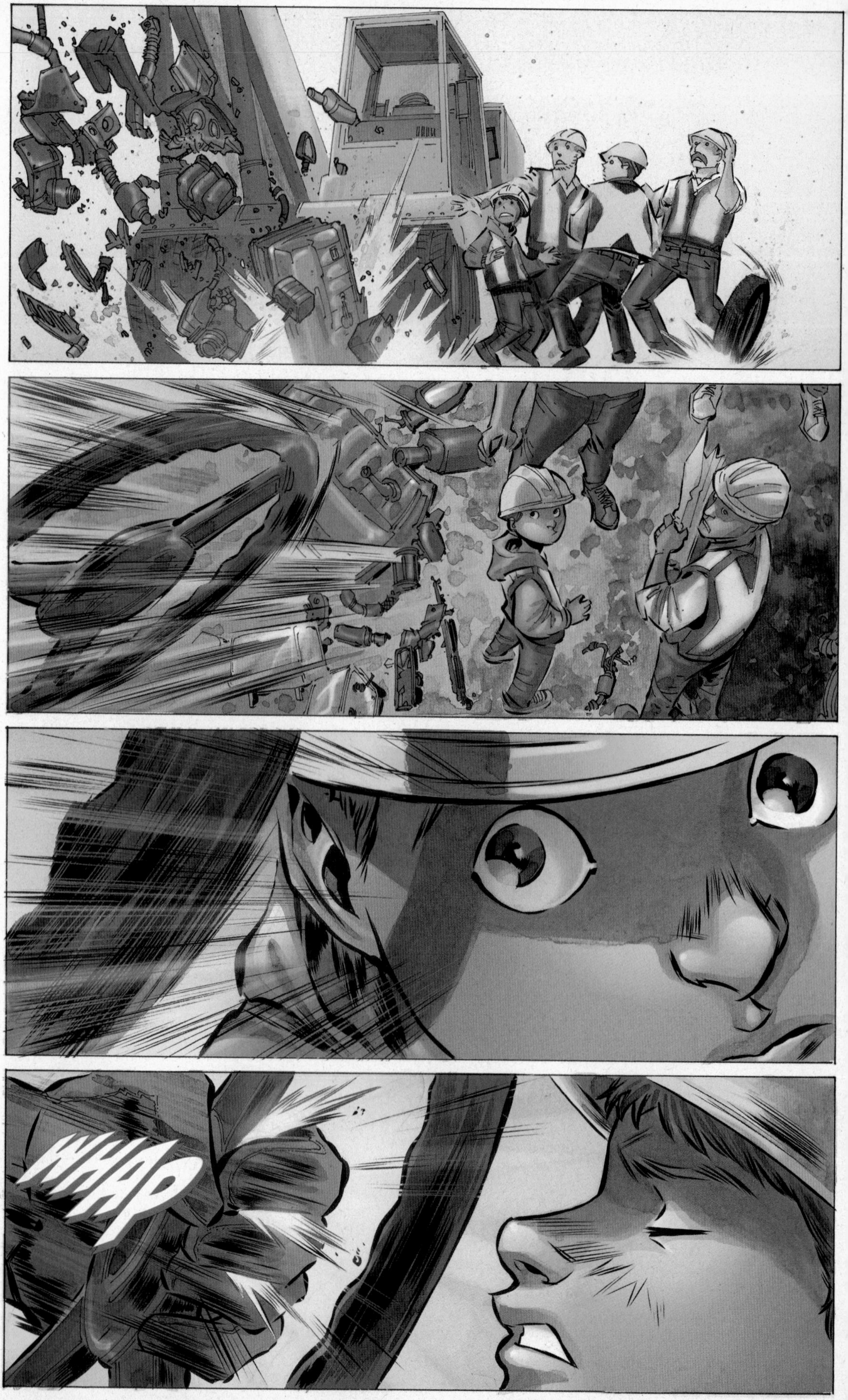
WHAP

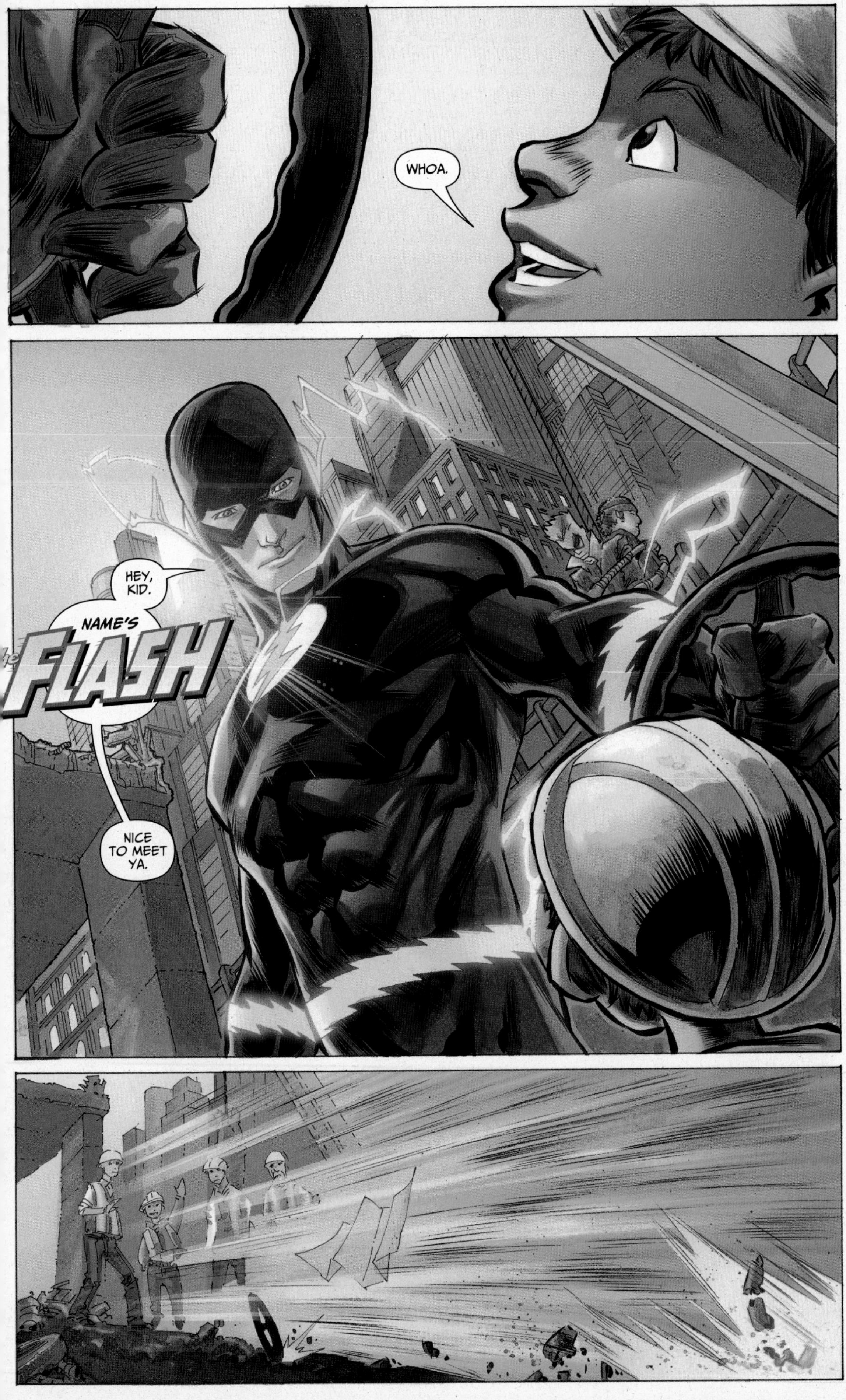
WHOA.
HEY, KID.
NAME'S
FLASH
NICE TO MEET YA.

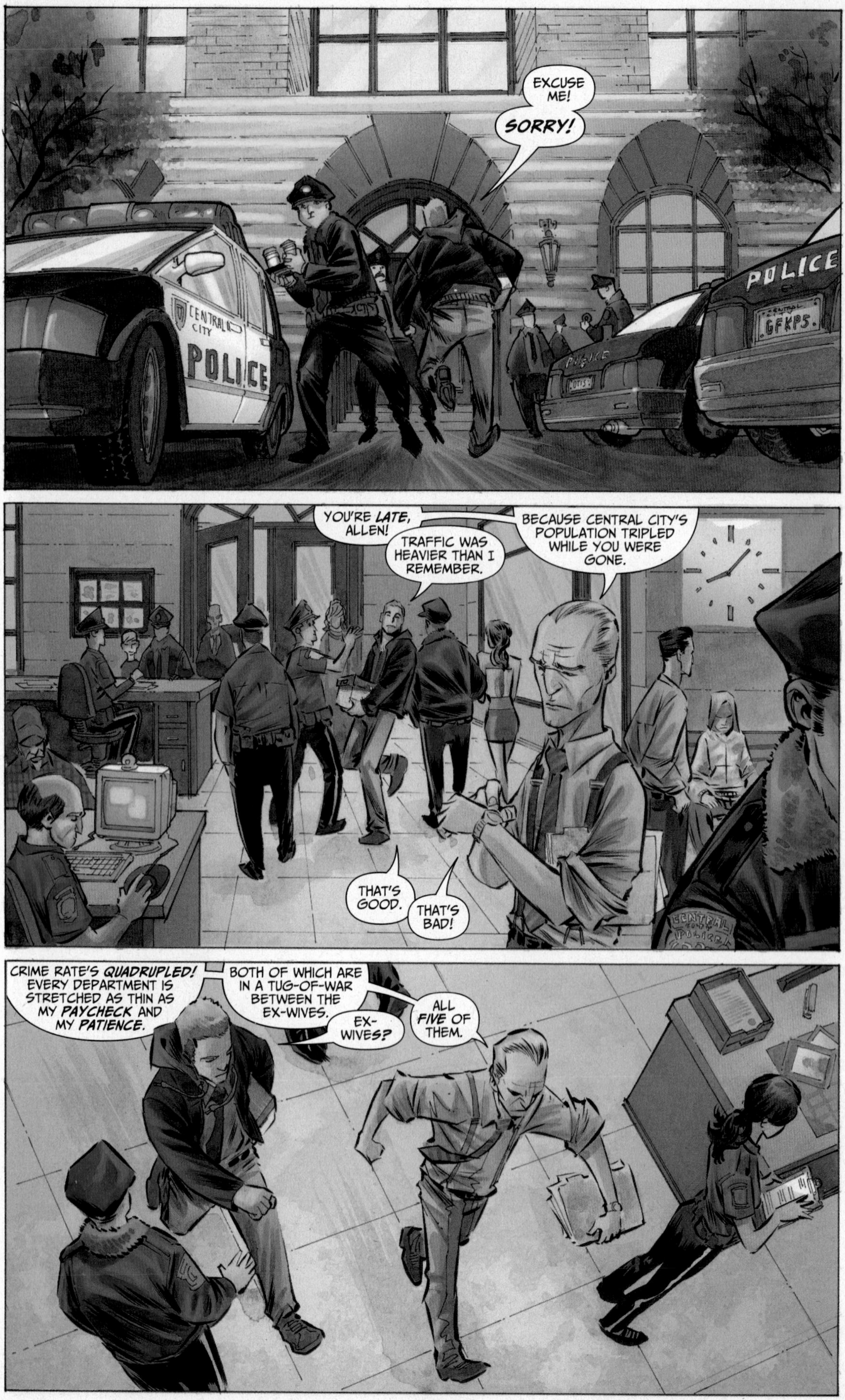

EXCUSE ME!
SORRY!
CENTRAL CITY
POLICE
POLICE
POLICE
GFKP5
YOU'RE LATE, ALLEN!
TRAFFIC WAS HEAVIER THAN I REMEMBER.
BECAUSE CENTRAL CITY'S POPULATION TRIPLED WHILE YOU WERE GONE.
THAT'S GOOD.
THAT'S BAD!
CRIME RATE'S QUADRUPLED! EVERY DEPARTMENT IS STRETCHED AS THIN AS MY PAYCHECK AND MY PATIENCE.
EX-WIVES?
BOTH OF WHICH ARE IN A TUG-OF-WAR BETWEEN THE EX-WIVES.
ALL FIVE OF THEM.

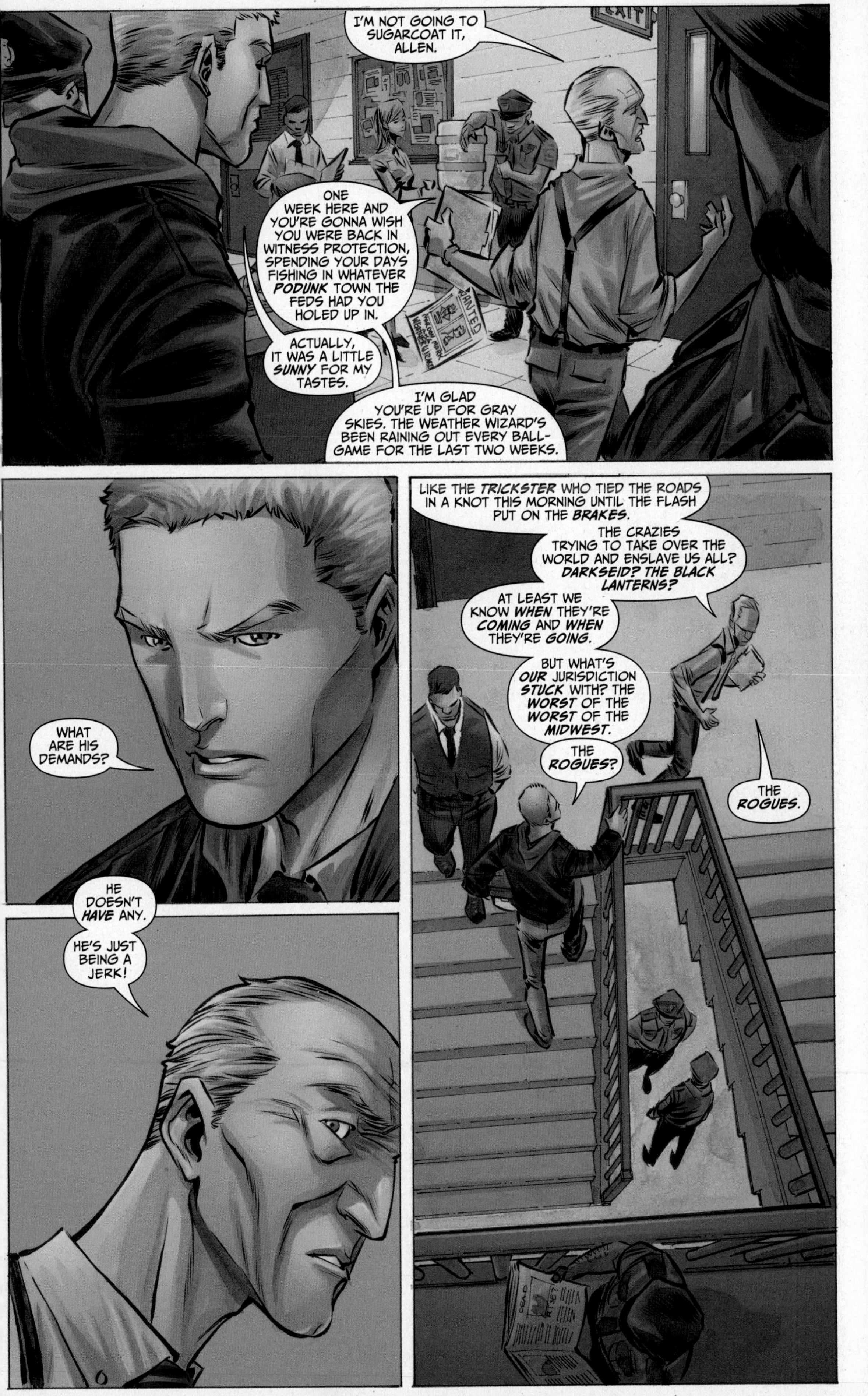
I'M NOT GOING TO SUGARCOAT IT, ALLEN.
ONE WEEK HERE AND YOU'RE GONNA WISH YOU WERE BACK IN WITNESS PROTECTION, SPENDING YOUR DAYS FISHING IN WHATEVER PODUNK TOWN THE FEDS HAD YOU HOLED UP IN.
ACTUALLY, IT WAS A LITTLE SUNNY FOR MY TASTES.
I'M GLAD YOU'RE UP FOR GRAY SKIES. THE WEATHER WIZARD'S BEEN RAINING OUT EVERY BALL-GAME FOR THE LAST TWO WEEKS.
WHAT ARE HIS DEMANDS?
HE DOESN'T HAVE ANY.
HE'S JUST BEING A JERK!
LIKE THE TRICKSTER WHO TIED THE ROADS IN A KNOT THIS MORNING UNTIL THE FLASH PUT ON THE BRAKES.
THE CRAZIES TRYING TO TAKE OVER THE WORLD AND ENSLAVE US ALL? DARKSEID? THE BLACK LANTERNS?
AT LEAST WE KNOW WHEN THEY'RE COMING AND WHEN THEY'RE GOING.
BUT WHAT'S OUR JURISDICTION STUCK WITH? THE WORST OF THE WORST OF THE MIDWEST.
THE ROGUES?
THE ROGUES.

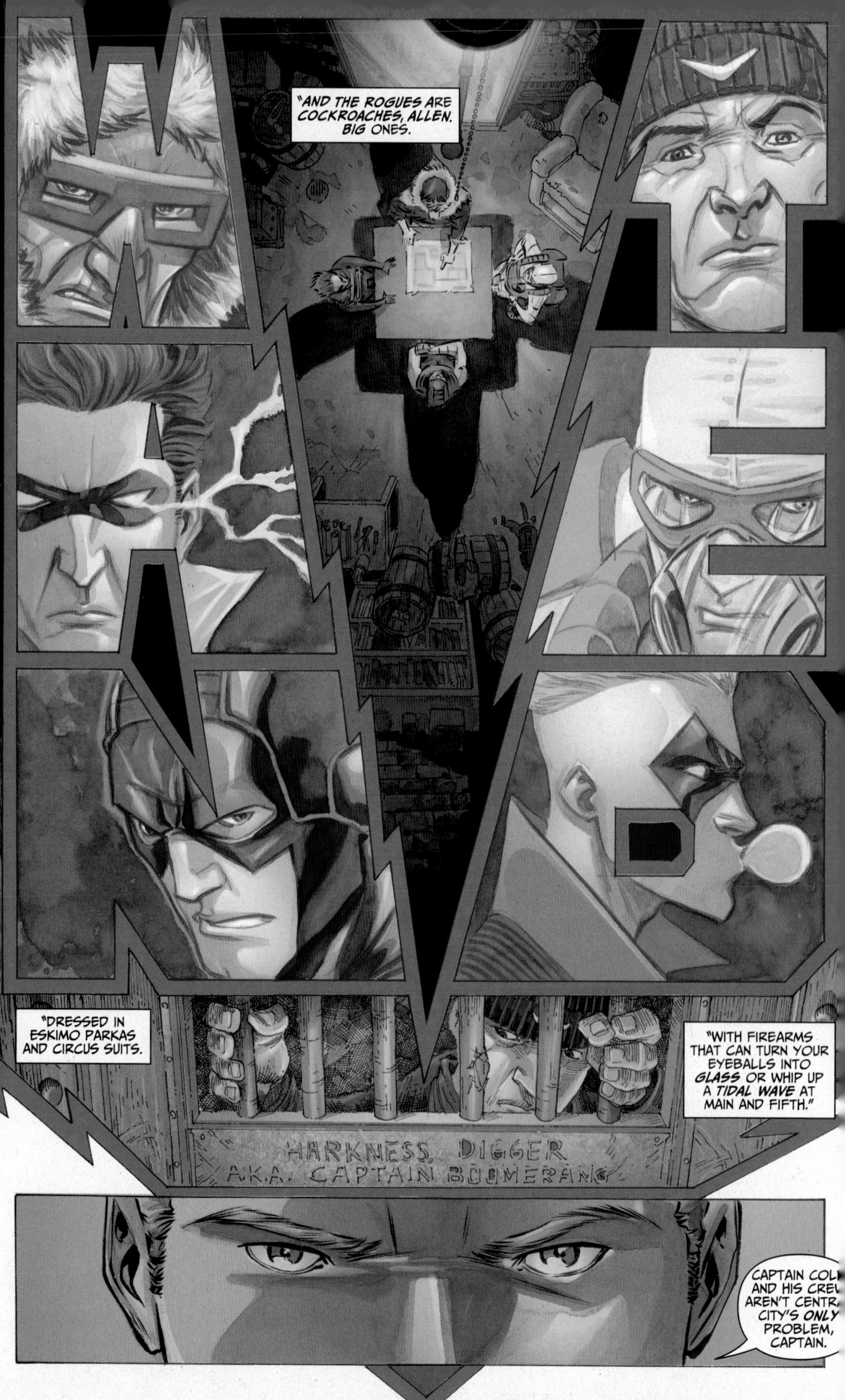
"AND THE ROGUES ARE COCKROACHES, ALLEN. BIG ONES.
"DRESSED IN ESKIMO PARKAS AND CIRCUS SUITS.
"WITH FIREARMS THAT CAN TURN YOUR EYEBALLS INTO GLASS OR WHIP UP A TIDAL WAVE AT MAIN AND FIFTH."
HARKNESS, DIGGER
A.K.A. CAPTAIN BOOMERANG
CAPTAIN COL AND HIS CREW AREN'T CENTR CITY'S ONLY PROBLEM, CAPTAIN.

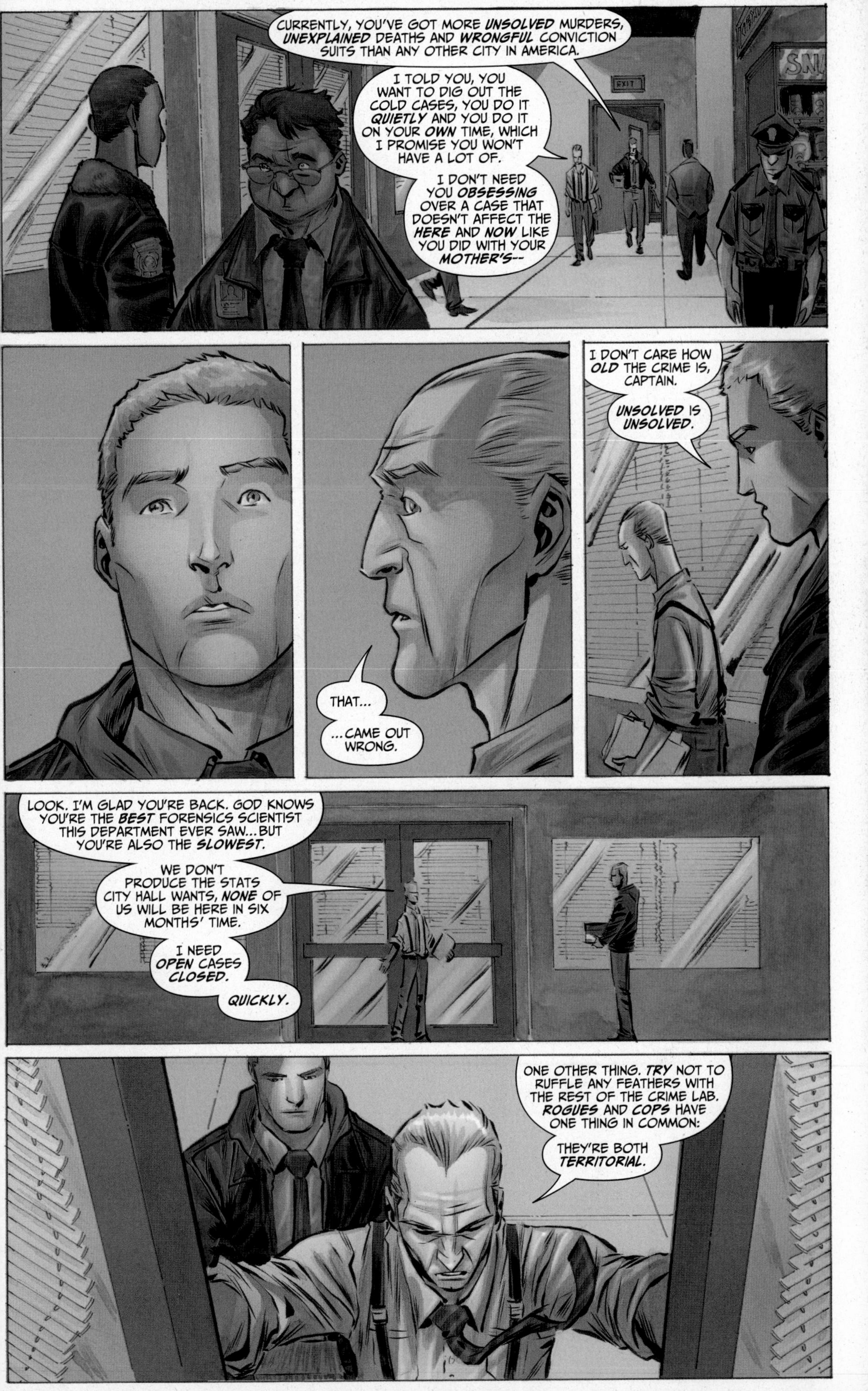
CURRENTLY, YOU'VE GOT MORE UNSOLVED MURDERS, UNEXPLAINED DEATHS AND WRONGFUL CONVICTION SUITS THAN ANY OTHER CITY IN AMERICA.
I TOLD YOU, YOU WANT TO DIG OUT THE COLD CASES, YOU DO IT QUIETLY AND YOU DO IT ON YOUR OWN TIME, WHICH I PROMISE YOU WON'T HAVE A LOT OF.
I DON'T NEED YOU OBSESSING OVER A CASE THAT DOESN'T AFFECT THE HERE AND NOW LIKE YOU DID WITH YOUR MOTHER'S--
THAT...
...CAME OUT WRONG.
I DON'T CARE HOW OLD THE CRIME IS, CAPTAIN.
UNSOLVED IS UNSOLVED.
LOOK. I'M GLAD YOU'RE BACK. GOD KNOWS YOU'RE THE BEST FORENSICS SCIENTIST THIS DEPARTMENT EVER SAW...BUT YOU'RE ALSO THE SLOWEST.
WE DON'T PRODUCE THE STATS CITY HALL WANTS, NONE OF US WILL BE HERE IN SIX MONTHS' TIME.
I NEED OPEN CASES CLOSED.
QUICKLY.
ONE OTHER THING. TRY NOT TO RUFFLE ANY FEATHERS WITH THE REST OF THE CRIME LAB. ROGUES AND COPS HAVE ONE THING IN COMMON:
THEY'RE BOTH TERRITORIAL.

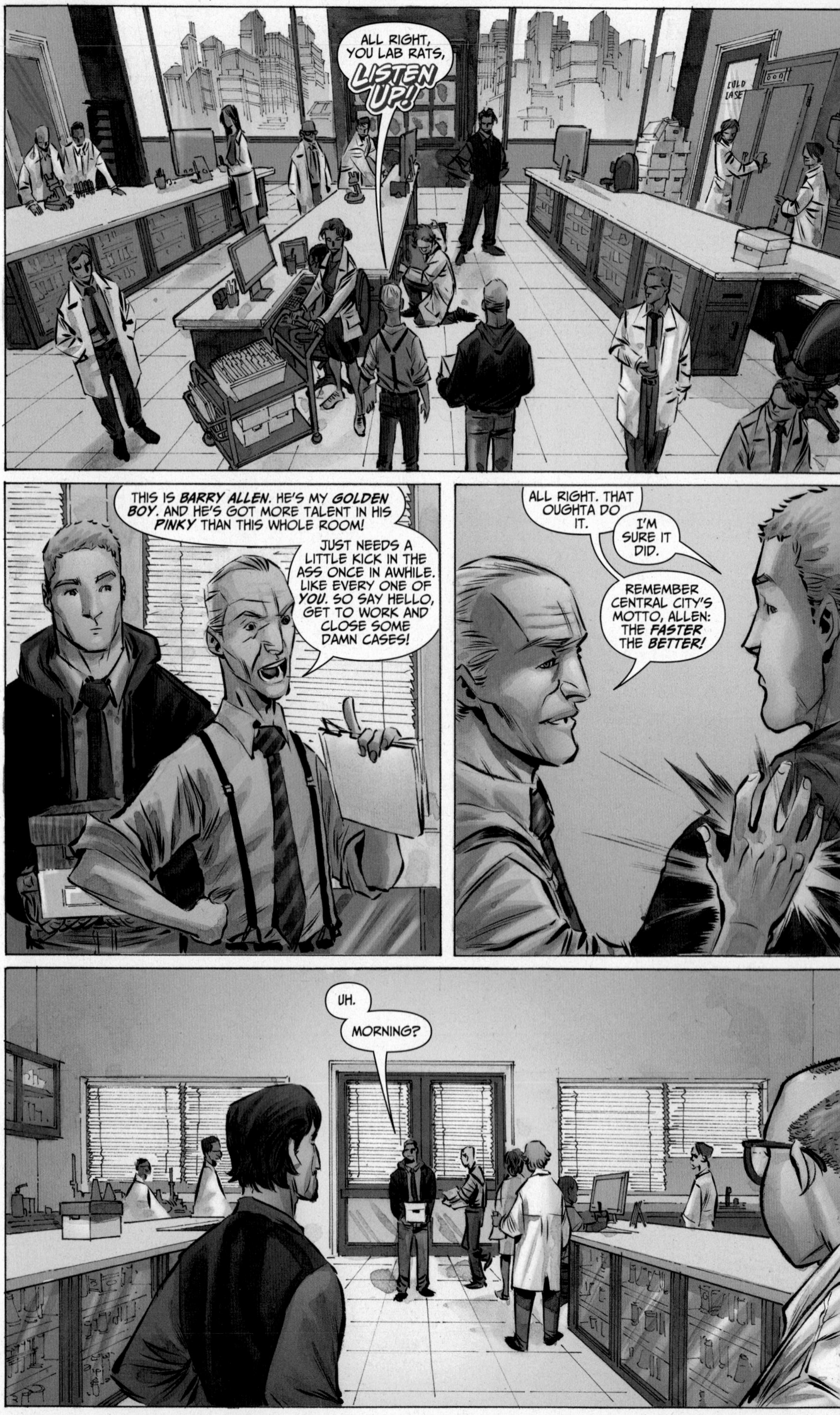
ALL RIGHT, YOU LAB RATS, LISTEN UP!
COLD CASE
THIS IS BARRY ALLEN. HE'S MY GOLDEN BOY. AND HE'S GOT MORE TALENT IN HIS PINKY THAN THIS WHOLE ROOM!
JUST NEEDS A LITTLE KICK IN THE ASS ONCE IN AWHILE. LIKE EVERY ONE OF YOU. SO SAY HELLO, GET TO WORK AND CLOSE SOME DAMN CASES!
ALL RIGHT. THAT OUGHTA DO IT.
I'M SURE IT DID.
REMEMBER CENTRAL CITY'S MOTTO, ALLEN: THE FASTER THE BETTER!
UH.
MORNING?

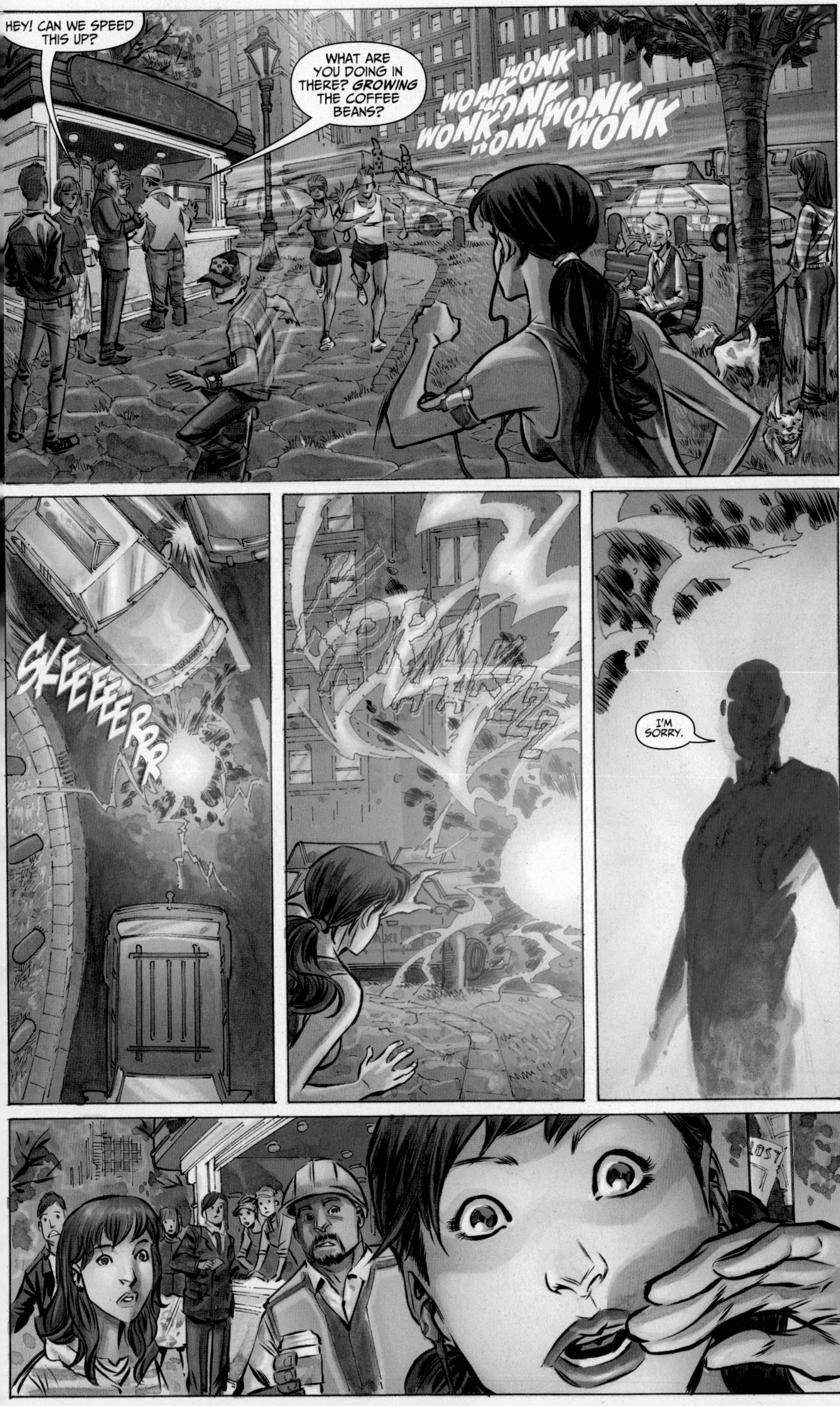
HEY! CAN WE SPEED THIS UP?
WHAT ARE YOU DOING IN THERE? GROWING THE COFFEE BEANS?
WONK WONK WONK WONK WONK WONK WONK WONK
SKEEEEERRR
I'M SORRY.
LOST

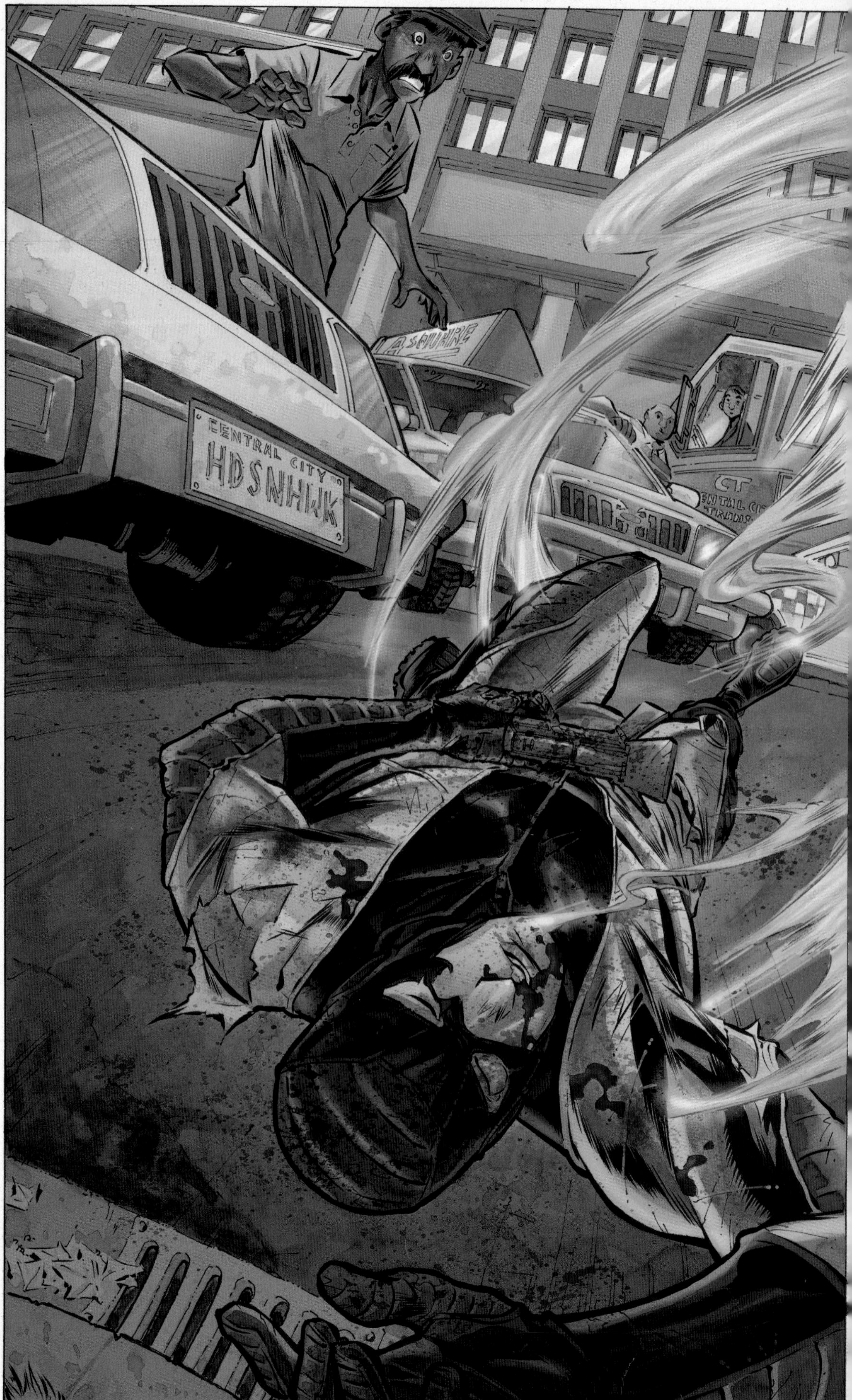
CENTRAL CITY
HDSNHWK

DOES ANYONE KNOW HOW YOU ADJUST THESE CHAIRS?

I BELIEVE THIS IS YOURS.

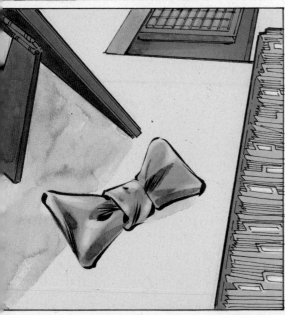

HEY, ALLEN.

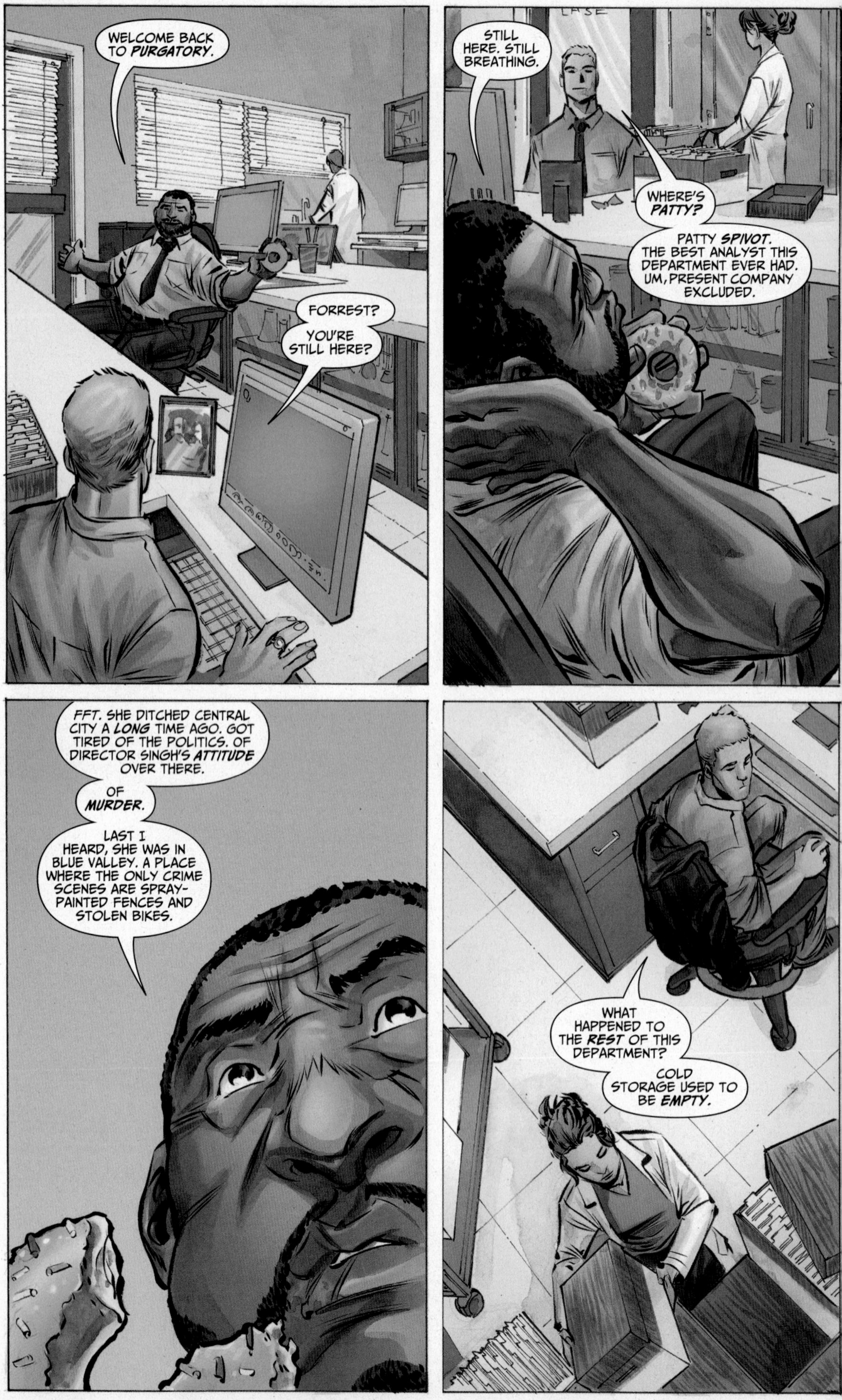
WELCOME BACK TO PURGATORY.
FORREST?
YOU'RE STILL HERE?
STILL HERE. STILL BREATHING.
WHERE'S PATTY?
PATTY SPIVOT. THE BEST ANALYST THIS DEPARTMENT EVER HAD. UM, PRESENT COMPANY EXCLUDED.
FFT. SHE DITCHED CENTRAL CITY A LONG TIME AGO. GOT TIRED OF THE POLITICS. OF DIRECTOR SINGH'S ATTITUDE OVER THERE.
OF MURDER.
LAST I HEARD, SHE WAS IN BLUE VALLEY. A PLACE WHERE THE ONLY CRIME SCENES ARE SPRAY-PAINTED FENCES AND STOLEN BIKES.
WHAT HAPPENED TO THE REST OF THIS DEPARTMENT?
COLD STORAGE USED TO BE EMPTY.

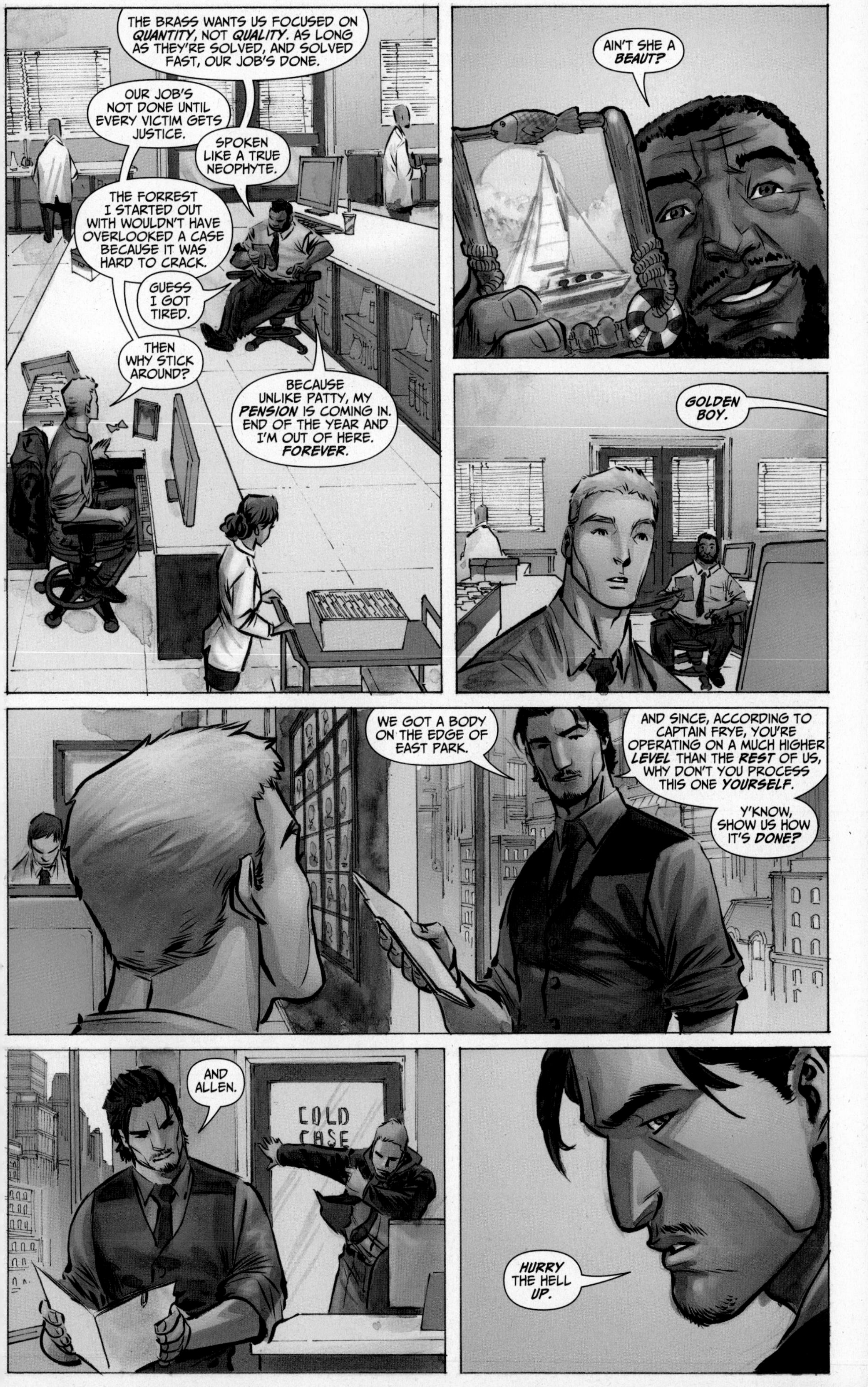
THE BRASS WANTS US FOCUSED ON QUANTITY, NOT QUALITY. AS LONG AS THEY'RE SOLVED, AND SOLVED FAST, OUR JOB'S DONE.
OUR JOB'S NOT DONE UNTIL EVERY VICTIM GETS JUSTICE.
SPOKEN LIKE A TRUE NEOPHYTE.
THE FORREST I STARTED OUT WITH WOULDN'T HAVE OVERLOOKED A CASE BECAUSE IT WAS HARD TO CRACK.
GUESS I GOT TIRED.
THEN WHY STICK AROUND?
BECAUSE UNLIKE PATTY, MY PENSION IS COMING IN. END OF THE YEAR AND I'M OUT OF HERE. FOREVER.
AIN'T SHE A BEAUT?
GOLDEN BOY.
WE GOT A BODY ON THE EDGE OF EAST PARK.
AND SINCE, ACCORDING TO CAPTAIN FRYE, YOU'RE OPERATING ON A MUCH HIGHER LEVEL THAN THE REST OF US, WHY DON'T YOU PROCESS THIS ONE YOURSELF.
Y'KNOW, SHOW US HOW IT'S DONE?
AND ALLEN.
COLD CASE
HURRY THE HELL UP.

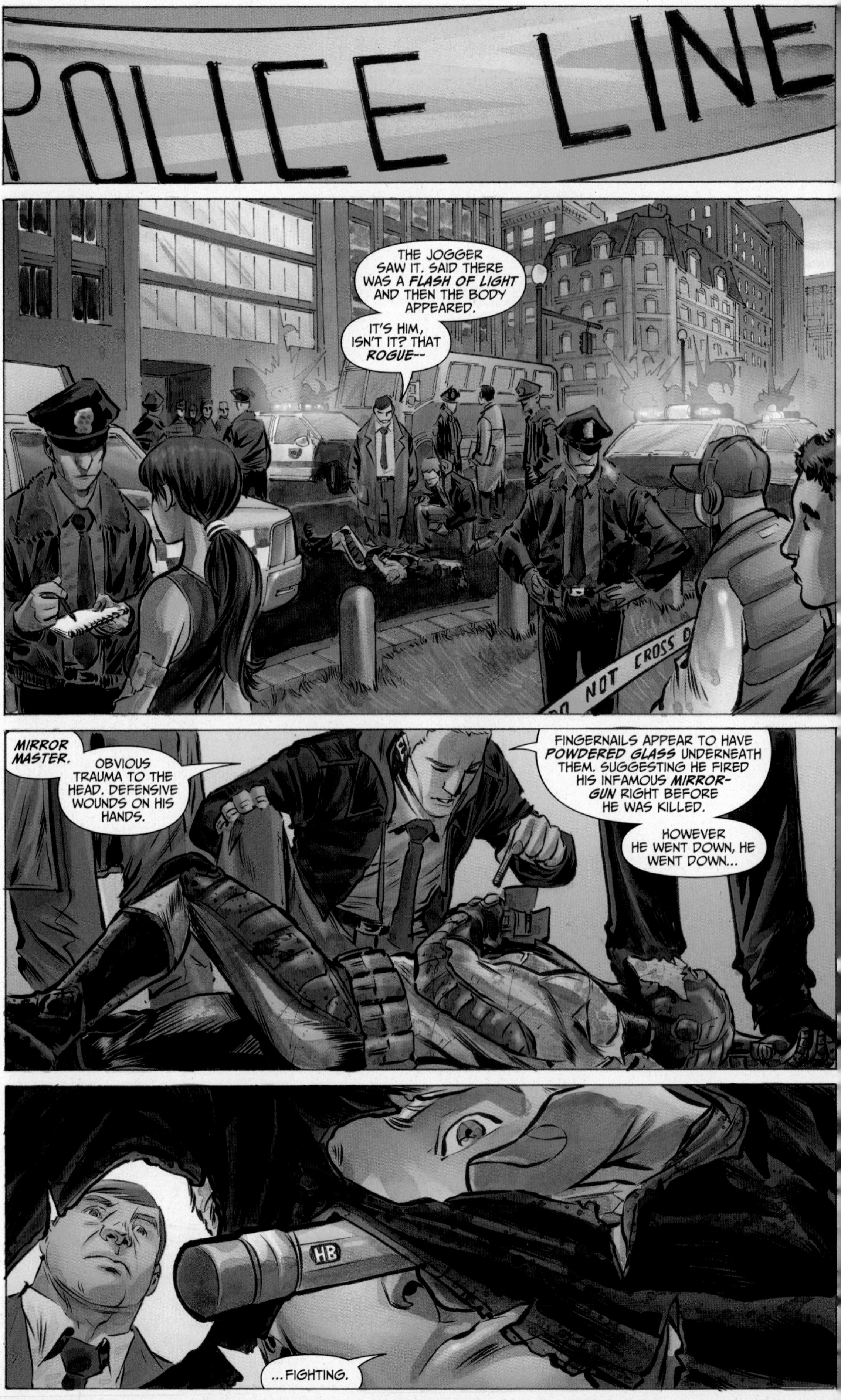
POLICE LINE
THE JOGGER SAW IT. SAID THERE WAS A FLASH OF LIGHT AND THEN THE BODY APPEARED.
IT'S HIM, ISN'T IT? THAT ROGUE--
NOT CROSS
MIRROR MASTER.
OBVIOUS TRAUMA TO THE HEAD. DEFENSIVE WOUNDS ON HIS HANDS.
FINGERNAILS APPEAR TO HAVE POWDERED GLASS UNDERNEATH THEM. SUGGESTING HE FIRED HIS INFAMOUS MIRROR-GUN RIGHT BEFORE HE WAS KILLED.
HOWEVER HE WENT DOWN, HE WENT DOWN...
HB
...FIGHTING.

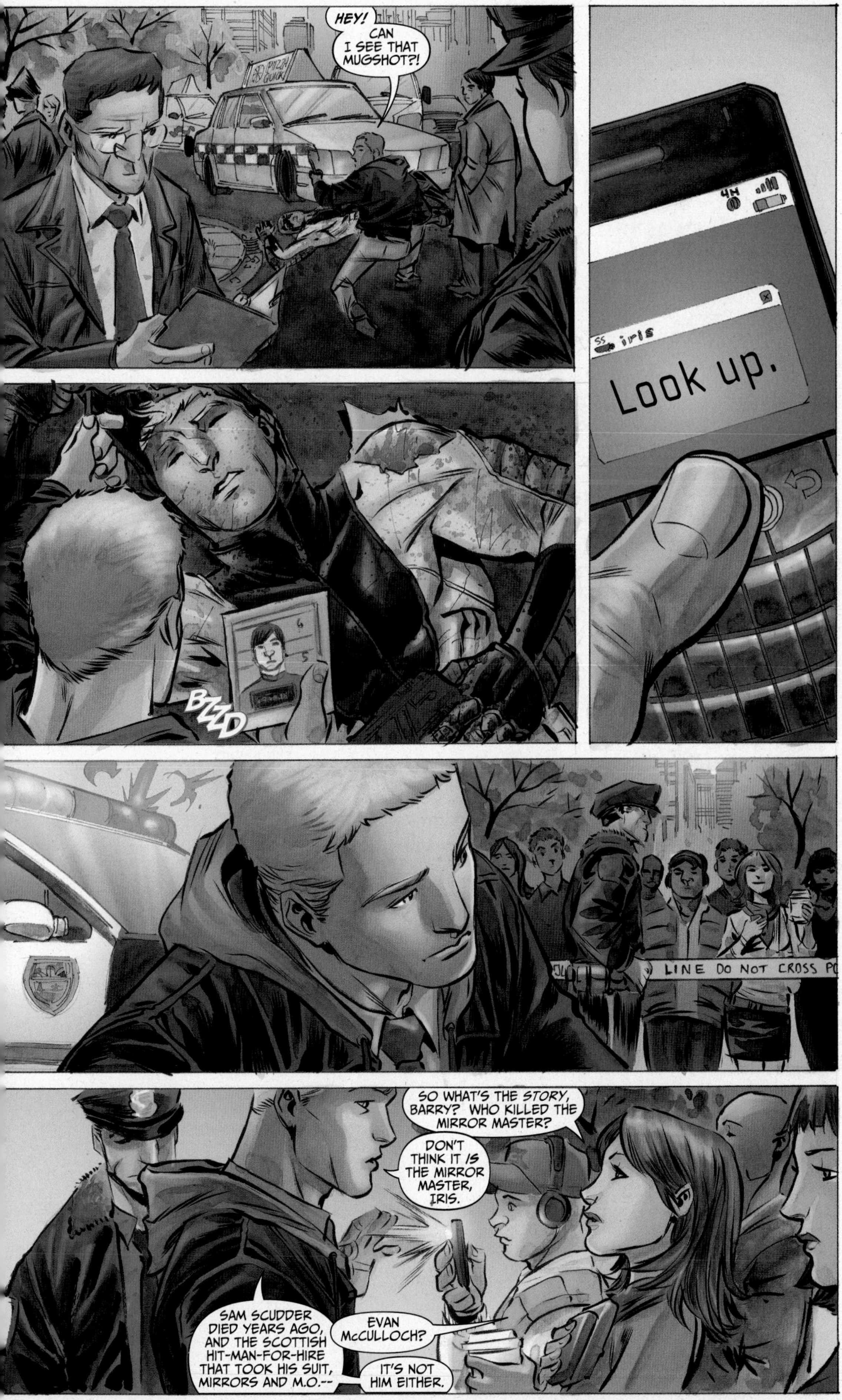
HEY! CAN I SEE THAT MUGSHOT?!
iris
Look up.
BZZD
LINE DO NOT CROSS PO
SO WHAT'S THE STORY, BARRY? WHO KILLED THE MIRROR MASTER?
DON'T THINK IT IS THE MIRROR MASTER, IRIS.
SAM SCUDDER DIED YEARS AGO, AND THE SCOTTISH HIT-MAN-FOR-HIRE THAT TOOK HIS SUIT, MIRRORS AND M.O.--
EVAN McCULLOCH?
IT'S NOT HIM EITHER.

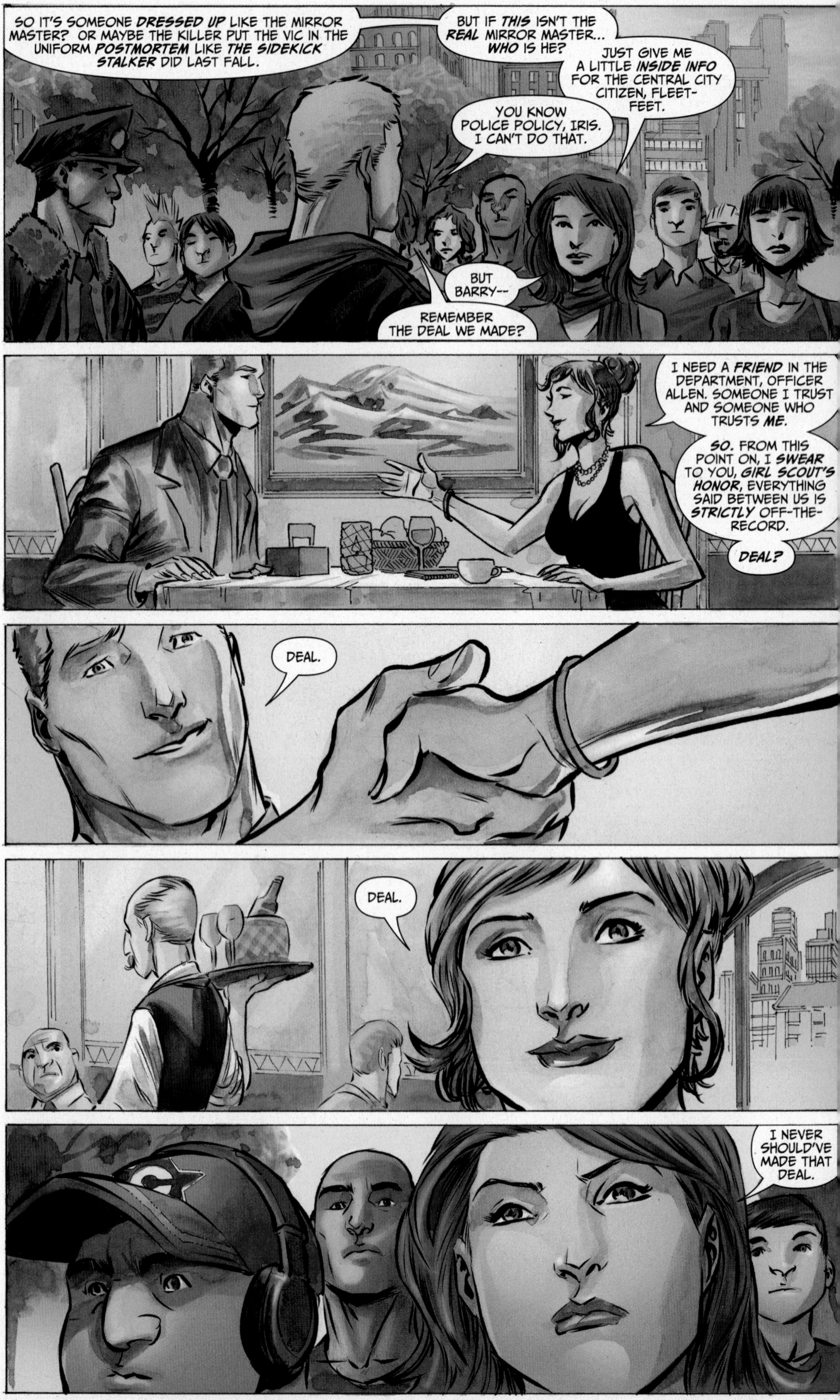
SO IT'S SOMEONE DRESSED UP LIKE THE MIRROR MASTER? OR MAYBE THE KILLER PUT THE VIC IN THE UNIFORM POSTMORTEM LIKE THE SIDEKICK STALKER DID LAST FALL.
BUT IF THIS ISN'T THE REAL MIRROR MASTER... WHO IS HE?
JUST GIVE ME A LITTLE INSIDE INFO FOR THE CENTRAL CITY CITIZEN, FLEET-FEET.
YOU KNOW POLICE POLICY, IRIS. I CAN'T DO THAT.
BUT BARRY--
REMEMBER THE DEAL WE MADE?
I NEED A FRIEND IN THE DEPARTMENT, OFFICER ALLEN. SOMEONE I TRUST AND SOMEONE WHO TRUSTS ME.
SO. FROM THIS POINT ON, I SWEAR TO YOU, GIRL SCOUT'S HONOR, EVERYTHING SAID BETWEEN US IS STRICTLY OFF-THE-RECORD.
DEAL?
DEAL.
DEAL.
I NEVER SHOULD'VE MADE THAT DEAL.

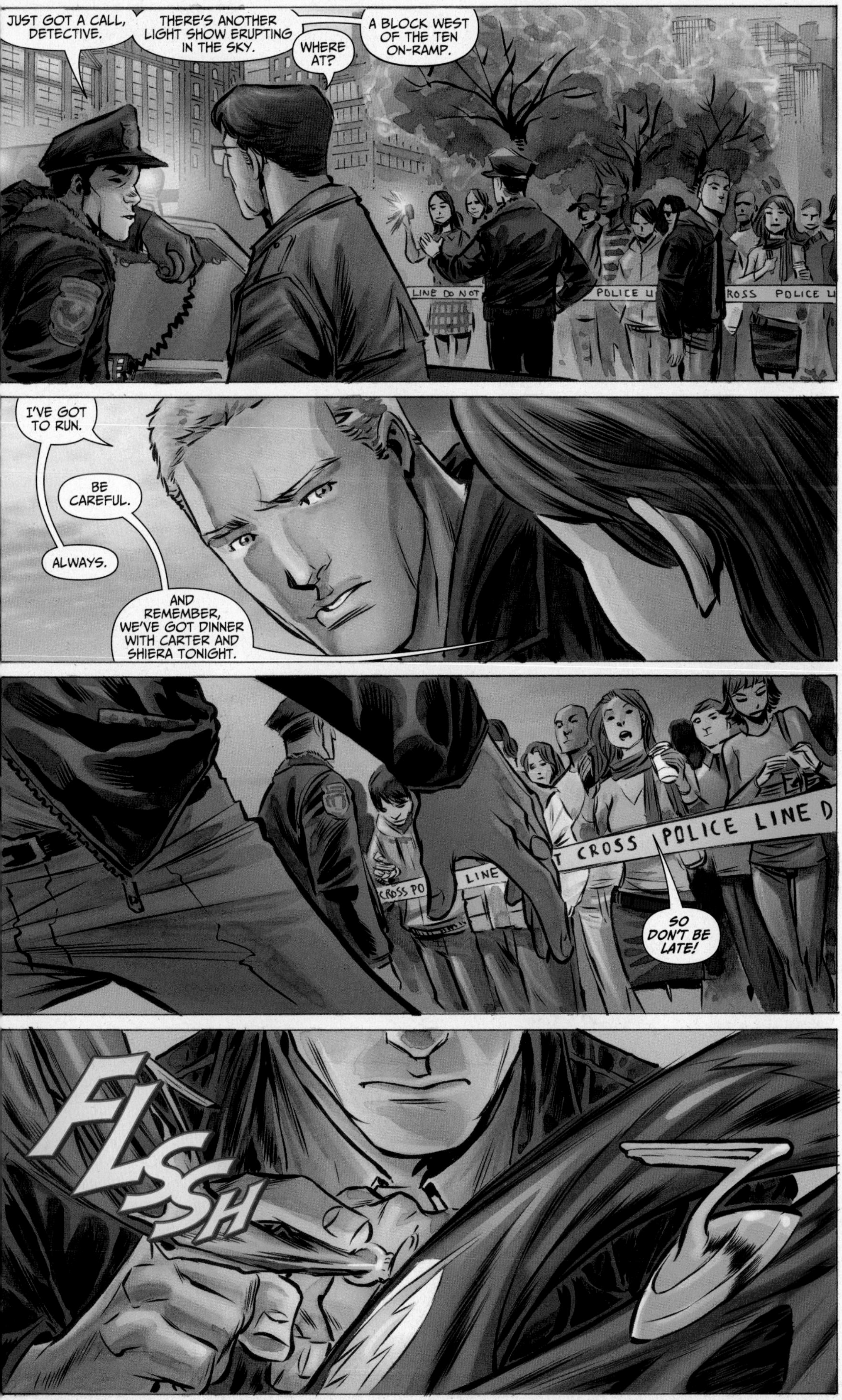
JUST GOT A CALL, DETECTIVE.
THERE'S ANOTHER LIGHT SHOW ERUPTING IN THE SKY.
WHERE AT?
A BLOCK WEST OF THE TEN ON-RAMP.
LINE DO NOT
I'VE GOT TO RUN.
BE CAREFUL.
ALWAYS.
AND REMEMBER, WE'VE GOT DINNER WITH CARTER AND SHIERA TONIGHT.
CROSS POLICE LINE
SO DON'T BE LATE!
FLSSH

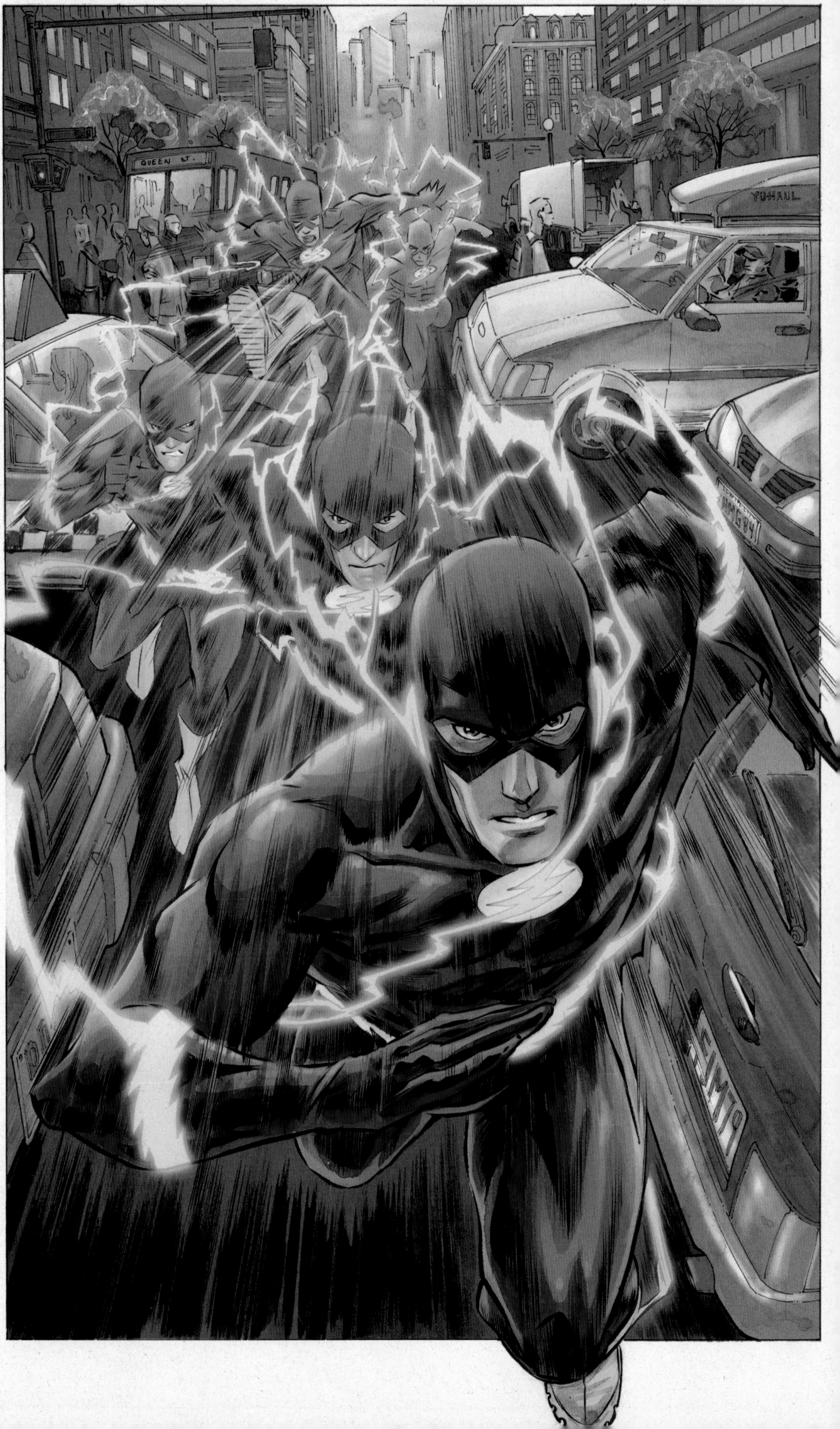
YUHAUL

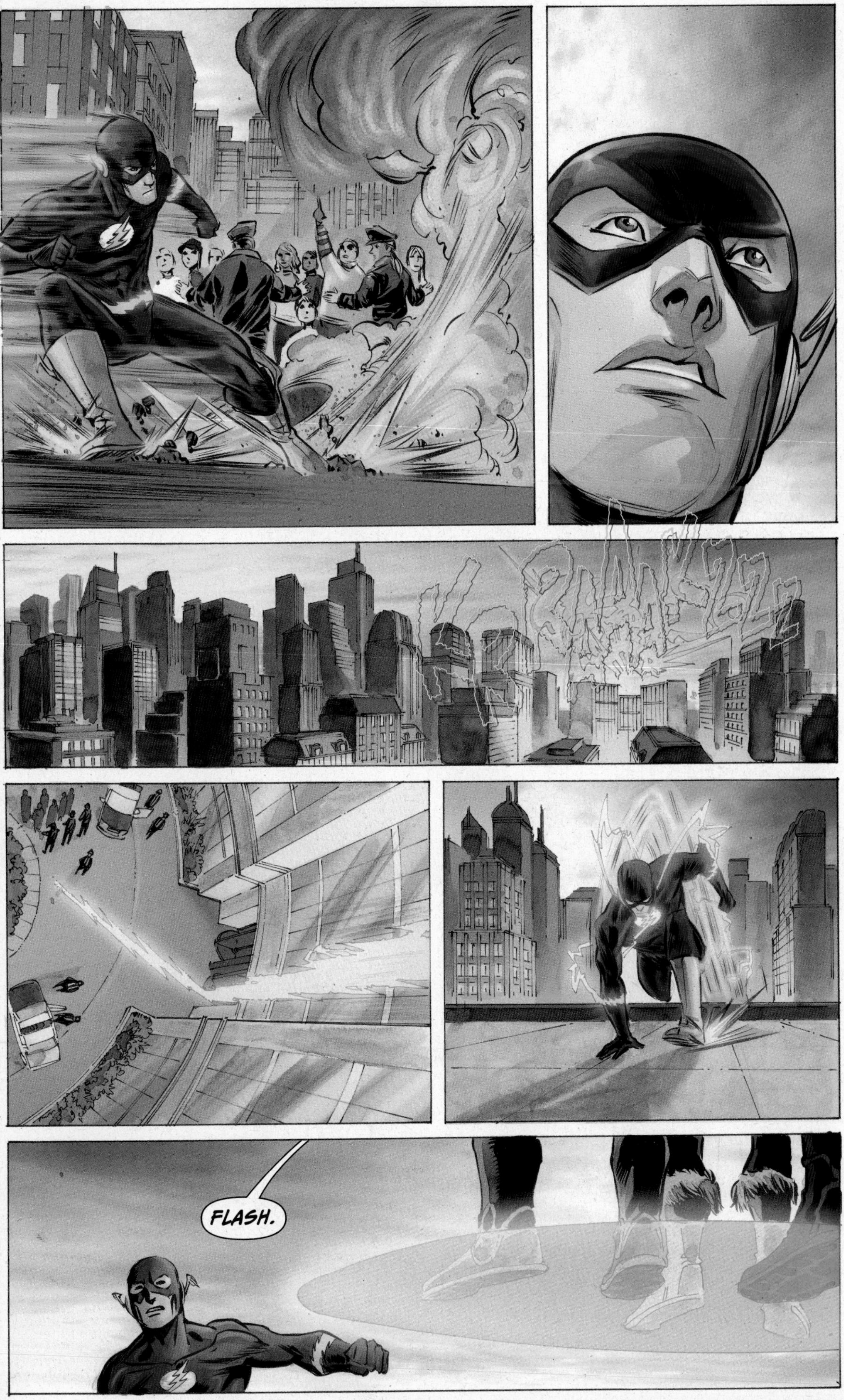
FLASH.

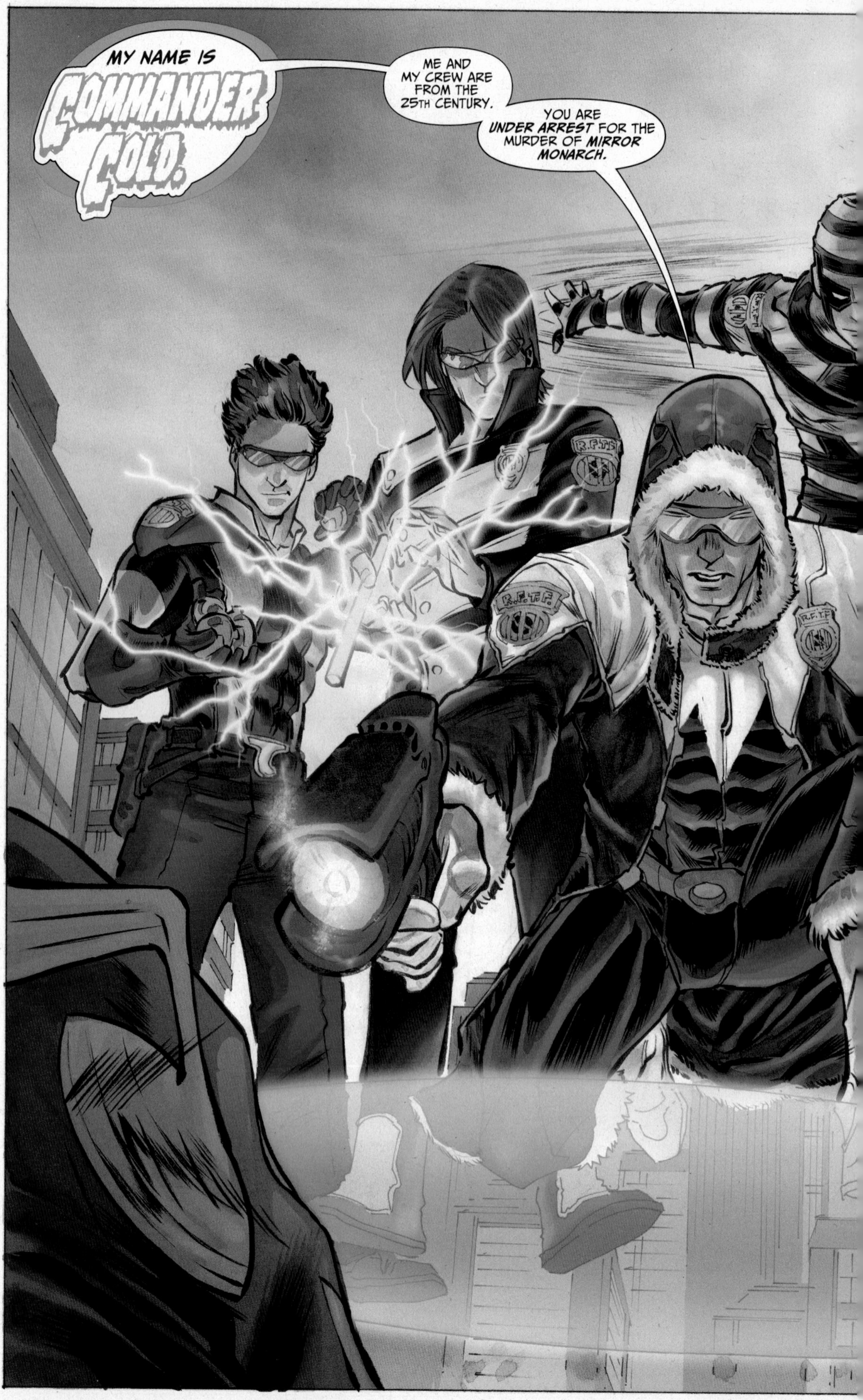
MY NAME IS
COMMANDER COLD.
ME AND MY CREW ARE FROM THE 25TH CENTURY.
YOU ARE UNDER ARREST FOR THE MURDER OF MIRROR MONARCH.

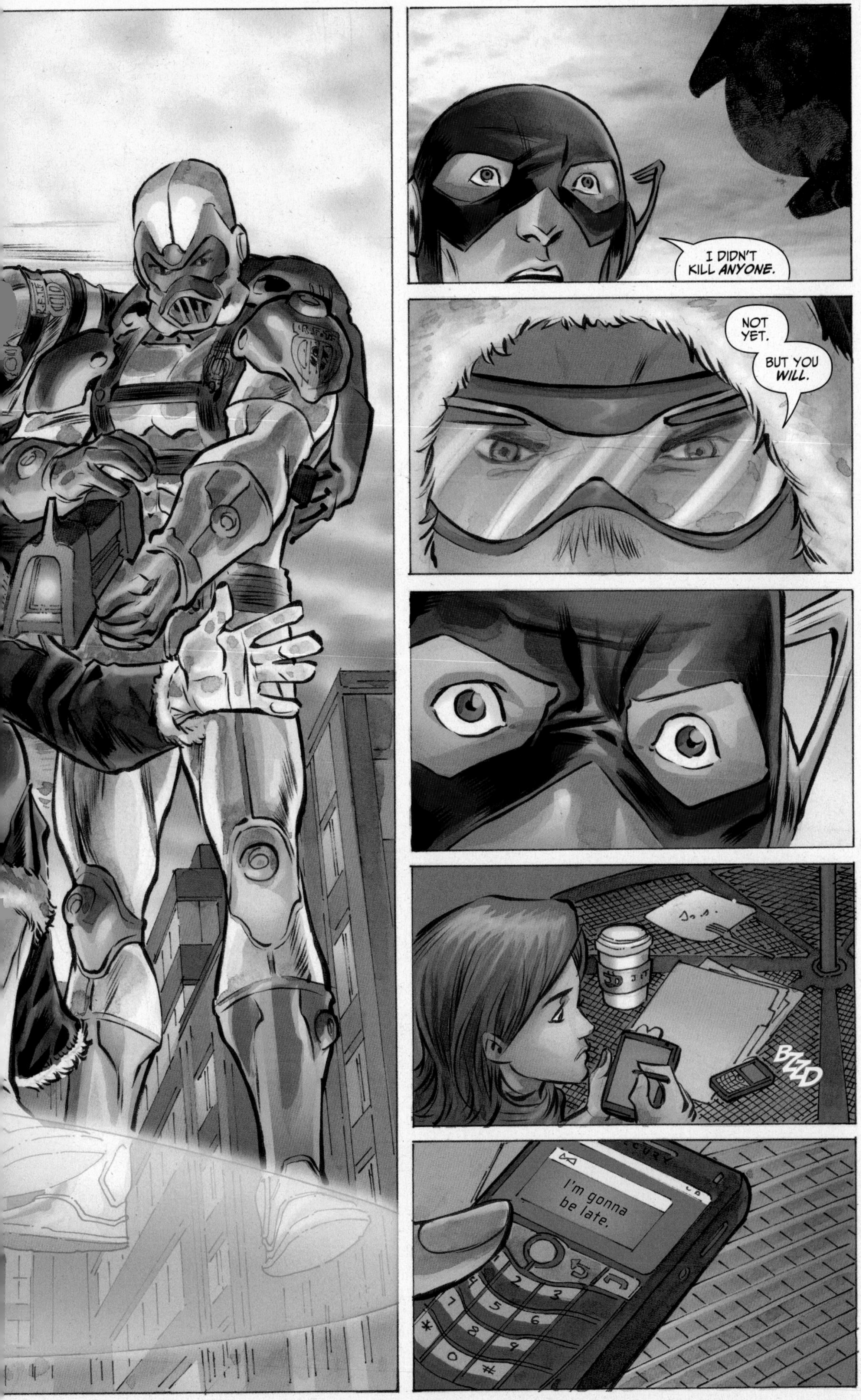
I DIDN'T KILL ANYONE.
NOT YET.
BUT YOU WILL.
BZZZD
I'm gonna be late.

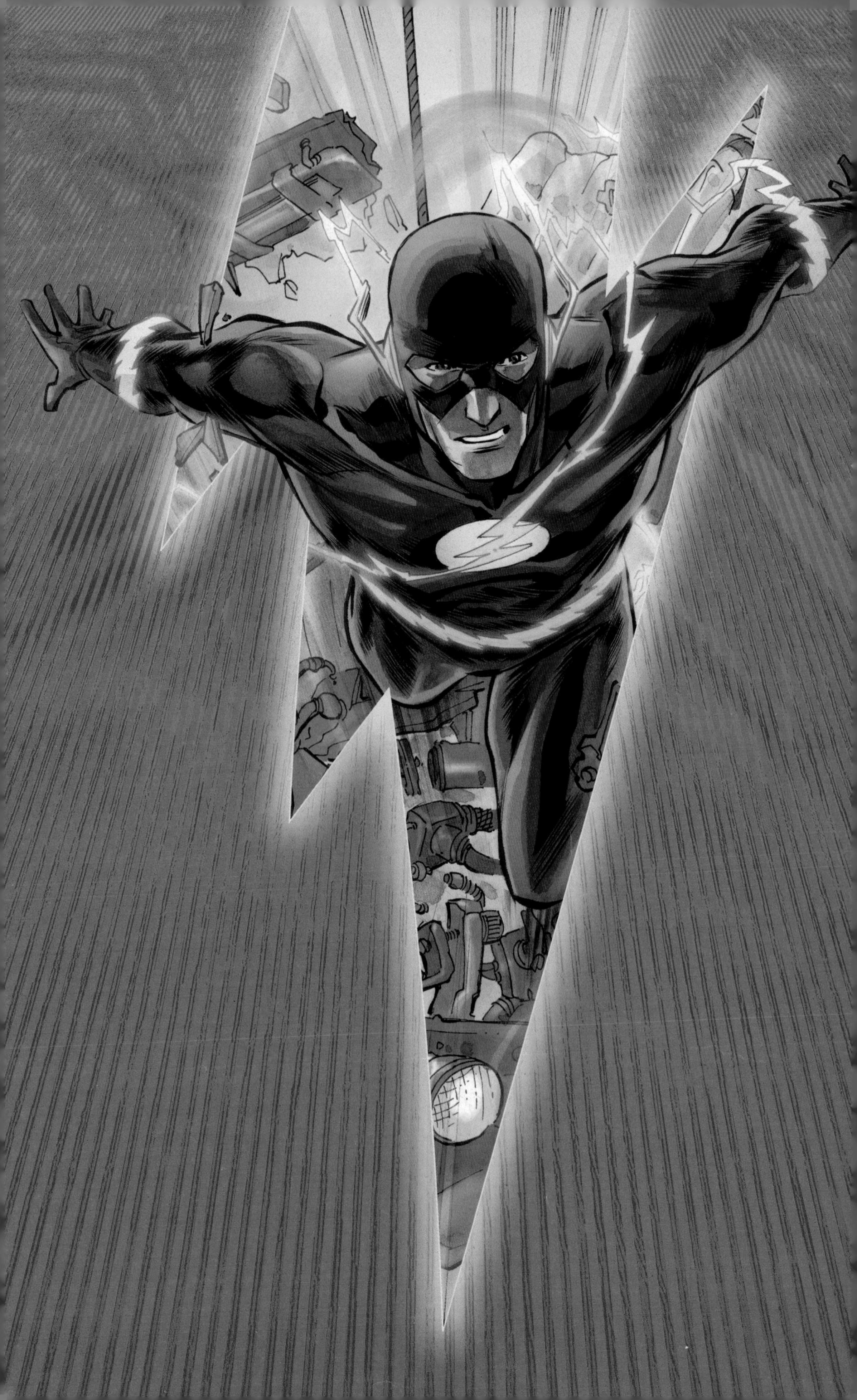

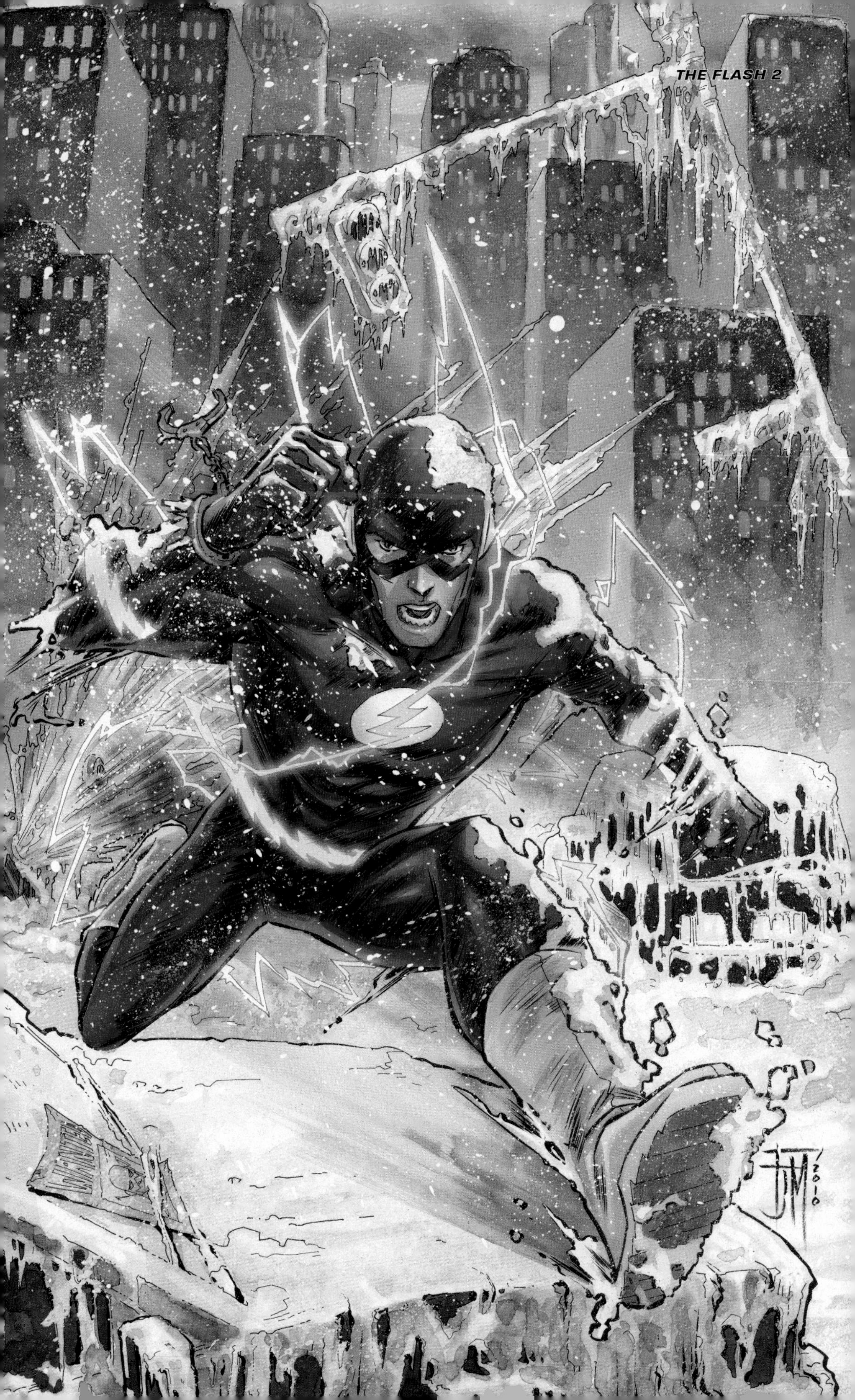

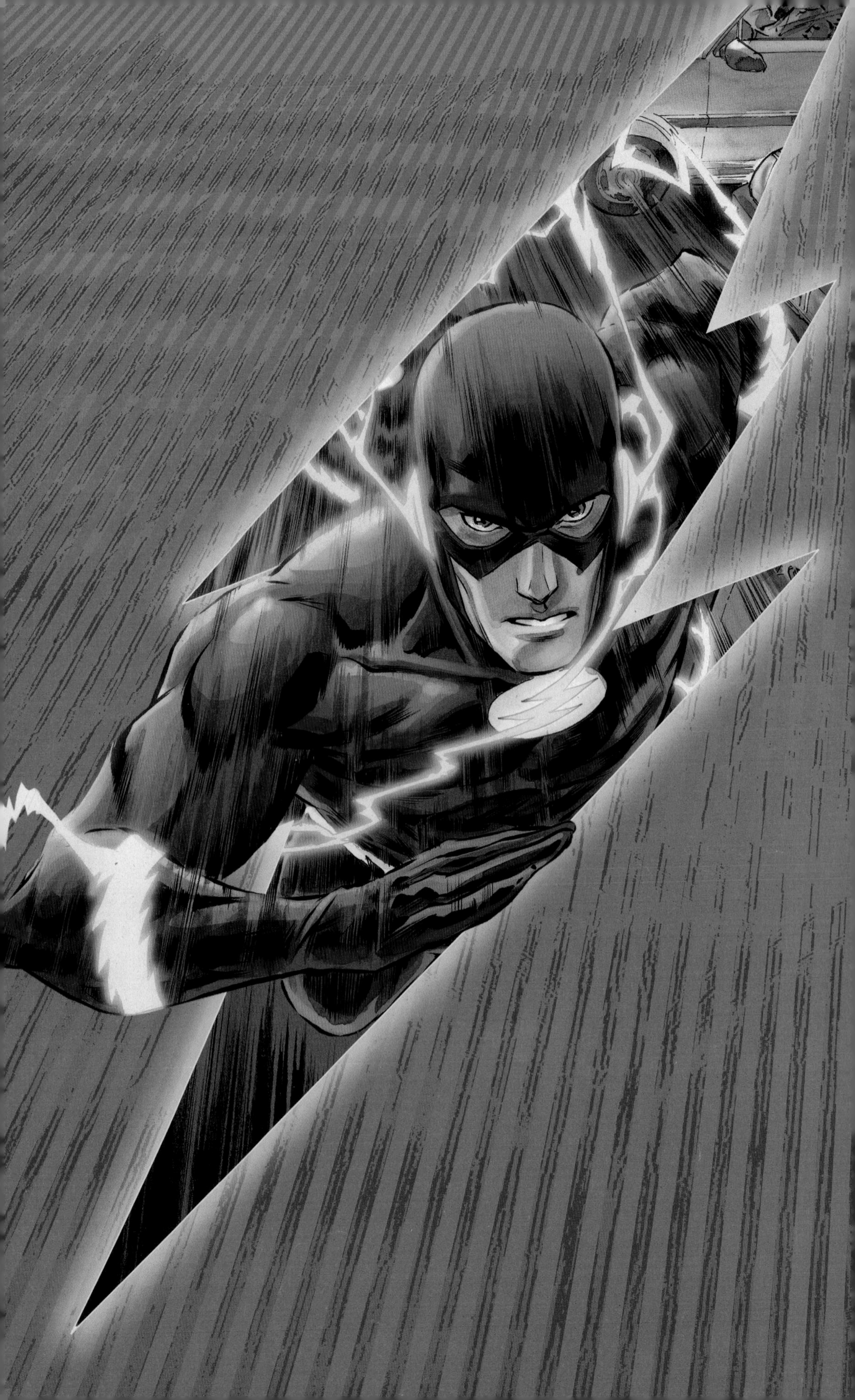

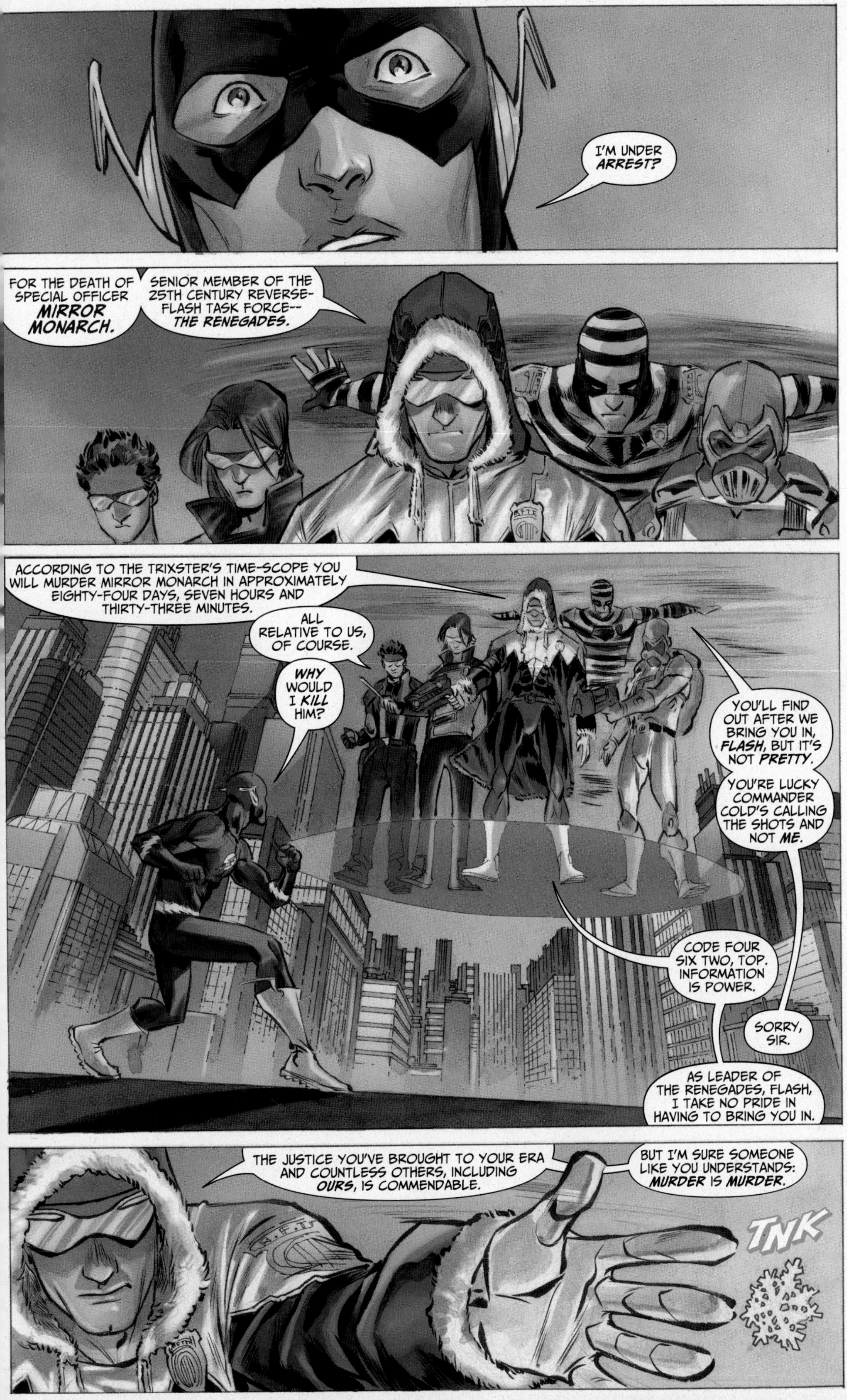
I'M UNDER ARREST?
FOR THE DEATH OF SPECIAL OFFICER MIRROR MONARCH.
SENIOR MEMBER OF THE 25TH CENTURY REVERSE-FLASH TASK FORCE-- THE RENEGADES.
ACCORDING TO THE TRIXSTER'S TIME-SCOPE YOU WILL MURDER MIRROR MONARCH IN APPROXIMATELY EIGHTY-FOUR DAYS, SEVEN HOURS AND THIRTY-THREE MINUTES.
ALL RELATIVE TO US, OF COURSE.
WHY WOULD I KILL HIM?
YOU'LL FIND OUT AFTER WE BRING YOU IN, FLASH, BUT IT'S NOT PRETTY.
YOU'RE LUCKY COMMANDER COLD'S CALLING THE SHOTS AND NOT ME.
CODE FOUR SIX TWO, TOP. INFORMATION IS POWER.
SORRY, SIR.
AS LEADER OF THE RENEGADES, FLASH, I TAKE NO PRIDE IN HAVING TO BRING YOU IN.
THE JUSTICE YOU'VE BROUGHT TO YOUR ERA AND COUNTLESS OTHERS, INCLUDING OURS, IS COMMENDABLE.
BUT I'M SURE SOMEONE LIKE YOU UNDERSTANDS: MURDER IS MURDER.
TNK

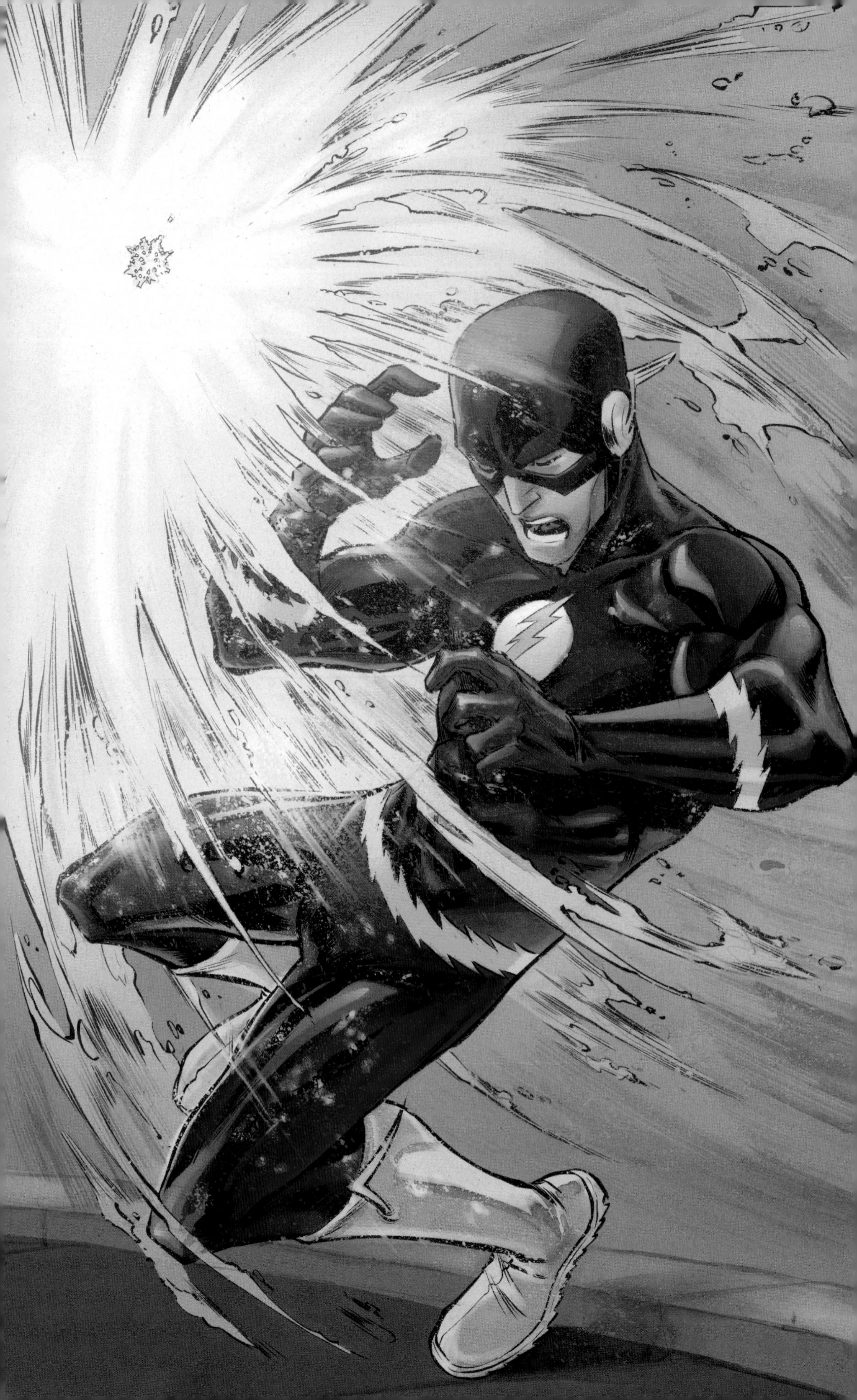

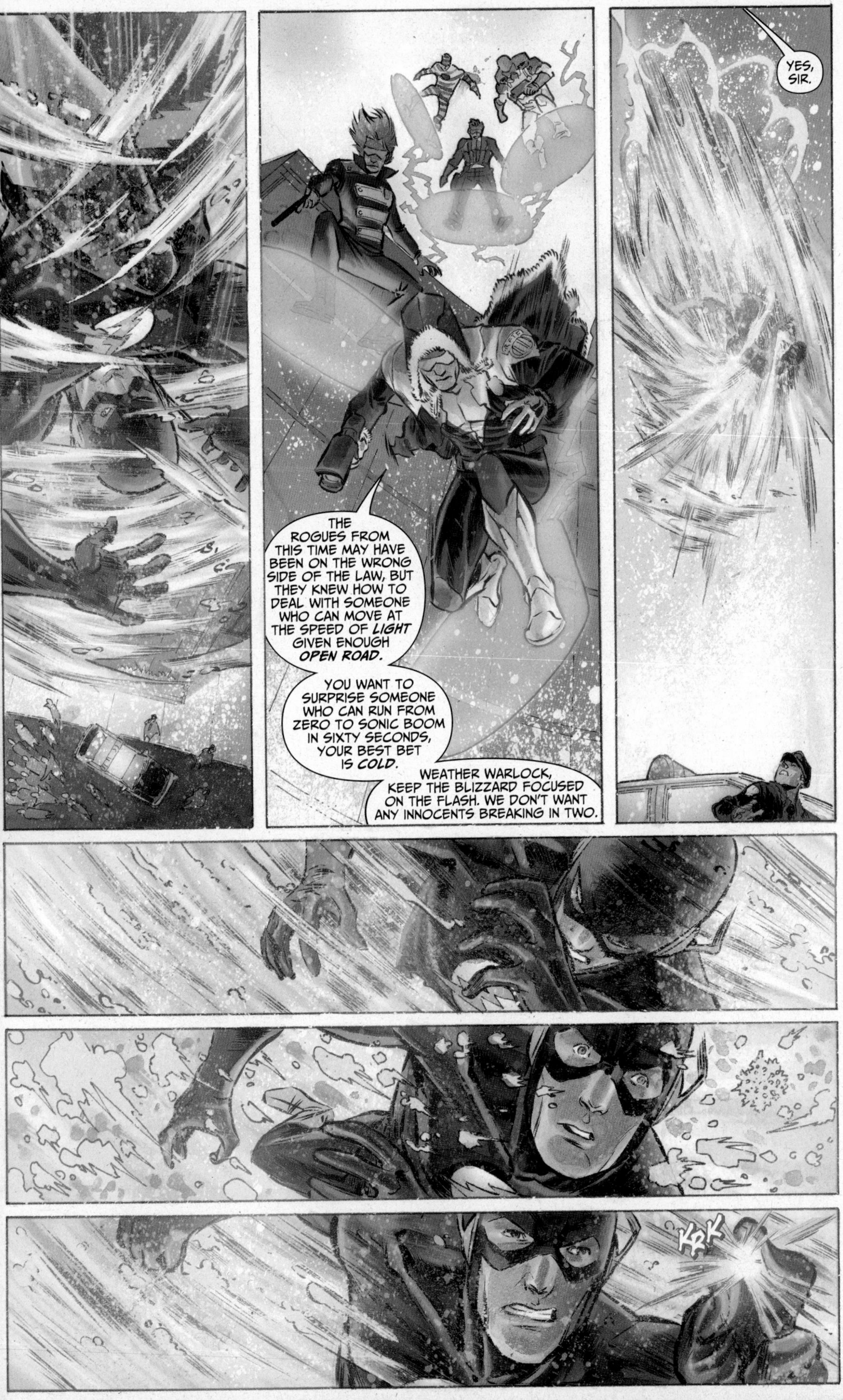
YES, SIR.
THE ROGUES FROM THIS TIME MAY HAVE BEEN ON THE WRONG SIDE OF THE LAW, BUT THEY KNEW HOW TO DEAL WITH SOMEONE WHO CAN MOVE AT THE SPEED OF LIGHT GIVEN ENOUGH OPEN ROAD.
YOU WANT TO SURPRISE SOMEONE WHO CAN RUN FROM ZERO TO SONIC BOOM IN SIXTY SECONDS, YOUR BEST BET IS COLD.
WEATHER WARLOCK, KEEP THE BLIZZARD FOCUSED ON THE FLASH. WE DON'T WANT ANY INNOCENTS BREAKING IN TWO.
KRK

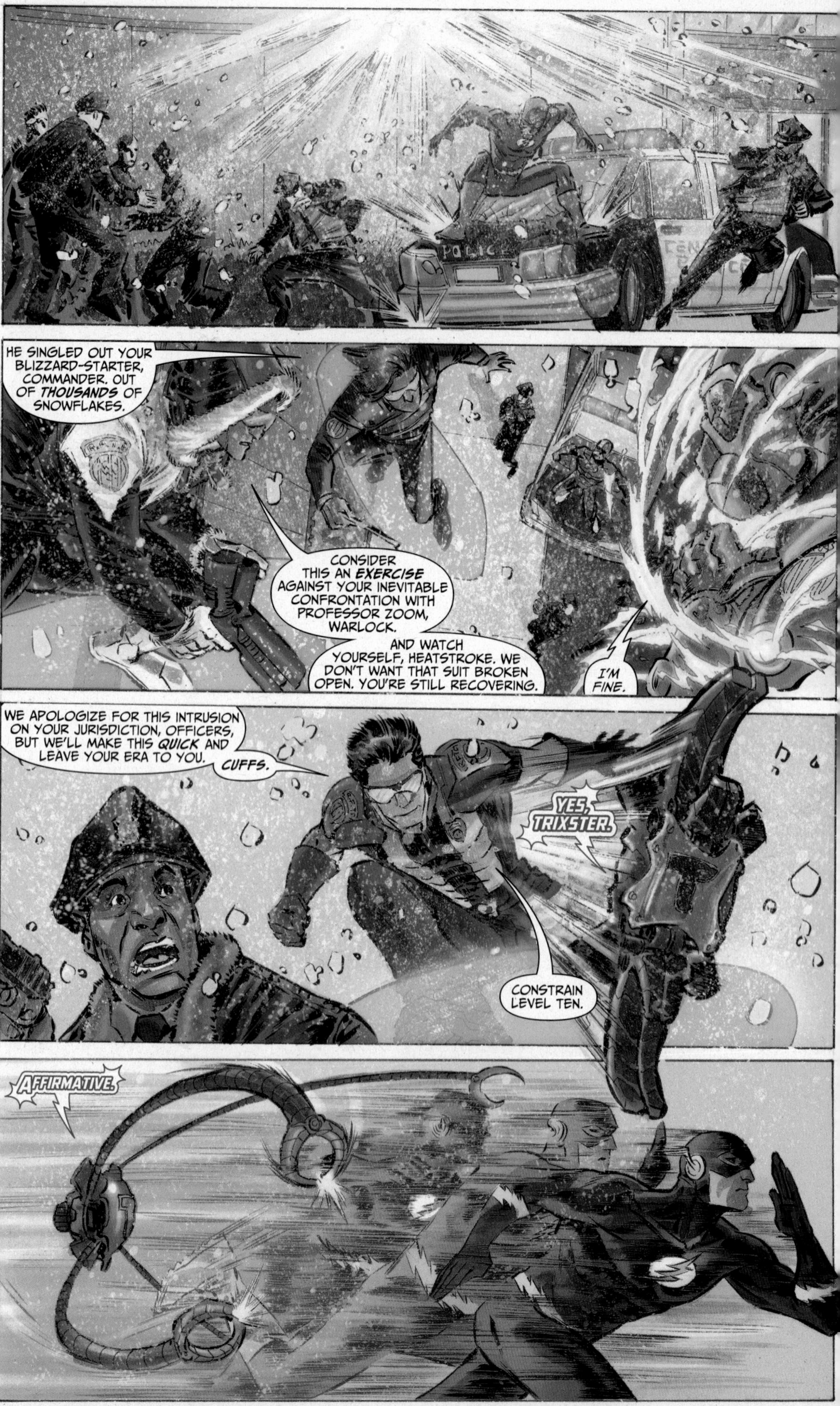
HE SINGLED OUT YOUR BLIZZARD-STARTER, COMMANDER. OUT OF THOUSANDS OF SNOWFLAKES.
CONSIDER THIS AN EXERCISE AGAINST YOUR INEVITABLE CONFRONTATION WITH PROFESSOR ZOOM, WARLOCK.
AND WATCH YOURSELF, HEATSTROKE. WE DON'T WANT THAT SUIT BROKEN OPEN. YOU'RE STILL RECOVERING.
I'M FINE.
WE APOLOGIZE FOR THIS INTRUSION ON YOUR JURISDICTION, OFFICERS, BUT WE'LL MAKE THIS QUICK AND LEAVE YOUR ERA TO YOU.
CUFFS.
YES, TRIXSTER.
CONSTRAIN LEVEL TEN.
AFFIRMATIVE.

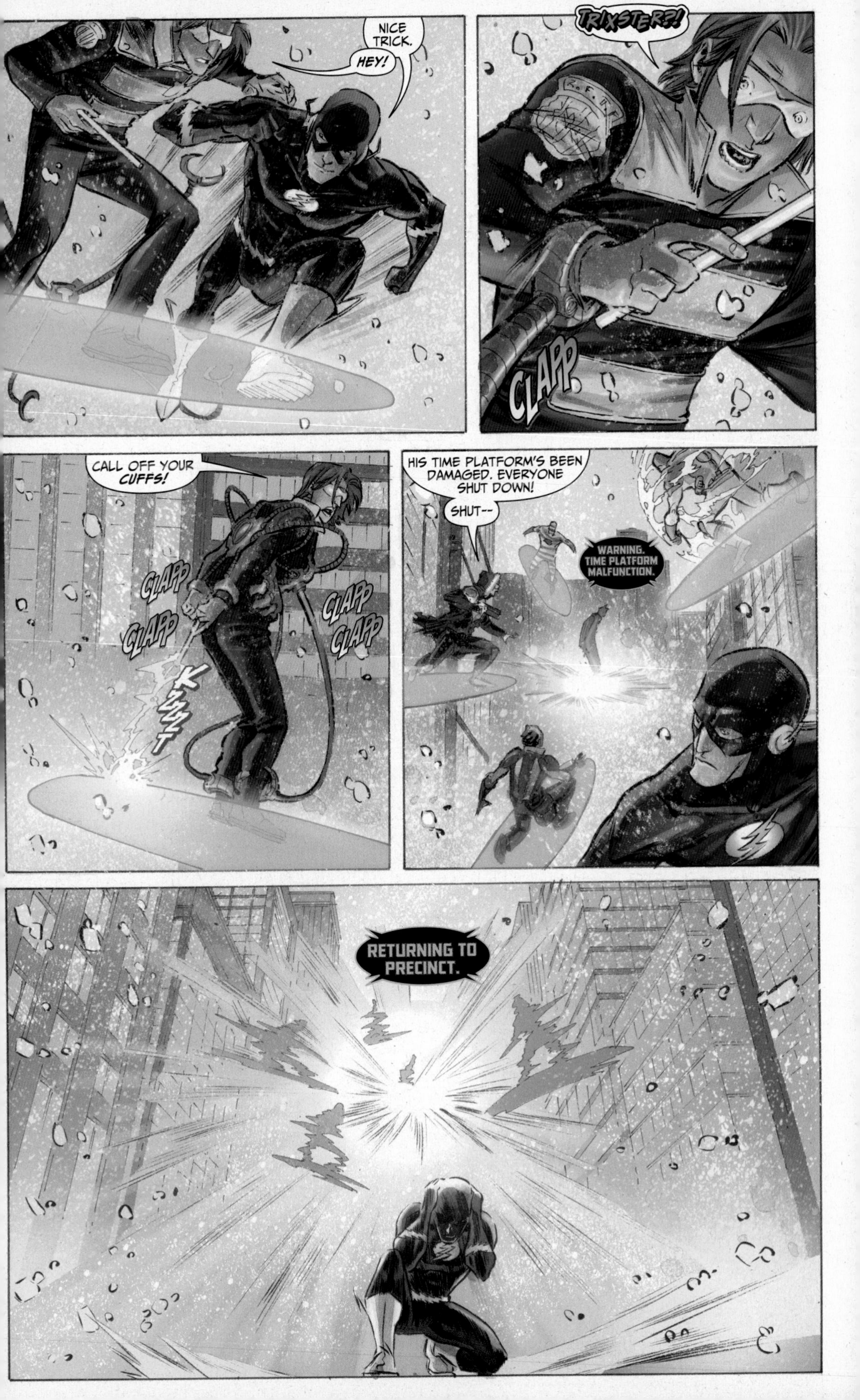
NICE TRICK.
HEY!
TRIXSTER?!
CLAPP
CALL OFF YOUR CUFFS!
CLAPP
CLAPP
CLAPP
CLAPP
KZZZT
HIS TIME PLATFORM'S BEEN DAMAGED. EVERYONE SHUT DOWN!
SHUT--
WARNING. TIME PLATFORM MALFUNCTION.
RETURNING TO PRECINCT.

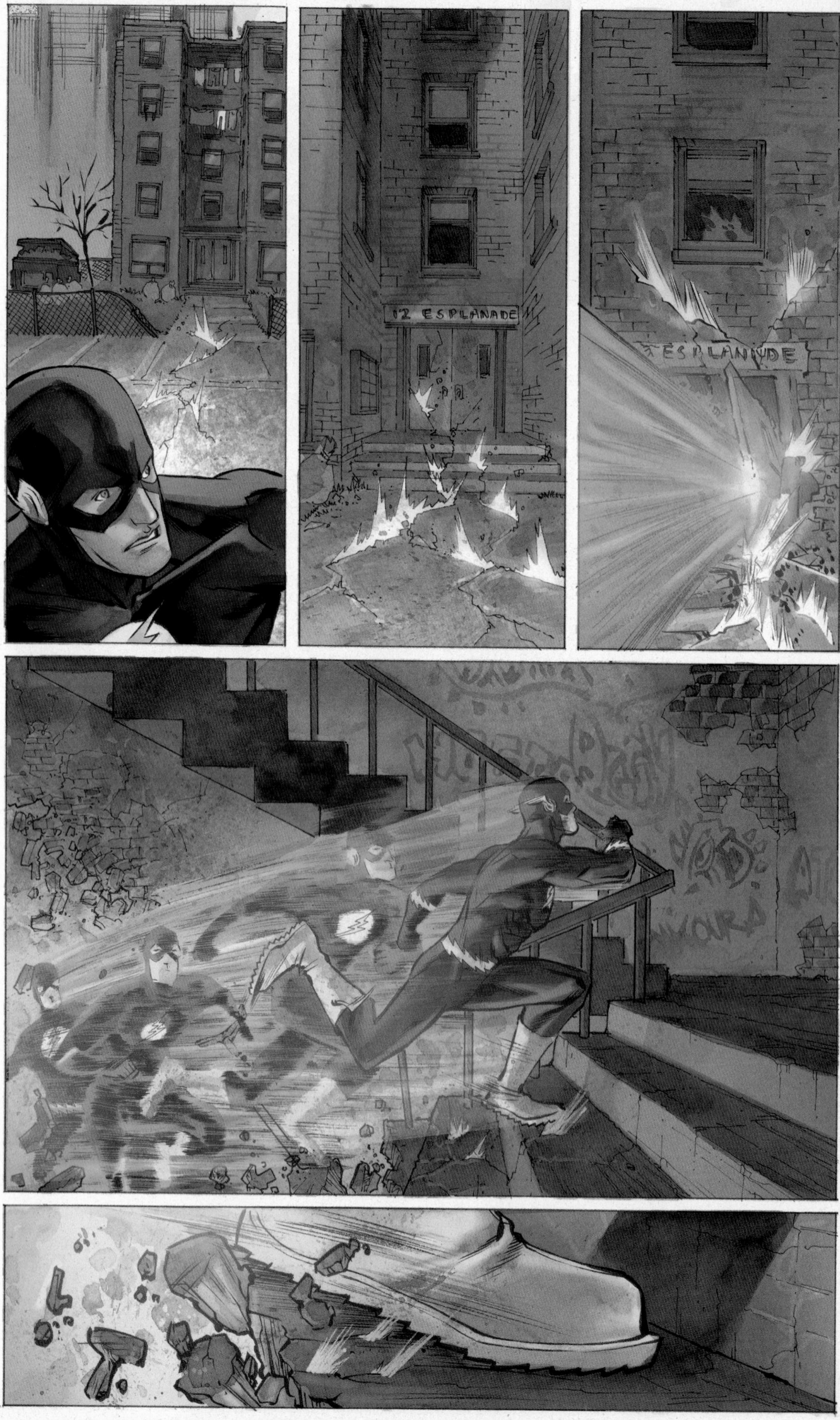
12 ESPLANADE

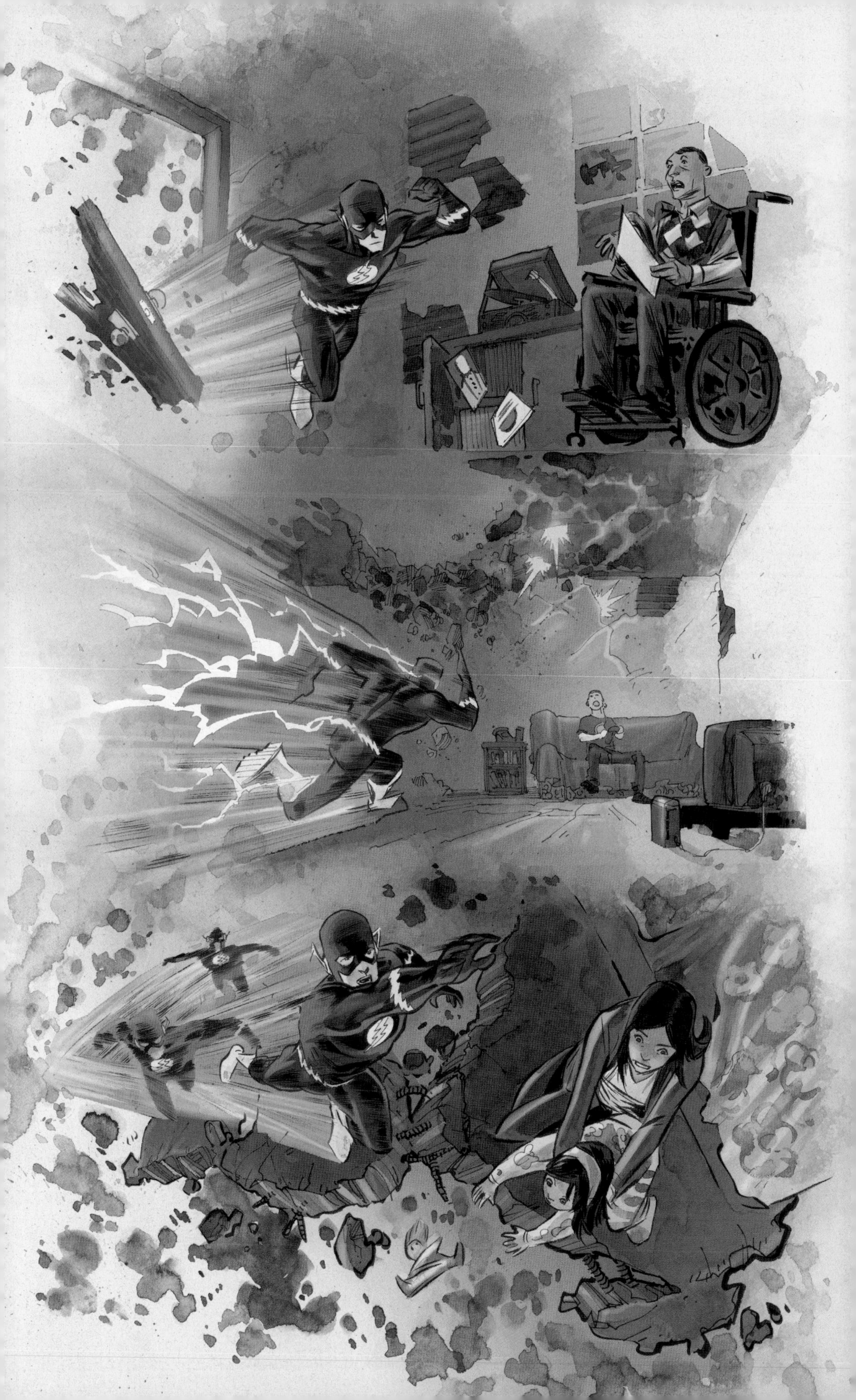

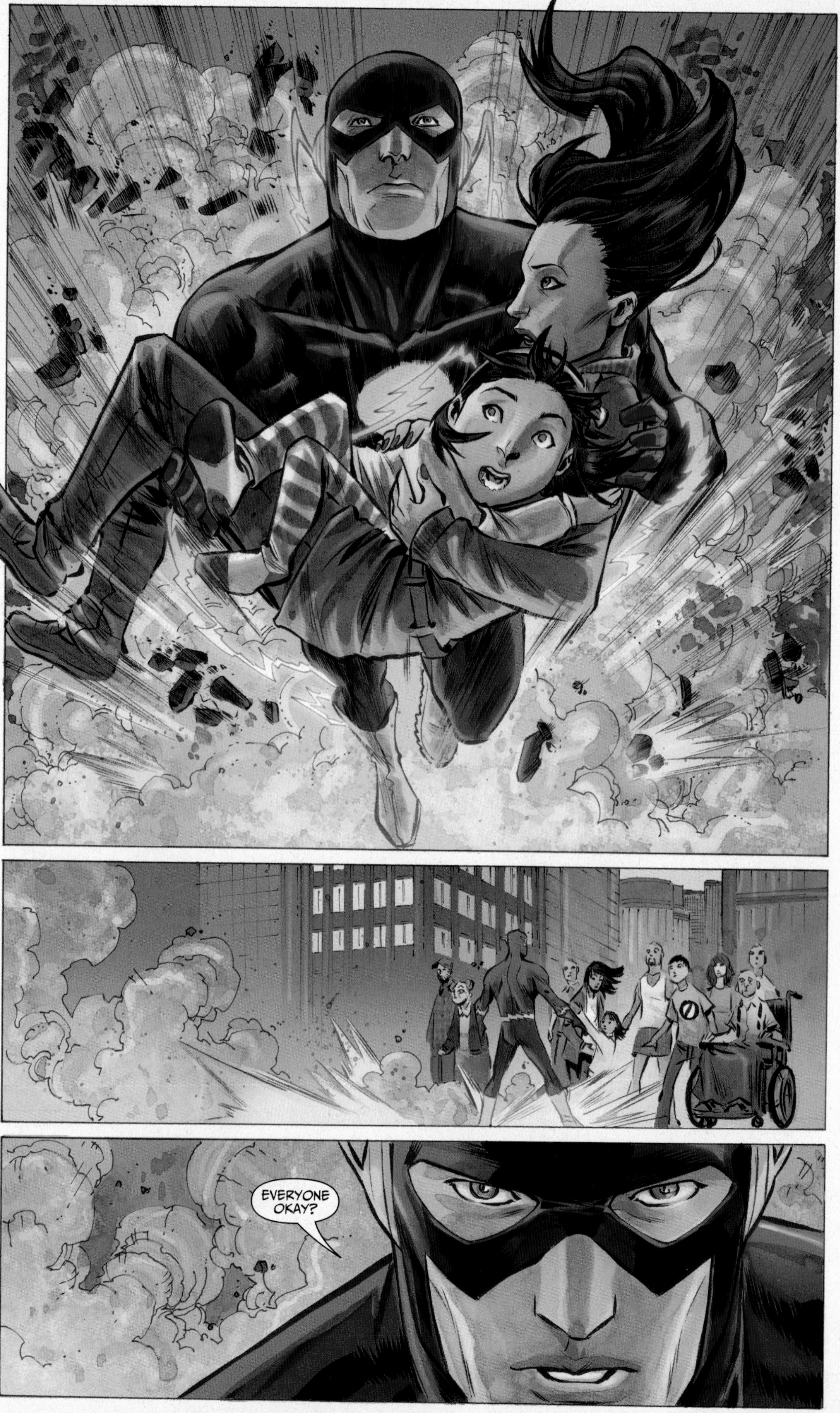
EVERYONE OKAY?

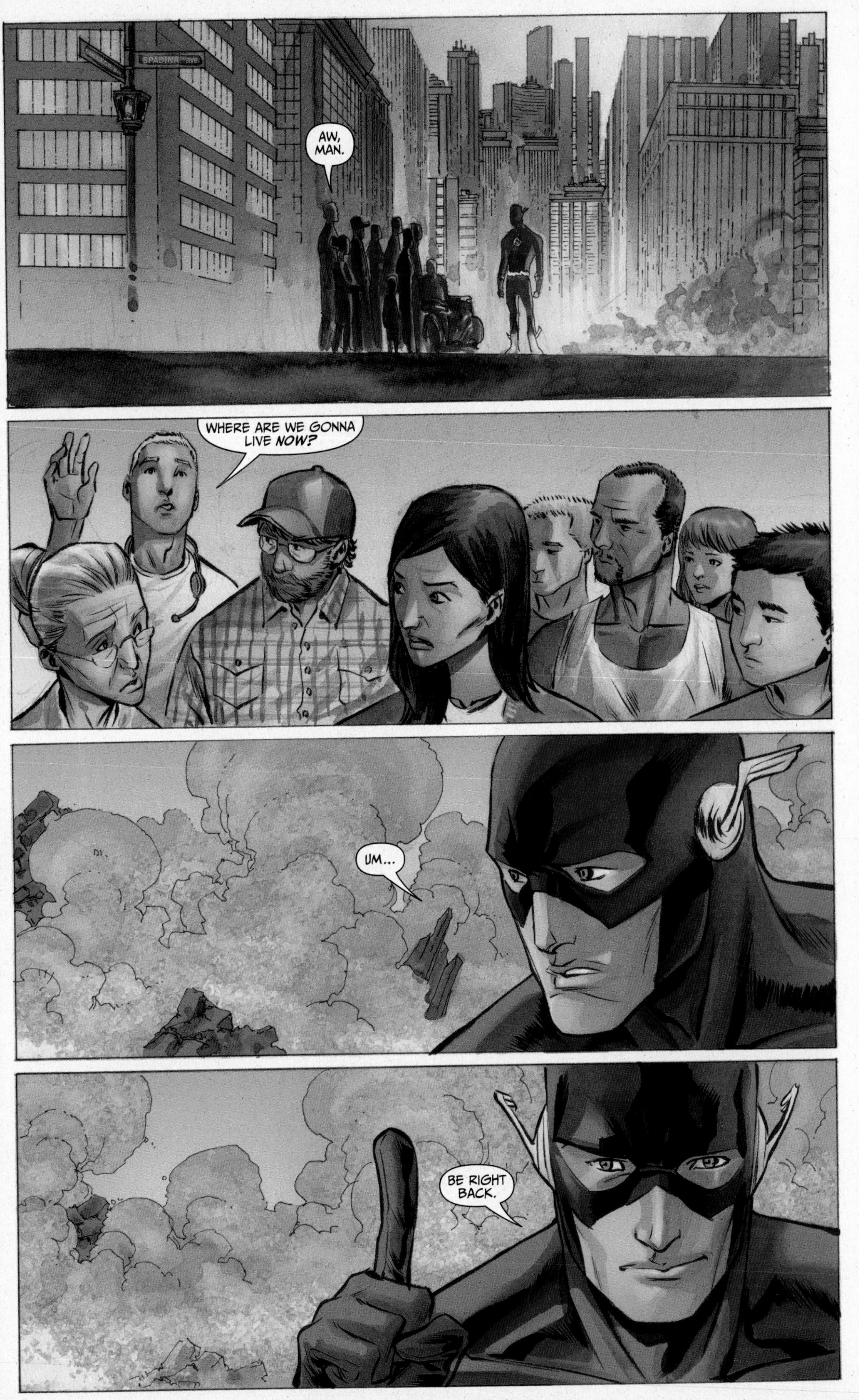
SPADINA AVE
AW, MAN.
WHERE ARE WE GONNA LIVE NOW?
UM...
BE RIGHT BACK.

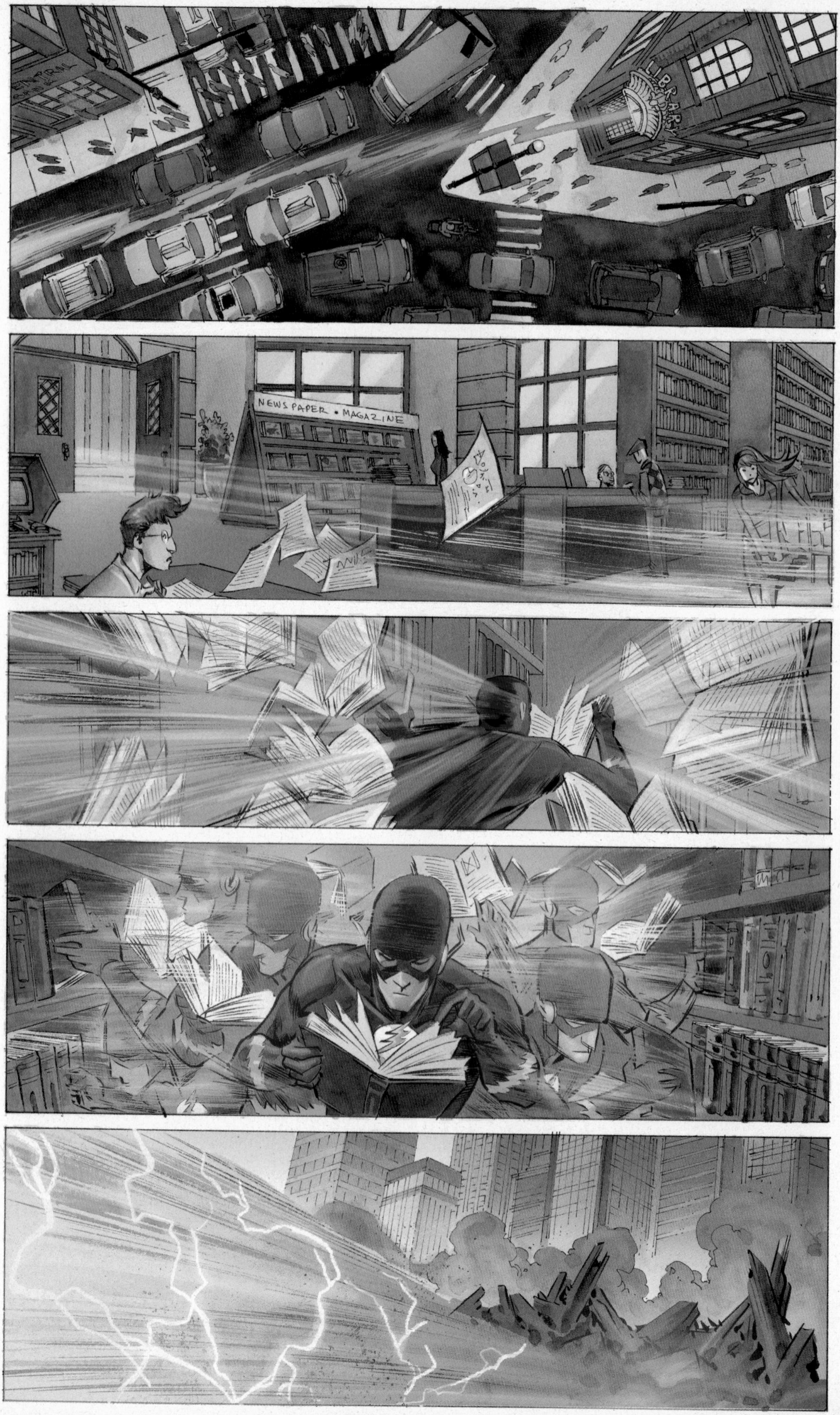
LIBRARY
NEWS PAPER • MAGAZINE

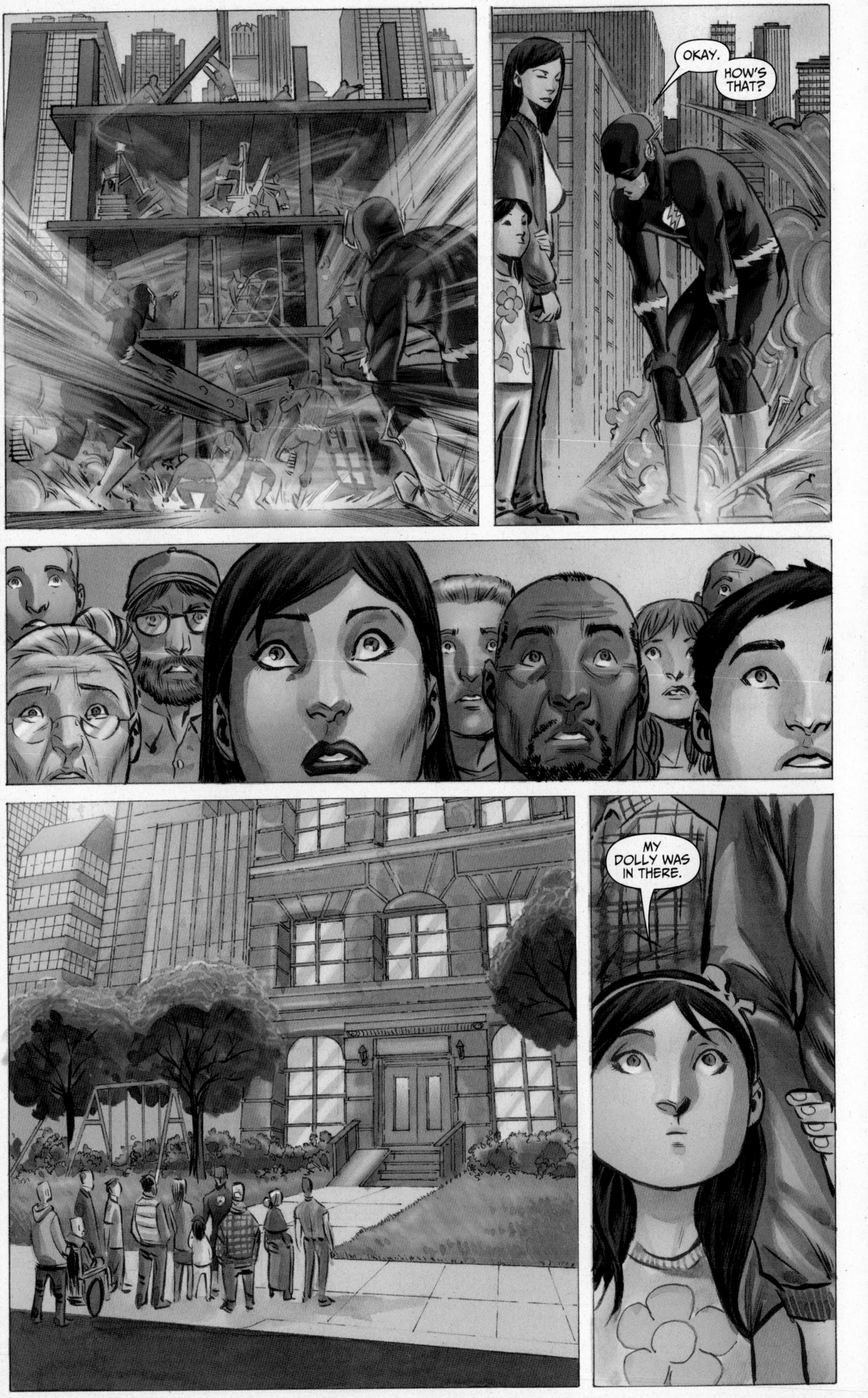
OKAY.
HOW'S THAT?
MY DOLLY WAS IN THERE.

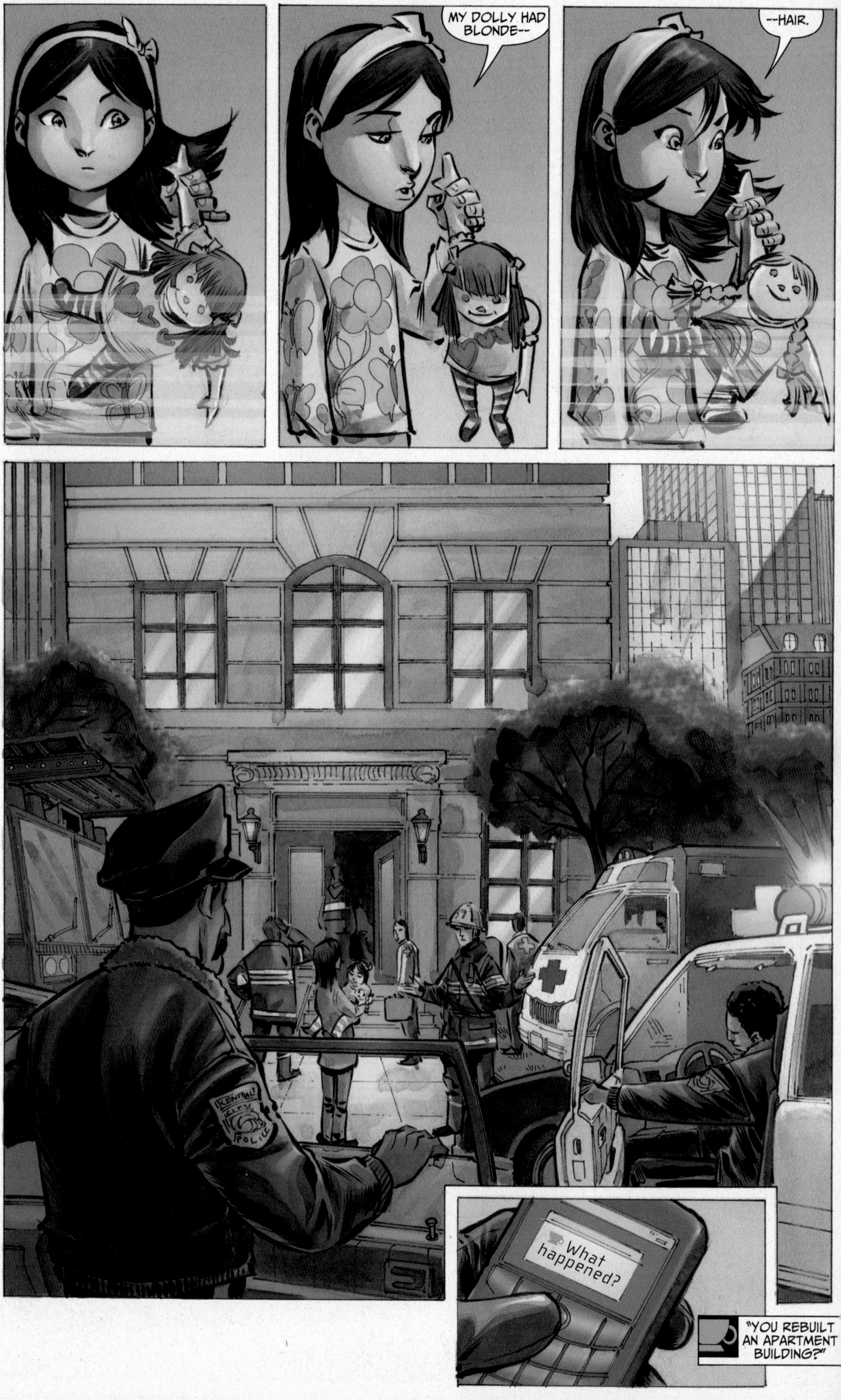
MY DOLLY HAD BLONDE--
--HAIR.
What happened?
"YOU REBUILT AN APARTMENT BUILDING?"

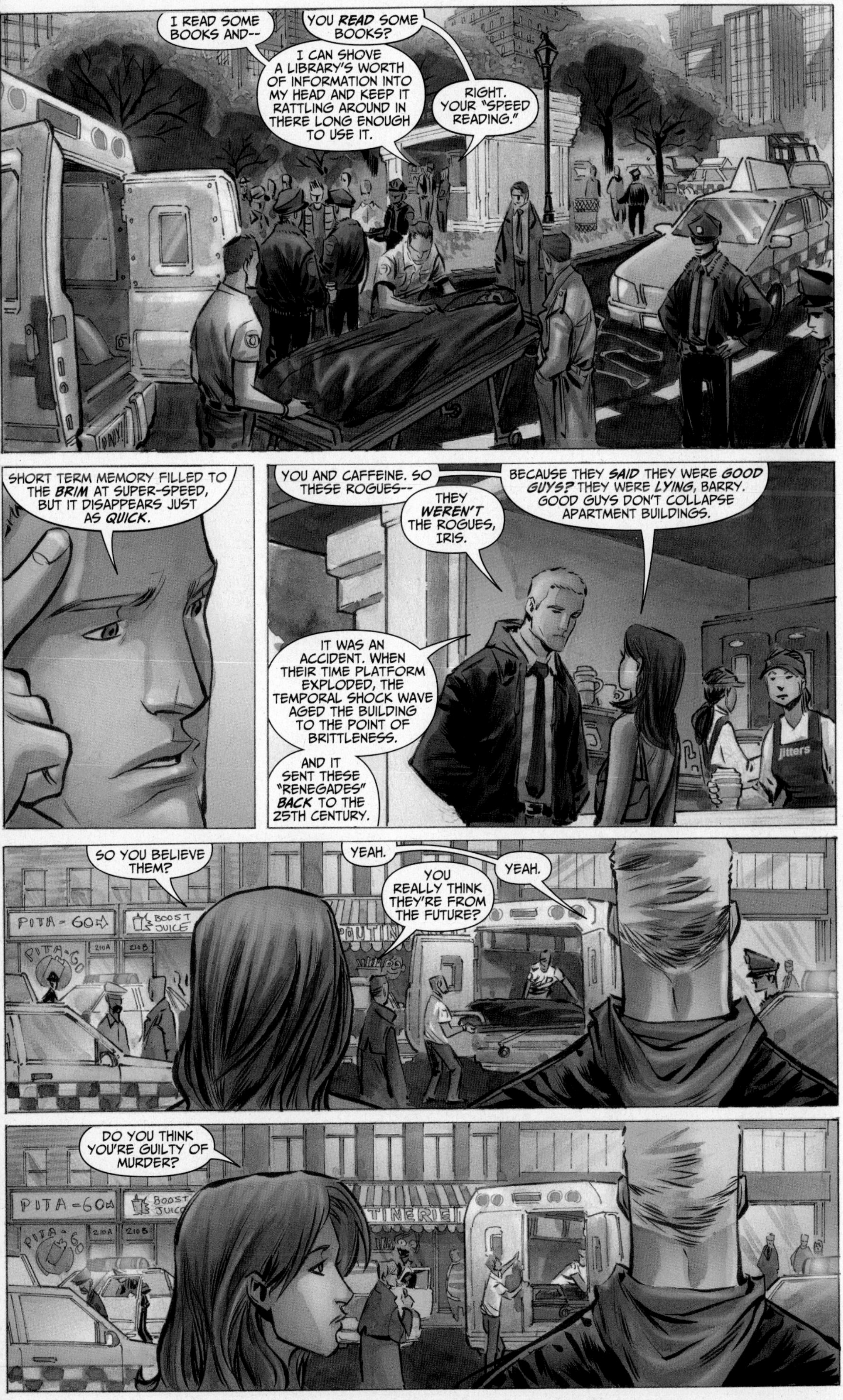
I READ SOME BOOKS AND--
YOU **READ** SOME BOOKS?
I CAN SHOVE A LIBRARY'S WORTH OF INFORMATION INTO MY HEAD AND KEEP IT RATTLING AROUND IN THERE LONG ENOUGH TO USE IT.
RIGHT. YOUR "SPEED READING."
SHORT TERM MEMORY FILLED TO THE **BRIM** AT SUPER-SPEED, BUT IT DISAPPEARS JUST AS **QUICK**.
YOU AND CAFFEINE. SO THESE ROGUES--
THEY **WEREN'T** THE ROGUES, IRIS.
BECAUSE THEY **SAID** THEY WERE **GOOD GUYS?** THEY WERE **LYING**, BARRY. GOOD GUYS DON'T COLLAPSE APARTMENT BUILDINGS.
IT WAS AN ACCIDENT. WHEN THEIR TIME PLATFORM EXPLODED, THE TEMPORAL SHOCK WAVE AGED THE BUILDING TO THE POINT OF BRITTLENESS.
AND IT SENT THESE "RENEGADES" **BACK** TO THE 25TH CENTURY.
jitters
SO YOU BELIEVE THEM?
YEAH.
YOU REALLY THINK THEY'RE FROM THE FUTURE?
YEAH.
PITA-GO
BOOST JUICE
210A
210B
DO YOU THINK YOU'RE GUILTY OF MURDER?

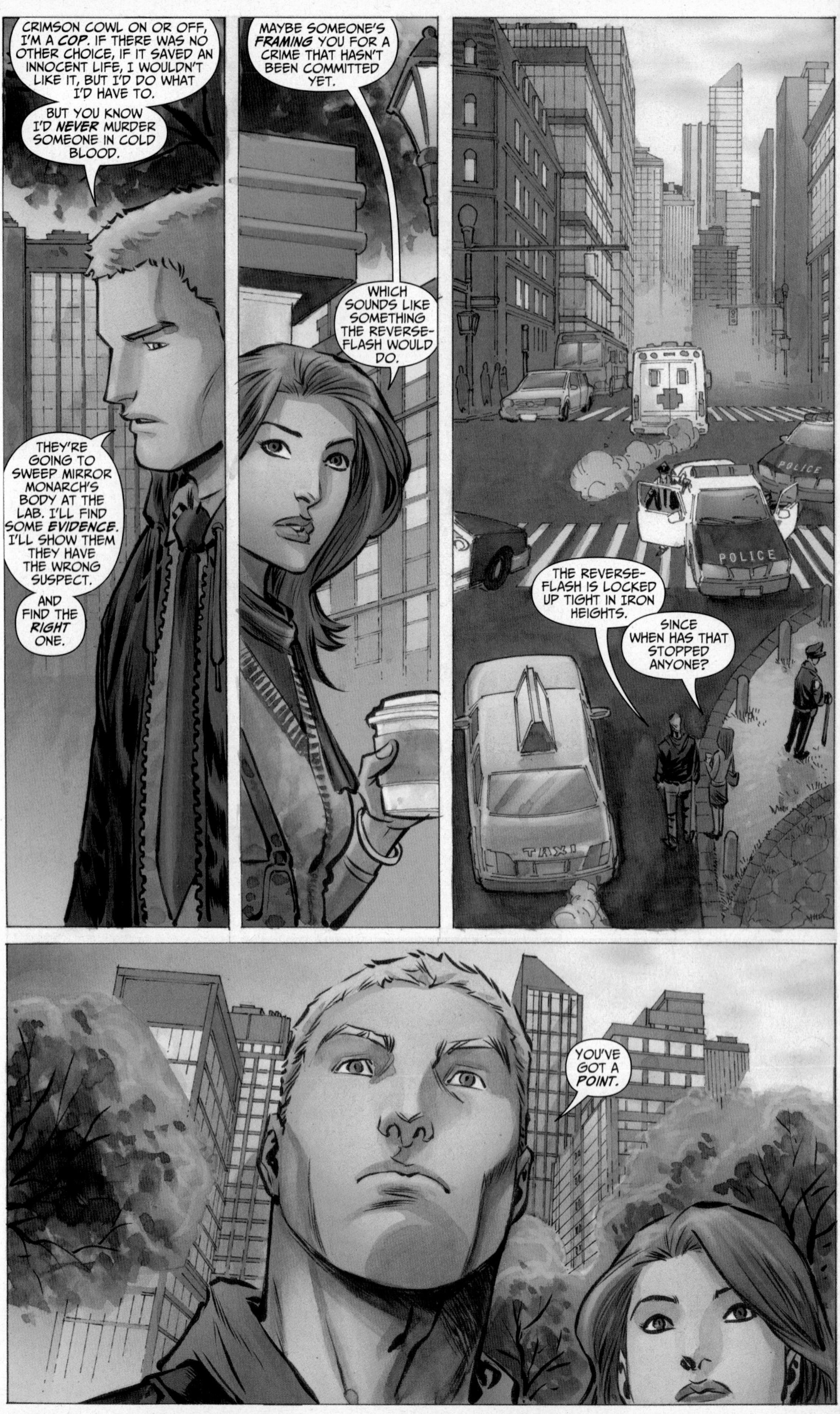

CRIMSON COWL ON OR OFF, I'M A COP. IF THERE WAS NO OTHER CHOICE, IF IT SAVED AN INNOCENT LIFE, I WOULDN'T LIKE IT, BUT I'D DO WHAT I'D HAVE TO.
BUT YOU KNOW I'D NEVER MURDER SOMEONE IN COLD BLOOD.
THEY'RE GOING TO SWEEP MIRROR MONARCH'S BODY AT THE LAB. I'LL FIND SOME EVIDENCE. I'LL SHOW THEM THEY HAVE THE WRONG SUSPECT.
AND FIND THE RIGHT ONE.
MAYBE SOMEONE'S FRAMING YOU FOR A CRIME THAT HASN'T BEEN COMMITTED YET.
WHICH SOUNDS LIKE SOMETHING THE REVERSE-FLASH WOULD DO.
POLICE
POLICE
THE REVERSE-FLASH IS LOCKED UP TIGHT IN IRON HEIGHTS.
SINCE WHEN HAS THAT STOPPED ANYONE?
TAXI
YOU'VE GOT A POINT.

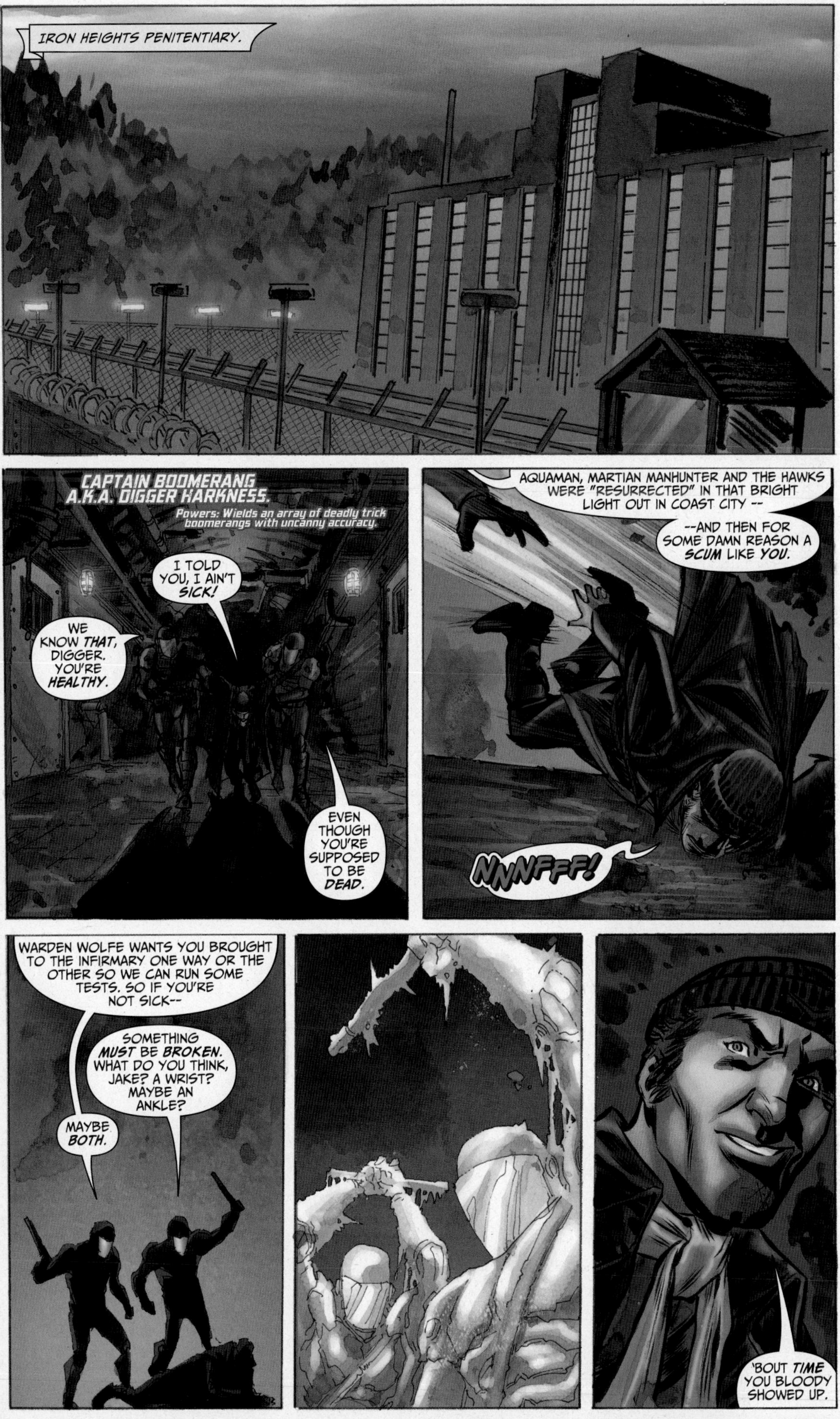
IRON HEIGHTS PENITENTIARY.
CAPTAIN BOOMERANG A.K.A. DIGGER HARKNESS.
Powers: Wields an array of deadly trick boomerangs with uncanny accuracy.
I TOLD YOU, I AIN'T SICK!
WE KNOW THAT, DIGGER. YOU'RE HEALTHY.
EVEN THOUGH YOU'RE SUPPOSED TO BE DEAD.
AQUAMAN, MARTIAN MANHUNTER AND THE HAWKS WERE "RESURRECTED" IN THAT BRIGHT LIGHT OUT IN COAST CITY --
--AND THEN FOR SOME DAMN REASON A SCUM LIKE YOU.
NNNFFF!
WARDEN WOLFE WANTS YOU BROUGHT TO THE INFIRMARY ONE WAY OR THE OTHER SO WE CAN RUN SOME TESTS. SO IF YOU'RE NOT SICK--
SOMETHING MUST BE BROKEN. WHAT DO YOU THINK, JAKE? A WRIST? MAYBE AN ANKLE?
MAYBE BOTH.
'BOUT TIME YOU BLOODY SHOWED UP.

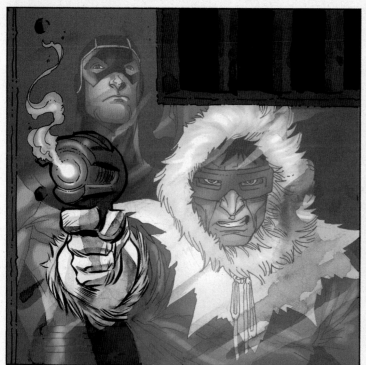

NOW LET'S GET THE HELL OUT OF--

--AAWW!

WHAT'S THE DEAL, MIRROR MASTER? LEMME *THROUGH*.

NO.

"*NO*"? THE ROGUES ALWAYS SPRING ONE ANOTHER, RIGHT, COLD? FIRST RULE WE ALL AGREED ON.

THE RULES HAVE *CHANGED*, DIGGER.

BEFORE YOU DIED, YOU GOT *LAZY*. YOU LET YOURSELF GO *PHYSICALLY* AND *MENTALLY* AND IN THE END, YOU WERE A *DISGRACE* TO YOURSELF AND TO US.

SO YOU'RE CASTING OFF OL' DIGGER, EH? THAT IT?

QUITE THE *OPPOSITE*, PAL. THE FLASH IS *BACK*. WE NEED CAPTAIN BOOMERANG *BACK*, TOO.

BUT YOU NEED TO PROVE THAT YOU'RE STILL A *ROGUE*.

AND HOW AM I SUPPOSED TO DO *THAT*?

THIS TIME, YOU BREAK OUT OF IRON HEIGHTS *YOURSELF*--

--AND THEN YOU MAKE THE FLASH *SWEAT*.

COLD?! MIRROR MASTER?!

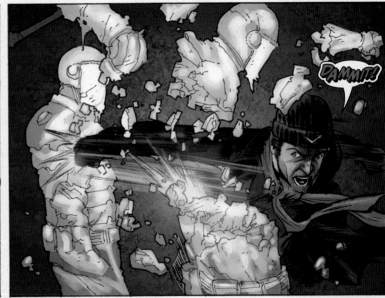

DAMMIT!

C'MON THEN. ALL OF Y--

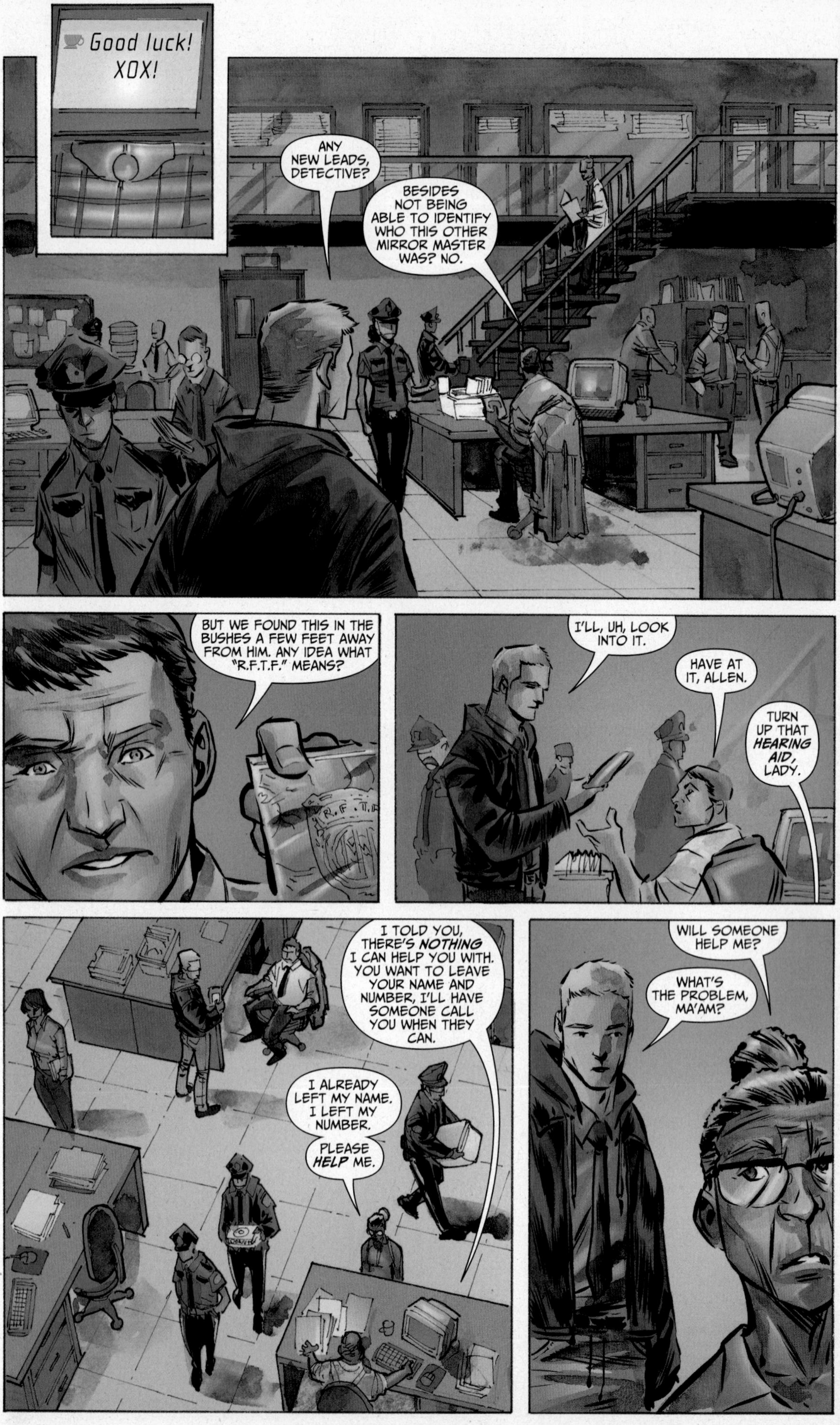
Good luck!
XOX!
ANY NEW LEADS, DETECTIVE?
BESIDES NOT BEING ABLE TO IDENTIFY WHO THIS OTHER MIRROR MASTER WAS? NO.
BUT WE FOUND THIS IN THE BUSHES A FEW FEET AWAY FROM HIM. ANY IDEA WHAT "R.F.T.F." MEANS?
I'LL, UH, LOOK INTO IT.
HAVE AT IT, ALLEN.
TURN UP THAT HEARING AID, LADY.
I TOLD YOU, THERE'S NOTHING I CAN HELP YOU WITH. YOU WANT TO LEAVE YOUR NAME AND NUMBER, I'LL HAVE SOMEONE CALL YOU WHEN THEY CAN.
I ALREADY LEFT MY NAME. I LEFT MY NUMBER.
PLEASE HELP ME.
WILL SOMEONE HELP ME?
WHAT'S THE PROBLEM, MA'AM?

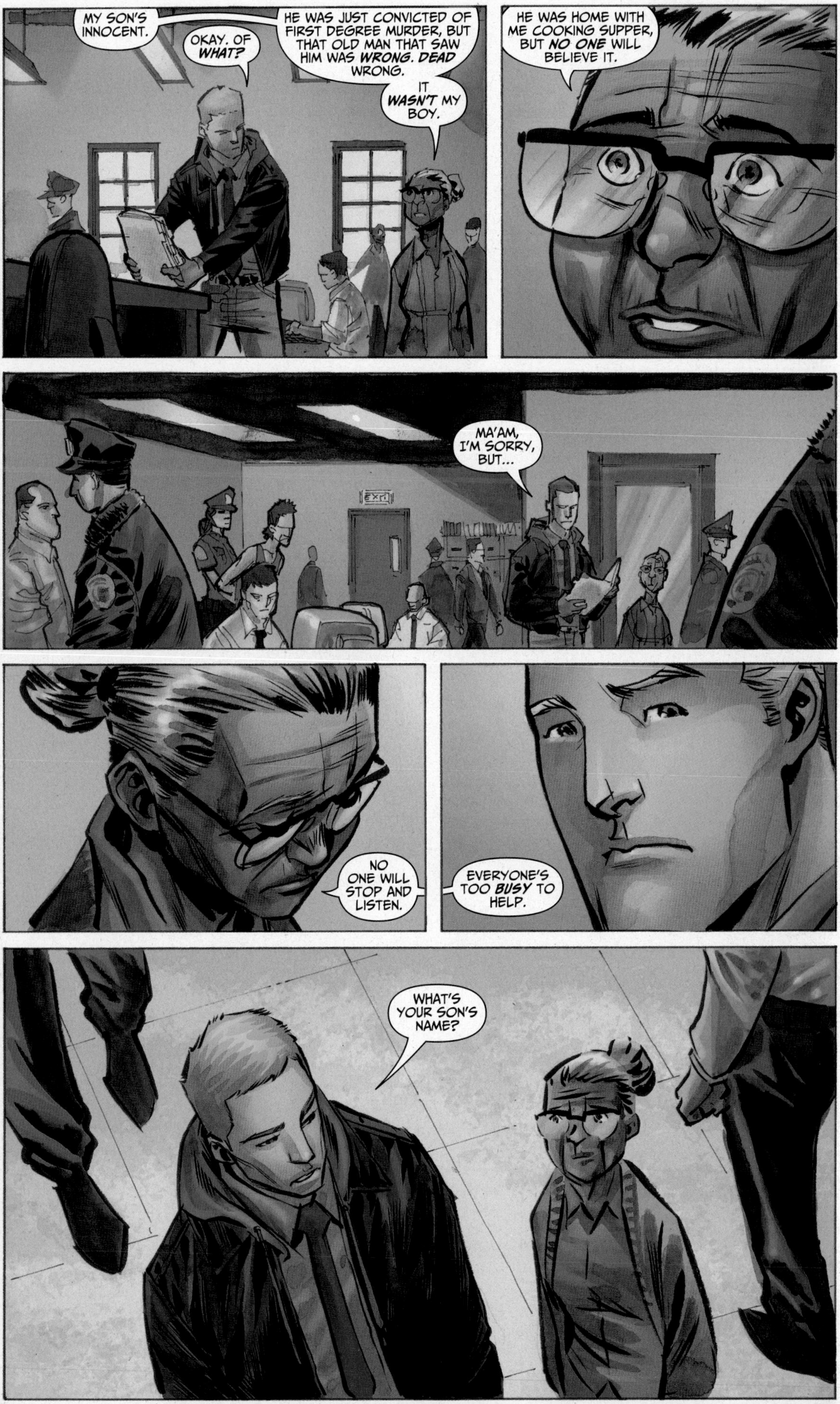
MY SON'S INNOCENT.
OKAY. OF *WHAT?*
HE WAS JUST CONVICTED OF FIRST DEGREE MURDER, BUT THAT OLD MAN THAT SAW HIM WAS *WRONG. DEAD* WRONG.
IT *WASN'T* MY BOY.
HE WAS HOME WITH ME COOKING SUPPER, BUT *NO ONE* WILL BELIEVE IT.
MA'AM, I'M SORRY, BUT...
EXIT
NO ONE WILL STOP AND LISTEN.
EVERYONE'S TOO *BUSY* TO HELP.
WHAT'S YOUR SON'S NAME?

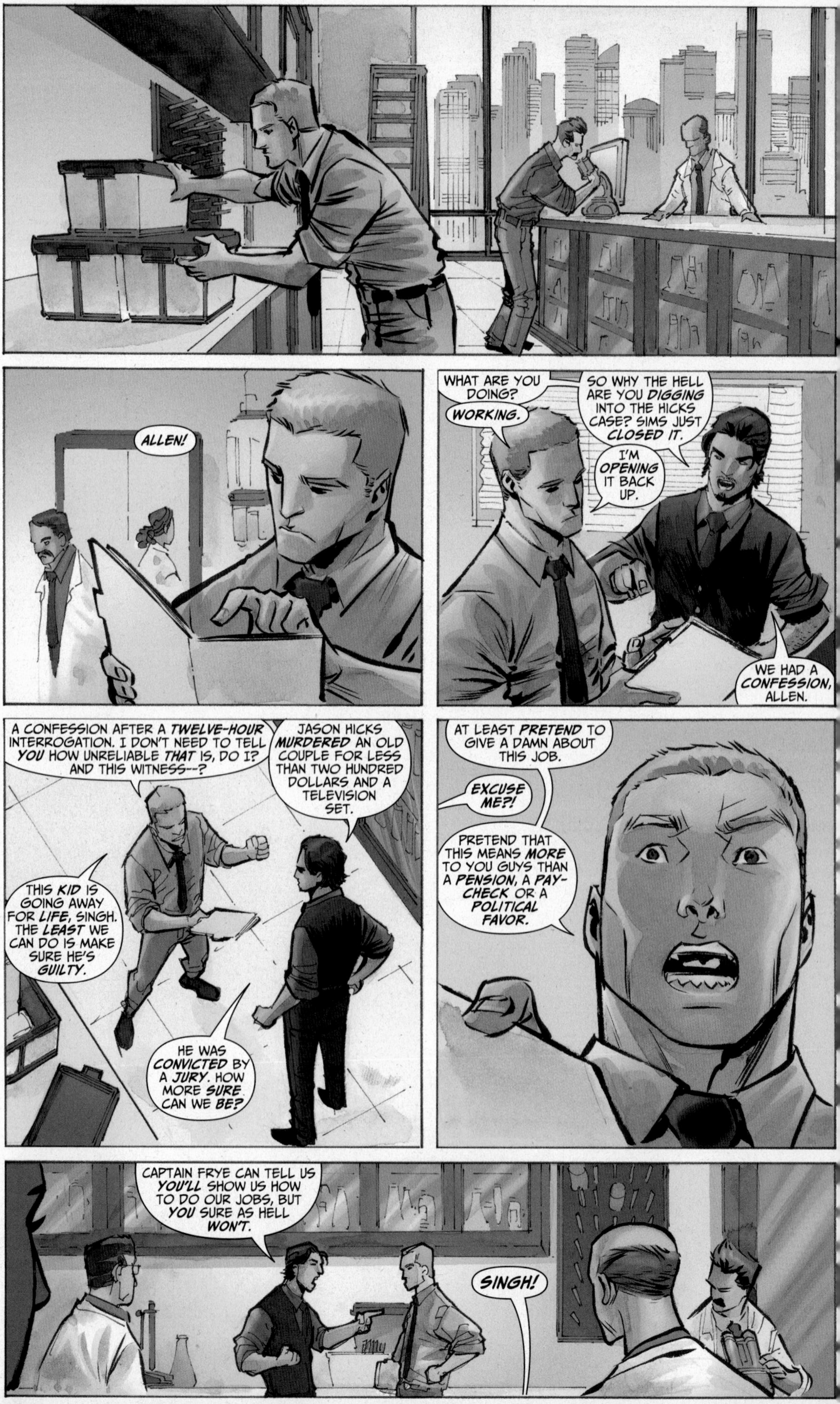
ALLEN!
WHAT ARE YOU DOING?
WORKING.
SO WHY THE HELL ARE YOU DIGGING INTO THE HICKS CASE? SIMS JUST CLOSED IT.
I'M OPENING IT BACK UP.
WE HAD A CONFESSION, ALLEN.
A CONFESSION AFTER A TWELVE-HOUR INTERROGATION. I DON'T NEED TO TELL YOU HOW UNRELIABLE THAT IS, DO I? AND THIS WITNESS--?
JASON HICKS MURDERED AN OLD COUPLE FOR LESS THAN TWO HUNDRED DOLLARS AND A TELEVISION SET.
THIS KID IS GOING AWAY FOR LIFE, SINGH. THE LEAST WE CAN DO IS MAKE SURE HE'S GUILTY.
HE WAS CONVICTED BY A JURY. HOW MORE SURE CAN WE BE?
AT LEAST PRETEND TO GIVE A DAMN ABOUT THIS JOB.
EXCUSE ME?!
PRETEND THAT THIS MEANS MORE TO YOU GUYS THAN A PENSION, A PAY-CHECK OR A POLITICAL FAVOR.
CAPTAIN FRYE CAN TELL US YOU'LL SHOW US HOW TO DO OUR JOBS, BUT YOU SURE AS HELL WON'T.
SINGH!

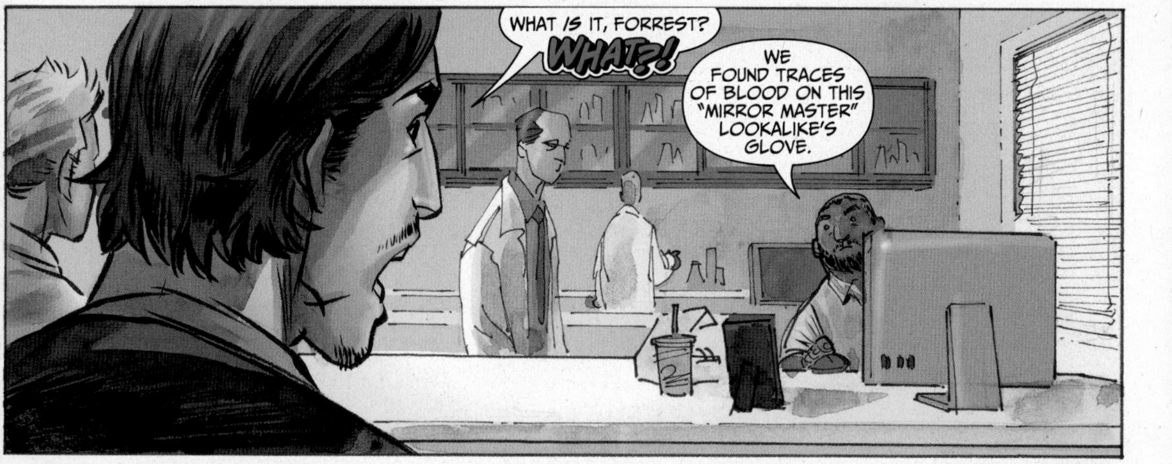
WHAT *IS* IT, FORREST? WHAT?!
WE FOUND TRACES OF BLOOD ON THIS "MIRROR MASTER" LOOKALIKE'S GLOVE.

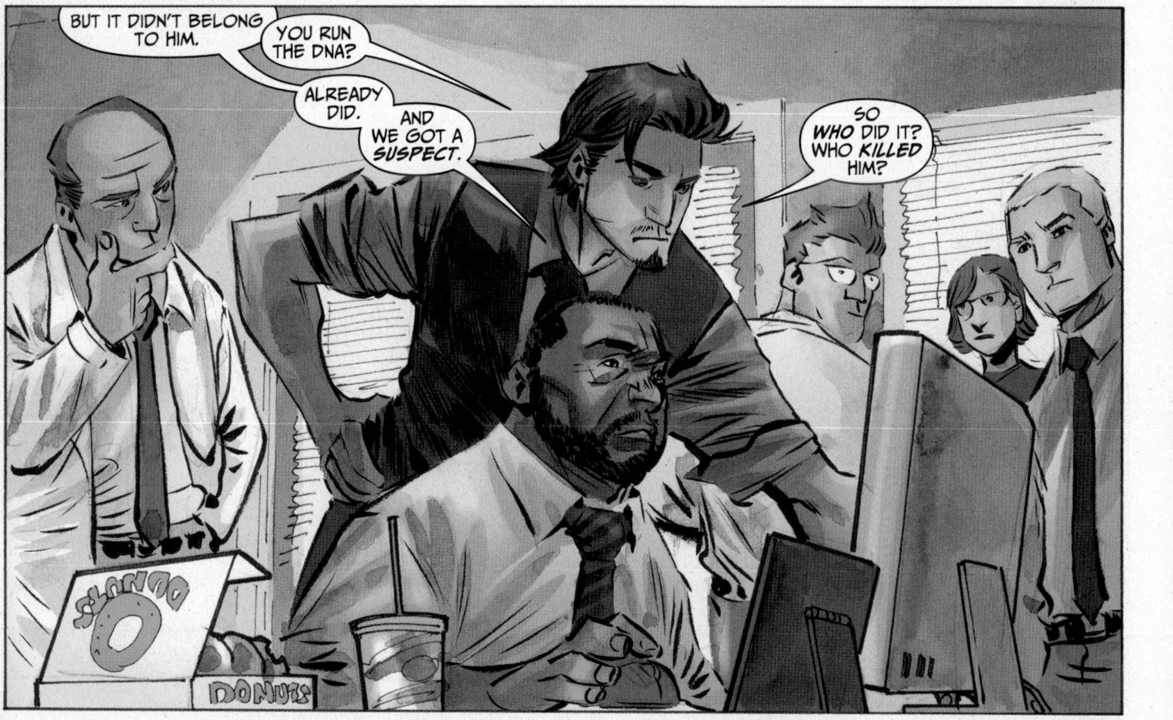
BUT IT DIDN'T BELONG TO HIM.
YOU RUN THE DNA?
ALREADY DID.
AND WE GOT A *SUSPECT*.
SO *WHO* DID IT? WHO *KILLED* HIM?
DONUTS

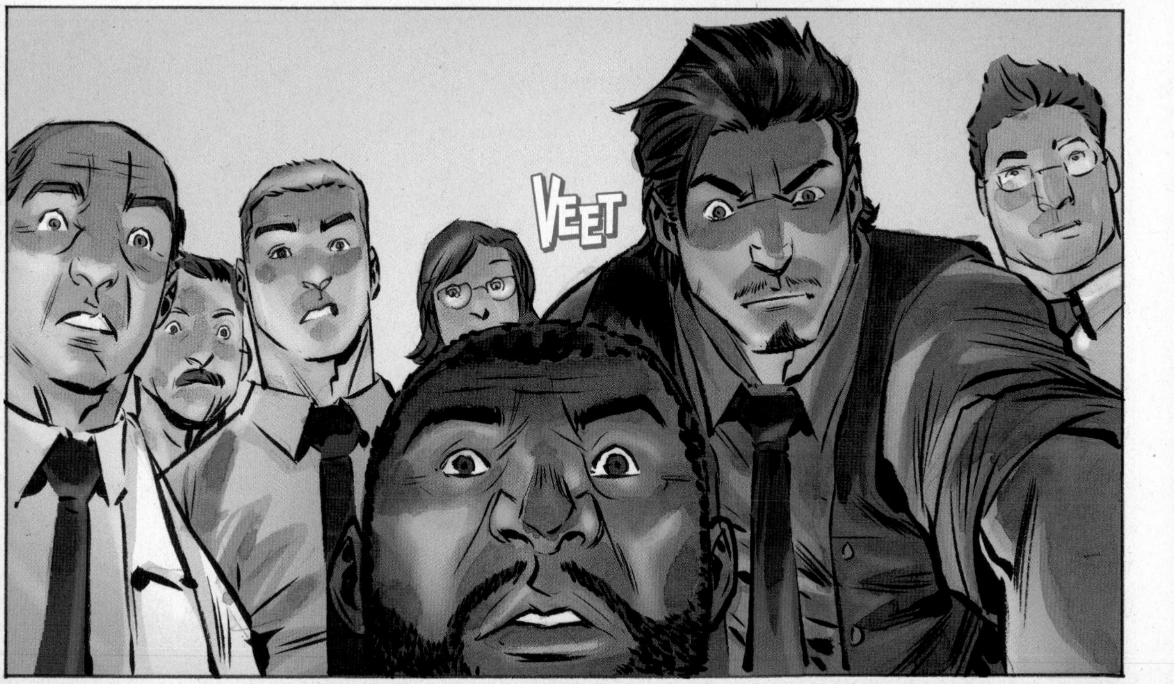
VEET

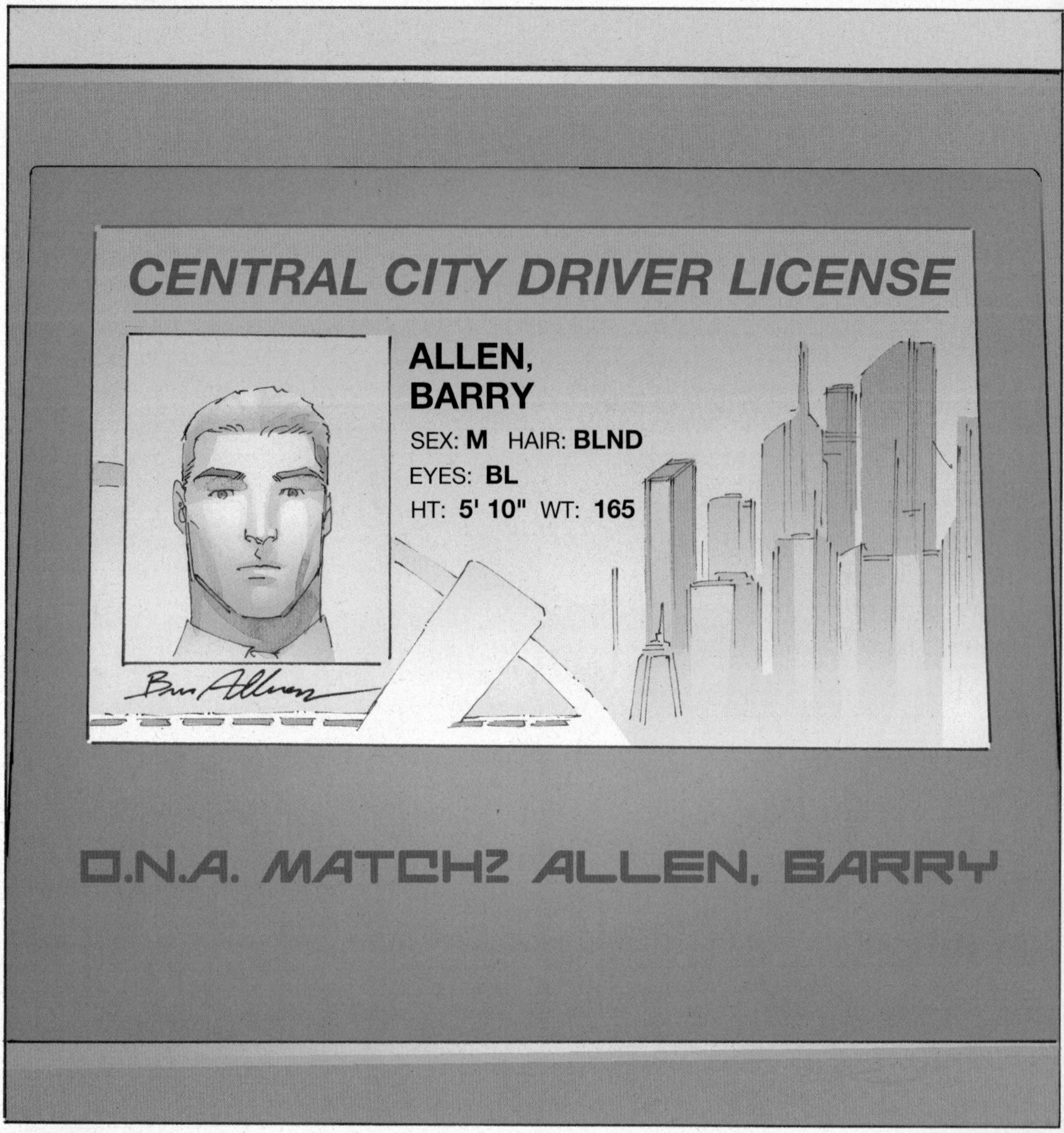
CENTRAL CITY DRIVER LICENSE
ALLEN, BARRY
SEX: M HAIR: BLND
EYES: BL
HT: 5' 10" WT: 165
D.N.A. MATCH: ALLEN, BARRY

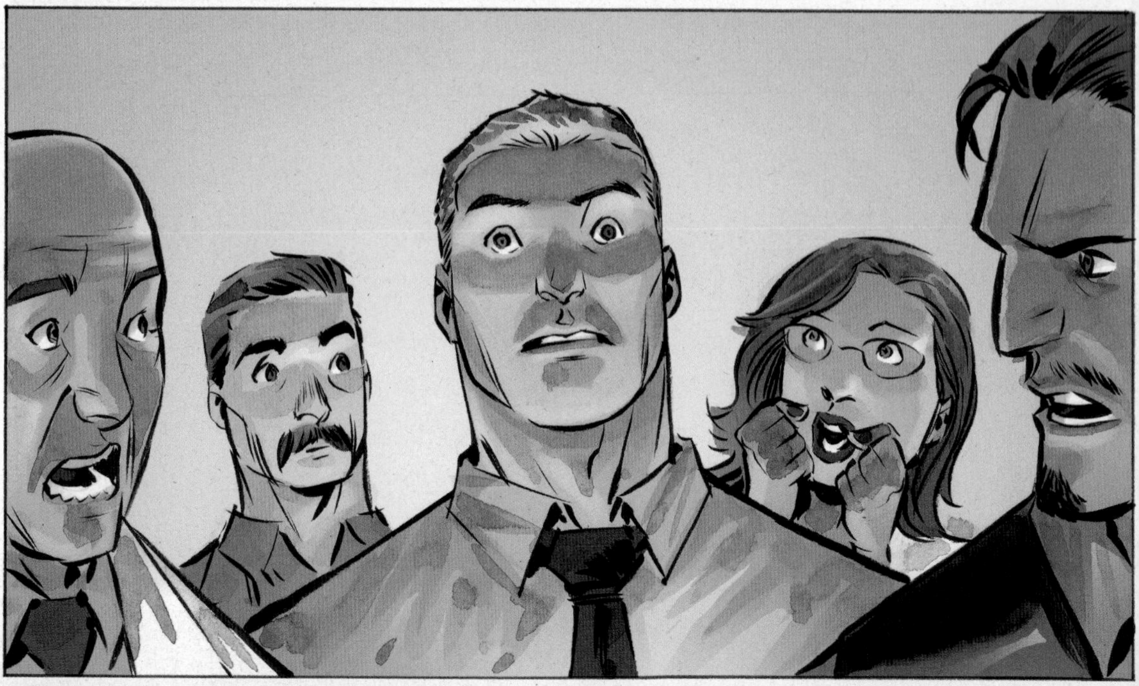

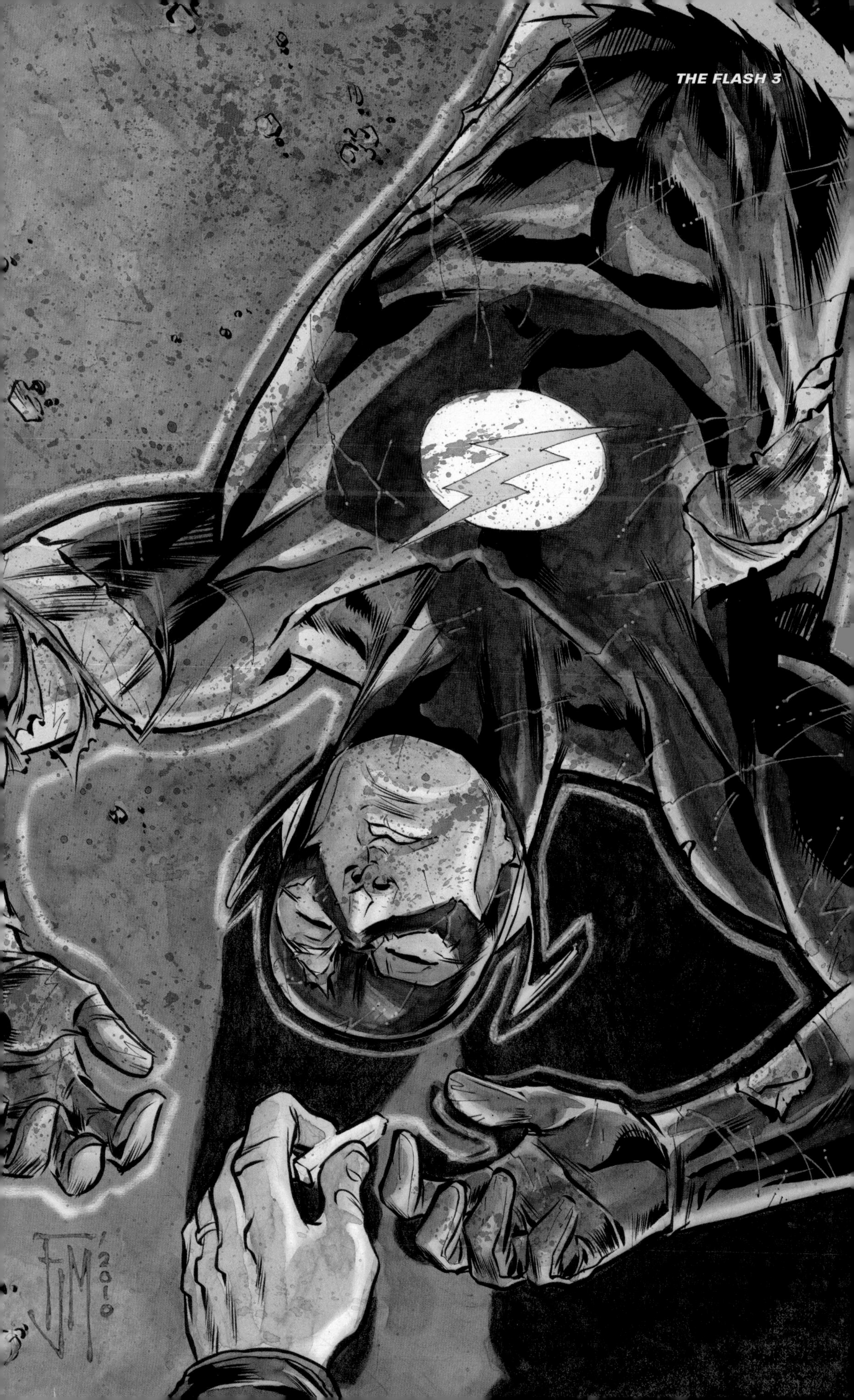
FJM
2010

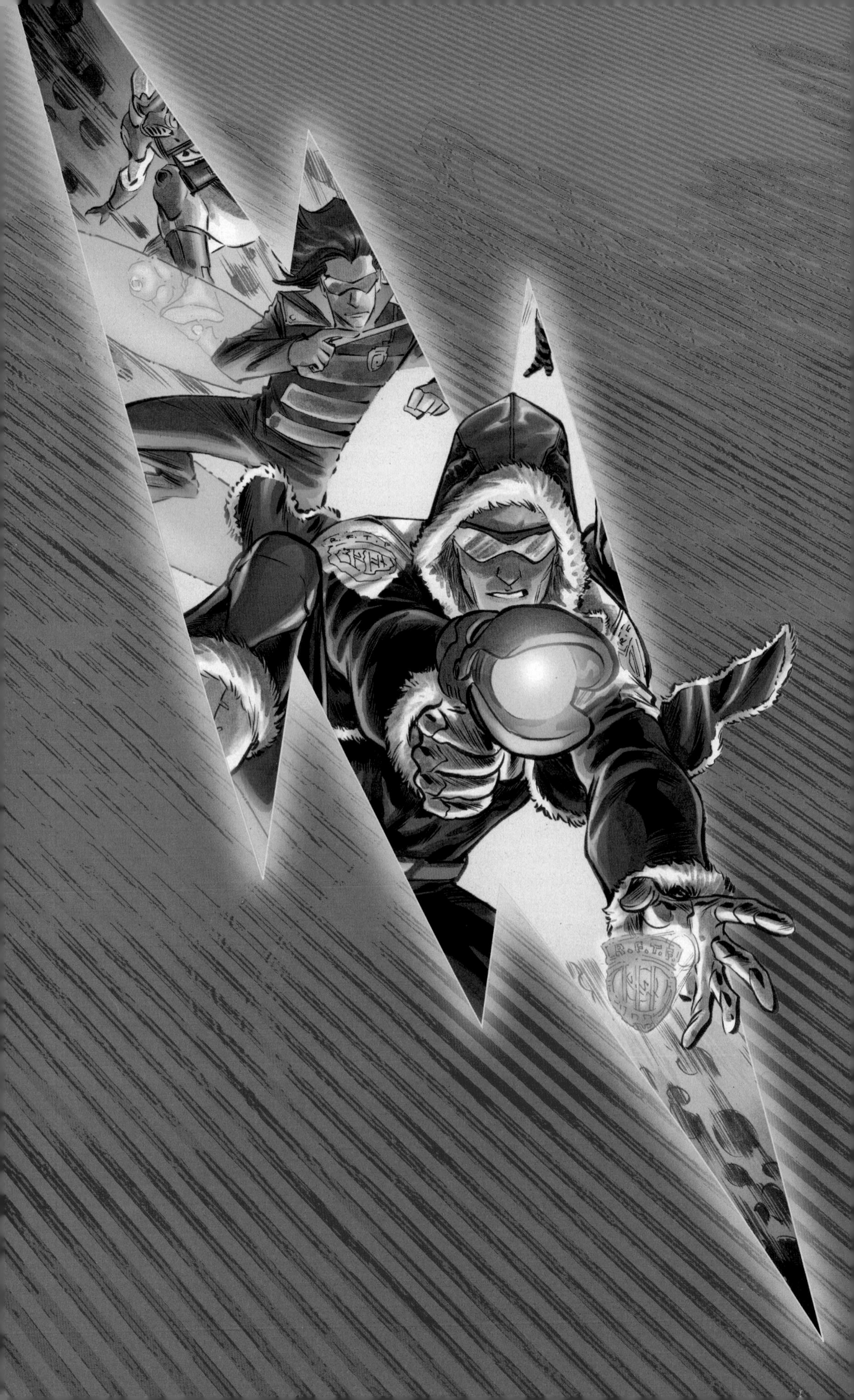

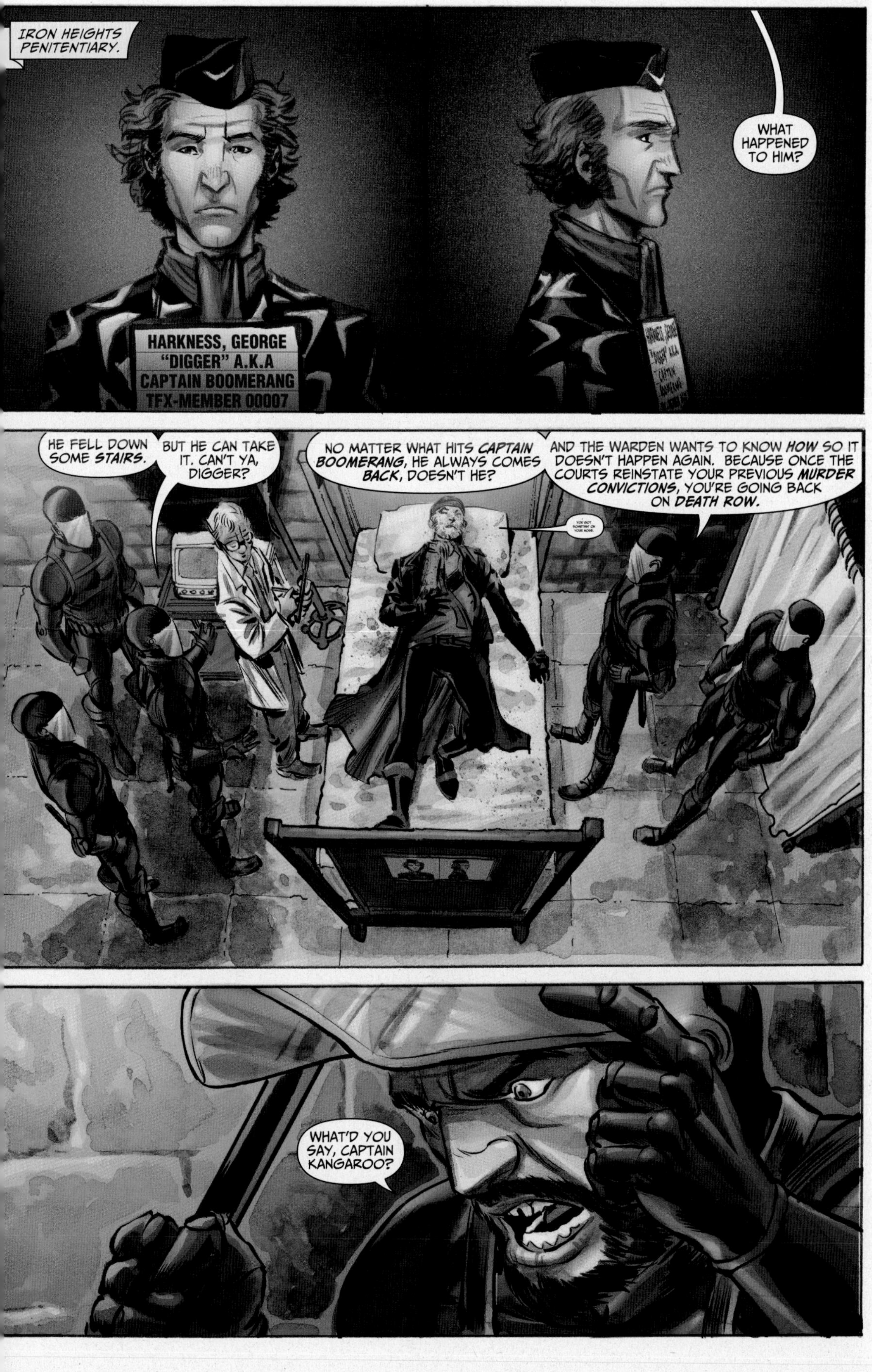
IRON HEIGHTS PENITENTIARY.
HARKNESS, GEORGE "DIGGER" A.K.A CAPTAIN BOOMERANG TFX-MEMBER 00007
WHAT HAPPENED TO HIM?
HE FELL DOWN SOME STAIRS.
BUT HE CAN TAKE IT. CAN'T YA, DIGGER?
NO MATTER WHAT HITS CAPTAIN BOOMERANG, HE ALWAYS COMES BACK, DOESN'T HE?
AND THE WARDEN WANTS TO KNOW HOW SO IT DOESN'T HAPPEN AGAIN. BECAUSE ONCE THE COURTS REINSTATE YOUR PREVIOUS MURDER CONVICTIONS, YOU'RE GOING BACK ON DEATH ROW.
YOU GOT SOMETHIN' ON YOUR NOSE.
WHAT'D YOU SAY, CAPTAIN KANGAROO?

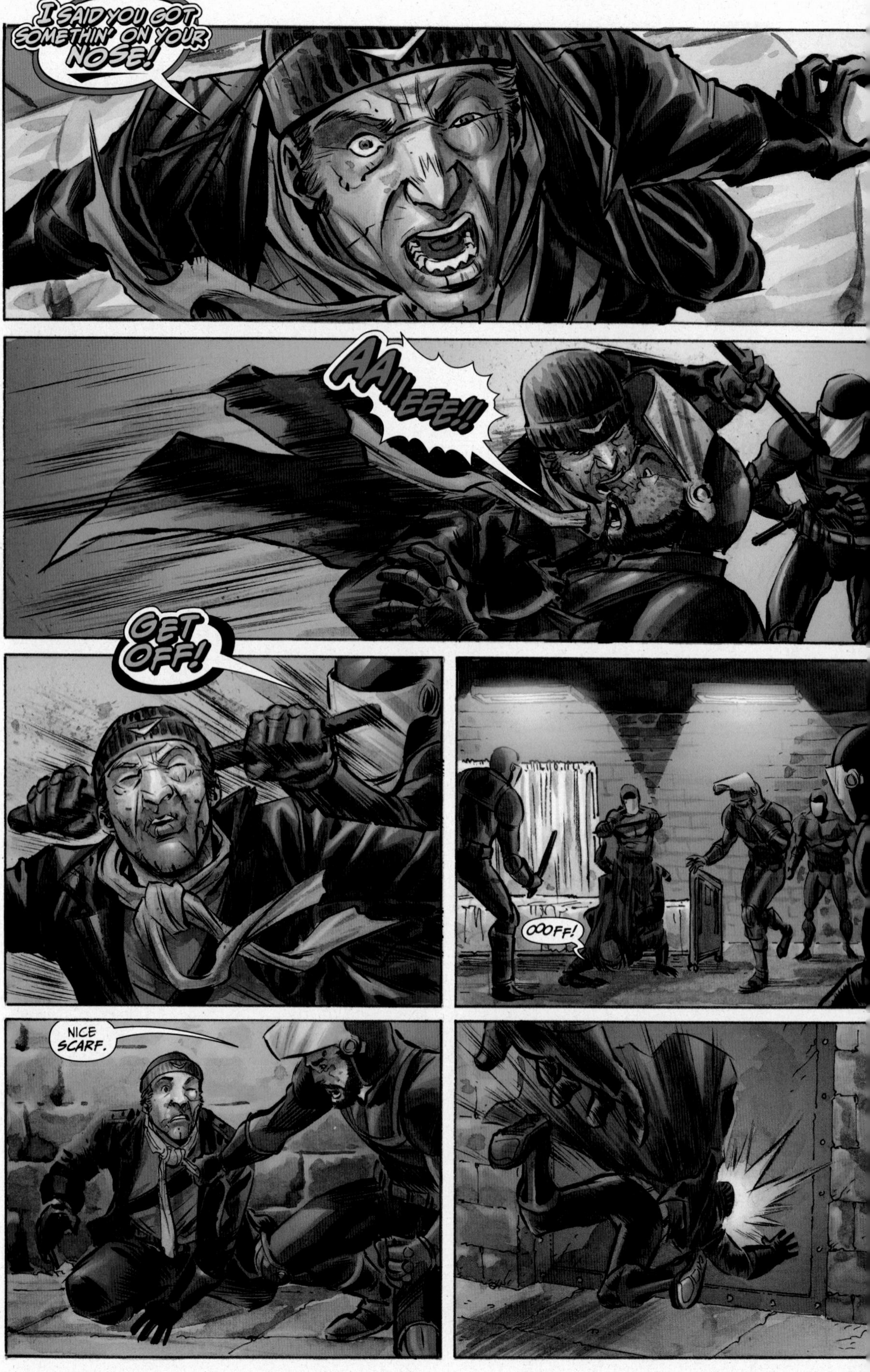
I SAID YOU GOT SOMETHIN' ON YOUR NOSE!
AAIIEEE!!
GET OFF!
OOOFF!
NICE SCARF.

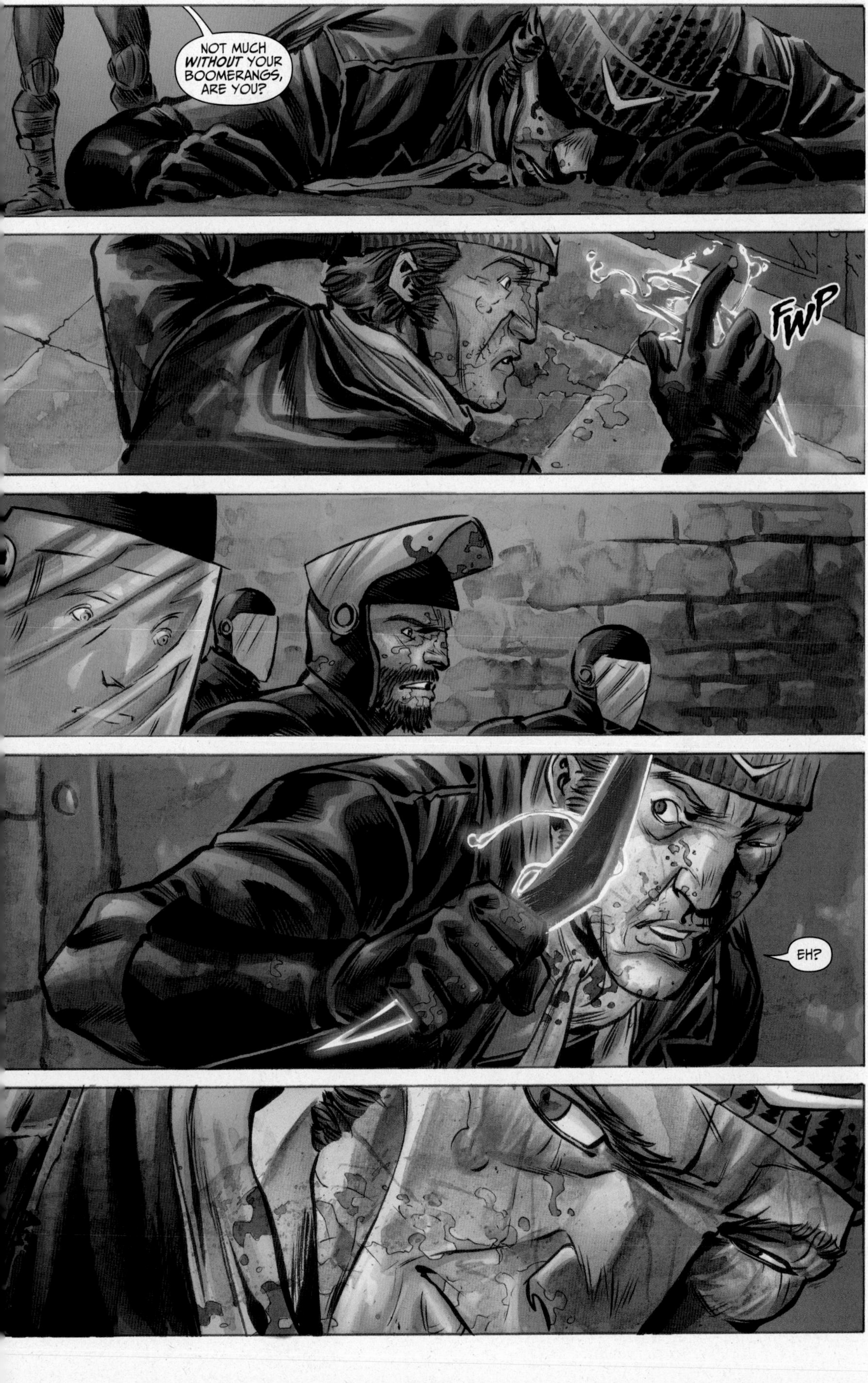
NOT MUCH *WITHOUT* YOUR BOOMERANGS, ARE YOU?
FWP
EH?

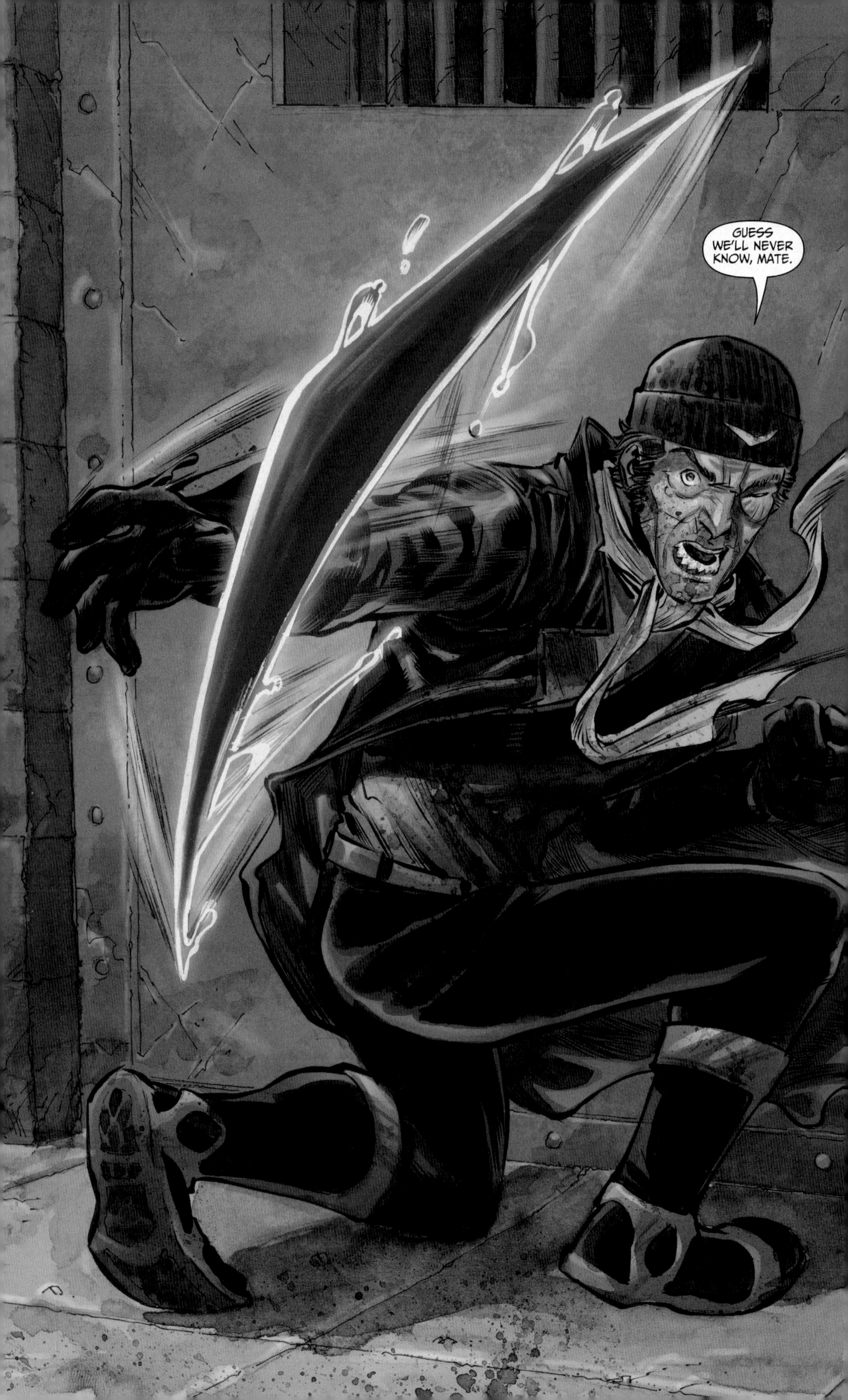
GUESS WE'LL NEVER KNOW, MATE.

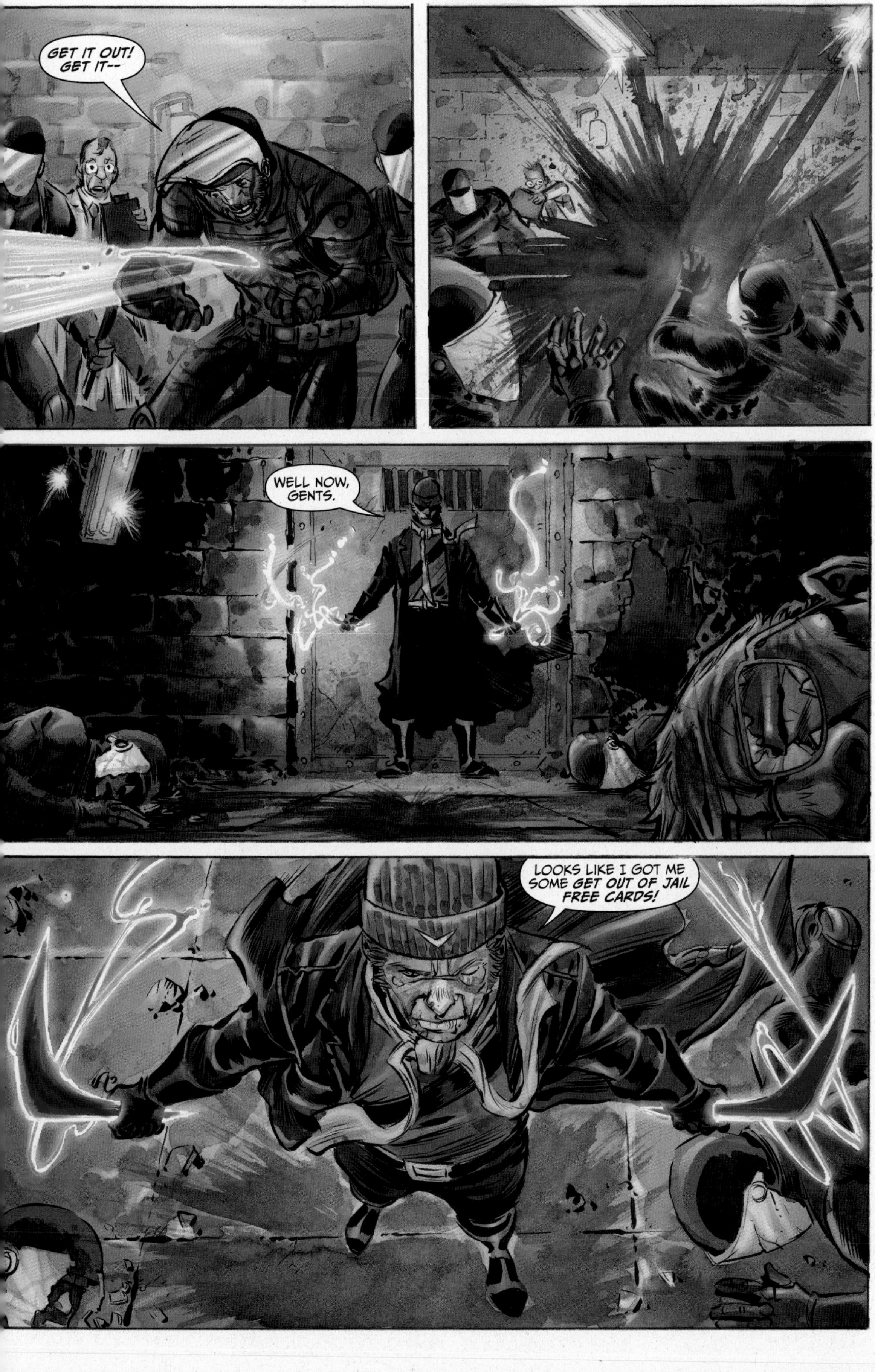
GET IT OUT! GET IT--
WELL NOW, GENTS.
LOOKS LIKE I GOT ME SOME GET OUT OF JAIL FREE CARDS!

"WHO ELSE WANTS ONE?"

MIRROR MASTER
...OPY
...EAT —
...REAL
...DENTITY
...NKNOWN.

YOU KILLED HIM, ALLEN.

CENTRAL CITY POLICE DEPARTMENT.

THE CRIME LAB.

I...I WOULDN'T...

BUT *THAT'S* WHAT THE *EVIDENCE* SAYS. *RIGHT*, FORREST?

THAT'S WHAT THE EVIDENCE SAYS, BUT--

AND YOU KNOW *WHY*, ALLEN?

NO.

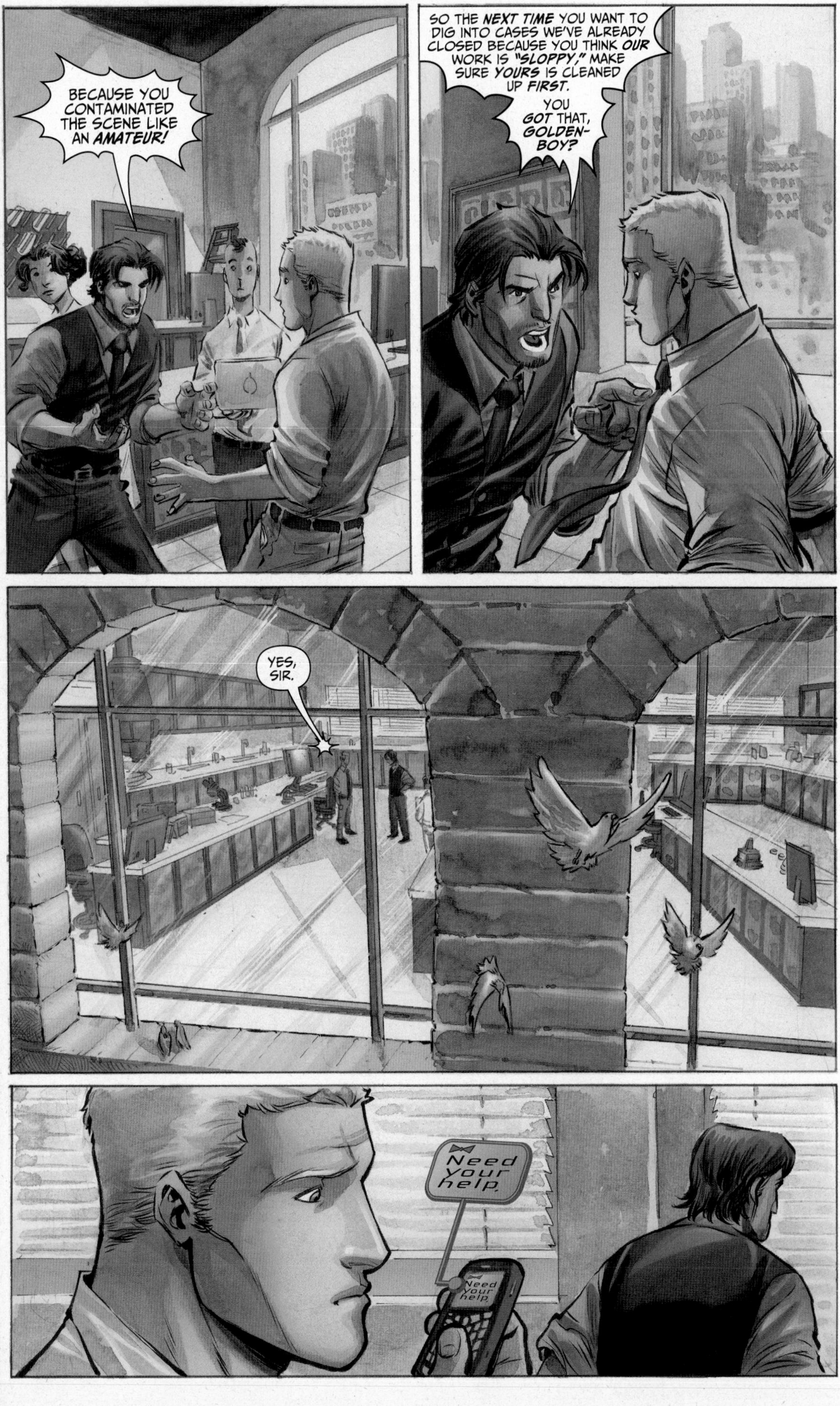
BECAUSE YOU CONTAMINATED THE SCENE LIKE AN AMATEUR!
SO THE NEXT TIME YOU WANT TO DIG INTO CASES WE'VE ALREADY CLOSED BECAUSE YOU THINK OUR WORK IS "SLOPPY," MAKE SURE YOURS IS CLEANED UP FIRST.
YOU GOT THAT, GOLDEN-BOY?
YES, SIR.
Need your help.
Need your help.

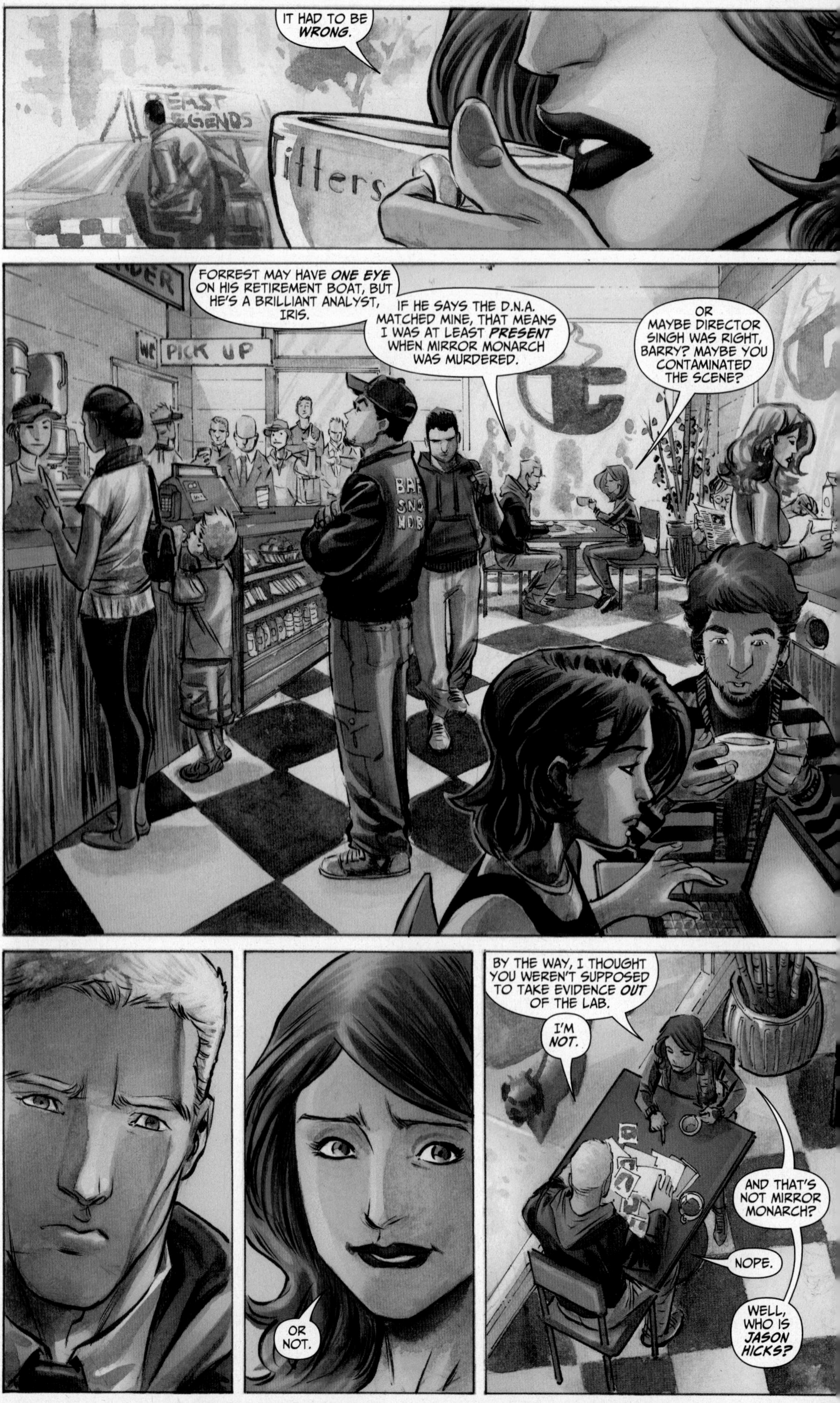
IT HAD TO BE *WRONG*.
BEAST LEGENDS
Titters
FORREST MAY HAVE *ONE EYE* ON HIS RETIREMENT BOAT, BUT HE'S A BRILLIANT ANALYST, IRIS.
IF HE SAYS THE D.N.A. MATCHED MINE, THAT MEANS I WAS AT LEAST *PRESENT* WHEN MIRROR MONARCH WAS MURDERED.
OR MAYBE DIRECTOR SINGH WAS RIGHT, BARRY? MAYBE YOU CONTAMINATED THE SCENE?
PICK UP
OR NOT.
BY THE WAY, I THOUGHT YOU WEREN'T SUPPOSED TO TAKE EVIDENCE *OUT* OF THE LAB.
I'M *NOT*.
AND THAT'S NOT MIRROR MONARCH?
NOPE.
WELL, WHO IS *JASON HICKS?*

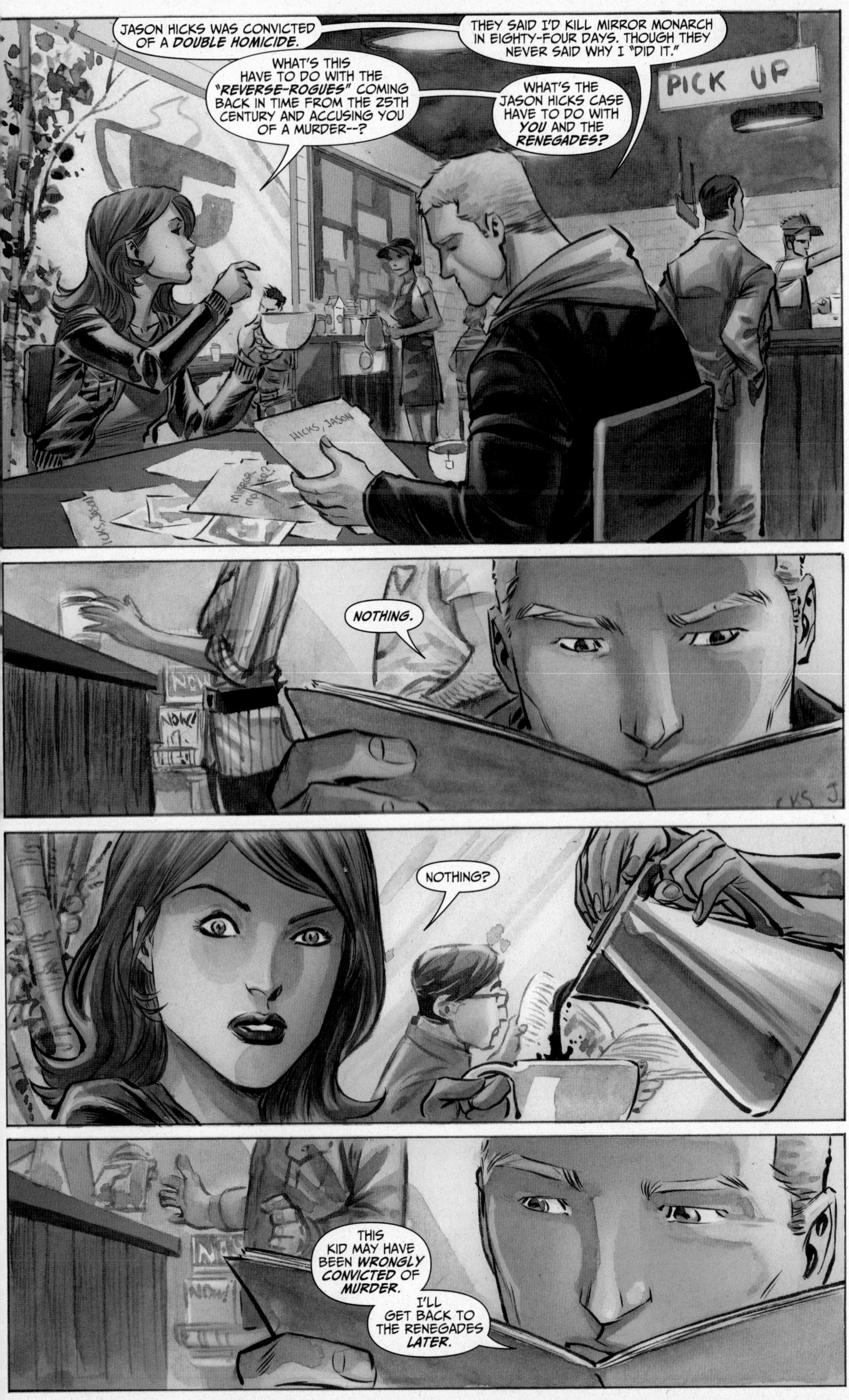

JASON HICKS WAS CONVICTED OF A *DOUBLE HOMICIDE*.
THEY SAID I'D KILL MIRROR MONARCH IN EIGHTY-FOUR DAYS. THOUGH THEY NEVER SAID WHY I "DID IT."
PICK UP
WHAT'S THIS HAVE TO DO WITH THE *"REVERSE-ROGUES"* COMING BACK IN TIME FROM THE 25TH CENTURY AND ACCUSING YOU OF A MURDER--?
WHAT'S THE JASON HICKS CASE HAVE TO DO WITH *YOU* AND THE *RENEGADES?*
HICKS, JASON
NOTHING.
NOTHING?
THIS KID MAY HAVE BEEN *WRONGLY CONVICTED* OF *MURDER*.
I'LL GET BACK TO THE RENEGADES *LATER*.

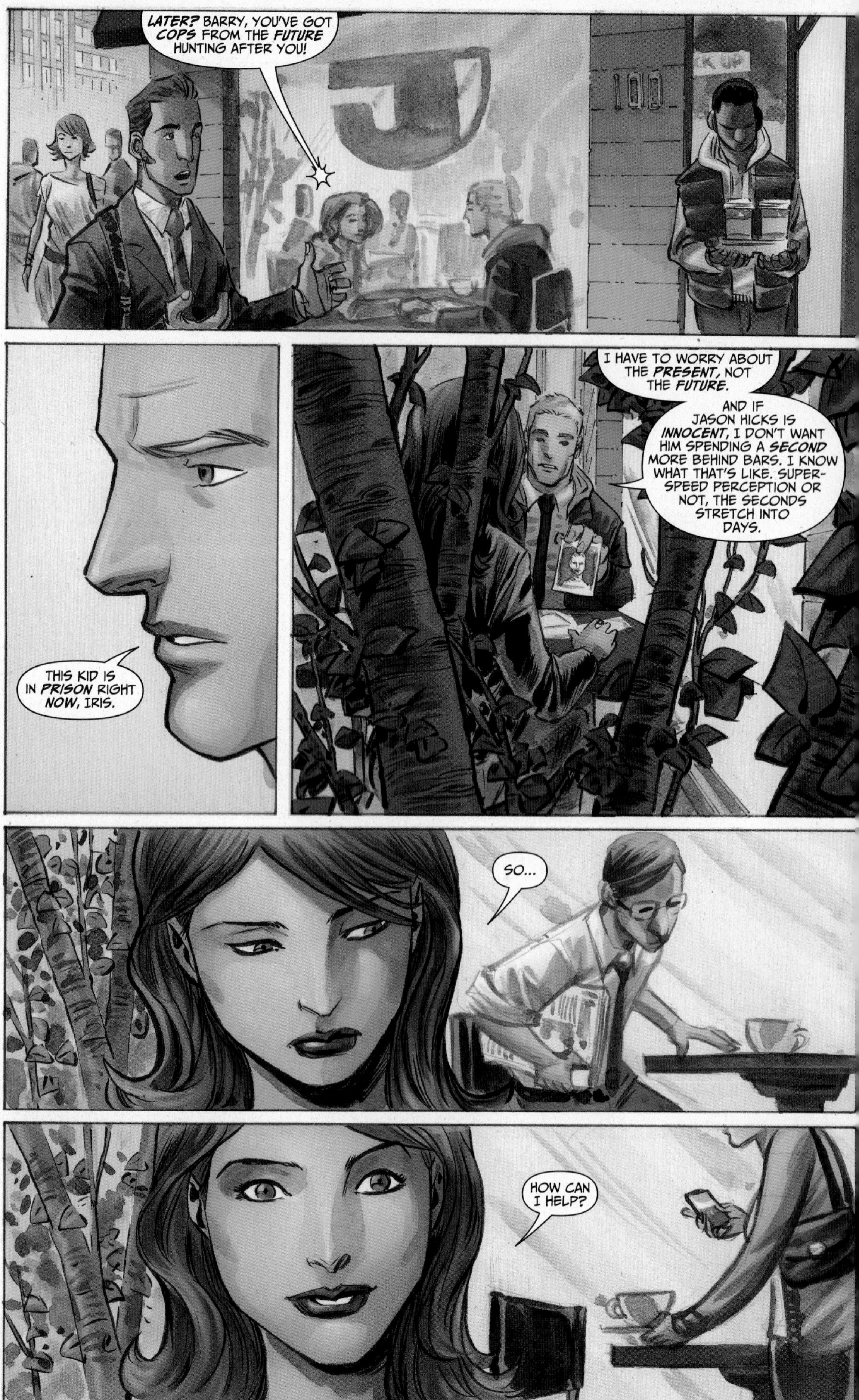

LATER? BARRY, YOU'VE GOT COPS FROM THE FUTURE HUNTING AFTER YOU!
100
THIS KID IS IN PRISON RIGHT NOW, IRIS.
I HAVE TO WORRY ABOUT THE PRESENT, NOT THE FUTURE.
AND IF JASON HICKS IS INNOCENT, I DON'T WANT HIM SPENDING A SECOND MORE BEHIND BARS. I KNOW WHAT THAT'S LIKE. SUPER-SPEED PERCEPTION OR NOT, THE SECONDS STRETCH INTO DAYS.
SO...
HOW CAN I HELP?

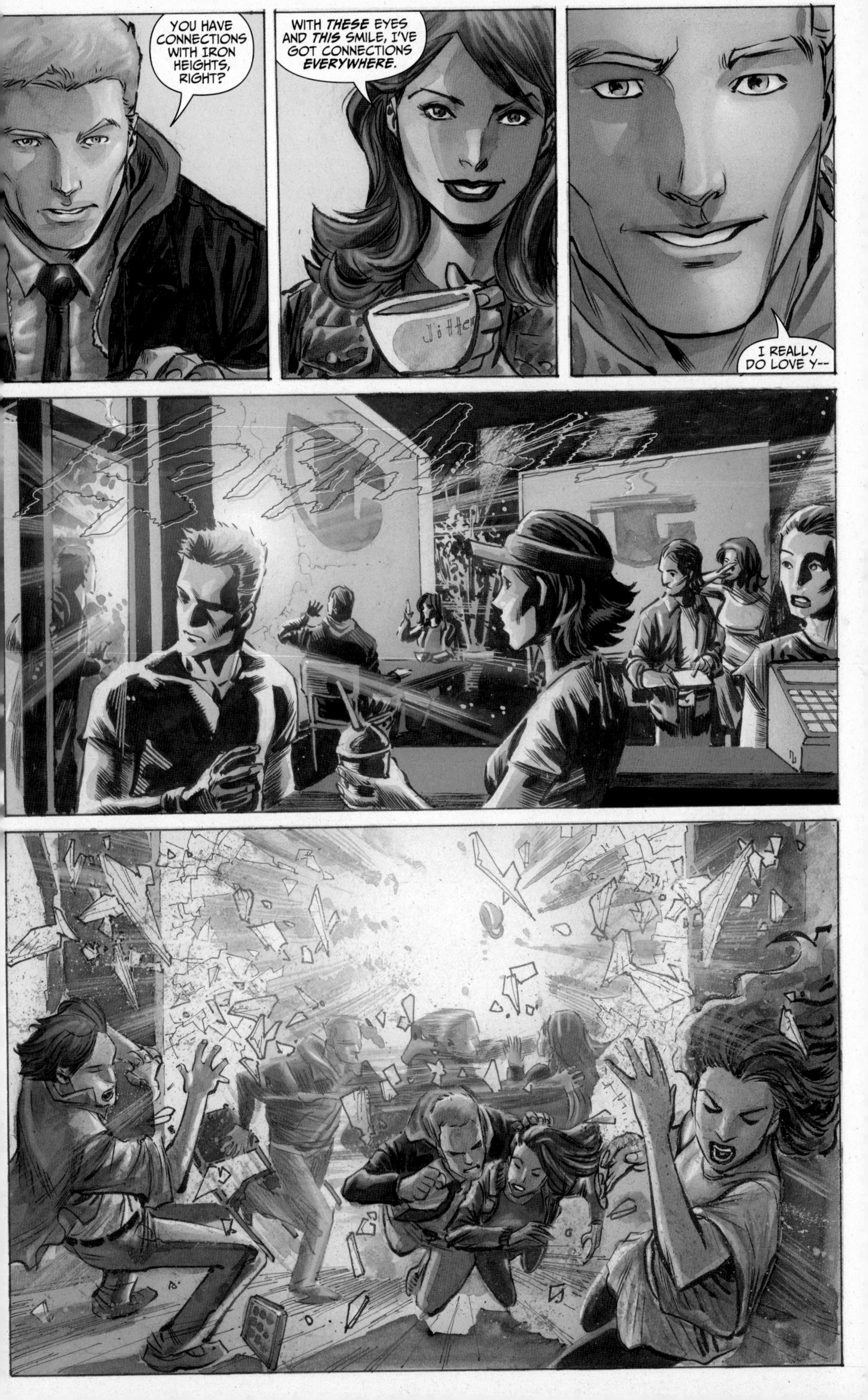
YOU HAVE CONNECTIONS WITH IRON HEIGHTS, RIGHT?
WITH *THESE* EYES AND *THIS* SMILE, I'VE GOT CONNECTIONS *EVERYWHERE*.
I REALLY DO LOVE Y--

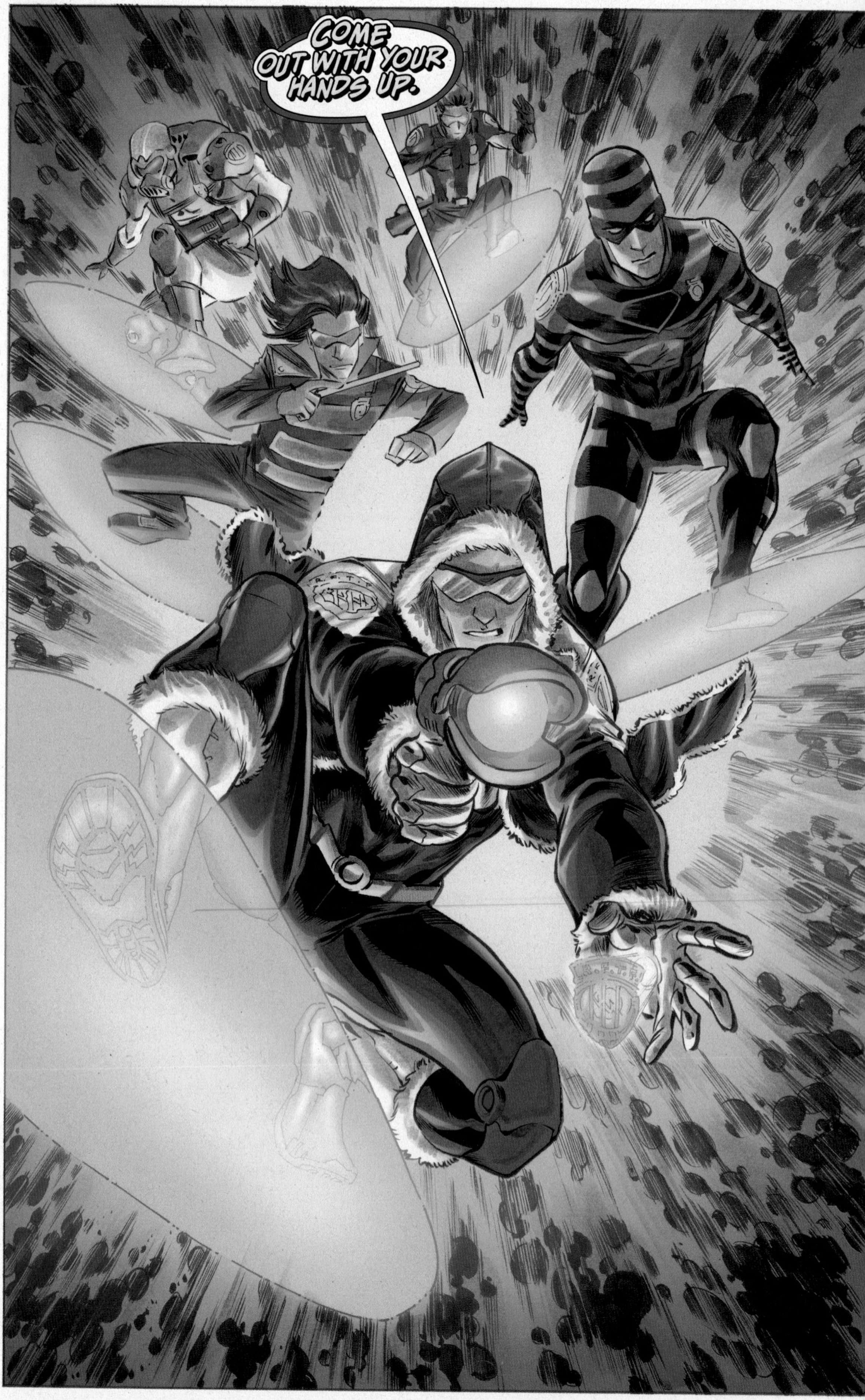
COME OUT WITH YOUR HANDS UP.

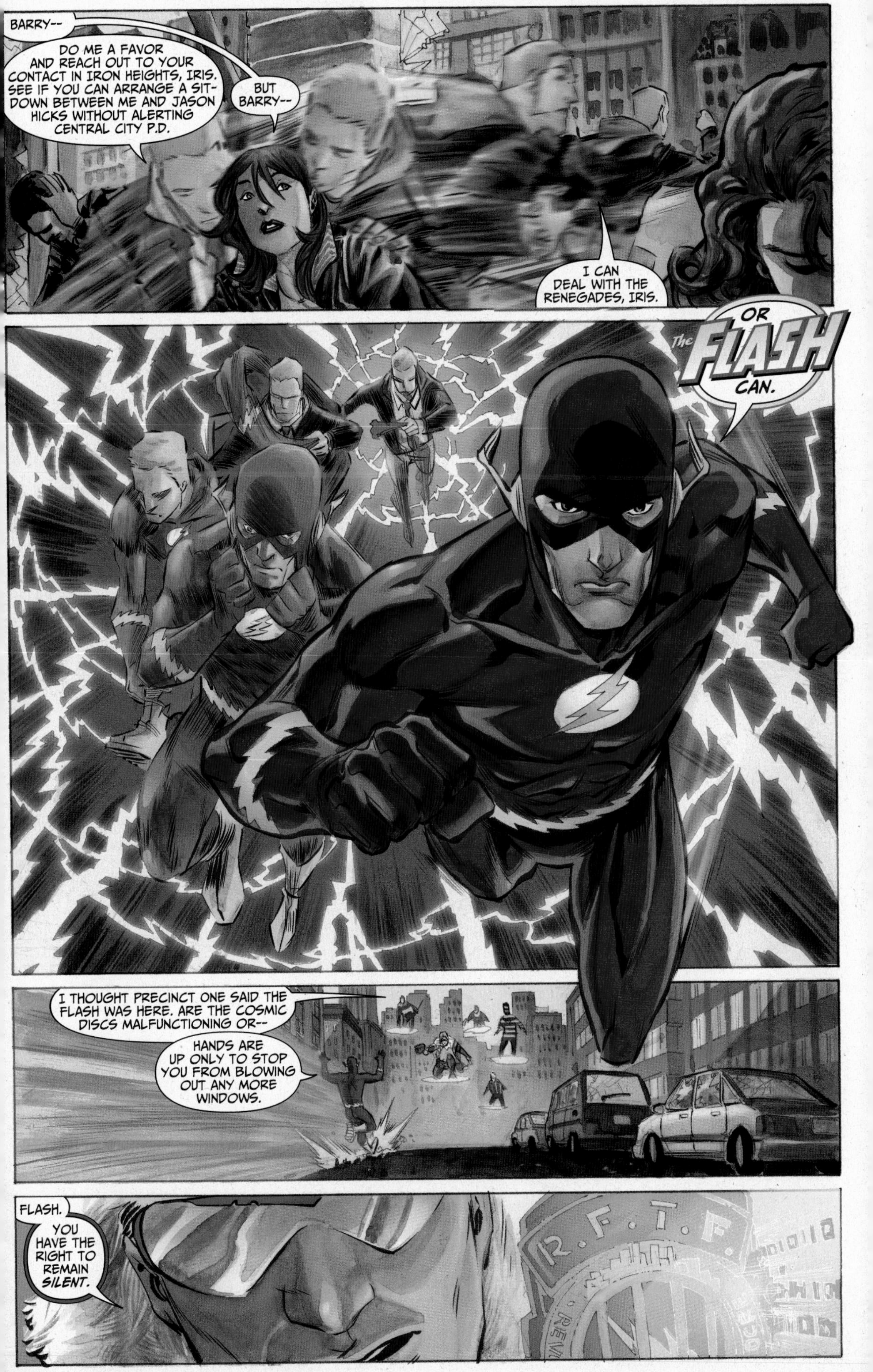
BARRY--
DO ME A FAVOR AND REACH OUT TO YOUR CONTACT IN IRON HEIGHTS, IRIS. SEE IF YOU CAN ARRANGE A SIT-DOWN BETWEEN ME AND JASON HICKS WITHOUT ALERTING CENTRAL CITY P.D.
BUT BARRY--
I CAN DEAL WITH THE RENEGADES, IRIS.
OR The FLASH CAN.
I THOUGHT PRECINCT ONE SAID THE FLASH WAS HERE. ARE THE COSMIC DISCS MALFUNCTIONING OR--
HANDS ARE UP ONLY TO STOP YOU FROM BLOWING OUT ANY MORE WINDOWS.
FLASH.
YOU HAVE THE RIGHT TO REMAIN SILENT.
R.F.T.F.

ANYTHING YOU SAY WILL BE RECORDED AND HELD AGAINST YOU IN THE TWENTY-FIFTH COURT OF LAWS.

YOU HAVE THE RIGHT TO ACCESS AN ATTORNEY. IF YOU ARE UNABLE TO ACCESS AN ATTORNEY ONE WILL BE PROGRAMMED FOR YOU. AND MOST OF ALL--

VEET

--YOU HAVE THE RIGHT TO A *SPEEDY* TRIAL. SOMETHING I DON'T THINK *ANYONE'S* USED TO IN *THIS* CENTURY.

THE WAY THINGS HAVE BEEN WORKING IN CENTRAL CITY LATELY, YOU'D BE SURPRISED. AND TO TELL YOU THE TRUTH, COMMANDER, I'M A LITTLE DISAPPOINTED.

I WAS HOPING IN THE FUTURE *INNOCENT* ARRESTS WOULD BE A THING LEFT IN THE *PAST.*

HOPING THE *ROGUES* WOULD BE TOO.

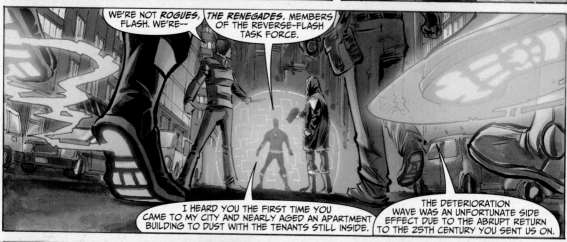

WE'RE NOT *ROGUES,* FLASH. WE'RE--

THE RENEGADES. MEMBERS OF THE REVERSE-FLASH TASK FORCE.

I HEARD YOU THE FIRST TIME YOU CAME TO MY CITY AND NEARLY AGED AN APARTMENT BUILDING TO DUST WITH THE TENANTS STILL INSIDE.

THE DETERIORATION WAVE WAS AN UNFORTUNATE SIDE EFFECT DUE TO THE ABRUPT RETURN TO THE 25TH CENTURY YOU SENT US ON.

IF I REMEMBER, IT WAS *YOUR* TRICKS THAT CAUSED IT.

I'VE GOT A FEW *TRICKS* OF MY OWN.

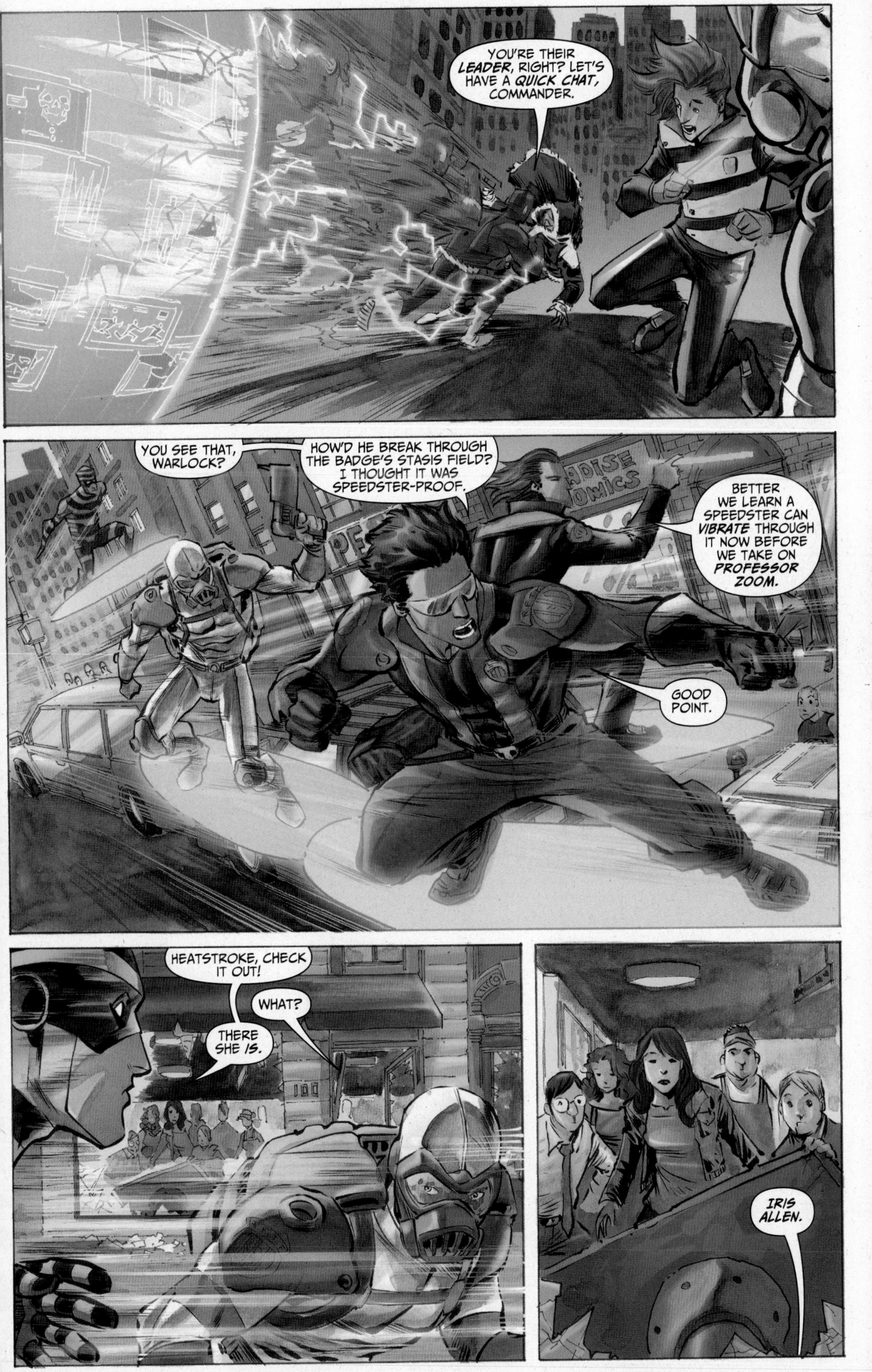
YOU'RE THEIR LEADER, RIGHT? LET'S HAVE A QUICK CHAT, COMMANDER.
YOU SEE THAT, WARLOCK?
HOW'D HE BREAK THROUGH THE BADGE'S STASIS FIELD? I THOUGHT IT WAS SPEEDSTER-PROOF.
BETTER WE LEARN A SPEEDSTER CAN VIBRATE THROUGH IT NOW BEFORE WE TAKE ON PROFESSOR ZOOM.
GOOD POINT.
HEATSTROKE, CHECK IT OUT!
WHAT?
THERE SHE IS.
IRIS ALLEN.

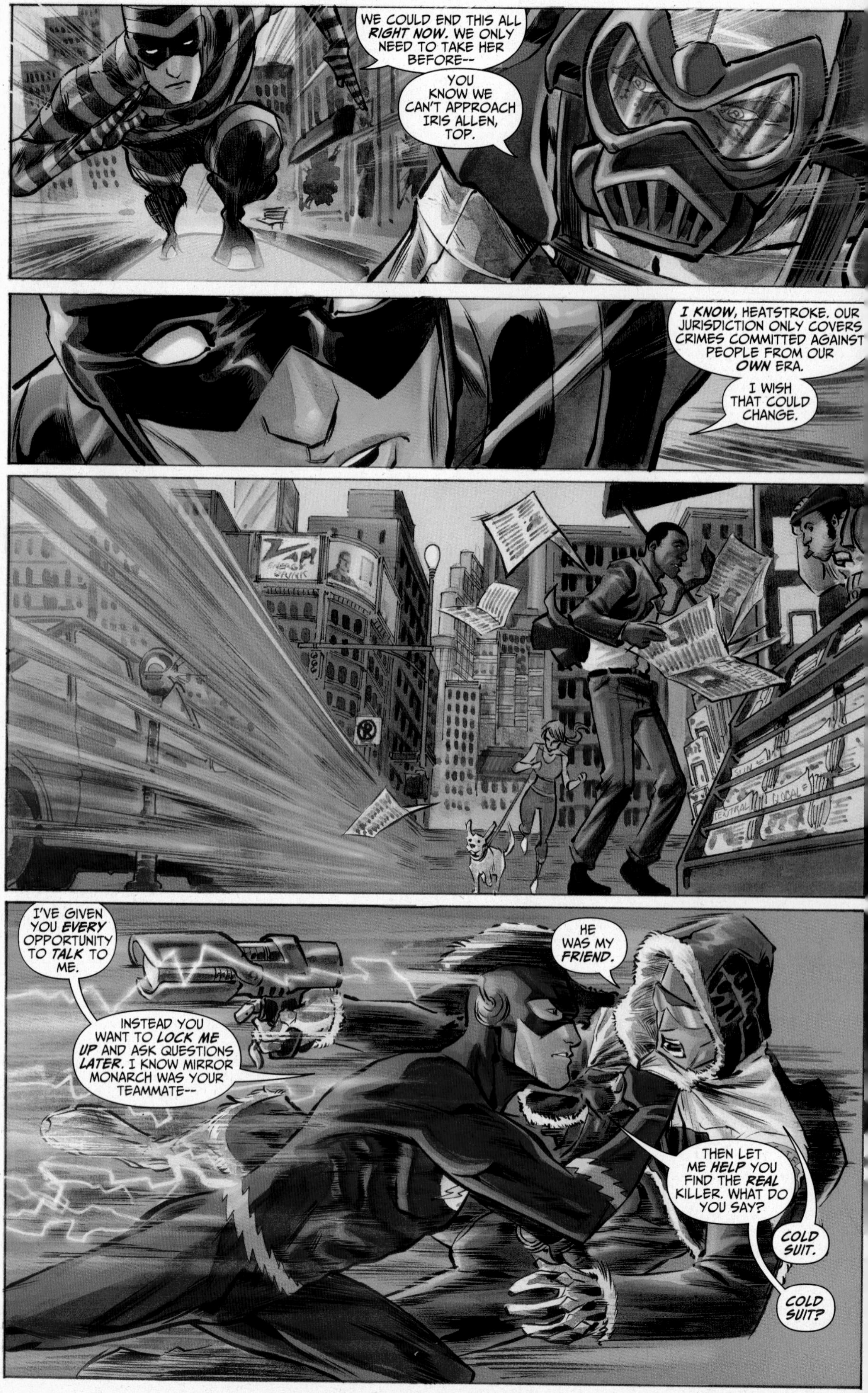
WE COULD END THIS ALL RIGHT NOW. WE ONLY NEED TO TAKE HER BEFORE--
YOU KNOW WE CAN'T APPROACH IRIS ALLEN, TOP.
I KNOW, HEATSTROKE. OUR JURISDICTION ONLY COVERS CRIMES COMMITTED AGAINST PEOPLE FROM OUR OWN ERA.
I WISH THAT COULD CHANGE.
ZAP!
CENTRAL
GLOBAL
I'VE GIVEN YOU EVERY OPPORTUNITY TO TALK TO ME.
INSTEAD YOU WANT TO LOCK ME UP AND ASK QUESTIONS LATER. I KNOW MIRROR MONARCH WAS YOUR TEAMMATE--
HE WAS MY FRIEND.
THEN LET ME HELP YOU FIND THE REAL KILLER. WHAT DO YOU SAY?
COLD SUIT.
COLD SUIT?

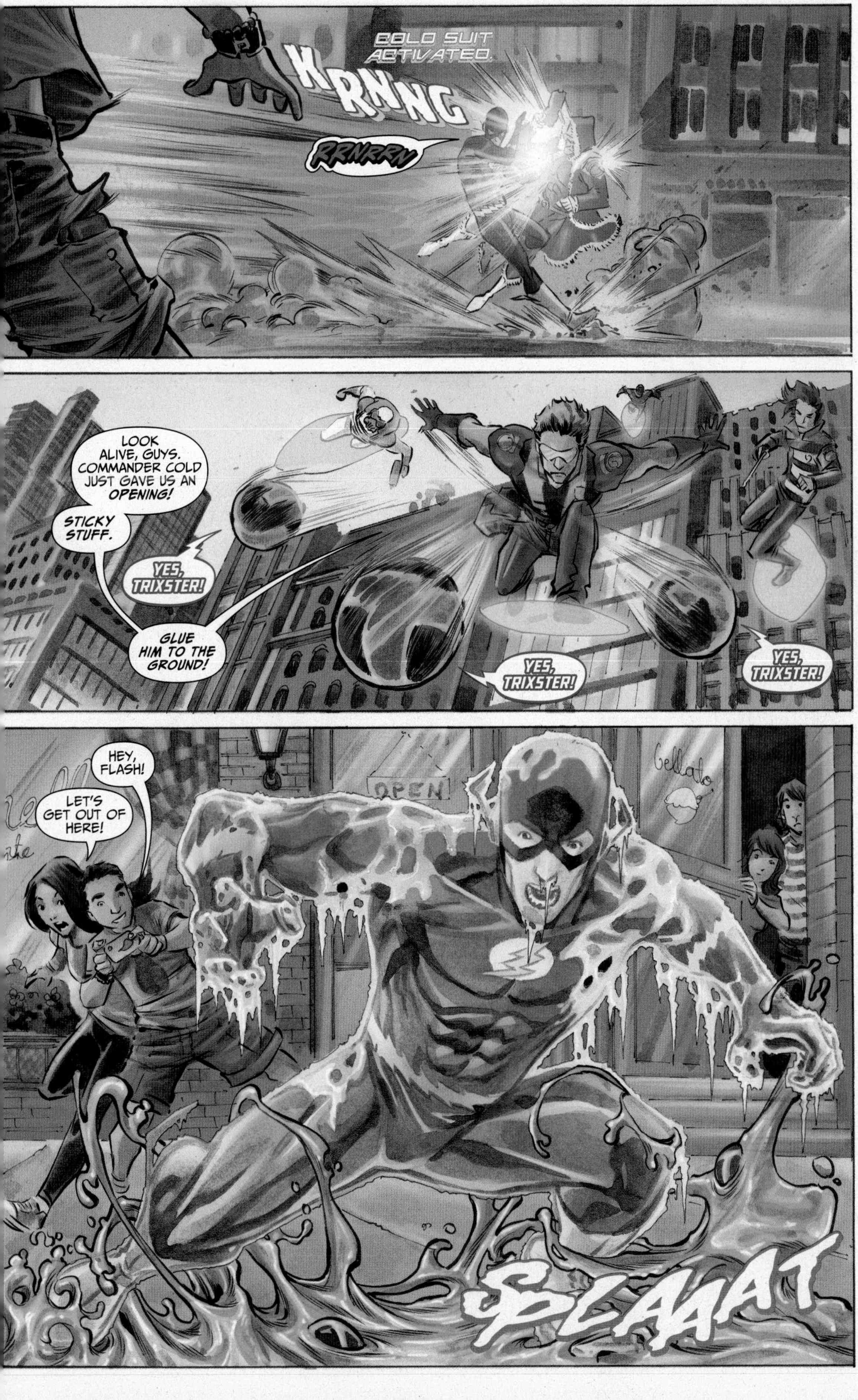
COLD SUIT ACTIVATED.
KRNNG
RRNRRN
LOOK ALIVE, GUYS. COMMANDER COLD JUST GAVE US AN *OPENING!*
STICKY STUFF.
GLUE HIM TO THE GROUND!
YES, TRIXSTER!
YES, TRIXSTER!
YES, TRIXSTER!
HEY, FLASH!
LET'S GET OUT OF HERE!
OPEN
Gellato
SLAAAT

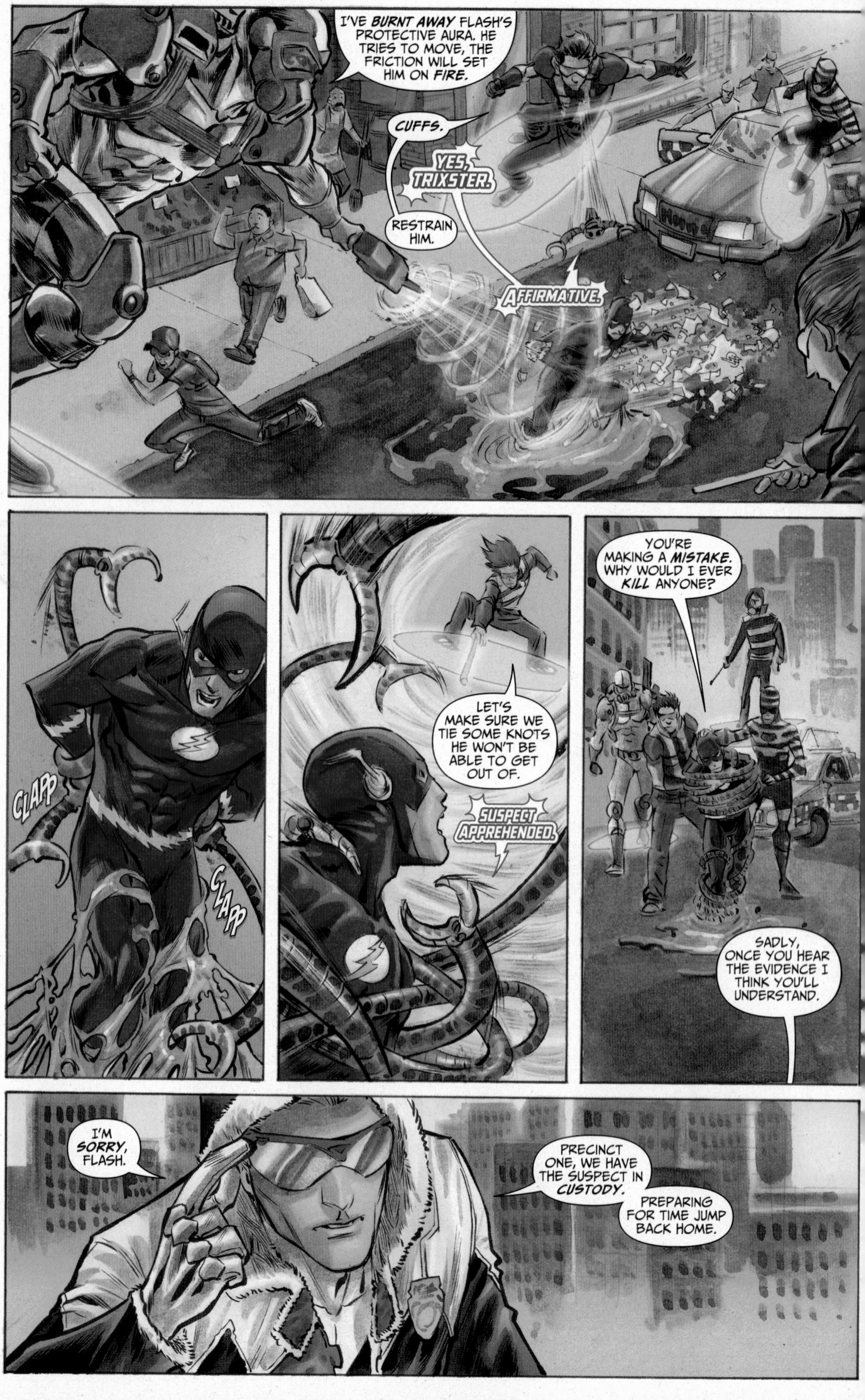

I'VE BURNT AWAY FLASH'S PROTECTIVE AURA. HE TRIES TO MOVE, THE FRICTION WILL SET HIM ON FIRE.
CUFFS.
YES, TRIXSTER.
RESTRAIN HIM.
AFFIRMATIVE.
CLAPP
CLAPP
LET'S MAKE SURE WE TIE SOME KNOTS HE WON'T BE ABLE TO GET OUT OF.
SUSPECT APPREHENDED.
YOU'RE MAKING A MISTAKE. WHY WOULD I EVER KILL ANYONE?
SADLY, ONCE YOU HEAR THE EVIDENCE I THINK YOU'LL UNDERSTAND.
I'M SORRY, FLASH.
PRECINCT ONE, WE HAVE THE SUSPECT IN CUSTODY.
PREPARING FOR TIME JUMP BACK HOME.

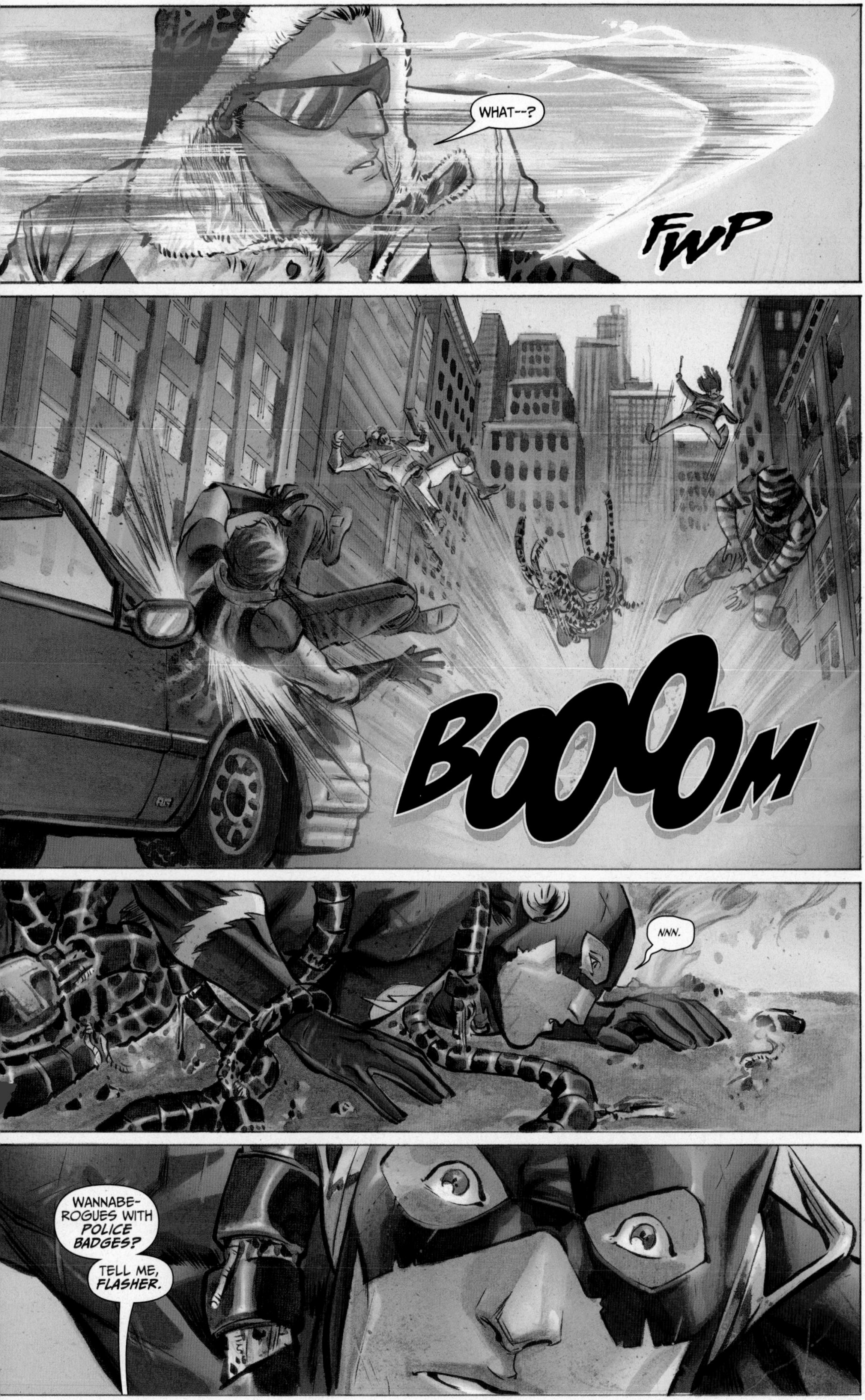
WHAT--?
FWP
BOOOOM
NNN.
WANNABE-ROGUES WITH POLICE BADGES?
TELL ME, FLASHER.

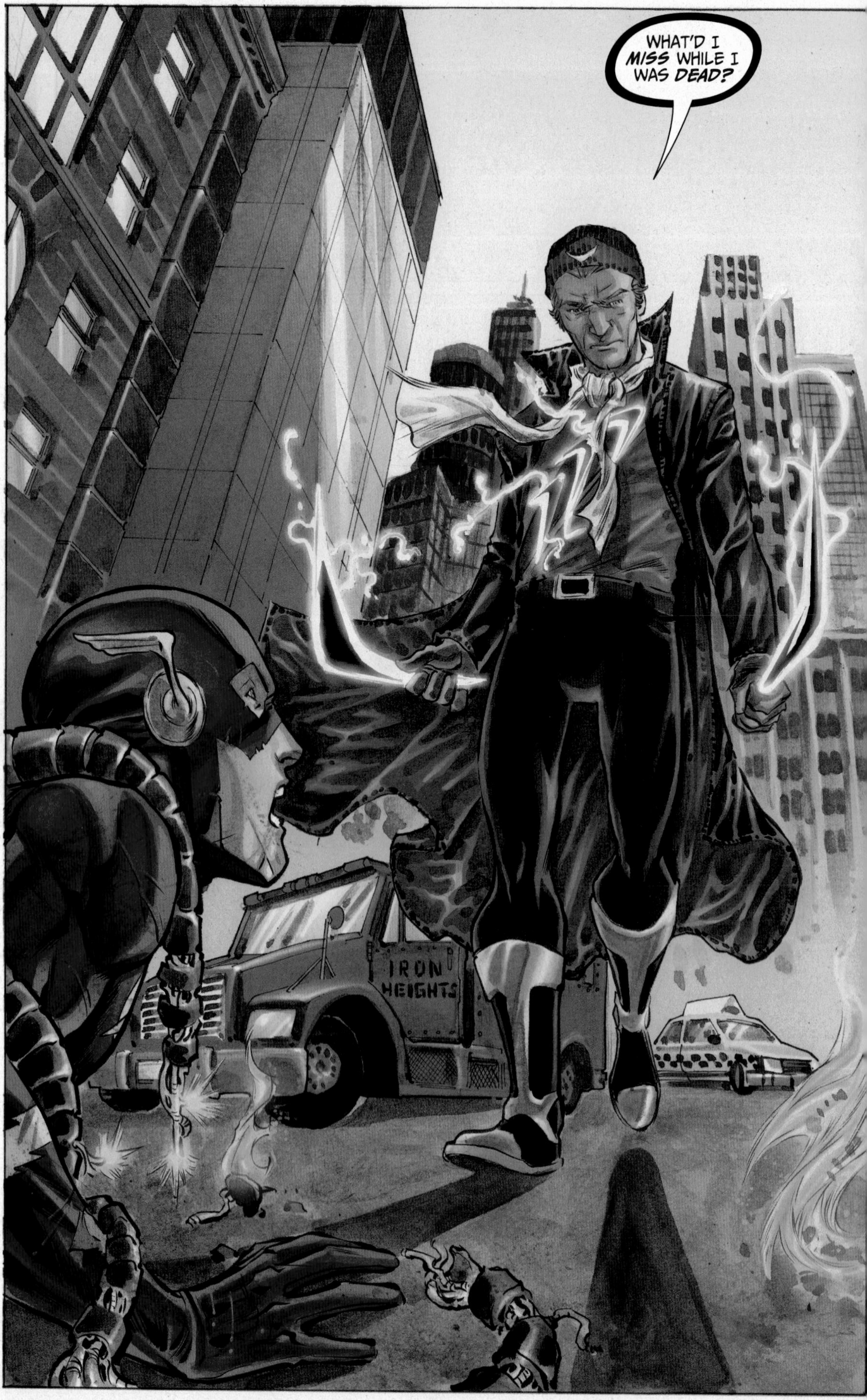
WHAT'D I *MISS* WHILE I WAS *DEAD?*
IRON HEIGHTS

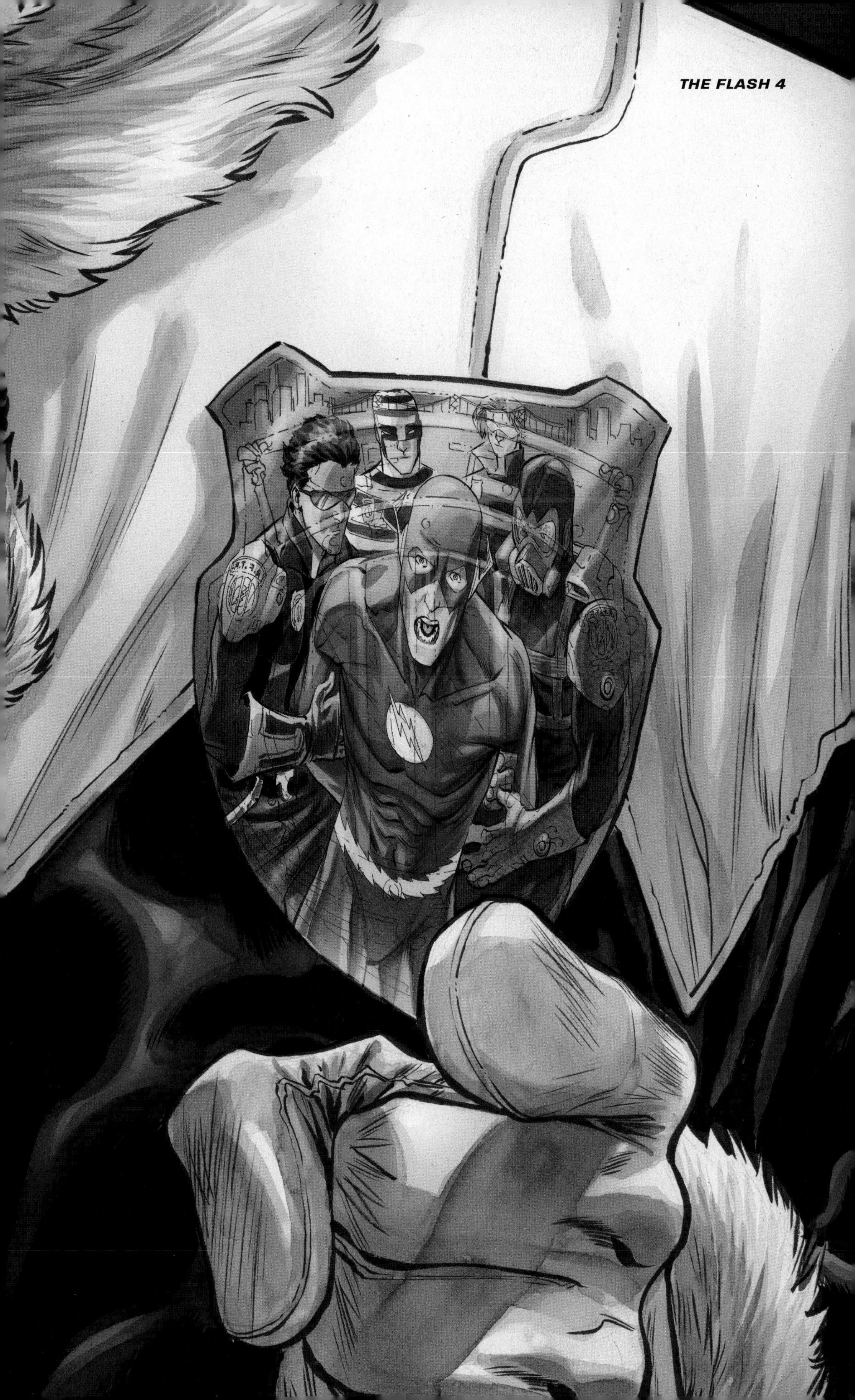
THE FLASH 4

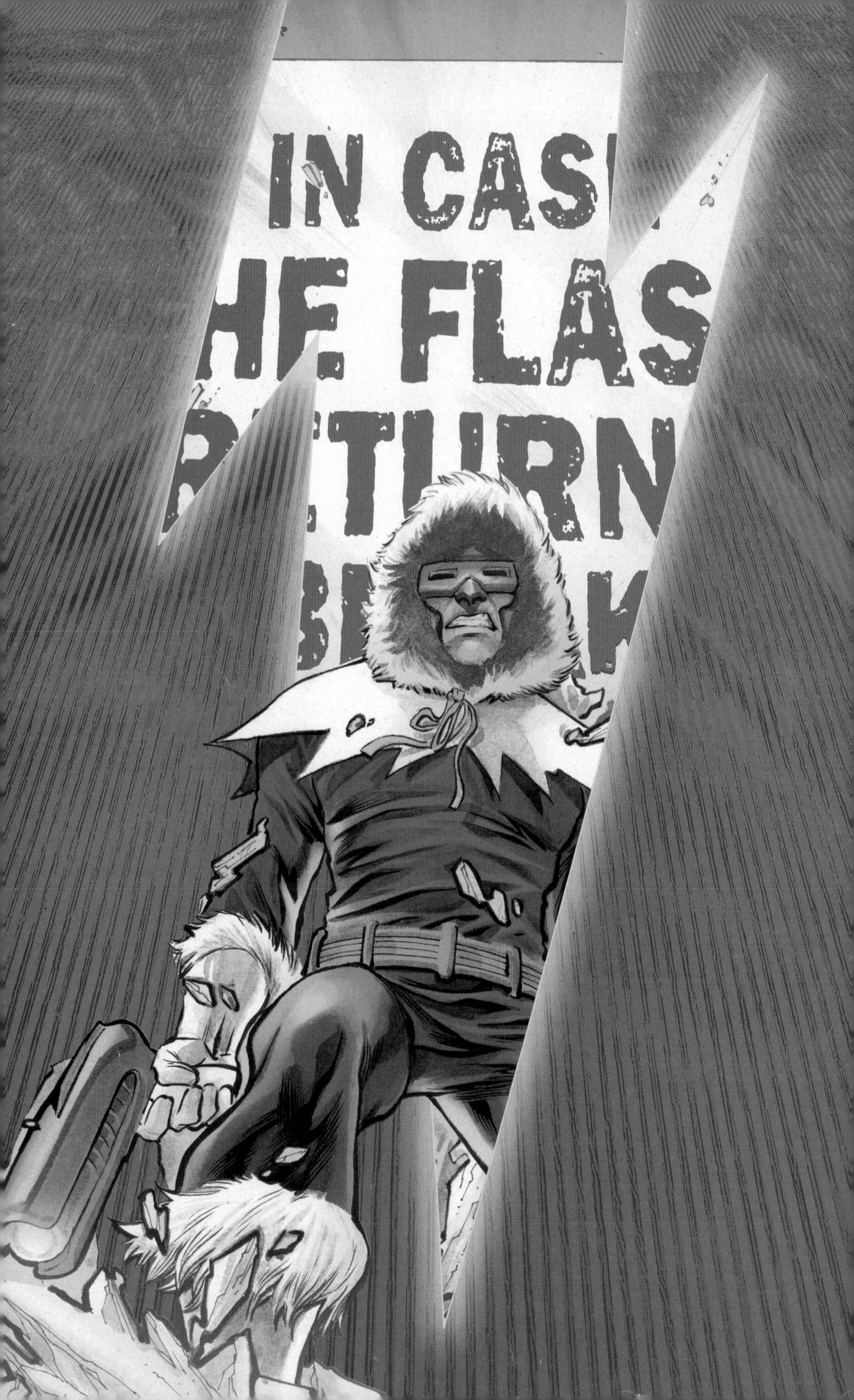
IN CAS
HE FLAS
ETURN

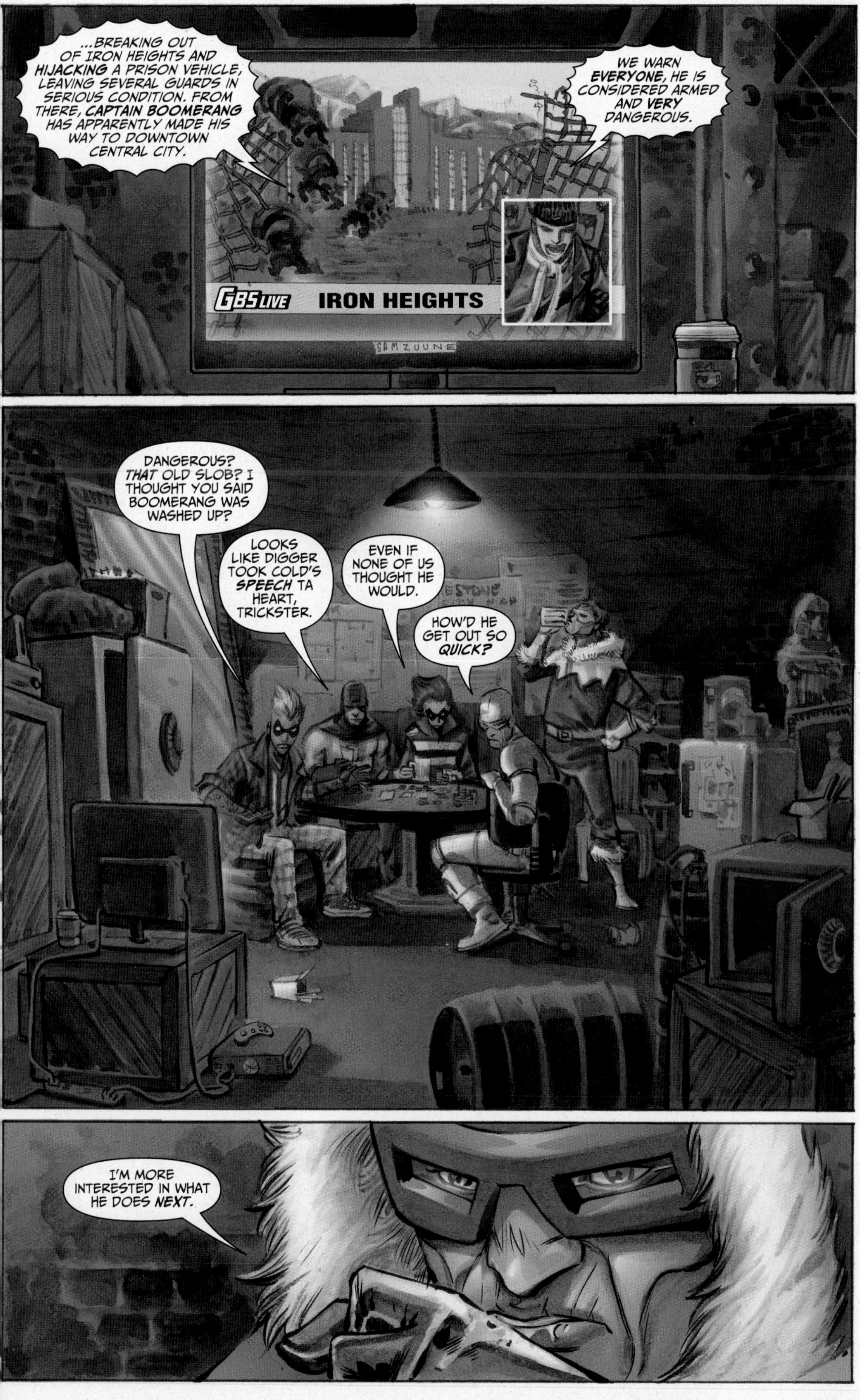
...BREAKING OUT OF IRON HEIGHTS AND HIJACKING A PRISON VEHICLE, LEAVING SEVERAL GUARDS IN SERIOUS CONDITION. FROM THERE, CAPTAIN BOOMERANG HAS APPARENTLY MADE HIS WAY TO DOWNTOWN CENTRAL CITY.
WE WARN EVERYONE, HE IS CONSIDERED ARMED AND VERY DANGEROUS.
GBS LIVE
IRON HEIGHTS
SAMZUUNE
DANGEROUS? THAT OLD SLOB? I THOUGHT YOU SAID BOOMERANG WAS WASHED UP?
LOOKS LIKE DIGGER TOOK COLD'S SPEECH TA HEART, TRICKSTER.
EVEN IF NONE OF US THOUGHT HE WOULD.
HOW'D HE GET OUT SO QUICK?
I'M MORE INTERESTED IN WHAT HE DOES NEXT.

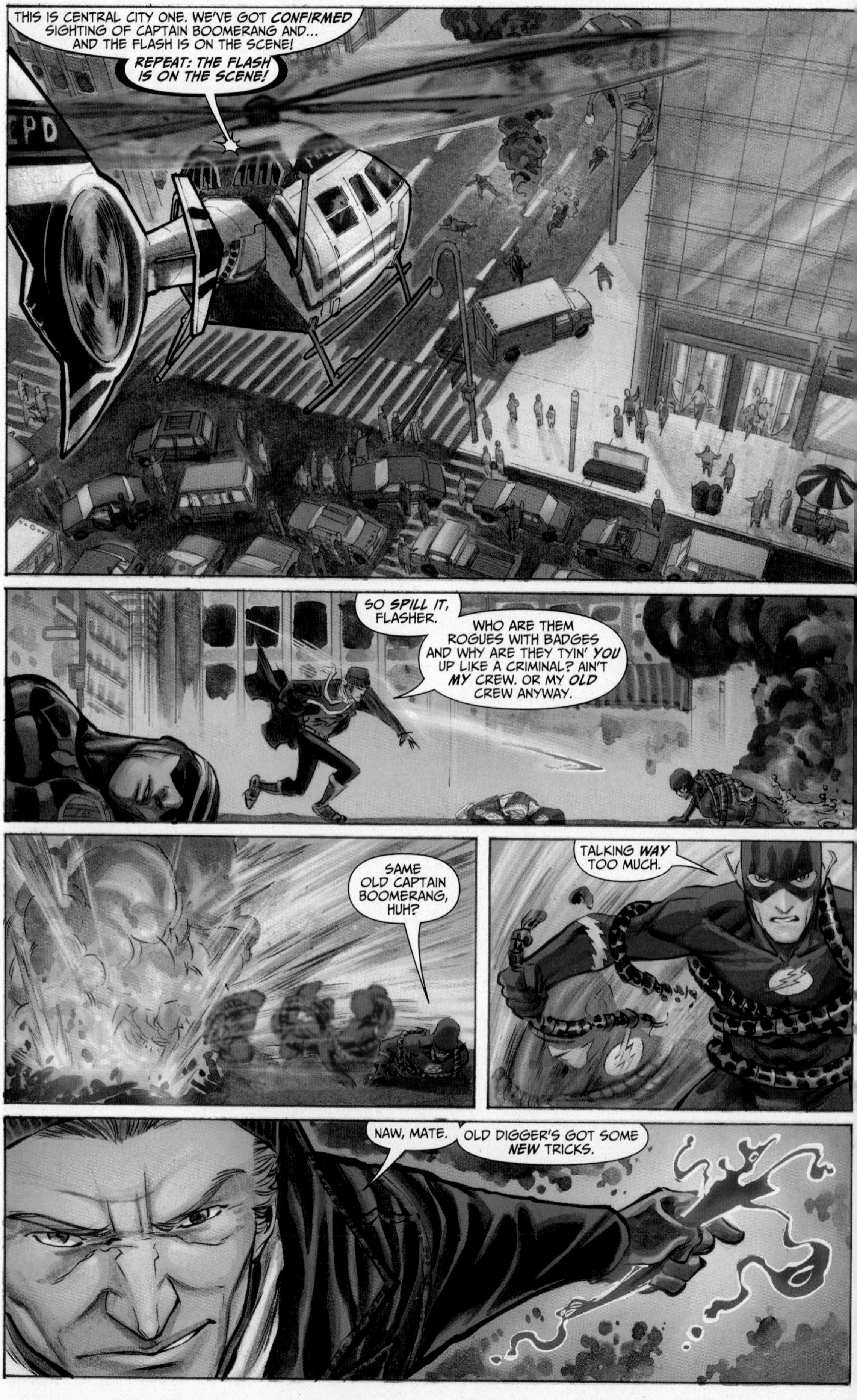
THIS IS CENTRAL CITY ONE. WE'VE GOT CONFIRMED SIGHTING OF CAPTAIN BOOMERANG AND... AND THE FLASH IS ON THE SCENE!
REPEAT: THE FLASH IS ON THE SCENE!
CPD
SO SPILL IT, FLASHER.
WHO ARE THEM ROGUES WITH BADGES AND WHY ARE THEY TYIN' YOU UP LIKE A CRIMINAL? AIN'T MY CREW. OR MY OLD CREW ANYWAY.
SAME OLD CAPTAIN BOOMERANG, HUH?
TALKING WAY TOO MUCH.
NAW, MATE.
OLD DIGGER'S GOT SOME NEW TRICKS.

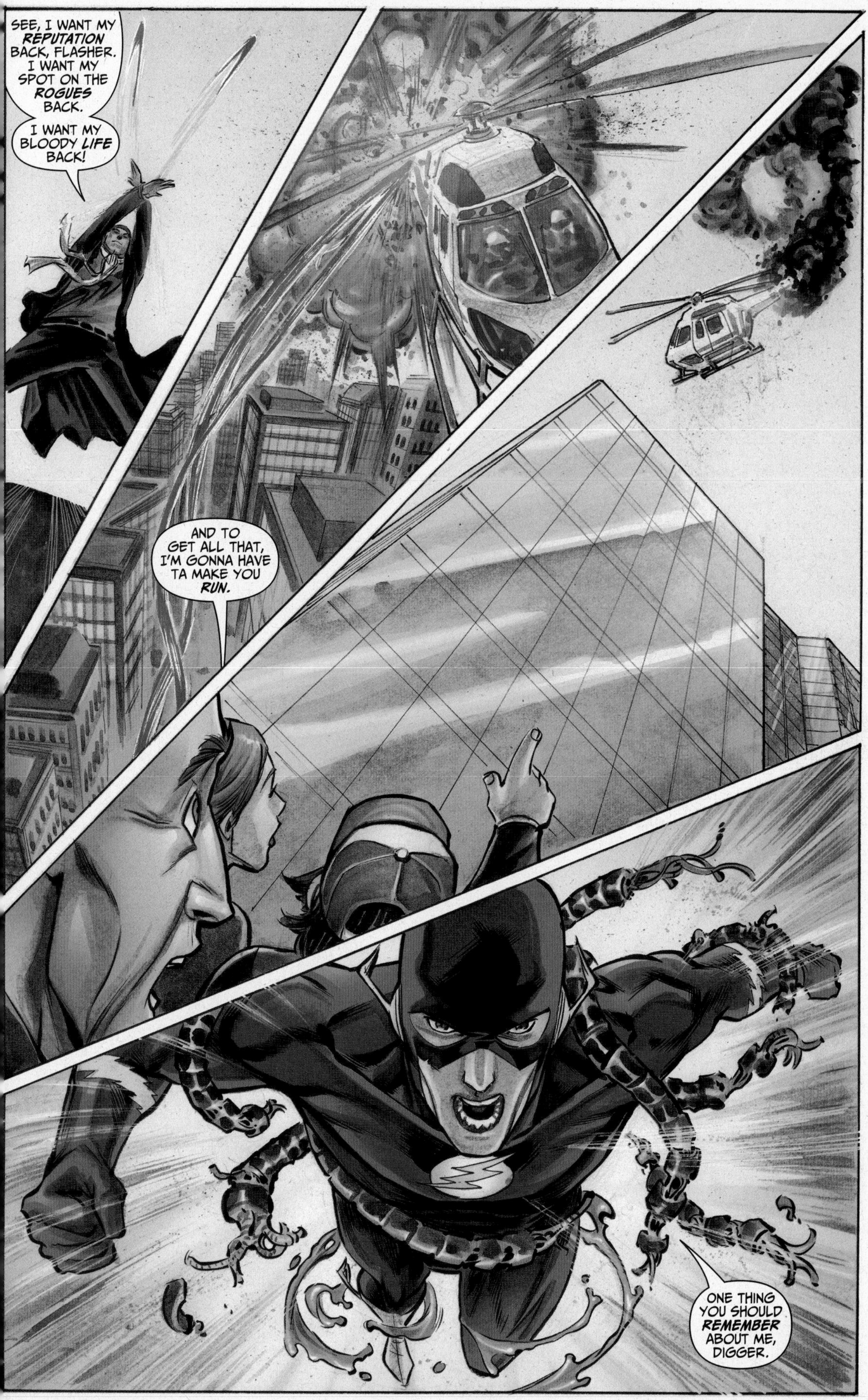
SEE, I WANT MY REPUTATION BACK, FLASHER. I WANT MY SPOT ON THE ROGUES BACK.
I WANT MY BLOODY LIFE BACK!
AND TO GET ALL THAT, I'M GONNA HAVE TA MAKE YOU RUN.
ONE THING YOU SHOULD REMEMBER ABOUT ME, DIGGER.

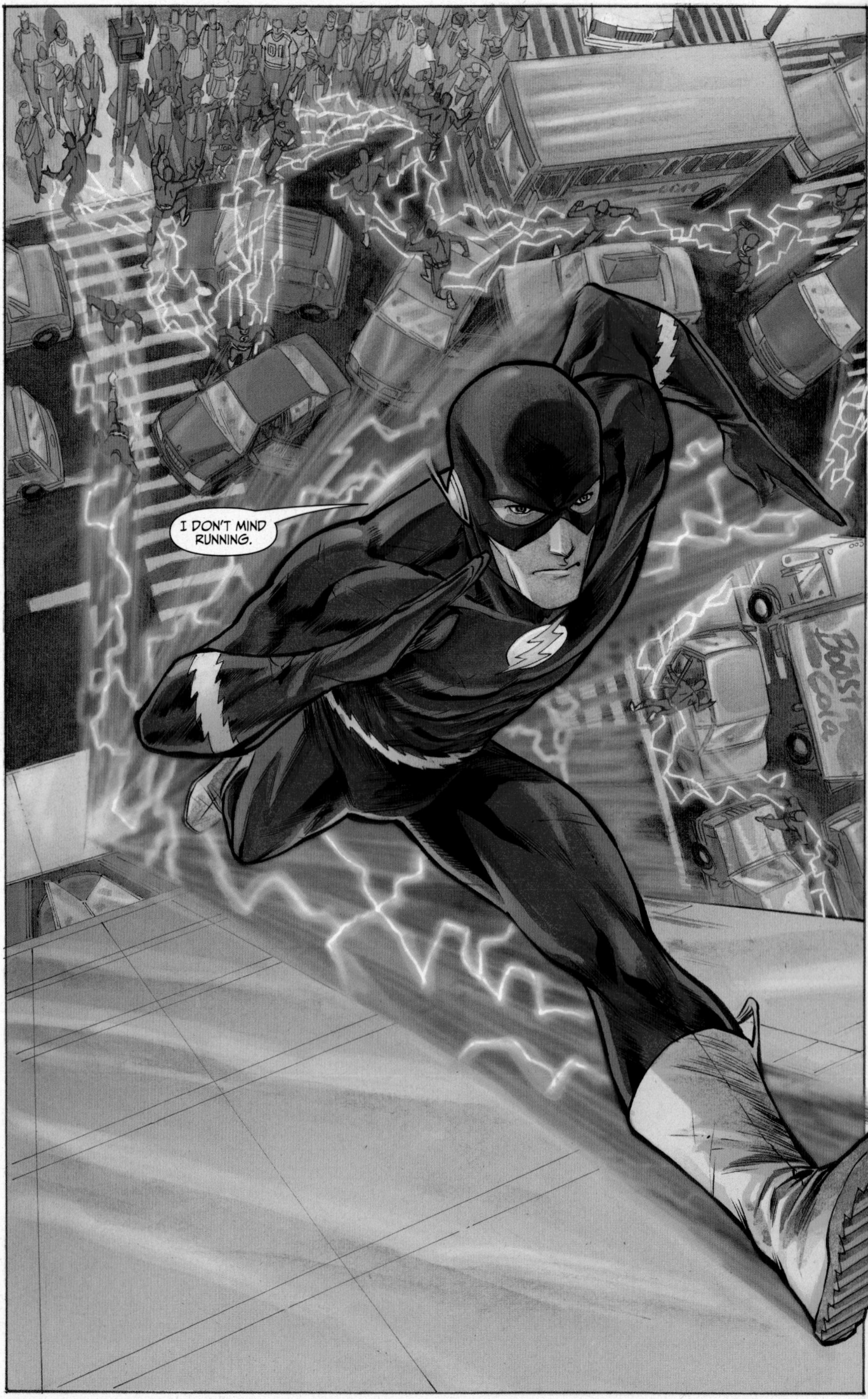

I DON'T MIND RUNNING.
BOOST Cola

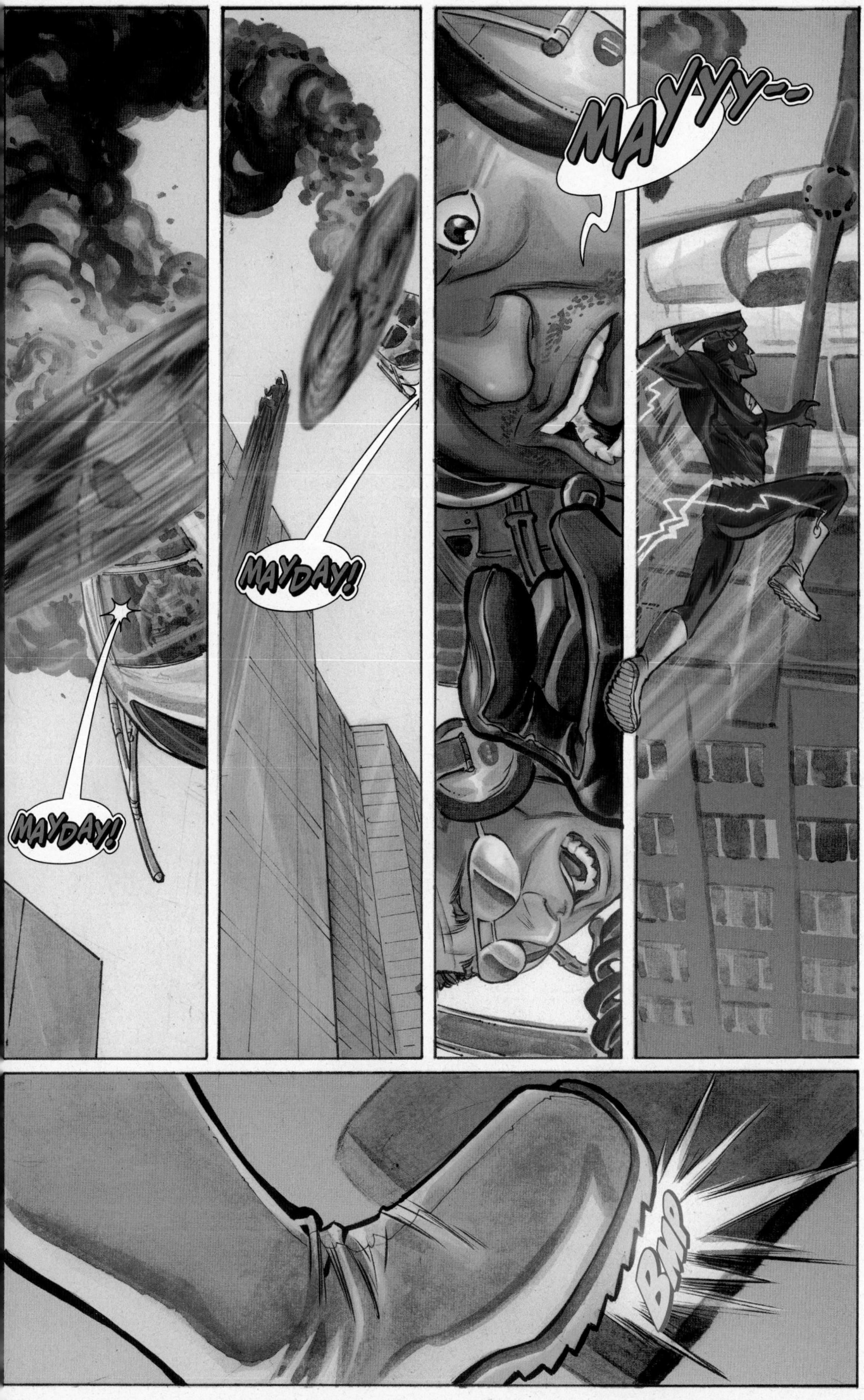
MAYDAY!
MAYDAY!
MAYYY--
BMP

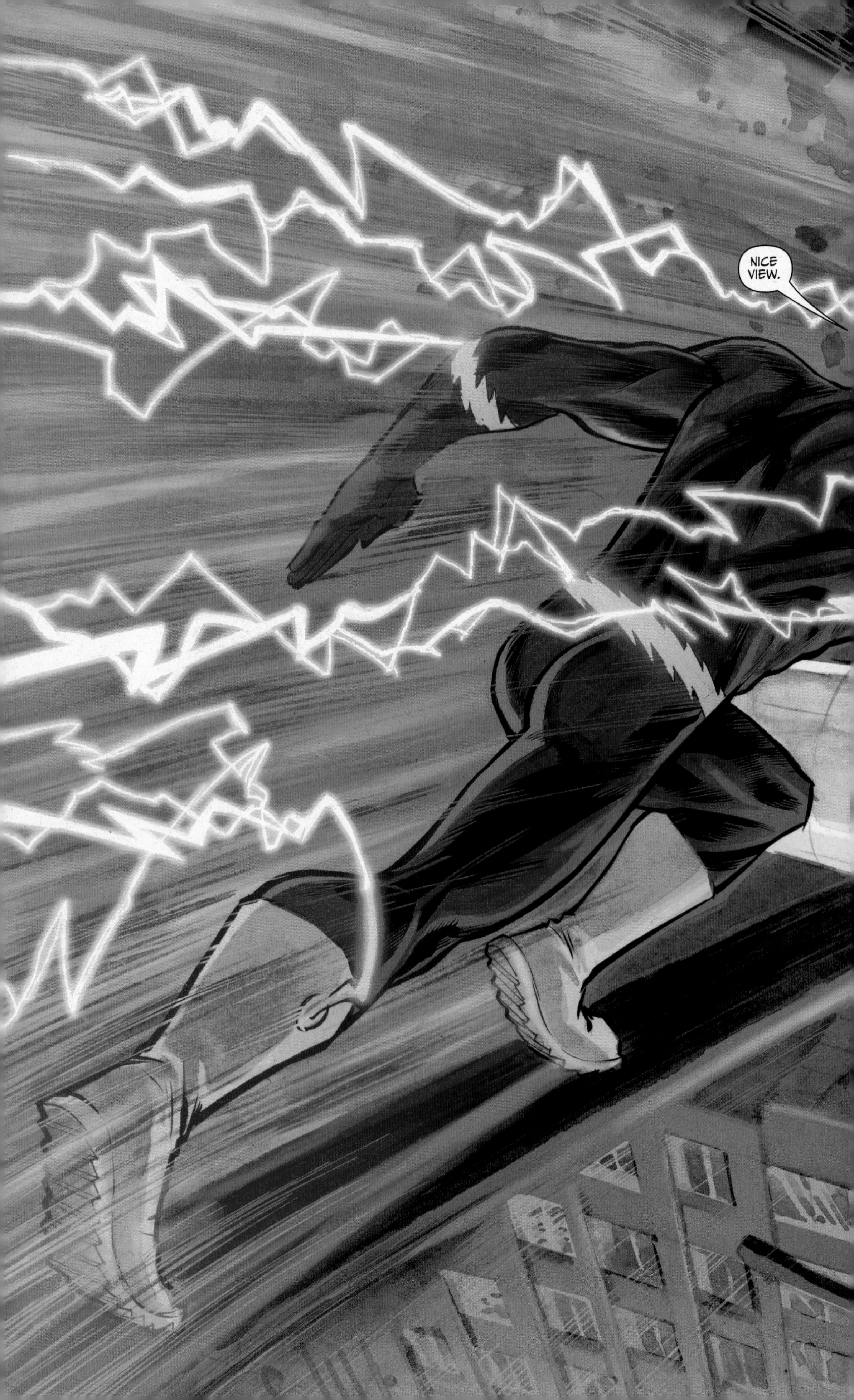
NICE VIEW.

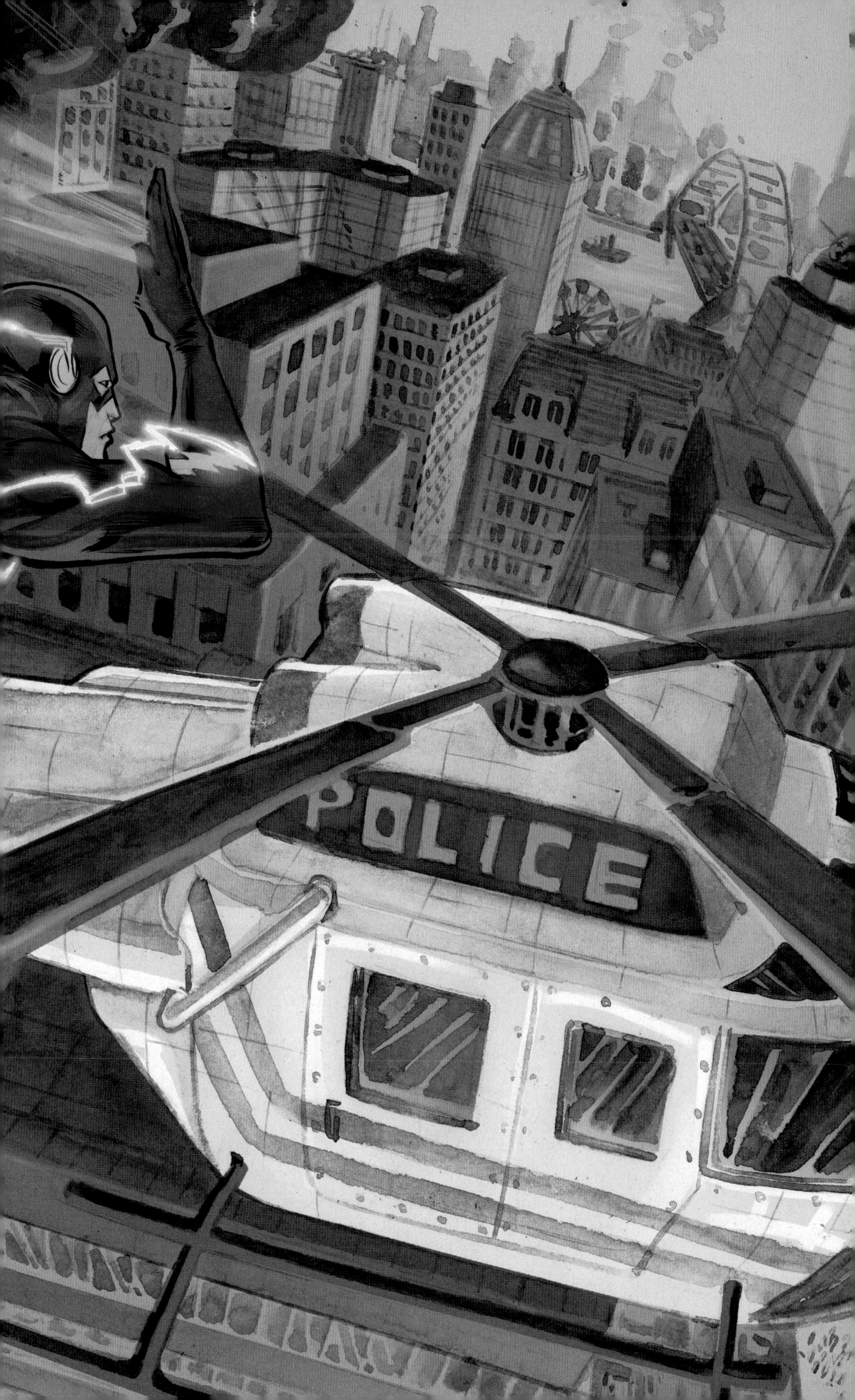
POLICE

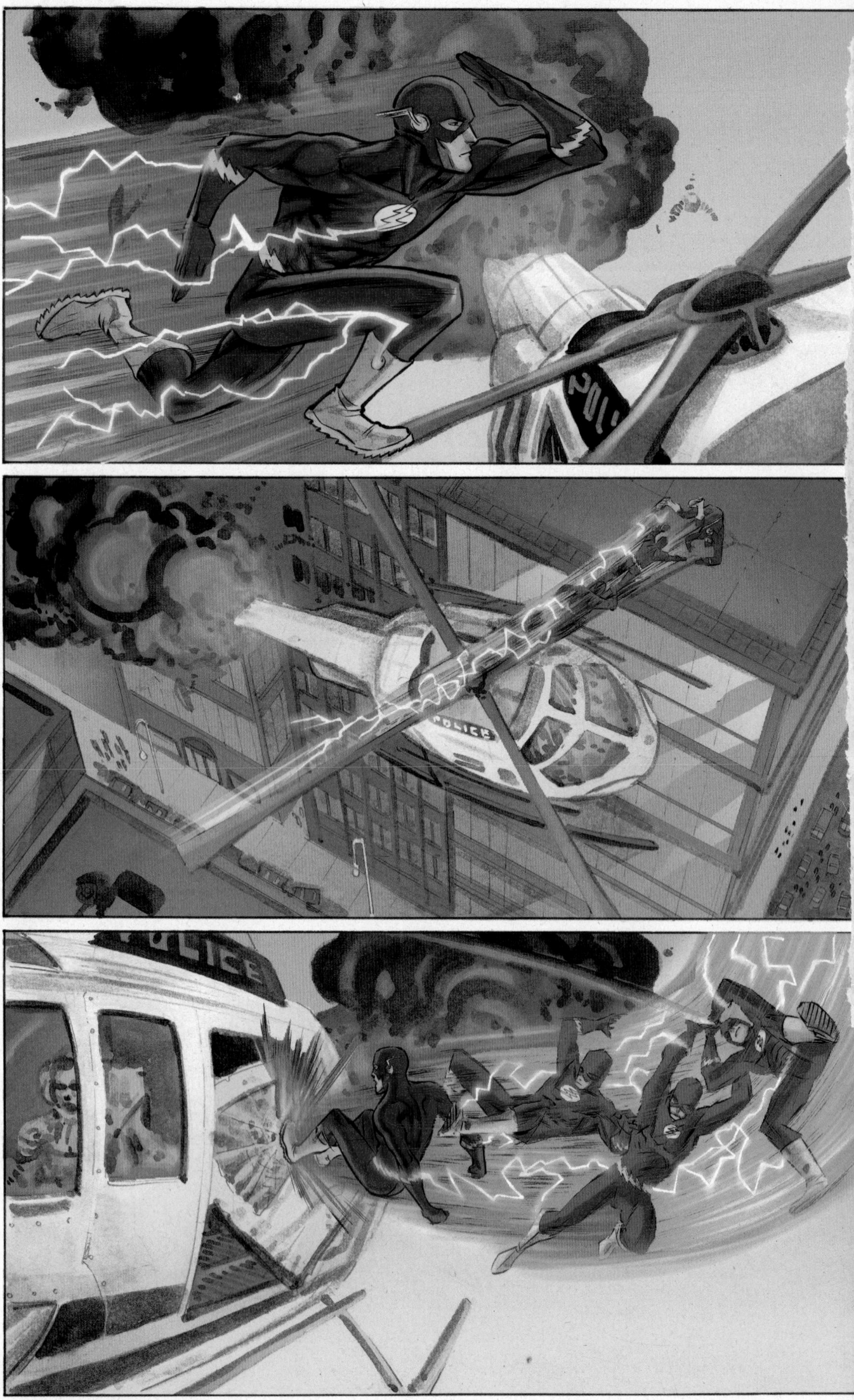
POLICE

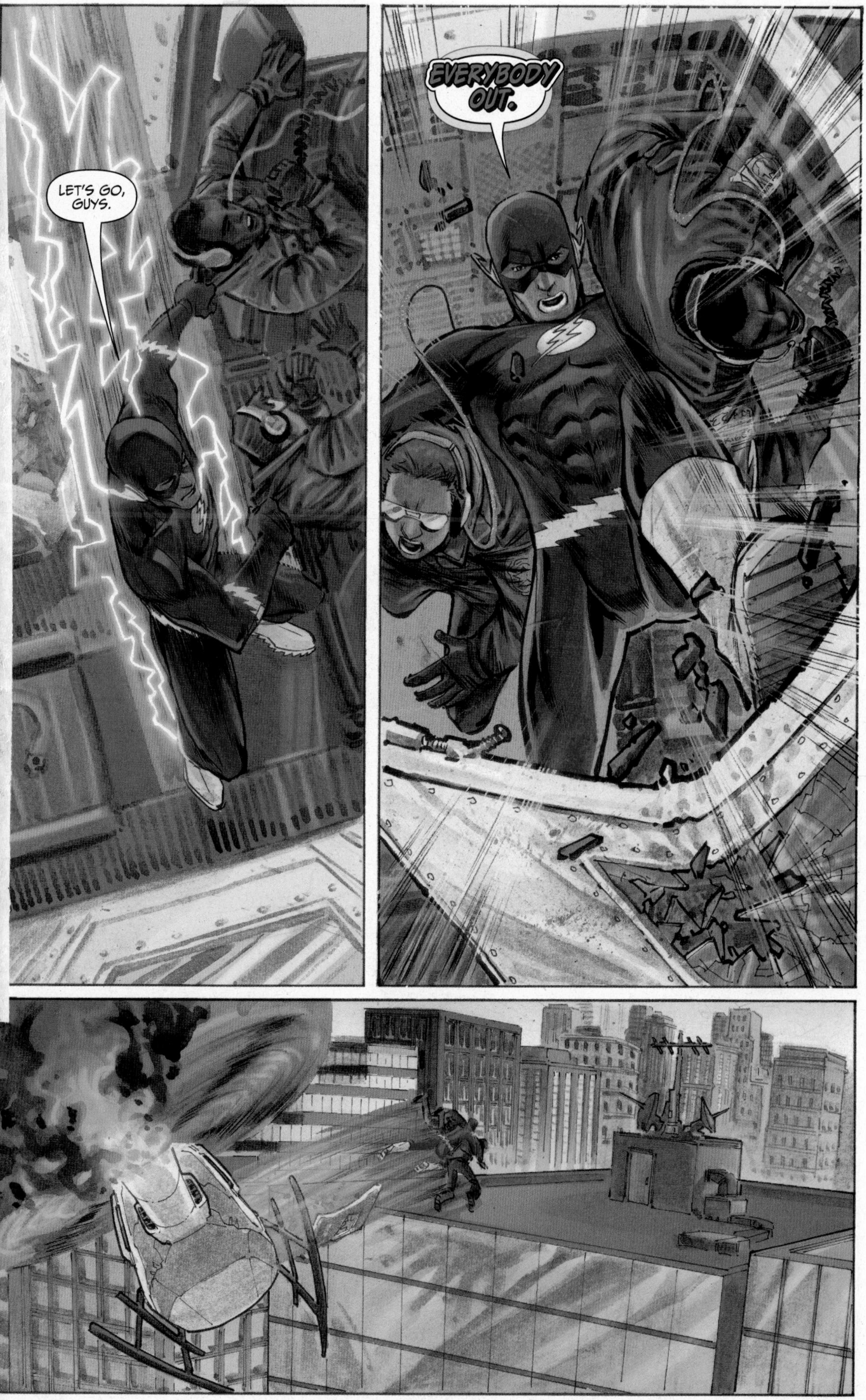
LET'S GO, GUYS.
EVERYBODY OUT.

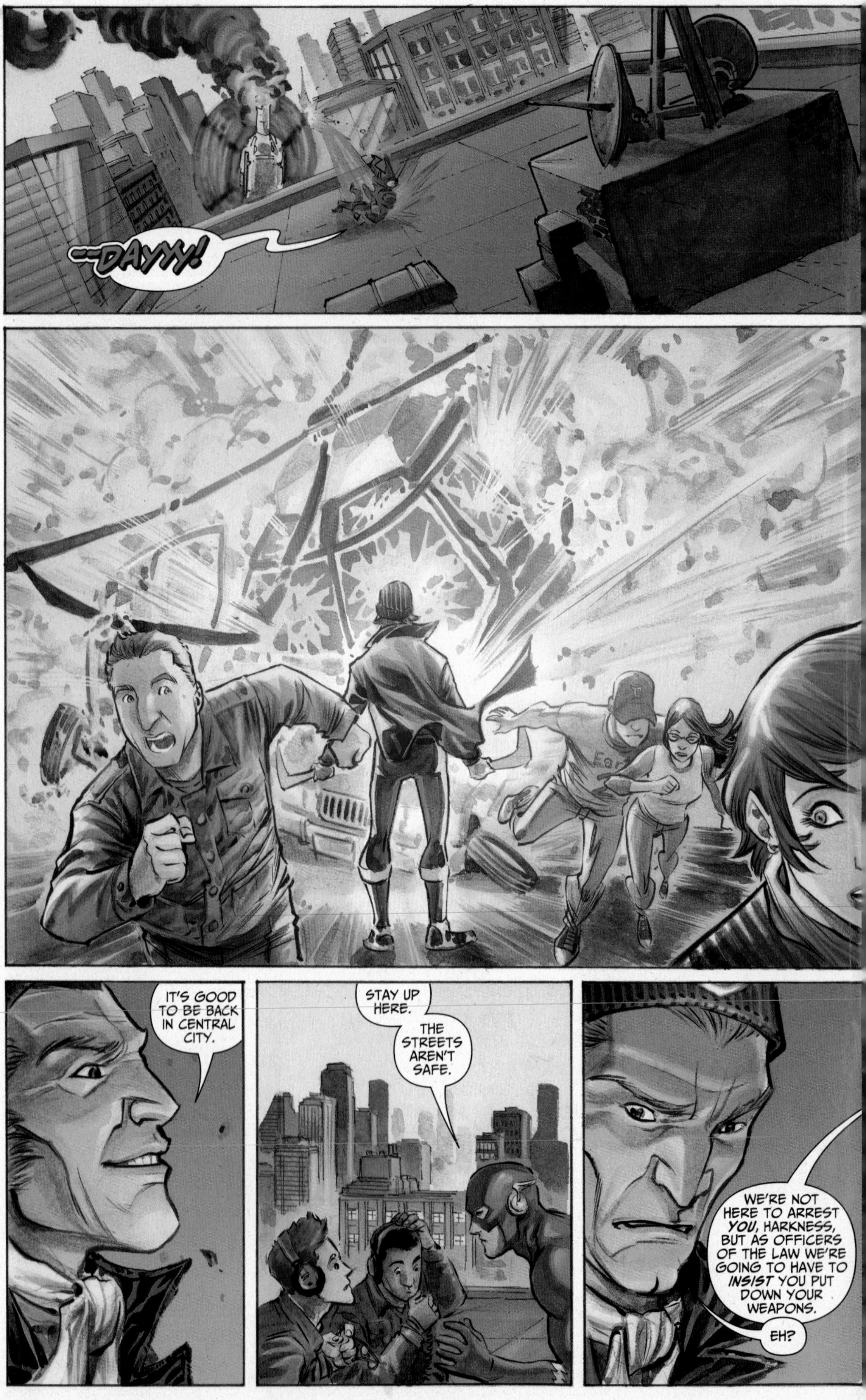
--DAYYY!
IT'S GOOD TO BE BACK IN CENTRAL CITY.
STAY UP HERE.
THE STREETS AREN'T SAFE.
WE'RE NOT HERE TO ARREST *YOU*, HARKNESS, BUT AS OFFICERS OF THE LAW WE'RE GOING TO HAVE TO *INSIST* YOU PUT DOWN YOUR WEAPONS.
EH?

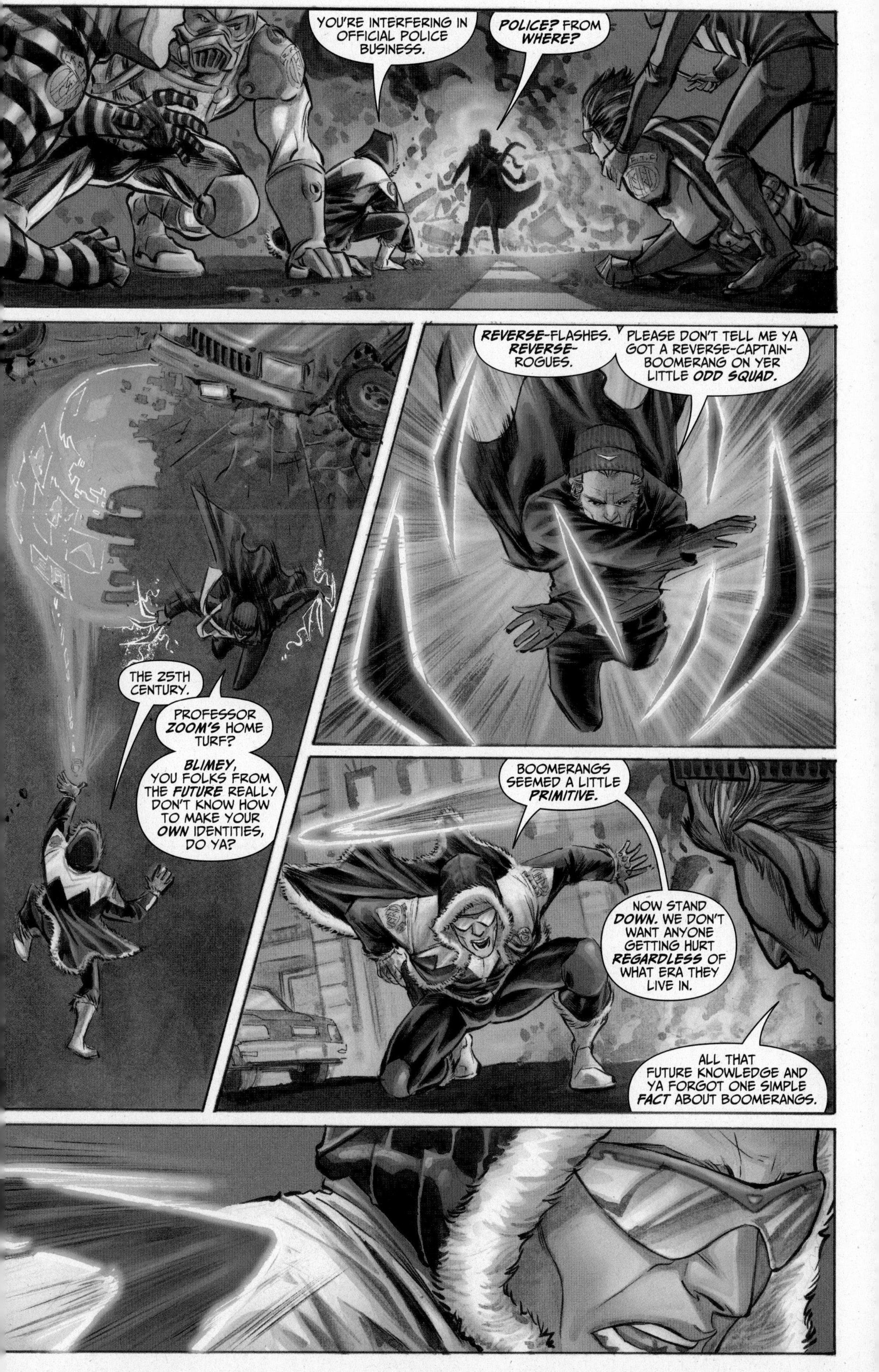

YOU'RE INTERFERING IN OFFICIAL POLICE BUSINESS.
POLICE? FROM WHERE?
THE 25TH CENTURY.
PROFESSOR ZOOM'S HOME TURF?
BLIMEY, YOU FOLKS FROM THE FUTURE REALLY DON'T KNOW HOW TO MAKE YOUR OWN IDENTITIES, DO YA?
REVERSE-FLASHES. REVERSE-ROGUES.
PLEASE DON'T TELL ME YA GOT A REVERSE-CAPTAIN-BOOMERANG ON YER LITTLE ODD SQUAD.
BOOMERANGS SEEMED A LITTLE PRIMITIVE.
NOW STAND DOWN. WE DON'T WANT ANYONE GETTING HURT REGARDLESS OF WHAT ERA THEY LIVE IN.
ALL THAT FUTURE KNOWLEDGE AND YA FORGOT ONE SIMPLE FACT ABOUT BOOMERANGS.

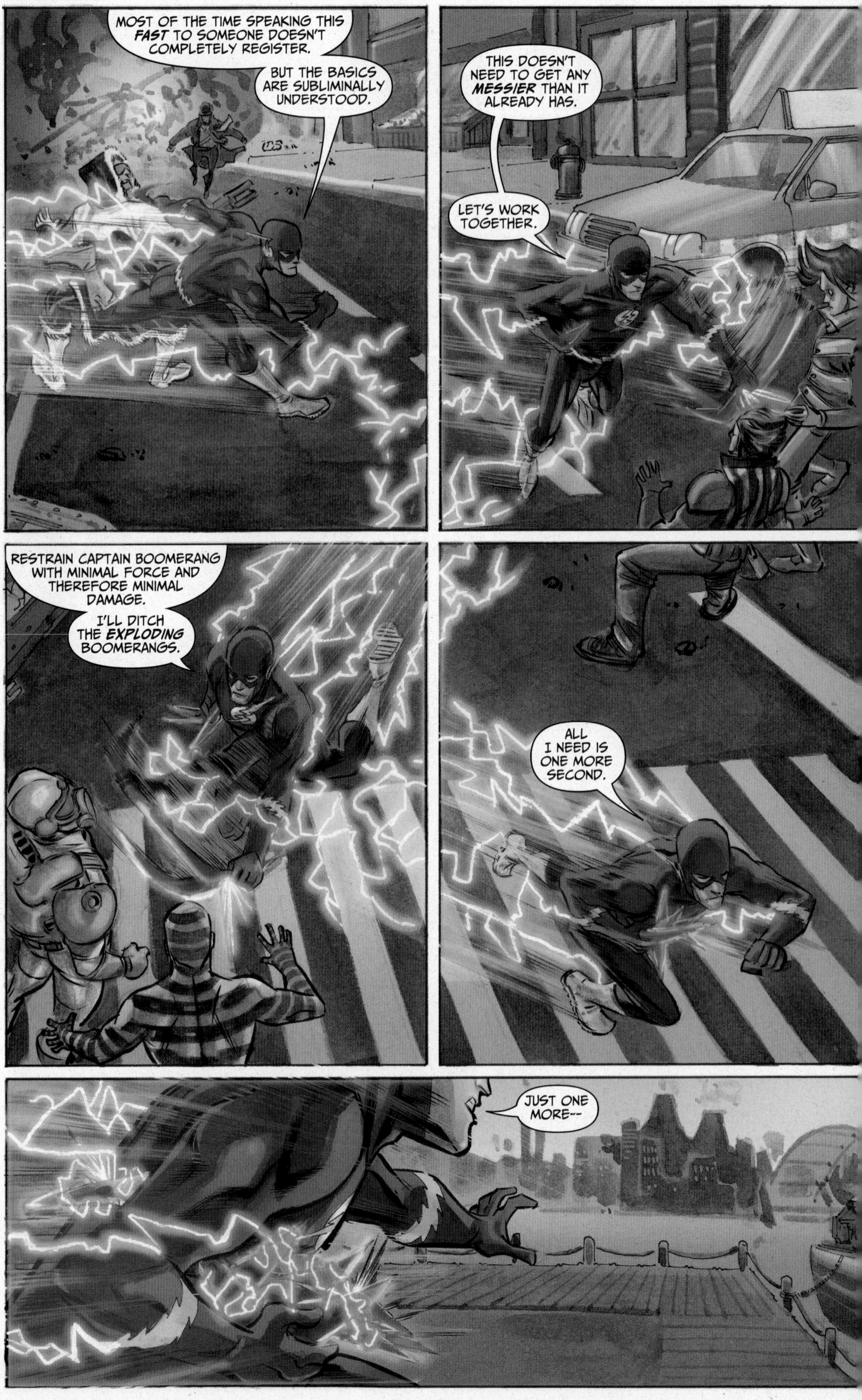
MOST OF THE TIME SPEAKING THIS FAST TO SOMEONE DOESN'T COMPLETELY REGISTER.
BUT THE BASICS ARE SUBLIMINALLY UNDERSTOOD.
THIS DOESN'T NEED TO GET ANY MESSIER THAN IT ALREADY HAS.
LET'S WORK TOGETHER.
RESTRAIN CAPTAIN BOOMERANG WITH MINIMAL FORCE AND THEREFORE MINIMAL DAMAGE.
I'LL DITCH THE EXPLODING BOOMERANGS.
ALL I NEED IS ONE MORE SECOND.
JUST ONE MORE--

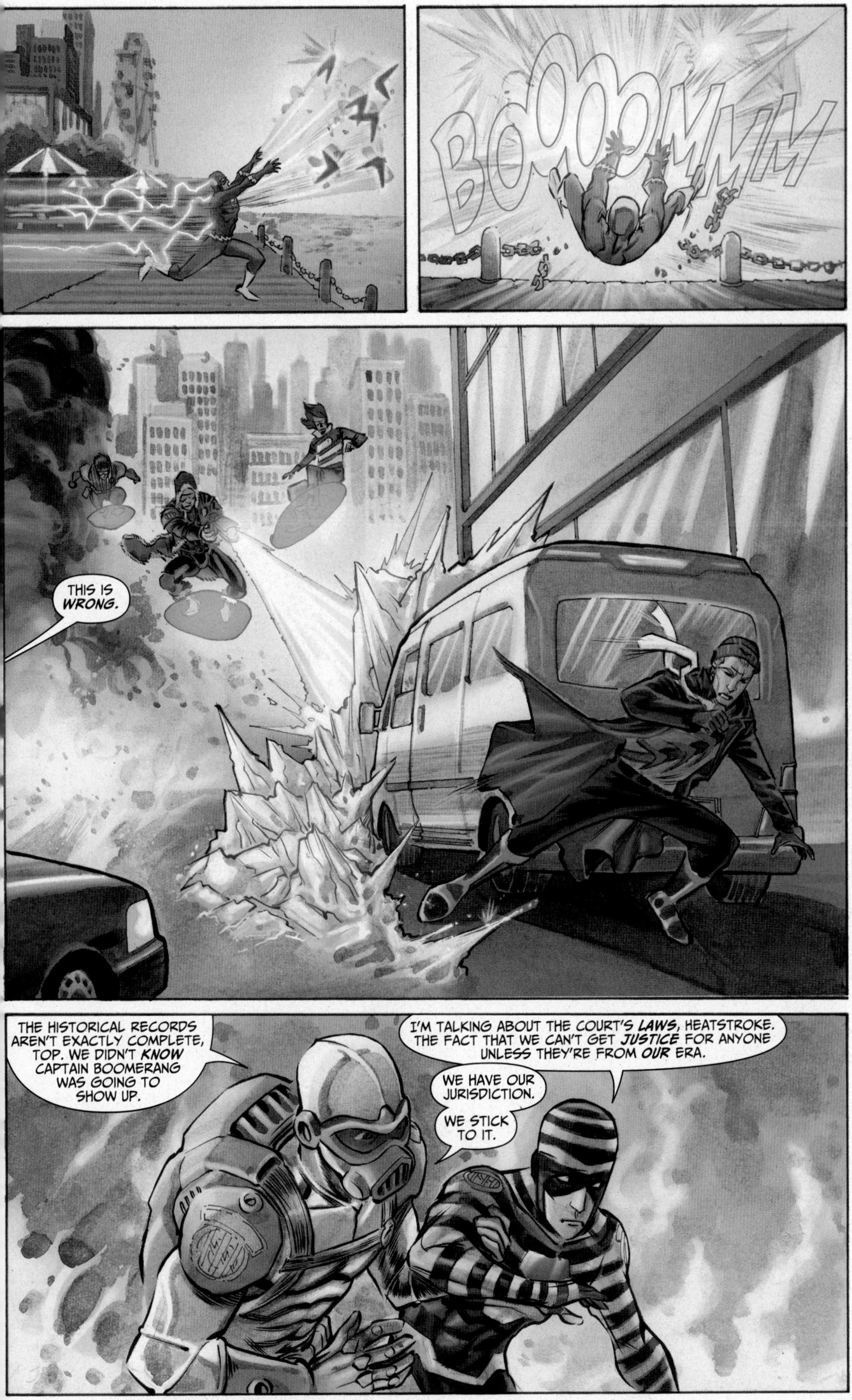
BOOOOMMM
THIS IS *WRONG*.
THE HISTORICAL RECORDS AREN'T EXACTLY COMPLETE, TOP. WE DIDN'T *KNOW* CAPTAIN BOOMERANG WAS GOING TO SHOW UP.
I'M TALKING ABOUT THE COURT'S *LAWS*, HEATSTROKE. THE FACT THAT WE CAN'T GET *JUSTICE* FOR ANYONE UNLESS THEY'RE FROM *OUR* ERA.
WE HAVE OUR JURISDICTION.
WE STICK TO IT.

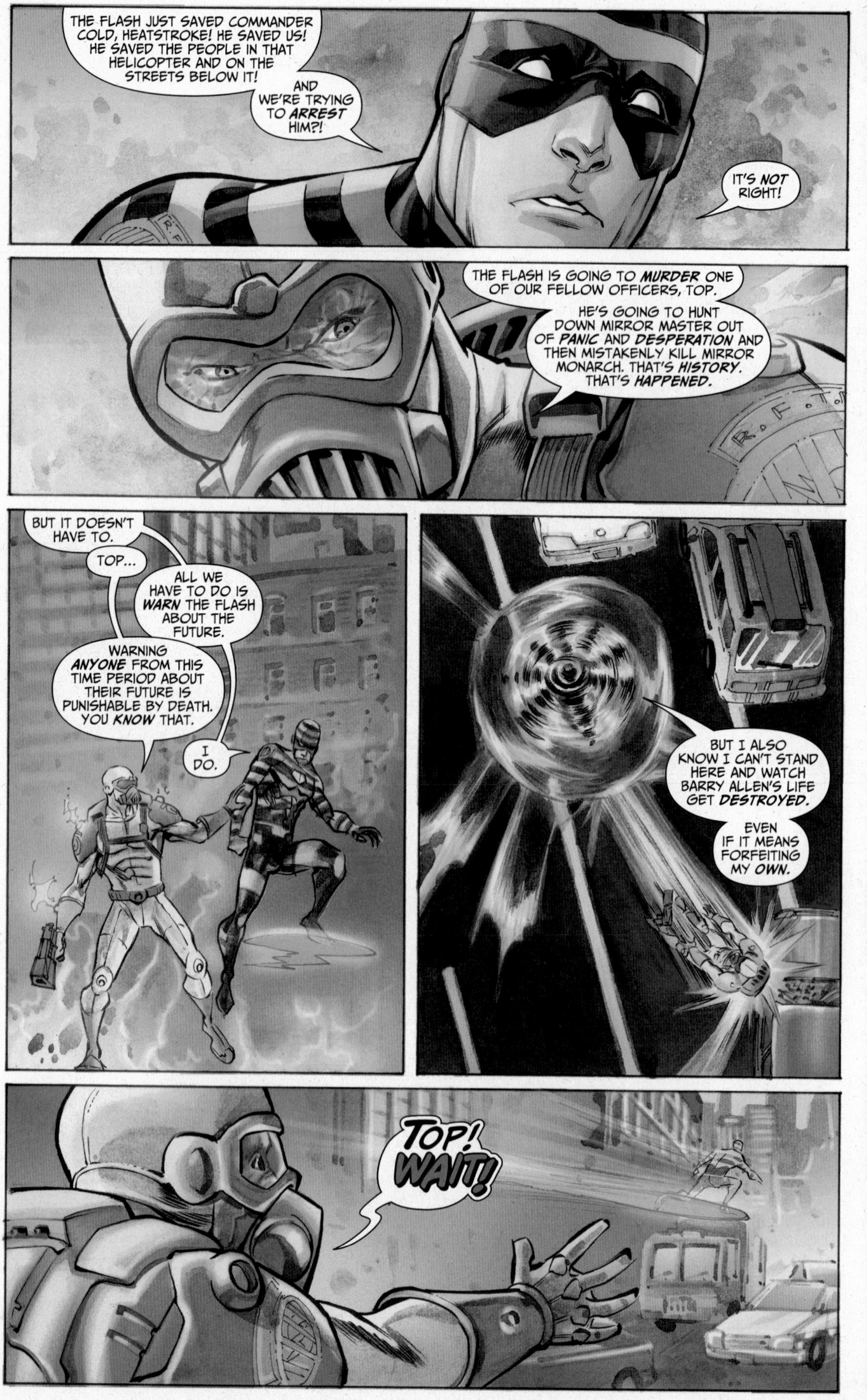
THE FLASH JUST SAVED COMMANDER COLD, HEATSTROKE! HE SAVED US! HE SAVED THE PEOPLE IN THAT HELICOPTER AND ON THE STREETS BELOW IT!
AND WE'RE TRYING TO ARREST HIM?!
IT'S NOT RIGHT!
THE FLASH IS GOING TO MURDER ONE OF OUR FELLOW OFFICERS, TOP.
HE'S GOING TO HUNT DOWN MIRROR MASTER OUT OF PANIC AND DESPERATION AND THEN MISTAKENLY KILL MIRROR MONARCH. THAT'S HISTORY. THAT'S HAPPENED.
BUT IT DOESN'T HAVE TO.
TOP...
ALL WE HAVE TO DO IS WARN THE FLASH ABOUT THE FUTURE.
WARNING ANYONE FROM THIS TIME PERIOD ABOUT THEIR FUTURE IS PUNISHABLE BY DEATH. YOU KNOW THAT.
I DO.
BUT I ALSO KNOW I CAN'T STAND HERE AND WATCH BARRY ALLEN'S LIFE GET DESTROYED.
EVEN IF IT MEANS FORFEITING MY OWN.
TOP! WAIT!

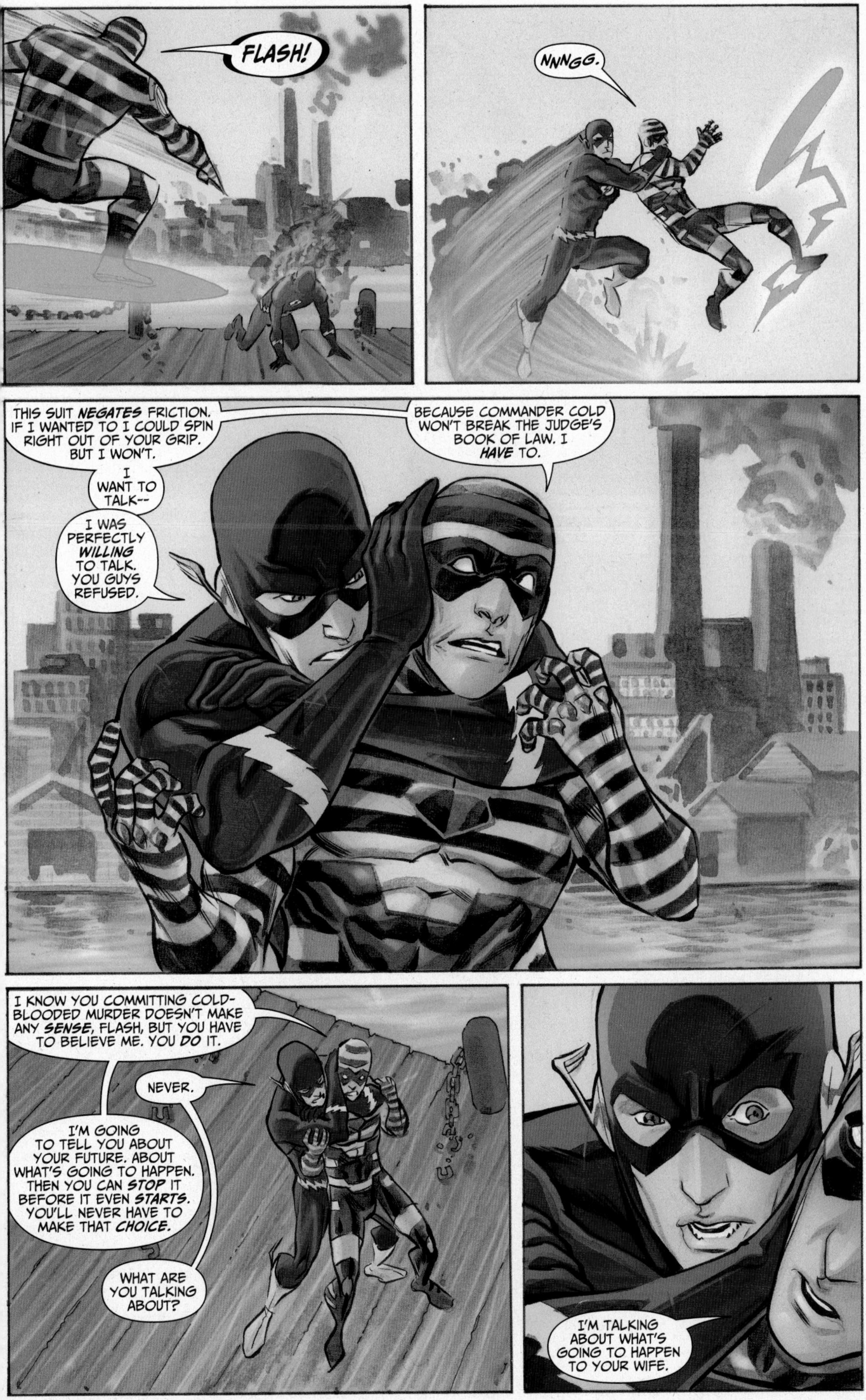
FLASH!
NNNGG.
THIS SUIT NEGATES FRICTION. IF I WANTED TO I COULD SPIN RIGHT OUT OF YOUR GRIP. BUT I WON'T.
I WANT TO TALK--
I WAS PERFECTLY WILLING TO TALK. YOU GUYS REFUSED.
BECAUSE COMMANDER COLD WON'T BREAK THE JUDGE'S BOOK OF LAW. I HAVE TO.
I KNOW YOU COMMITTING COLD-BLOODED MURDER DOESN'T MAKE ANY SENSE, FLASH, BUT YOU HAVE TO BELIEVE ME. YOU DO IT.
NEVER.
I'M GOING TO TELL YOU ABOUT YOUR FUTURE. ABOUT WHAT'S GOING TO HAPPEN. THEN YOU CAN STOP IT BEFORE IT EVEN STARTS. YOU'LL NEVER HAVE TO MAKE THAT CHOICE.
WHAT ARE YOU TALKING ABOUT?
I'M TALKING ABOUT WHAT'S GOING TO HAPPEN TO YOUR WIFE.

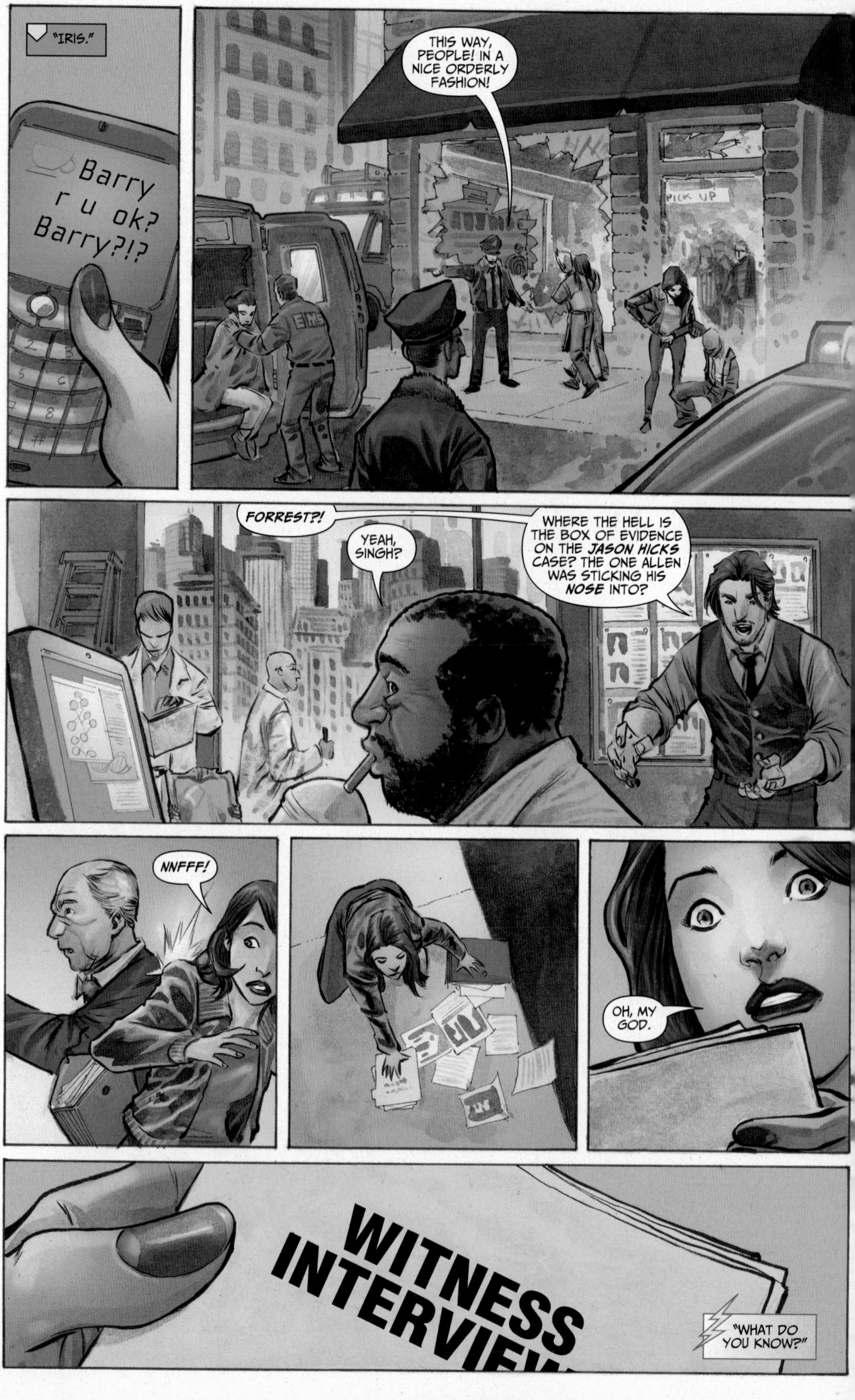
"IRIS."
Barry
r u ok?
Barry?!?
THIS WAY, PEOPLE! IN A NICE ORDERLY FASHION!
PICK UP
EMS
FORREST?!
YEAH, SINGH?
WHERE THE HELL IS THE BOX OF EVIDENCE ON THE JASON HICKS CASE? THE ONE ALLEN WAS STICKING HIS NOSE INTO?
NNFFF!
OH, MY GOD.
WITNESS
INTERVIEW
"WHAT DO YOU KNOW?"

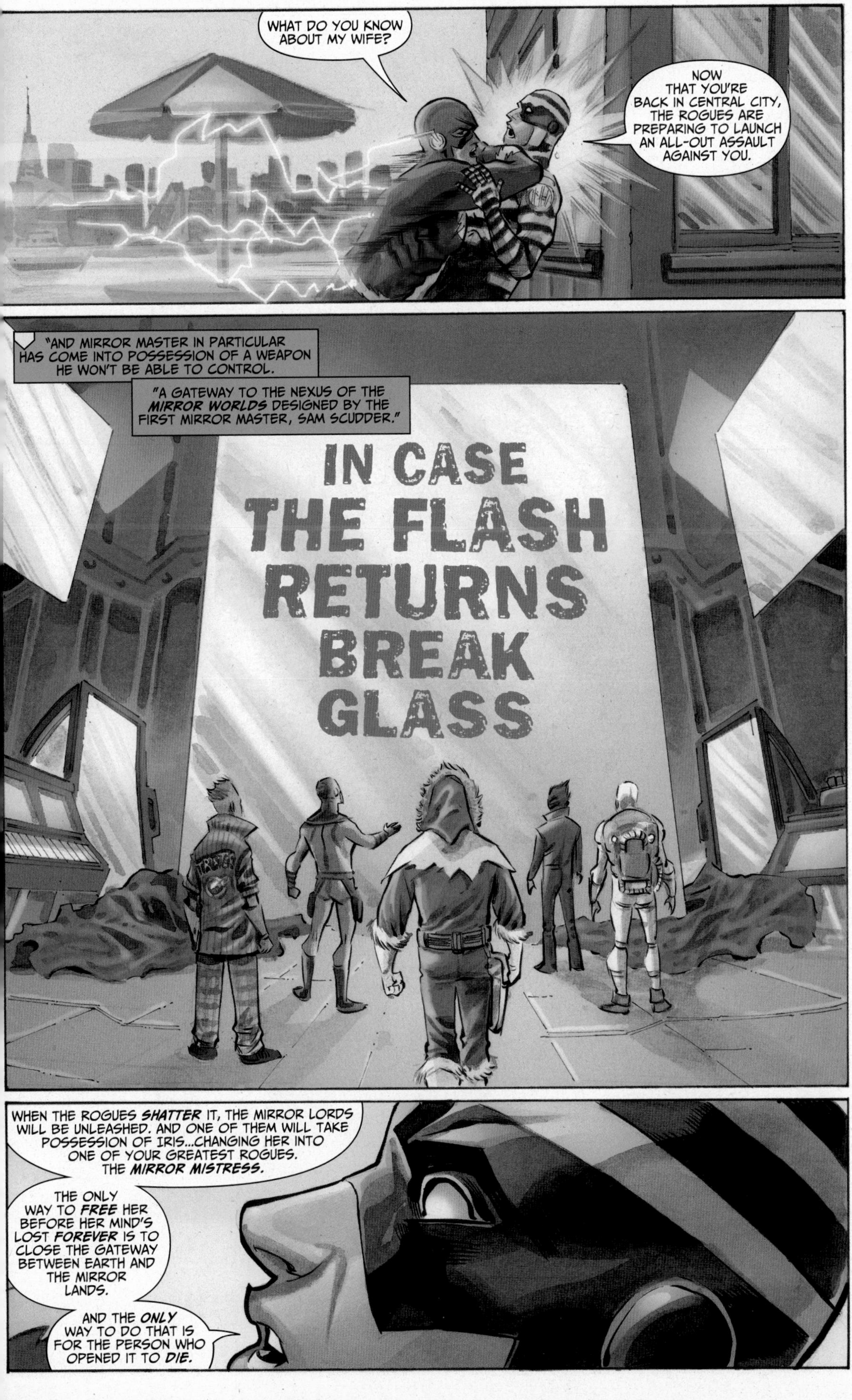
WHAT DO YOU KNOW ABOUT MY WIFE?
NOW THAT YOU'RE BACK IN CENTRAL CITY, THE ROGUES ARE PREPARING TO LAUNCH AN ALL-OUT ASSAULT AGAINST YOU.
"AND MIRROR MASTER IN PARTICULAR HAS COME INTO POSSESSION OF A WEAPON HE WON'T BE ABLE TO CONTROL.
"A GATEWAY TO THE NEXUS OF THE *MIRROR WORLDS* DESIGNED BY THE FIRST MIRROR MASTER, SAM SCUDDER."
IN CASE THE FLASH RETURNS BREAK GLASS
WHEN THE ROGUES *SHATTER* IT, THE MIRROR LORDS WILL BE UNLEASHED. AND ONE OF THEM WILL TAKE POSSESSION OF IRIS...CHANGING HER INTO ONE OF YOUR GREATEST ROGUES. THE *MIRROR MISTRESS.*
THE ONLY WAY TO *FREE* HER BEFORE HER MIND'S LOST *FOREVER* IS TO CLOSE THE GATEWAY BETWEEN EARTH AND THE MIRROR LANDS.
AND THE *ONLY* WAY TO DO THAT IS FOR THE PERSON WHO OPENED IT TO *DIE.*

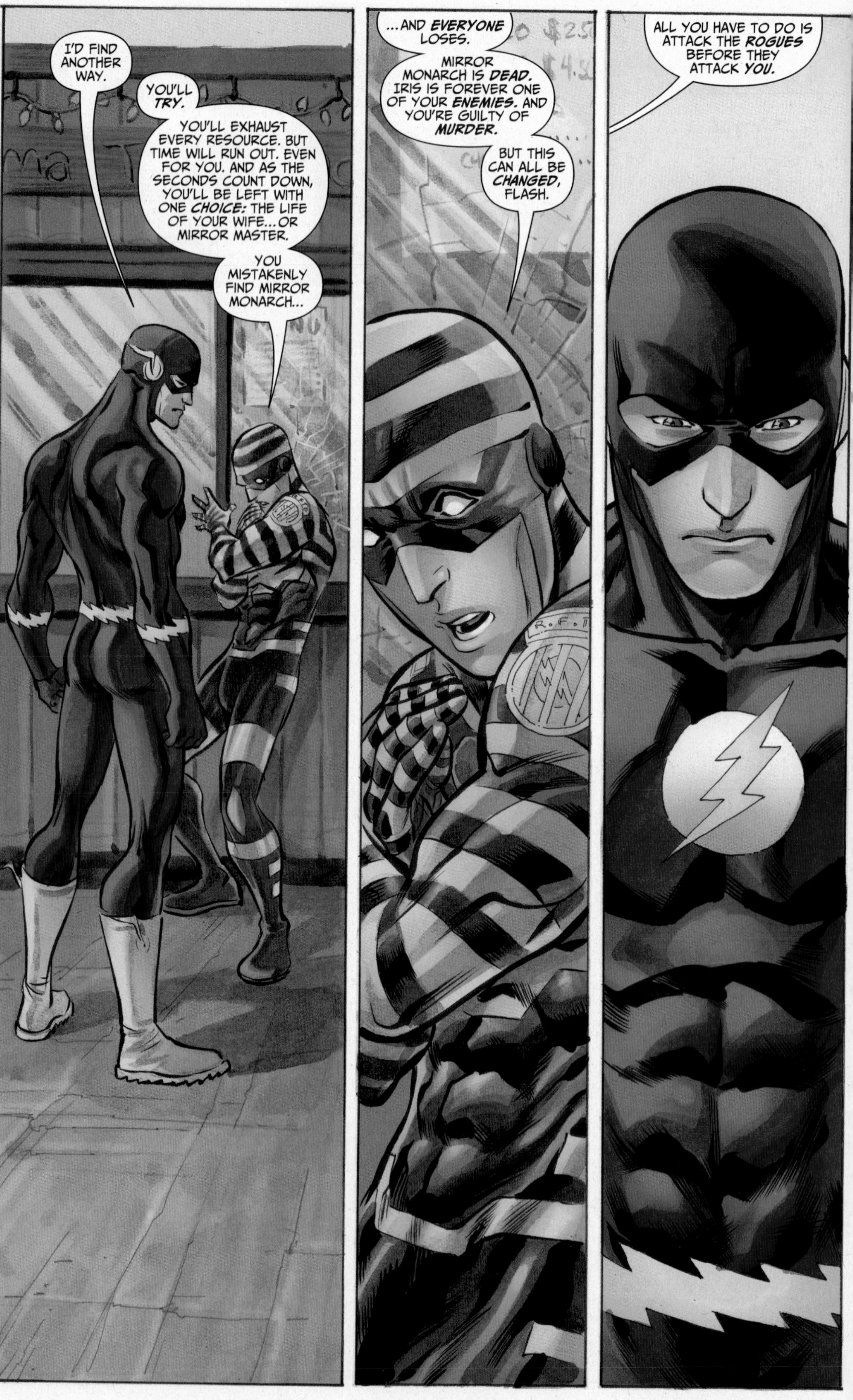
I'D FIND ANOTHER WAY.
YOU'LL TRY.
YOU'LL EXHAUST EVERY RESOURCE. BUT TIME WILL RUN OUT. EVEN FOR YOU. AND AS THE SECONDS COUNT DOWN, YOU'LL BE LEFT WITH ONE CHOICE: THE LIFE OF YOUR WIFE...OR MIRROR MASTER.
YOU MISTAKENLY FIND MIRROR MONARCH...
...AND EVERYONE LOSES.
MIRROR MONARCH IS DEAD. IRIS IS FOREVER ONE OF YOUR ENEMIES. AND YOU'RE GUILTY OF MURDER.
BUT THIS CAN ALL BE CHANGED, FLASH.
ALL YOU HAVE TO DO IS ATTACK THE ROGUES BEFORE THEY ATTACK YOU.

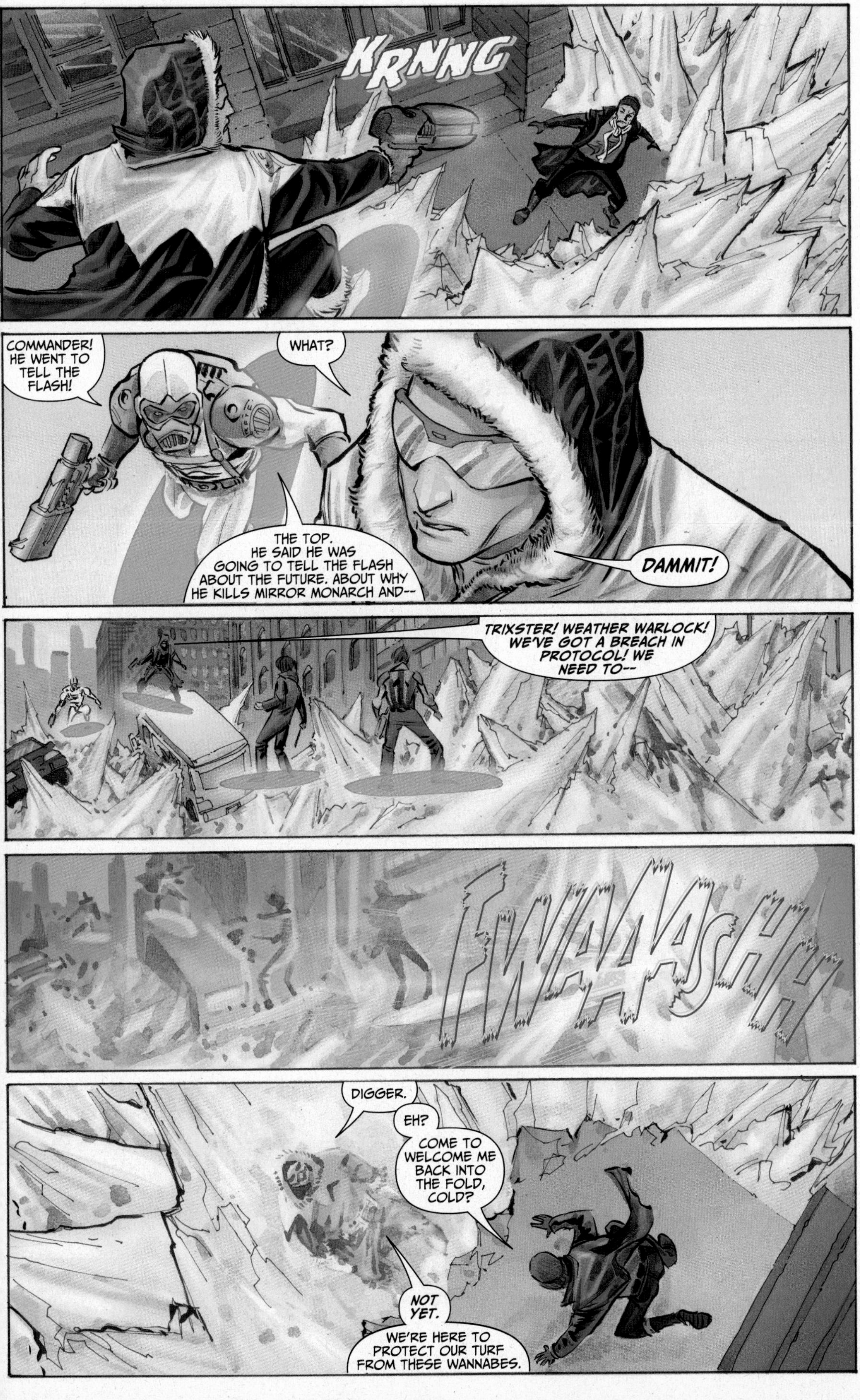
KRNNG
COMMANDER! HE WENT TO TELL THE FLASH!
WHAT?
THE TOP. HE SAID HE WAS GOING TO TELL THE FLASH ABOUT THE FUTURE. ABOUT WHY HE KILLS MIRROR MONARCH AND--
DAMMIT!
TRIXSTER! WEATHER WARLOCK! WE'VE GOT A BREACH IN PROTOCOL! WE NEED TO--
FWAAASHH
DIGGER.
EH?
COME TO WELCOME ME BACK INTO THE FOLD, COLD?
NOT YET.
WE'RE HERE TO PROTECT OUR TURF FROM THESE WANNABES.

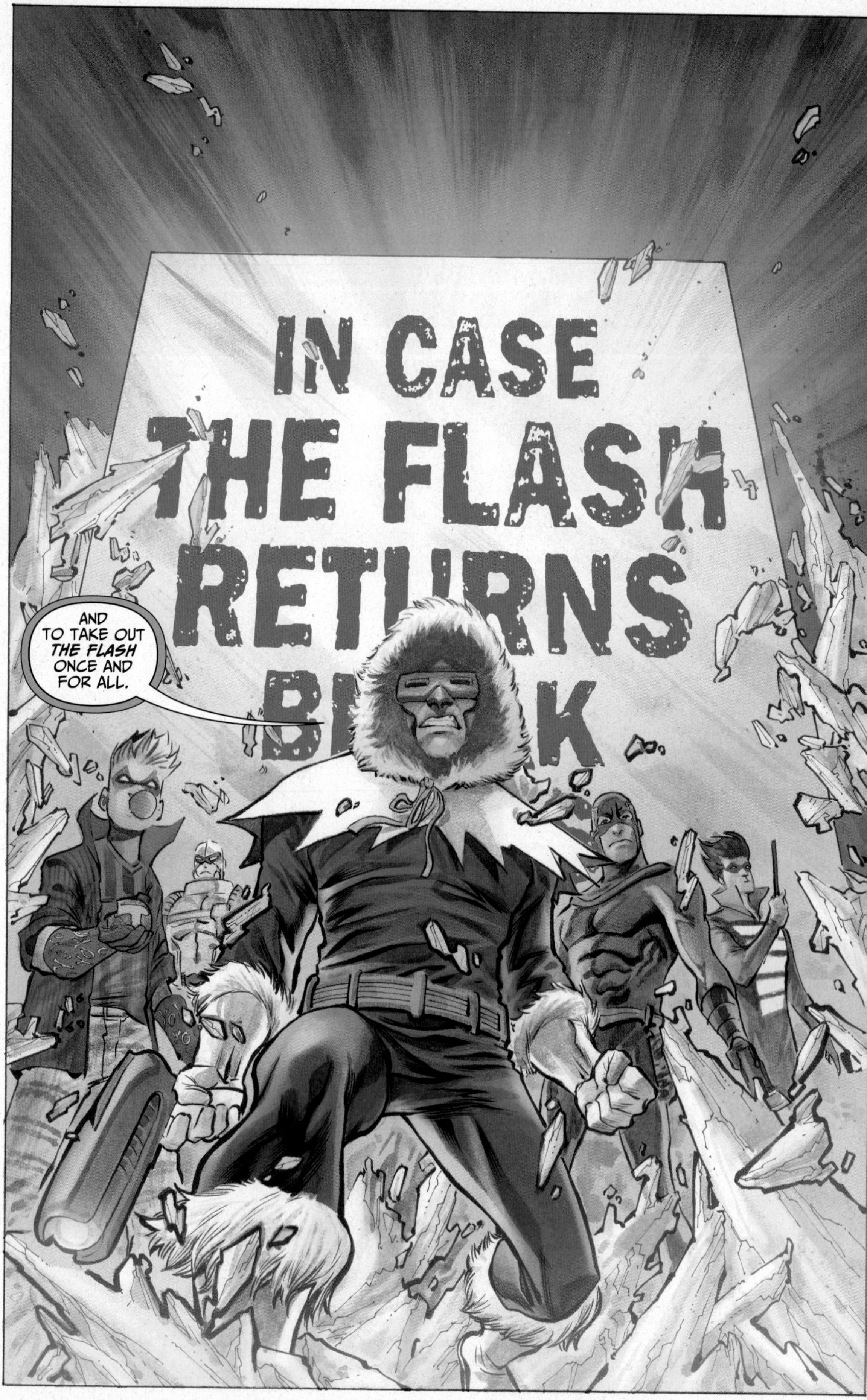
IN CASE THE FLASH RETURNS B K
AND TO TAKE OUT *THE FLASH* ONCE AND FOR ALL.
YO YO YO

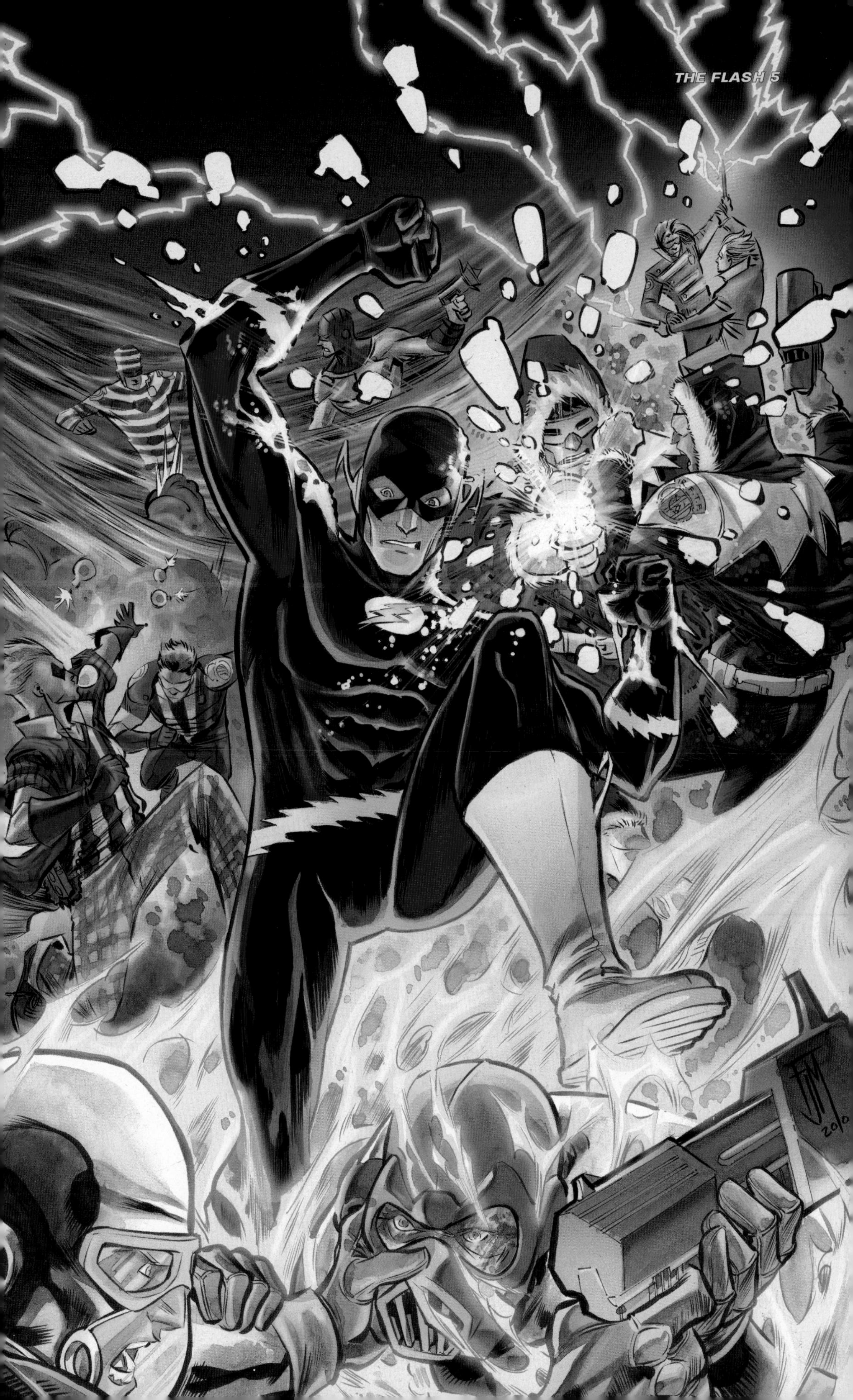

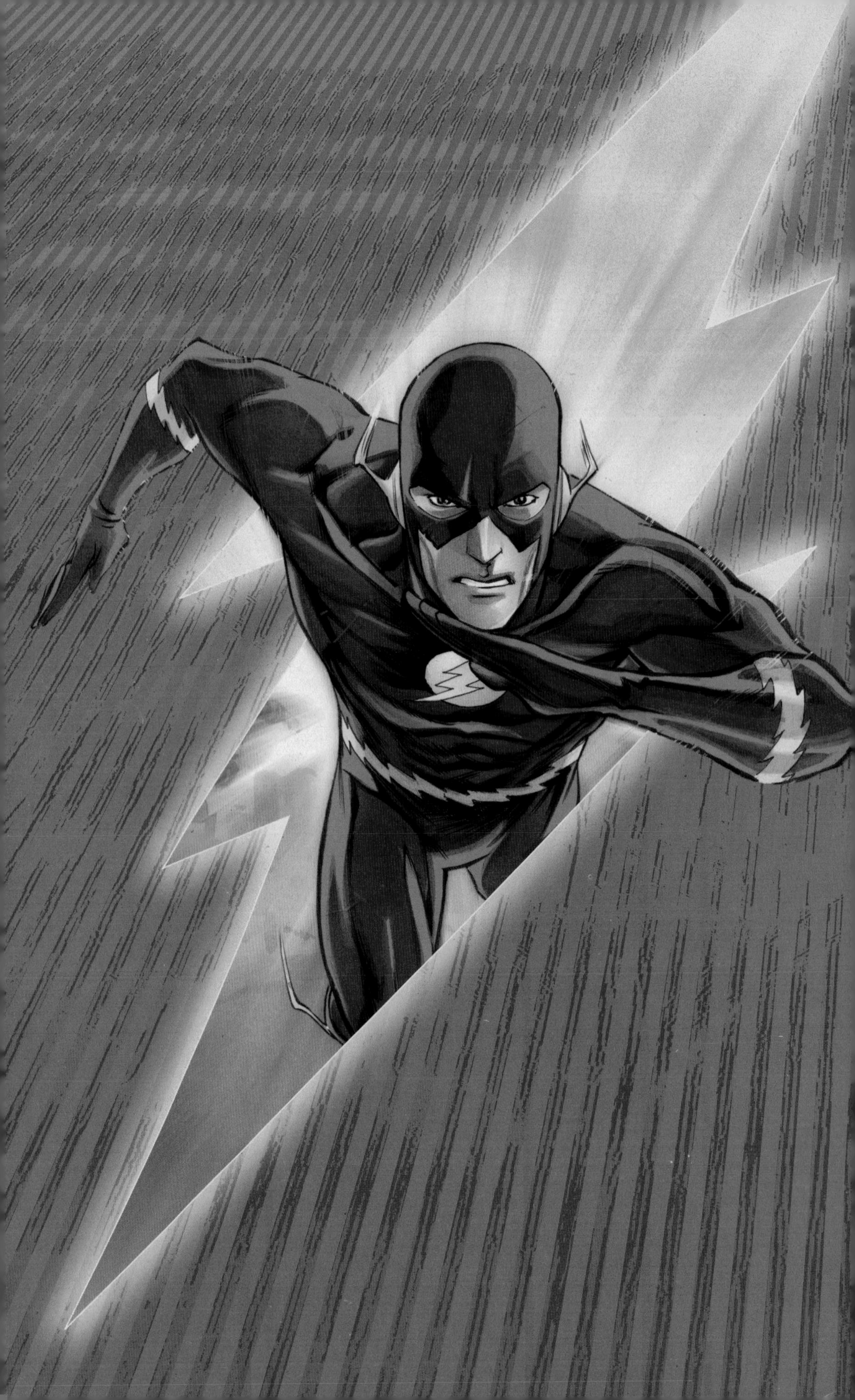

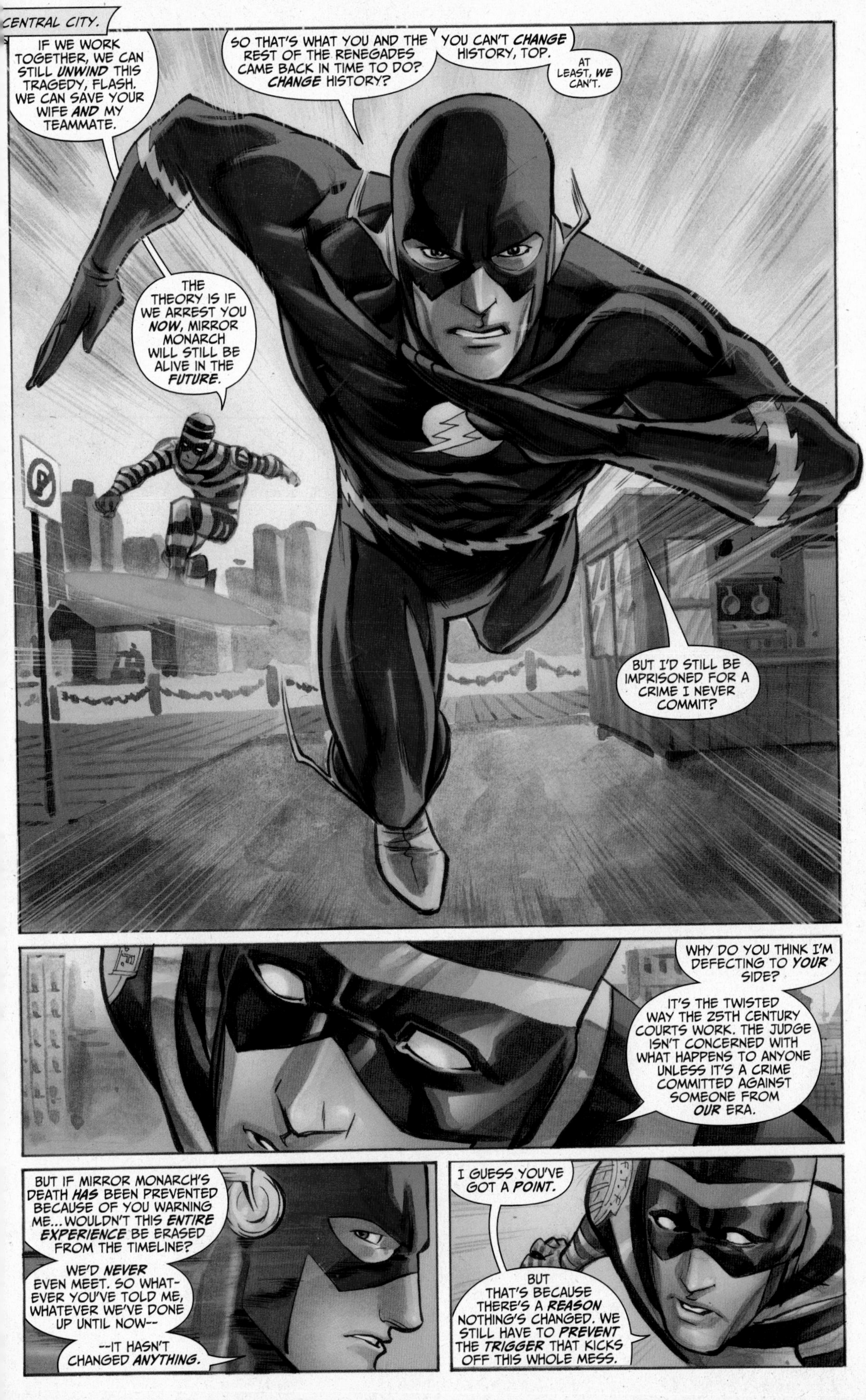

CENTRAL CITY.
IF WE WORK TOGETHER, WE CAN STILL UNWIND THIS TRAGEDY, FLASH. WE CAN SAVE YOUR WIFE AND MY TEAMMATE.
SO THAT'S WHAT YOU AND THE REST OF THE RENEGADES CAME BACK IN TIME TO DO? CHANGE HISTORY?
YOU CAN'T CHANGE HISTORY, TOP.
AT LEAST, WE CAN'T.
THE THEORY IS IF WE ARREST YOU NOW, MIRROR MONARCH WILL STILL BE ALIVE IN THE FUTURE.
BUT I'D STILL BE IMPRISONED FOR A CRIME I NEVER COMMIT?
WHY DO YOU THINK I'M DEFECTING TO YOUR SIDE?
IT'S THE TWISTED WAY THE 25TH CENTURY COURTS WORK. THE JUDGE ISN'T CONCERNED WITH WHAT HAPPENS TO ANYONE UNLESS IT'S A CRIME COMMITTED AGAINST SOMEONE FROM OUR ERA.
BUT IF MIRROR MONARCH'S DEATH HAS BEEN PREVENTED BECAUSE OF YOU WARNING ME...WOULDN'T THIS ENTIRE EXPERIENCE BE ERASED FROM THE TIMELINE?
WE'D NEVER EVEN MEET. SO WHAT-EVER YOU'VE TOLD ME, WHATEVER WE'VE DONE UP UNTIL NOW--
--IT HASN'T CHANGED ANYTHING.
I GUESS YOU'VE GOT A POINT.
BUT THAT'S BECAUSE THERE'S A REASON NOTHING'S CHANGED. WE STILL HAVE TO PREVENT THE TRIGGER THAT KICKS OFF THIS WHOLE MESS.

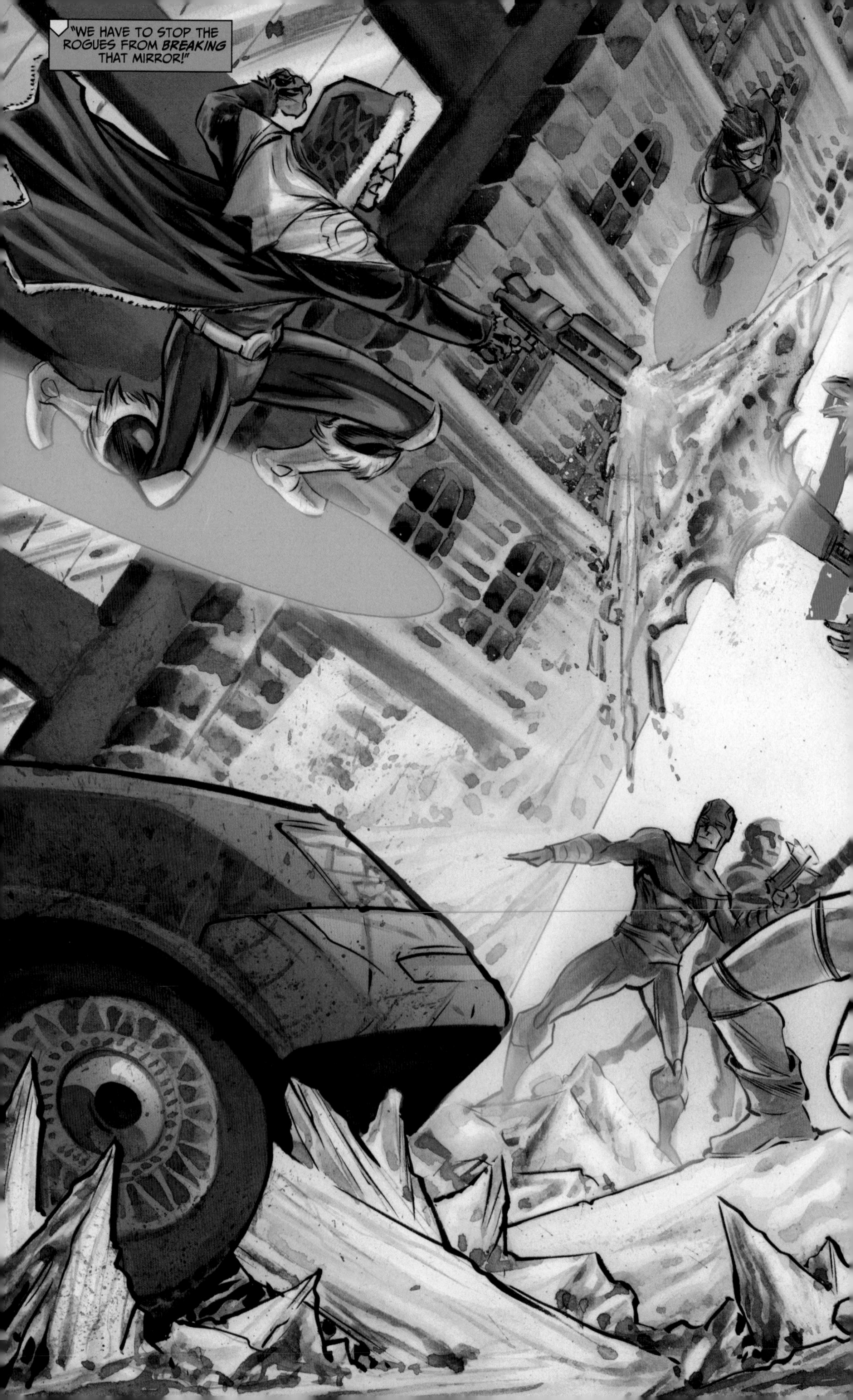
"WE HAVE TO STOP THE ROGUES FROM *BREAKING* THAT MIRROR!"

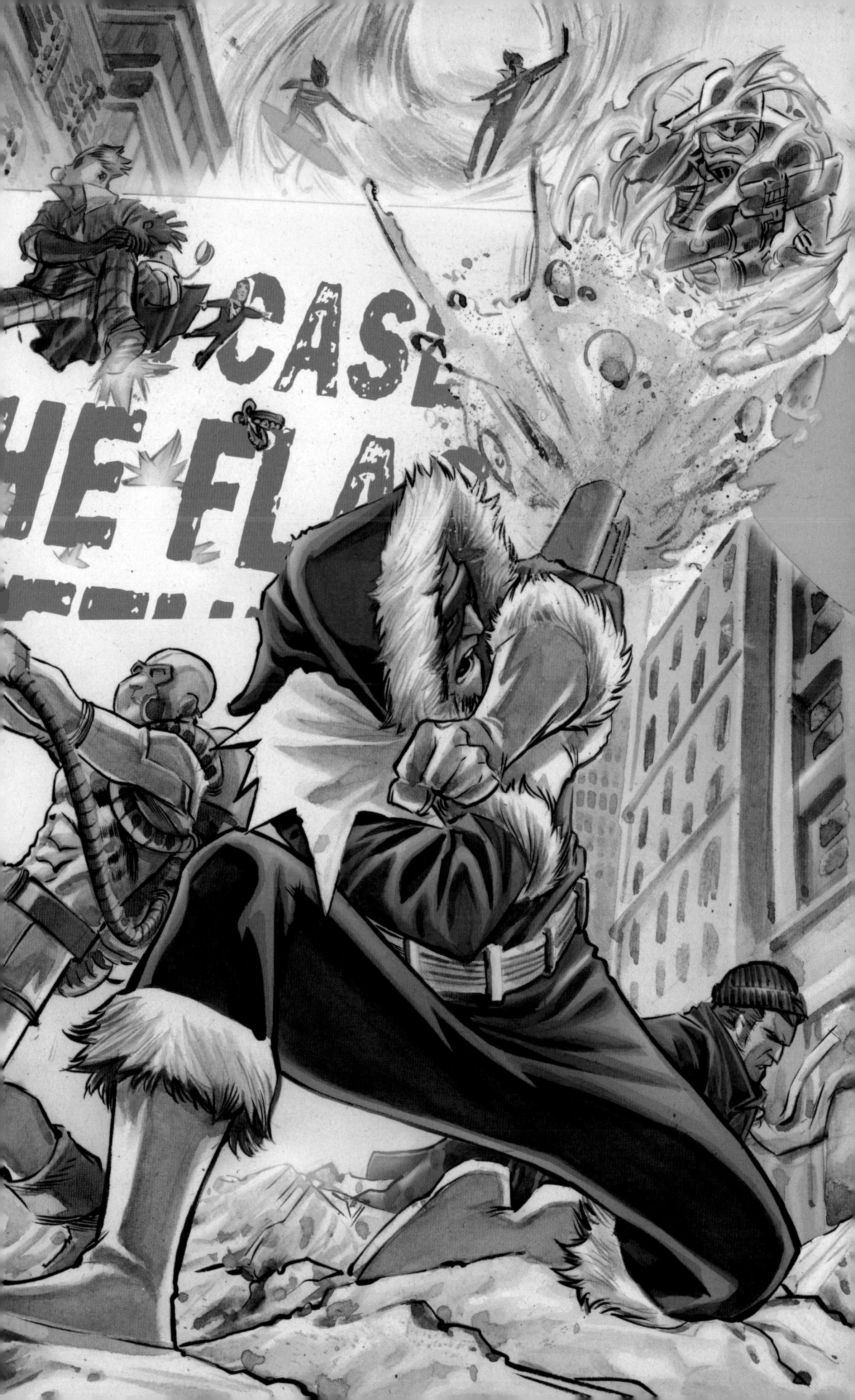

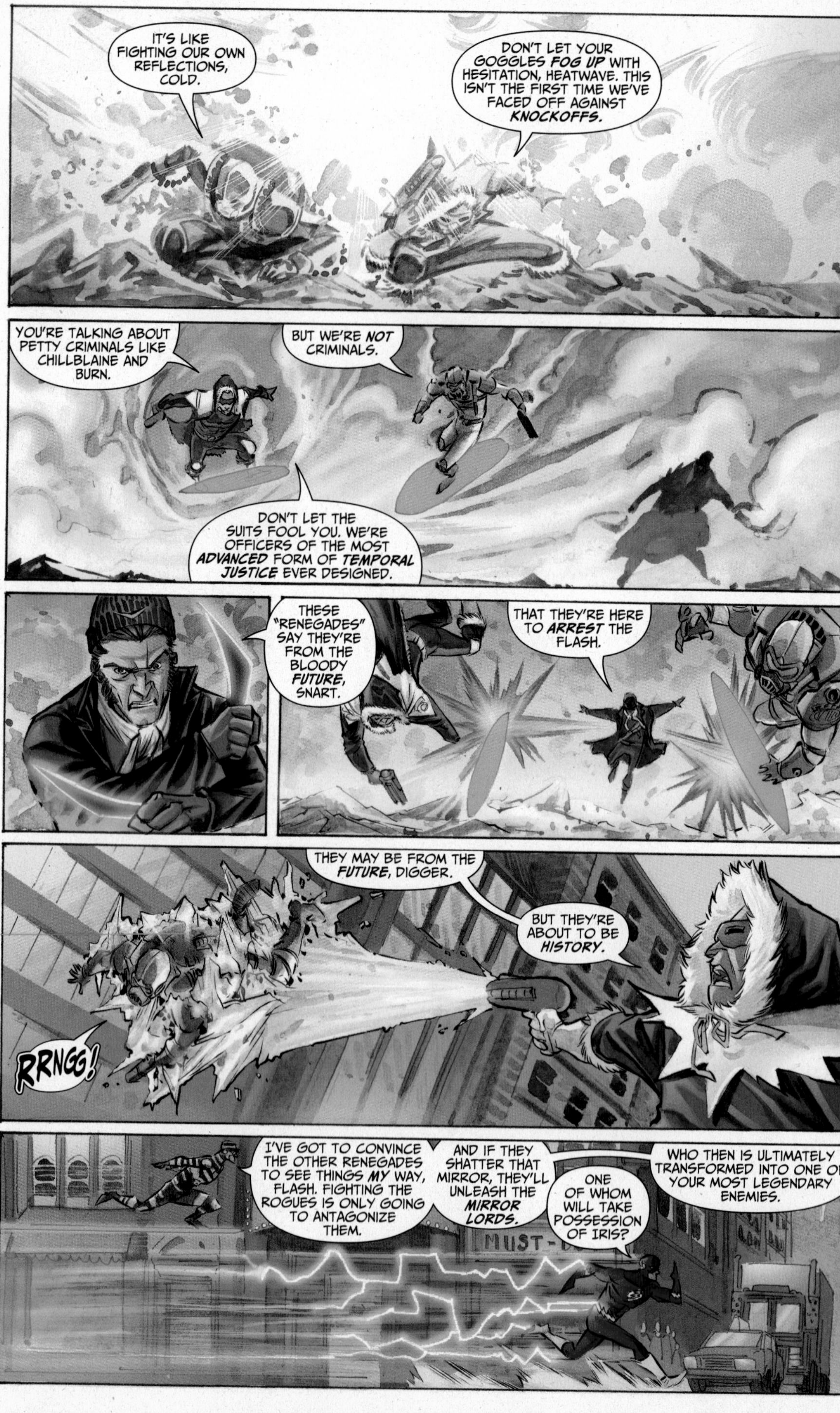
IT'S LIKE FIGHTING OUR OWN REFLECTIONS, COLD.
DON'T LET YOUR GOGGLES FOG UP WITH HESITATION, HEATWAVE. THIS ISN'T THE FIRST TIME WE'VE FACED OFF AGAINST KNOCKOFFS.
YOU'RE TALKING ABOUT PETTY CRIMINALS LIKE CHILLBLAINE AND BURN.
BUT WE'RE NOT CRIMINALS.
DON'T LET THE SUITS FOOL YOU. WE'RE OFFICERS OF THE MOST ADVANCED FORM OF TEMPORAL JUSTICE EVER DESIGNED.
THESE "RENEGADES" SAY THEY'RE FROM THE BLOODY FUTURE, SNART.
THAT THEY'RE HERE TO ARREST THE FLASH.
THEY MAY BE FROM THE FUTURE, DIGGER.
BUT THEY'RE ABOUT TO BE HISTORY.
RRNGG!
I'VE GOT TO CONVINCE THE OTHER RENEGADES TO SEE THINGS MY WAY, FLASH. FIGHTING THE ROGUES IS ONLY GOING TO ANTAGONIZE THEM.
AND IF THEY SHATTER THAT MIRROR, THEY'LL UNLEASH THE MIRROR LORDS.
ONE OF WHOM WILL TAKE POSSESSION OF IRIS?
WHO THEN IS ULTIMATELY TRANSFORMED INTO ONE OF YOUR MOST LEGENDARY ENEMIES.
MUST-

HEY, McCULLOCH! WHAT ARE YOU WAITING FOR?!

IN CASE THE FLASH RETURNS BREAK GLASS

BREAK THE GLASS ALREADY! I WANNA SEE WHAT HAPPENS!

IN CASE THE FLASH RETURNS BREAK G

AYE, KID. LET'S SEE WOT KINDA BAD LUCK SCUDDER'S MIRROR C'N UNLEASH--

ACCENT'S KIND OF THICK. WHAT IS IT? SCOTTISH?

WOT?

I HEARD SOMEONE HAD TAKEN OVER FOR SAM SCUDDER.

YOU'RE SHORTER THAN HE WAS.

AND LESS PREPARED.

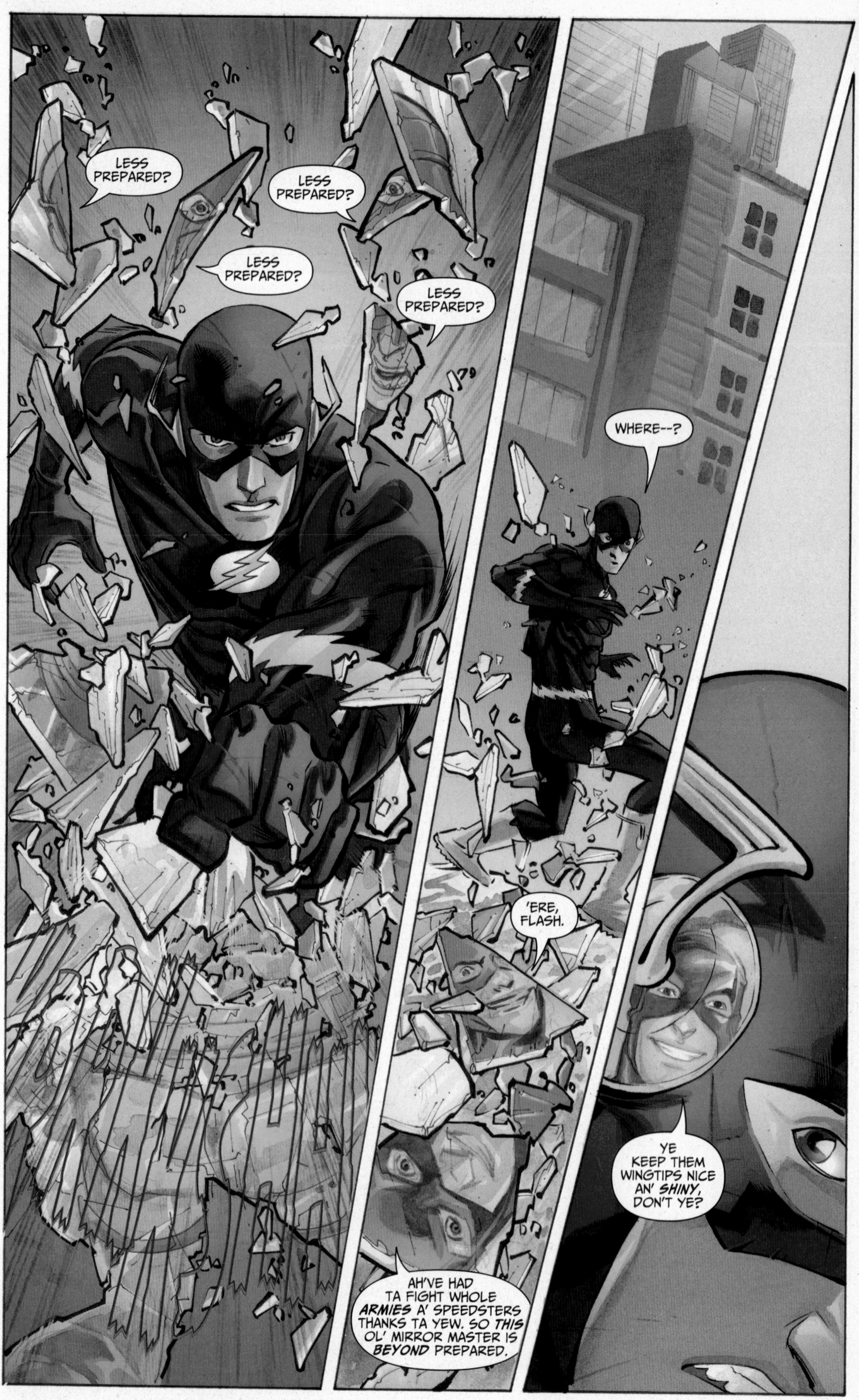
LESS PREPARED?
LESS PREPARED?
LESS PREPARED?
LESS PREPARED?
WHERE--?
'ERE, FLASH.
AH'VE HAD TA FIGHT WHOLE ARMIES A' SPEEDSTERS THANKS TA YEW. SO THIS OL' MIRROR MASTER IS BEYOND PREPARED.
YE KEEP THEM WINGTIPS NICE AN' SHINY, DON'T YE?

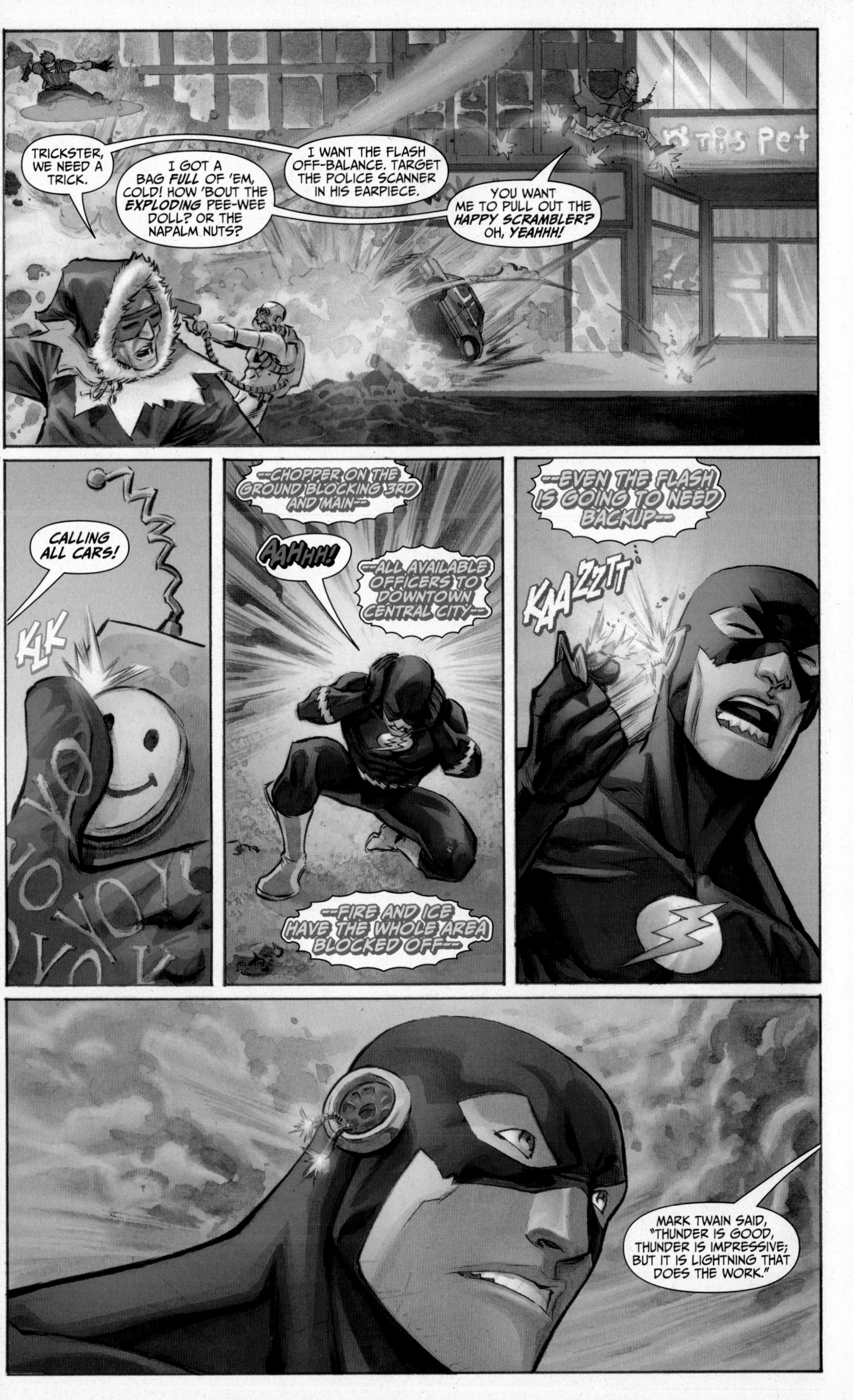
TRICKSTER, WE NEED A TRICK.
I GOT A BAG FULL OF 'EM, COLD! HOW 'BOUT THE EXPLODING PEE-WEE DOLL? OR THE NAPALM NUTS?
I WANT THE FLASH OFF-BALANCE. TARGET THE POLICE SCANNER IN HIS EARPIECE.
YOU WANT ME TO PULL OUT THE HAPPY SCRAMBLER? OH, YEAHHH!
CALLING ALL CARS!
KLK
--CHOPPER ON THE GROUND BLOCKING 3RD AND MAIN--
AAHHH!
--ALL AVAILABLE OFFICERS TO DOWNTOWN CENTRAL CITY--
--FIRE AND ICE HAVE THE WHOLE AREA BLOCKED OFF--
--EVEN THE FLASH IS GOING TO NEED BACKUP--
KAAZZTT
MARK TWAIN SAID, "THUNDER IS GOOD, THUNDER IS IMPRESSIVE; BUT IT IS LIGHTNING THAT DOES THE WORK."

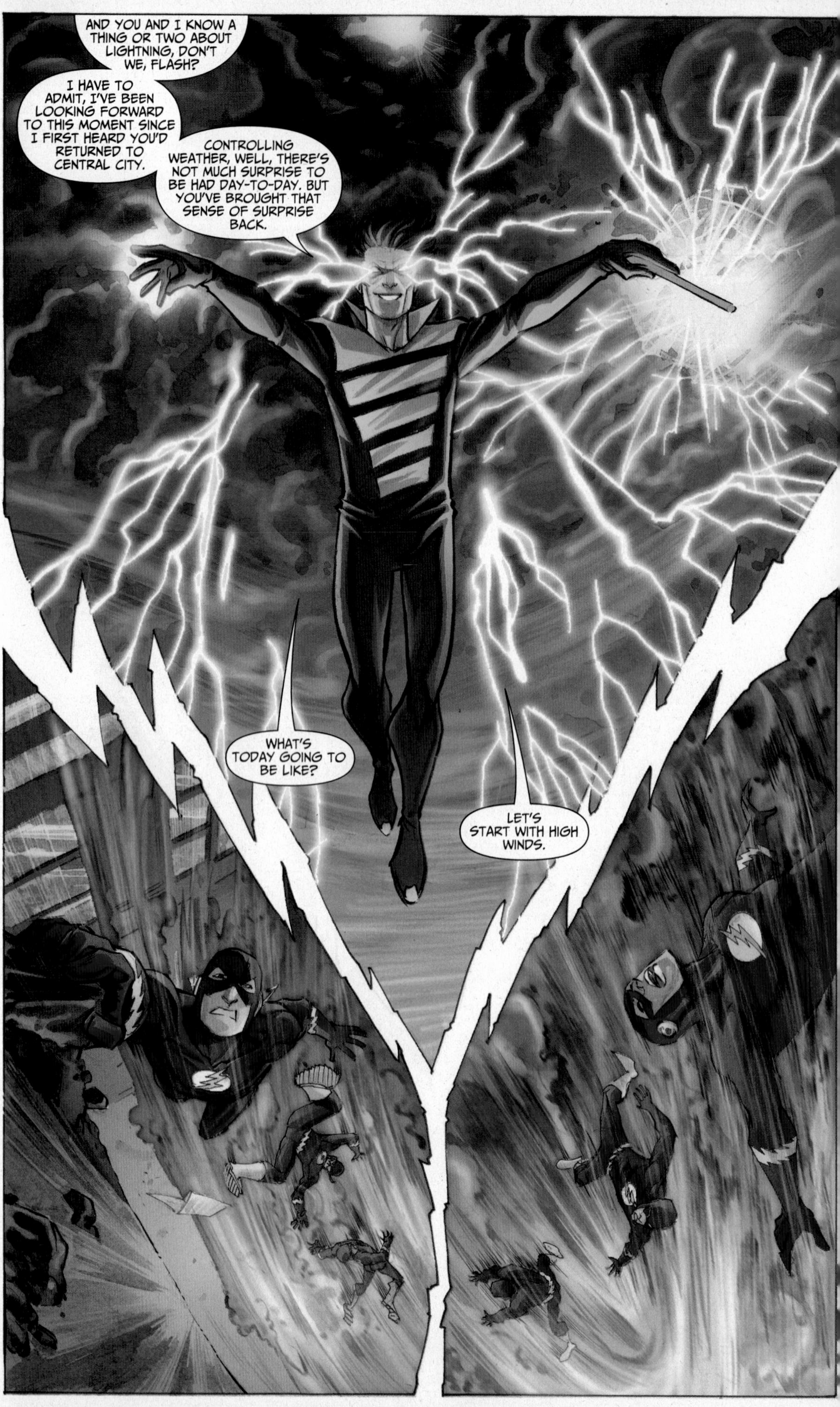
AND YOU AND I KNOW A THING OR TWO ABOUT LIGHTNING, DON'T WE, FLASH?
I HAVE TO ADMIT, I'VE BEEN LOOKING FORWARD TO THIS MOMENT SINCE I FIRST HEARD YOU'D RETURNED TO CENTRAL CITY.
CONTROLLING WEATHER, WELL, THERE'S NOT MUCH SURPRISE TO BE HAD DAY-TO-DAY. BUT YOU'VE BROUGHT THAT SENSE OF SURPRISE BACK.
WHAT'S TODAY GOING TO BE LIKE?
LET'S START WITH HIGH WINDS.

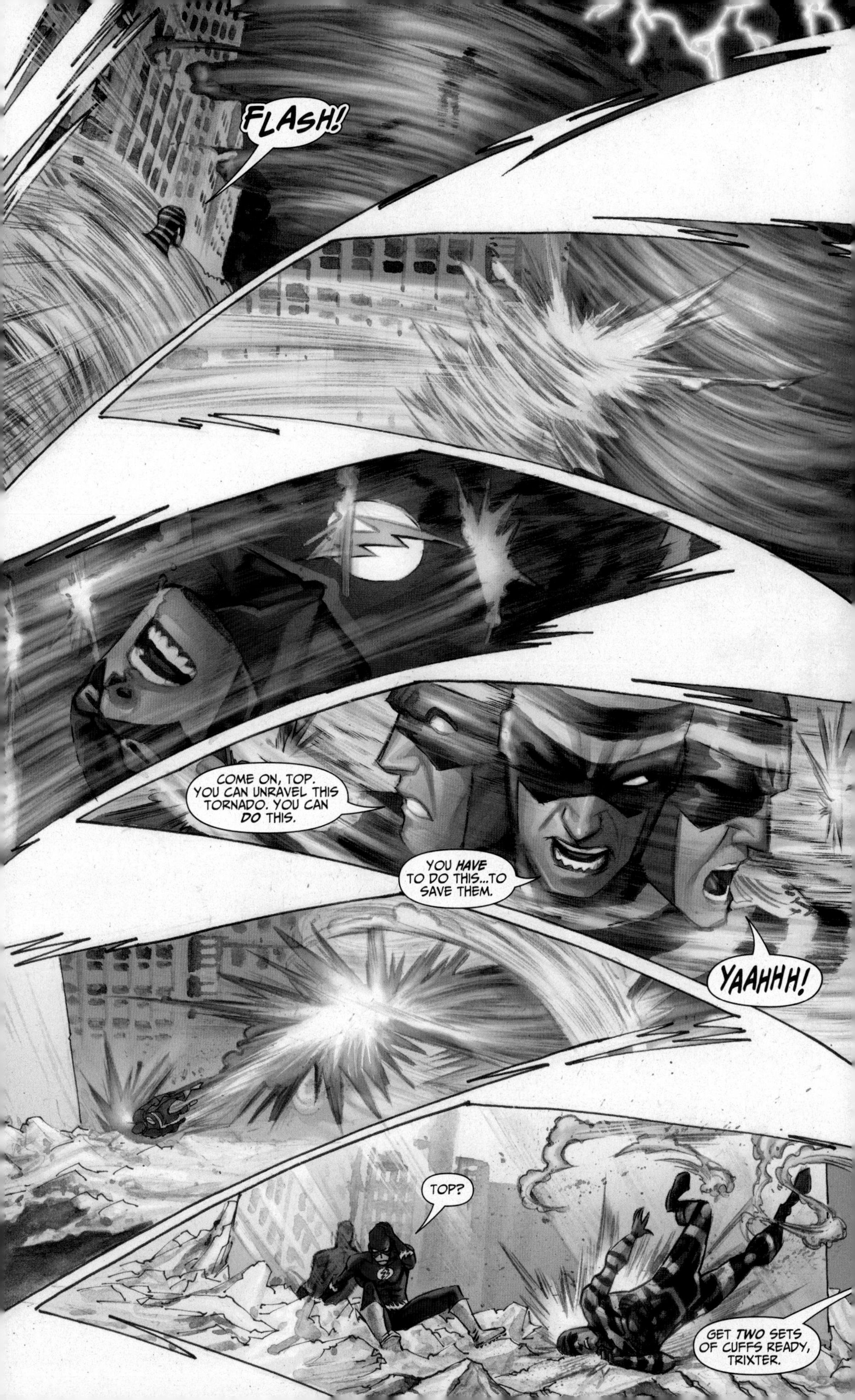
FLASH!
COME ON, TOP. YOU CAN UNRAVEL THIS TORNADO. YOU CAN DO THIS.
YOU HAVE TO DO THIS...TO SAVE THEM.
YAAHHH!
TOP?
GET TWO SETS OF CUFFS READY, TRIXTER.

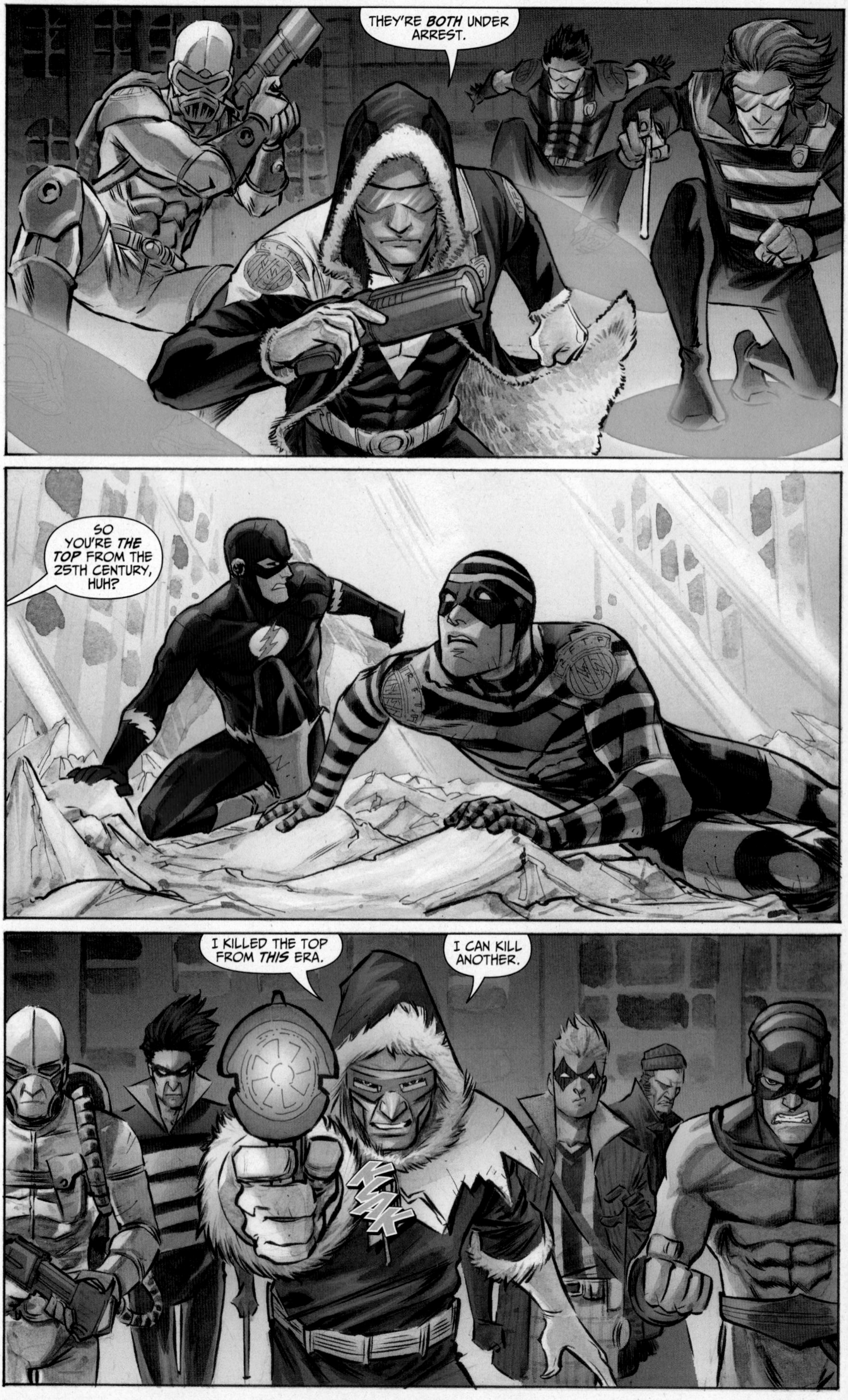
THEY'RE *BOTH* UNDER ARREST.
SO YOU'RE *THE TOP* FROM THE 25TH CENTURY, HUH?
I KILLED THE TOP FROM *THIS* ERA.
I CAN KILL ANOTHER.
KLAK

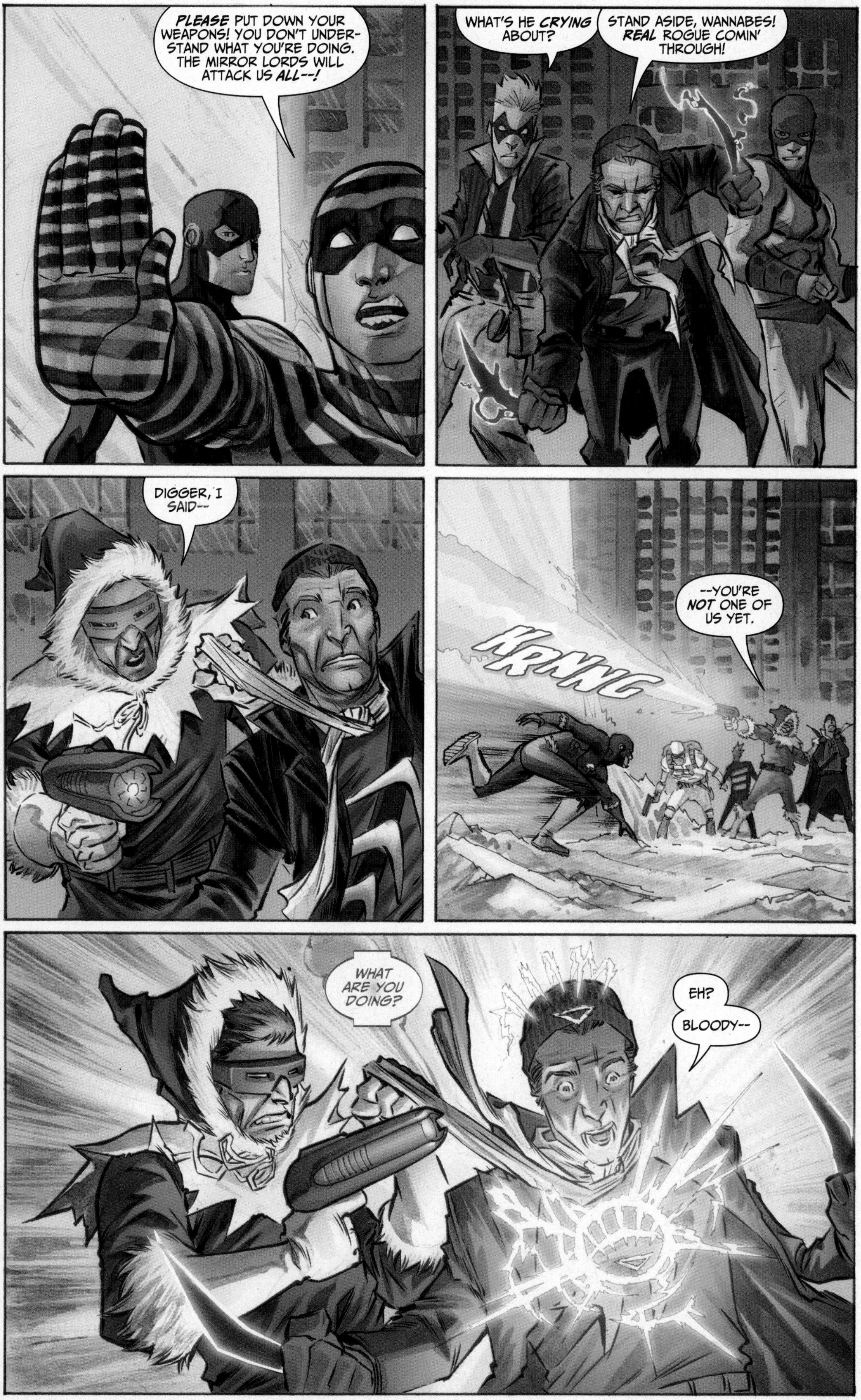
PLEASE PUT DOWN YOUR WEAPONS! YOU DON'T UNDERSTAND WHAT YOU'RE DOING. THE MIRROR LORDS WILL ATTACK US ALL--!
WHAT'S HE CRYING ABOUT?
STAND ASIDE, WANNABES! REAL ROGUE COMIN' THROUGH!
DIGGER, I SAID--
KRNNG
--YOU'RE NOT ONE OF US YET.
WHAT ARE YOU DOING?
EH?
BLOODY--

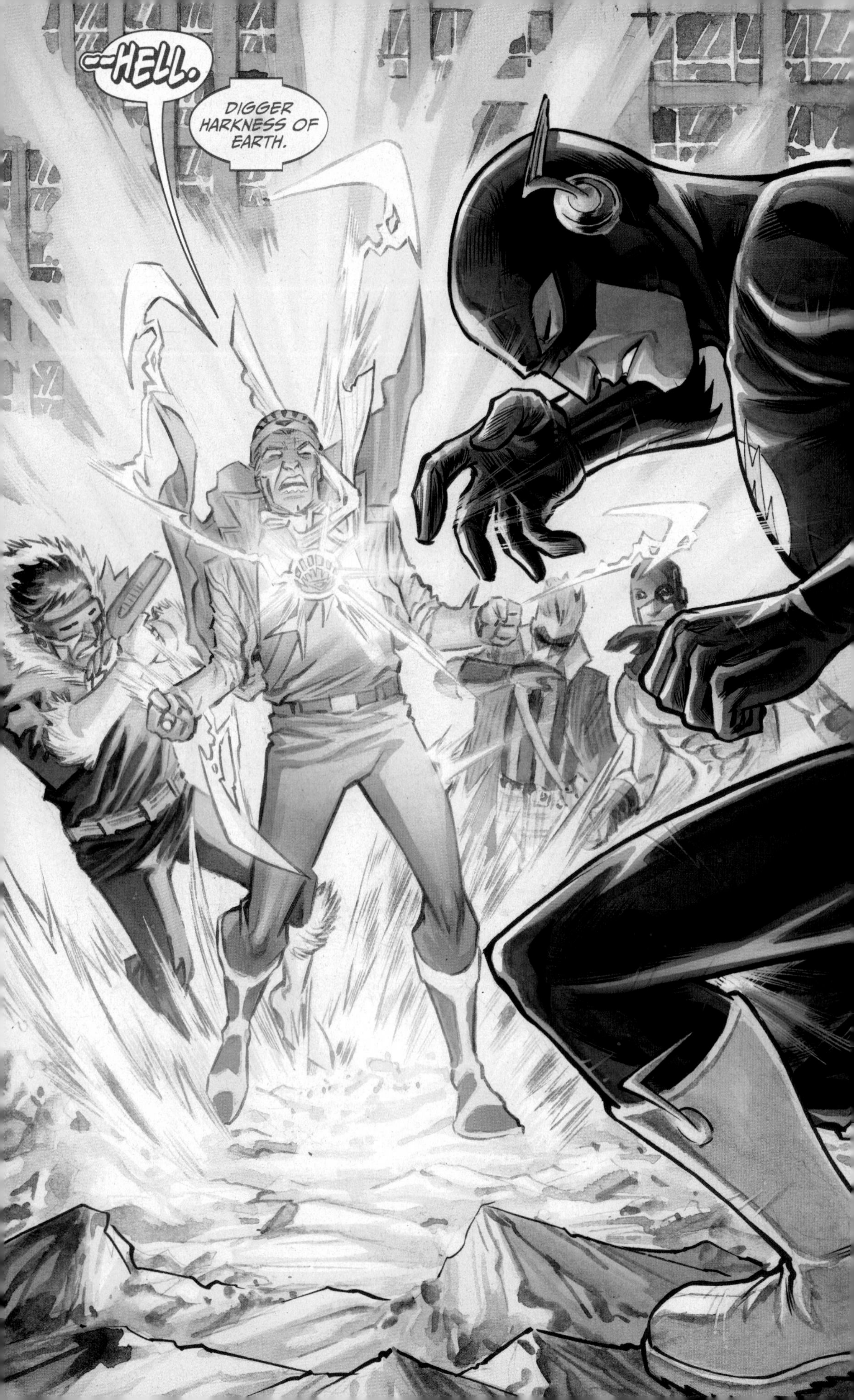
--HELL.
DIGGER HARKNESS OF EARTH.

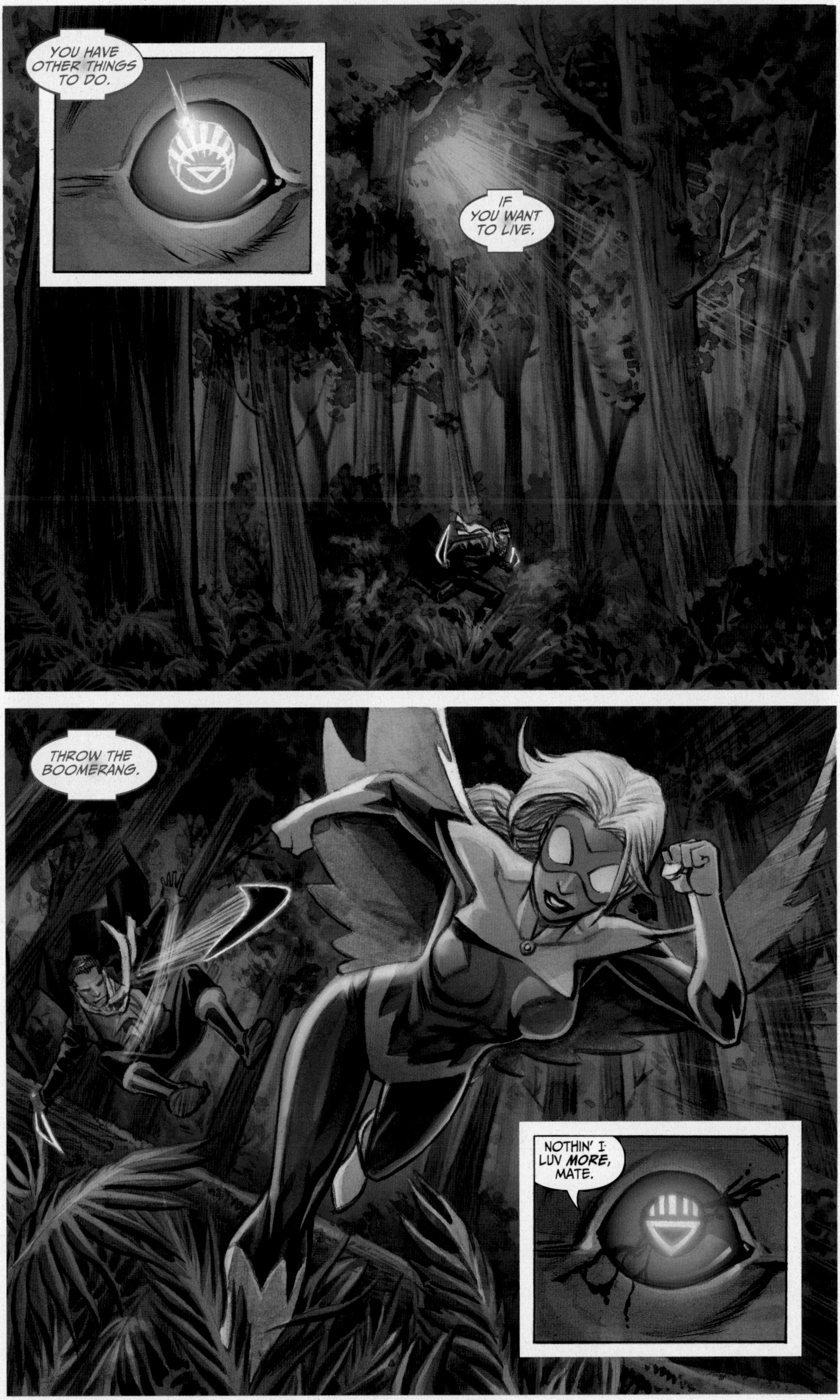
YOU HAVE OTHER THINGS TO DO.
IF YOU WANT TO LIVE.
THROW THE BOOMERANG.
NOTHIN' I LUV MORE, MATE.

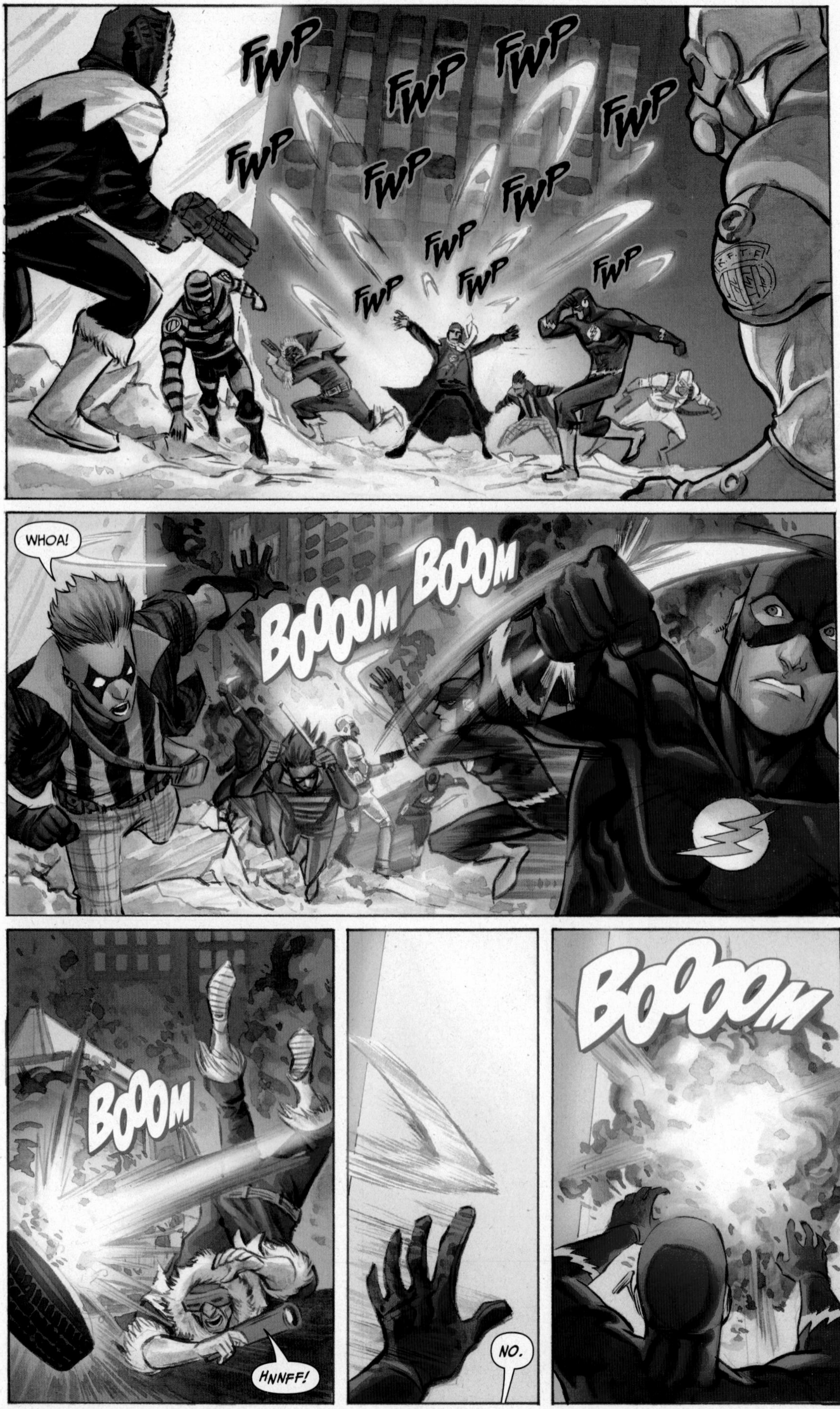
FWP
FWP
FWP
FWP
FWP
FWP
FWP
FWP
FWP
FWP
FWP
WHOA!
BOOOOM BOOOM
BOOOM
HNNFF!
NO.
BOOOOM

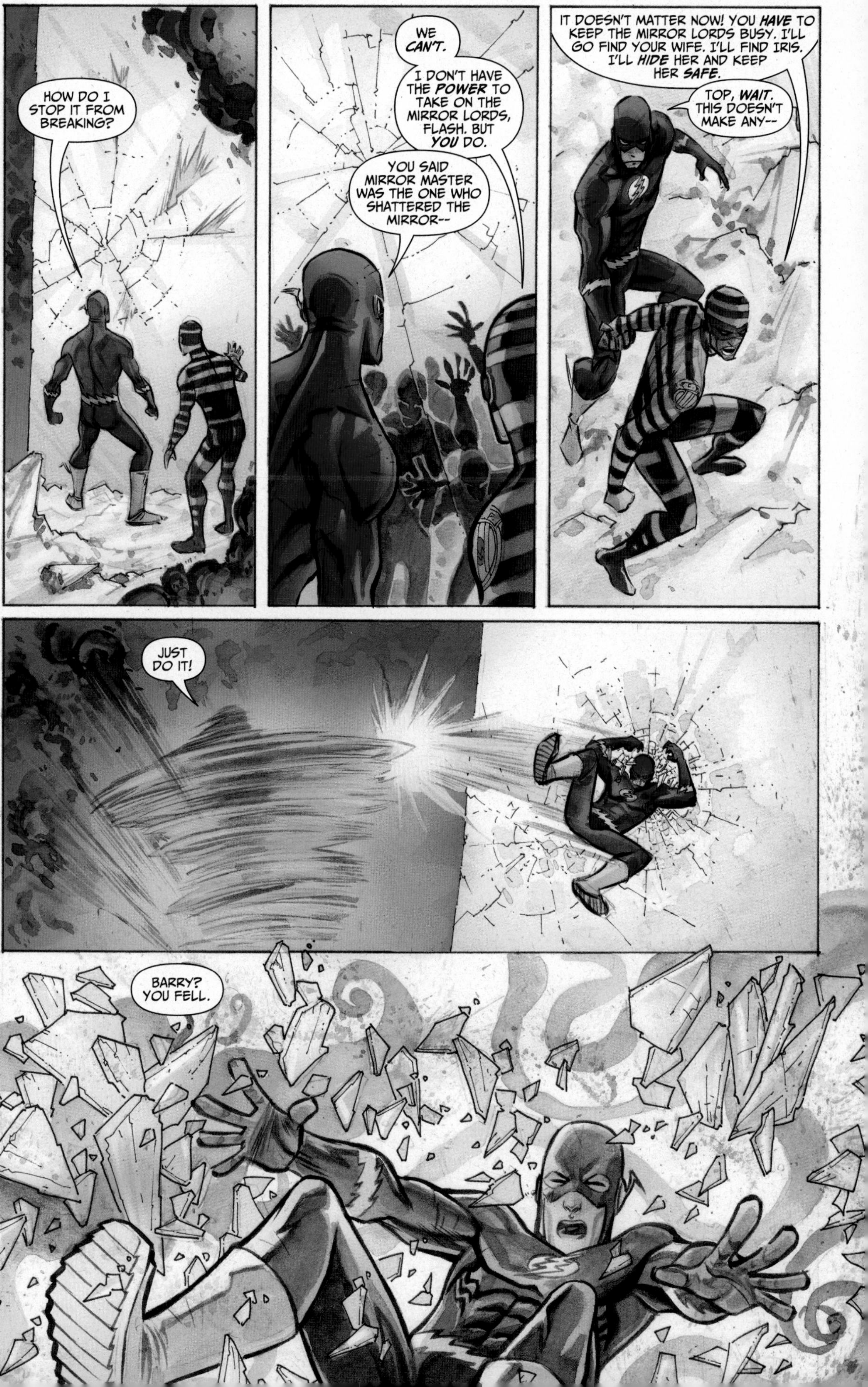
HOW DO I STOP IT FROM BREAKING?
WE CAN'T.
I DON'T HAVE THE POWER TO TAKE ON THE MIRROR LORDS, FLASH. BUT YOU DO.
YOU SAID MIRROR MASTER WAS THE ONE WHO SHATTERED THE MIRROR--
IT DOESN'T MATTER NOW! YOU HAVE TO KEEP THE MIRROR LORDS BUSY. I'LL GO FIND YOUR WIFE. I'LL FIND IRIS. I'LL HIDE HER AND KEEP HER SAFE.
TOP, WAIT. THIS DOESN'T MAKE ANY--
JUST DO IT!
BARRY? YOU FELL.

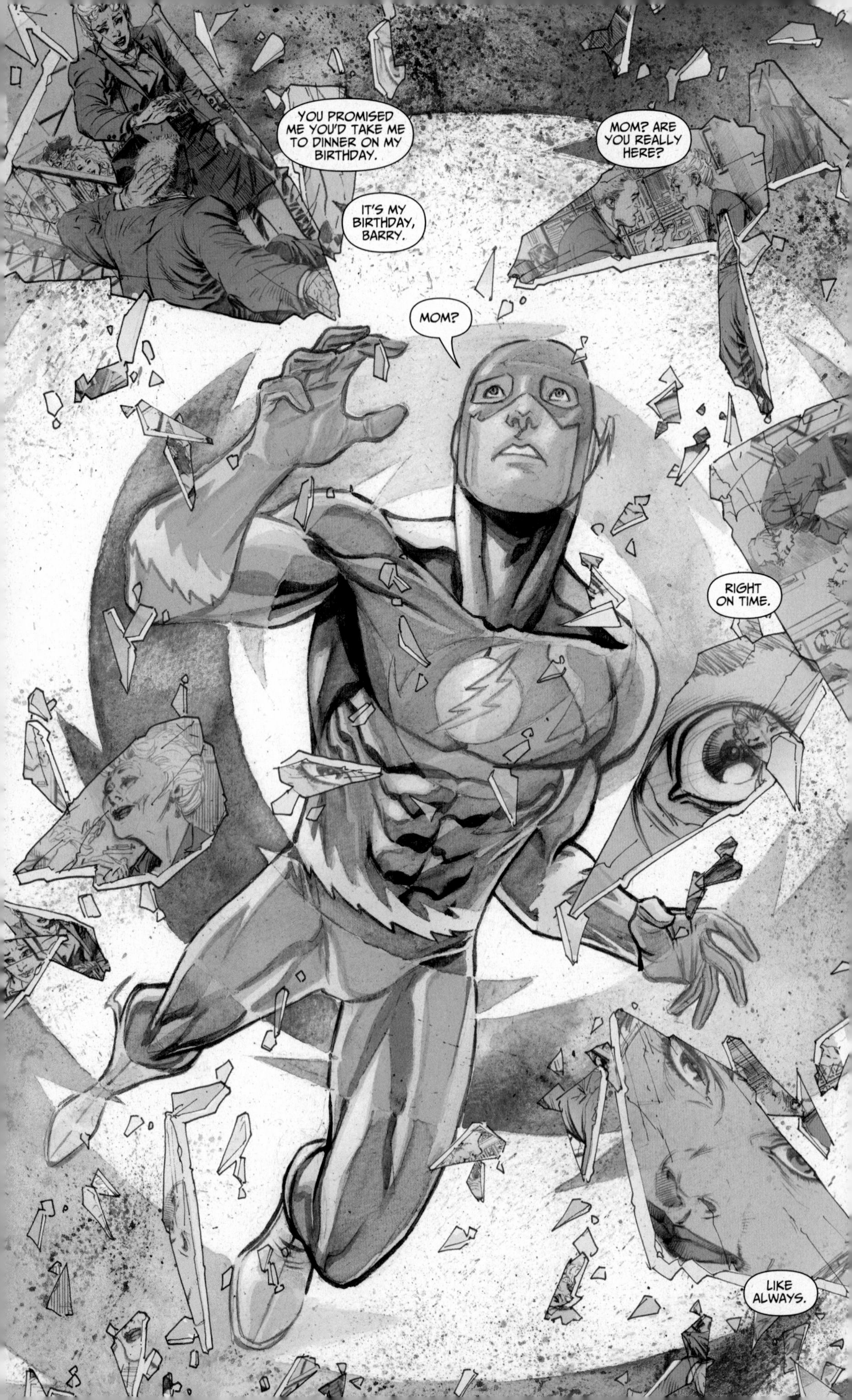
YOU PROMISED ME YOU'D TAKE ME TO DINNER ON MY BIRTHDAY.
IT'S MY BIRTHDAY, BARRY.
MOM? ARE YOU REALLY HERE?
MOM?
RIGHT ON TIME.
LIKE ALWAYS.

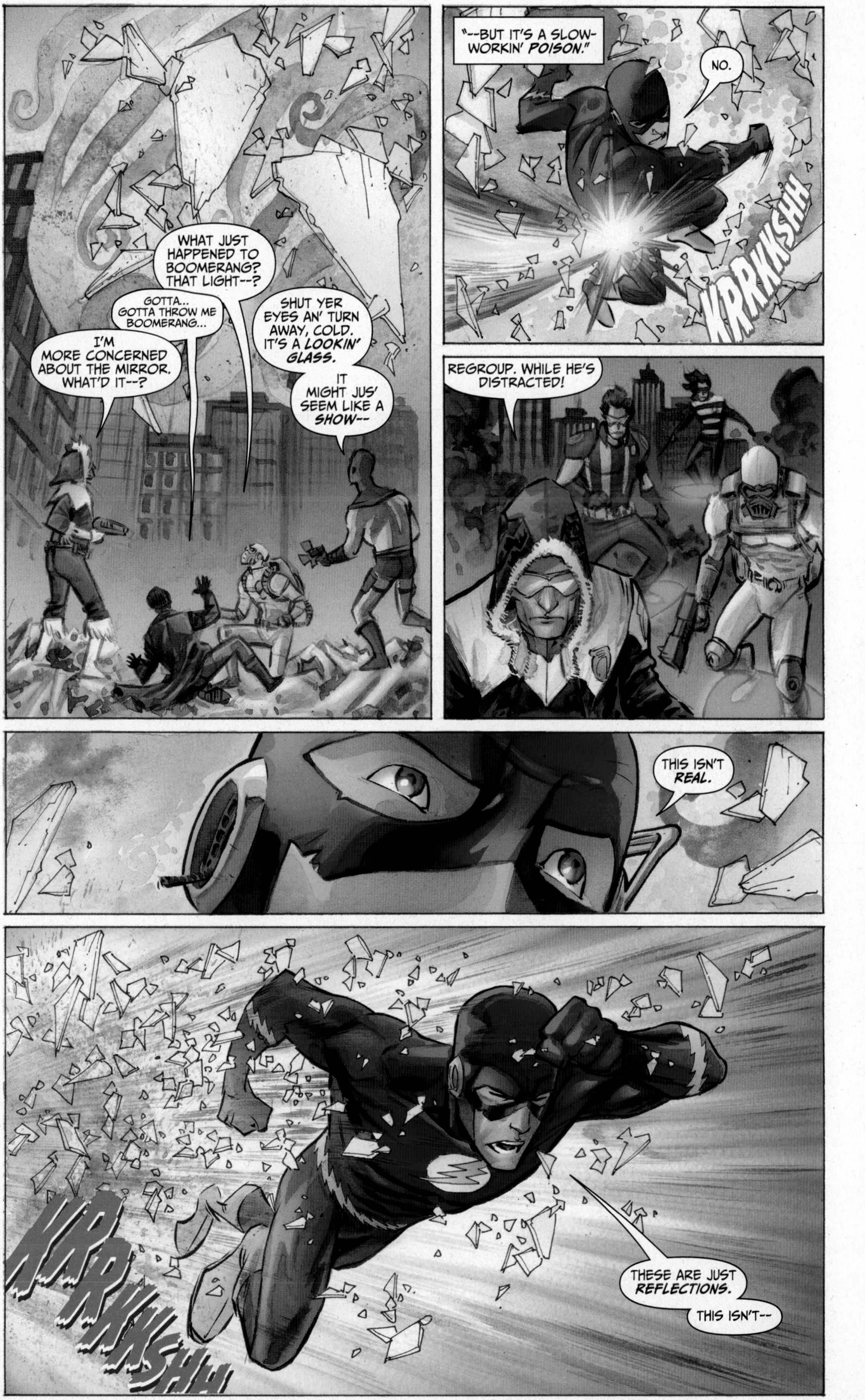
WHAT JUST HAPPENED TO BOOMERANG? THAT LIGHT--?
GOTTA... GOTTA THROW ME BOOMERANG...
I'M MORE CONCERNED ABOUT THE MIRROR. WHAT'D IT--?
SHUT YER EYES AN' TURN AWAY, COLD. IT'S A LOOKIN' GLASS.
IT MIGHT JUS' SEEM LIKE A SHOW--
"--BUT IT'S A SLOW-WORKIN' POISON."
NO.
KRRKKSHH
REGROUP. WHILE HE'S DISTRACTED!
THIS ISN'T REAL.
KRRKKSHH
THESE ARE JUST REFLECTIONS.
THIS ISN'T--

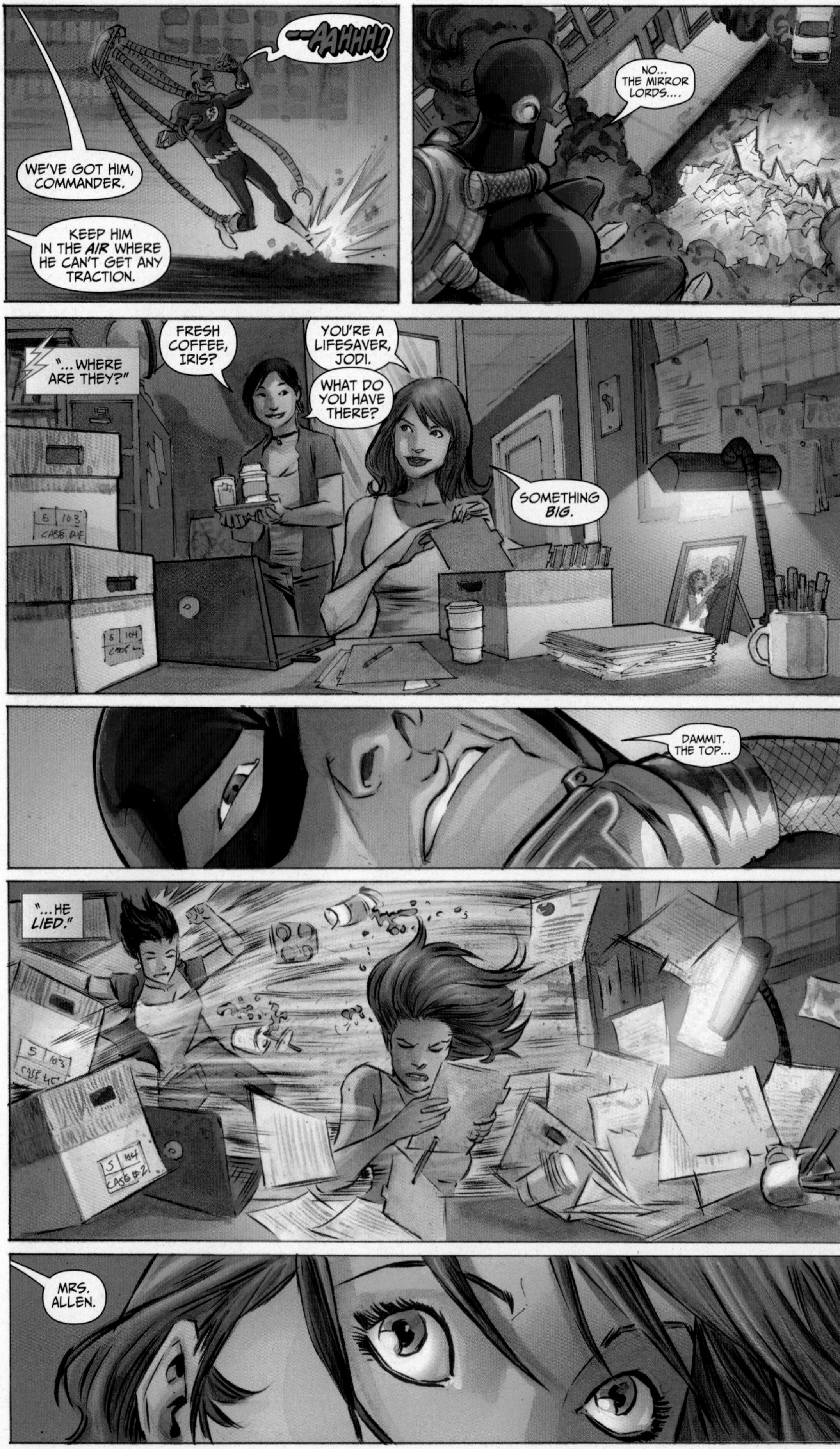
--AAHHH!
WE'VE GOT HIM, COMMANDER.
KEEP HIM IN THE *AIR* WHERE HE CAN'T GET ANY TRACTION.
NO... THE MIRROR LORDS....
"...WHERE ARE THEY?"
FRESH COFFEE, IRIS?
YOU'RE A LIFESAVER, JODI.
WHAT DO YOU HAVE THERE?
SOMETHING *BIG*.
DAMMIT. THE TOP...
"...HE *LIED*."
MRS. ALLEN.

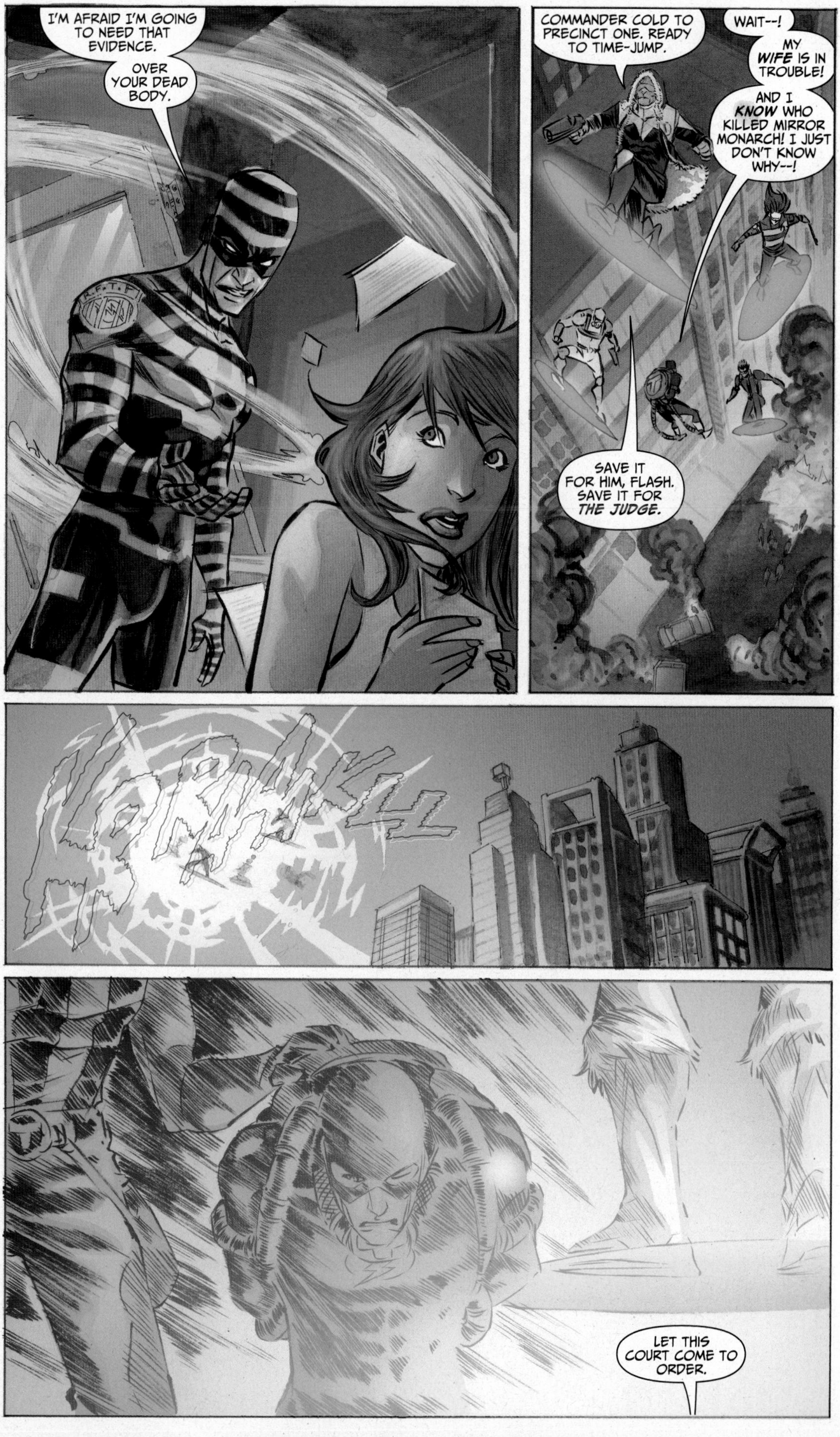

I'M AFRAID I'M GOING TO NEED THAT EVIDENCE.
OVER YOUR DEAD BODY.
COMMANDER COLD TO PRECINCT ONE. READY TO TIME-JUMP.
WAIT--!
MY WIFE IS IN TROUBLE!
AND I KNOW WHO KILLED MIRROR MONARCH! I JUST DON'T KNOW WHY--!
SAVE IT FOR HIM, FLASH. SAVE IT FOR THE JUDGE.
LET THIS COURT COME TO ORDER.

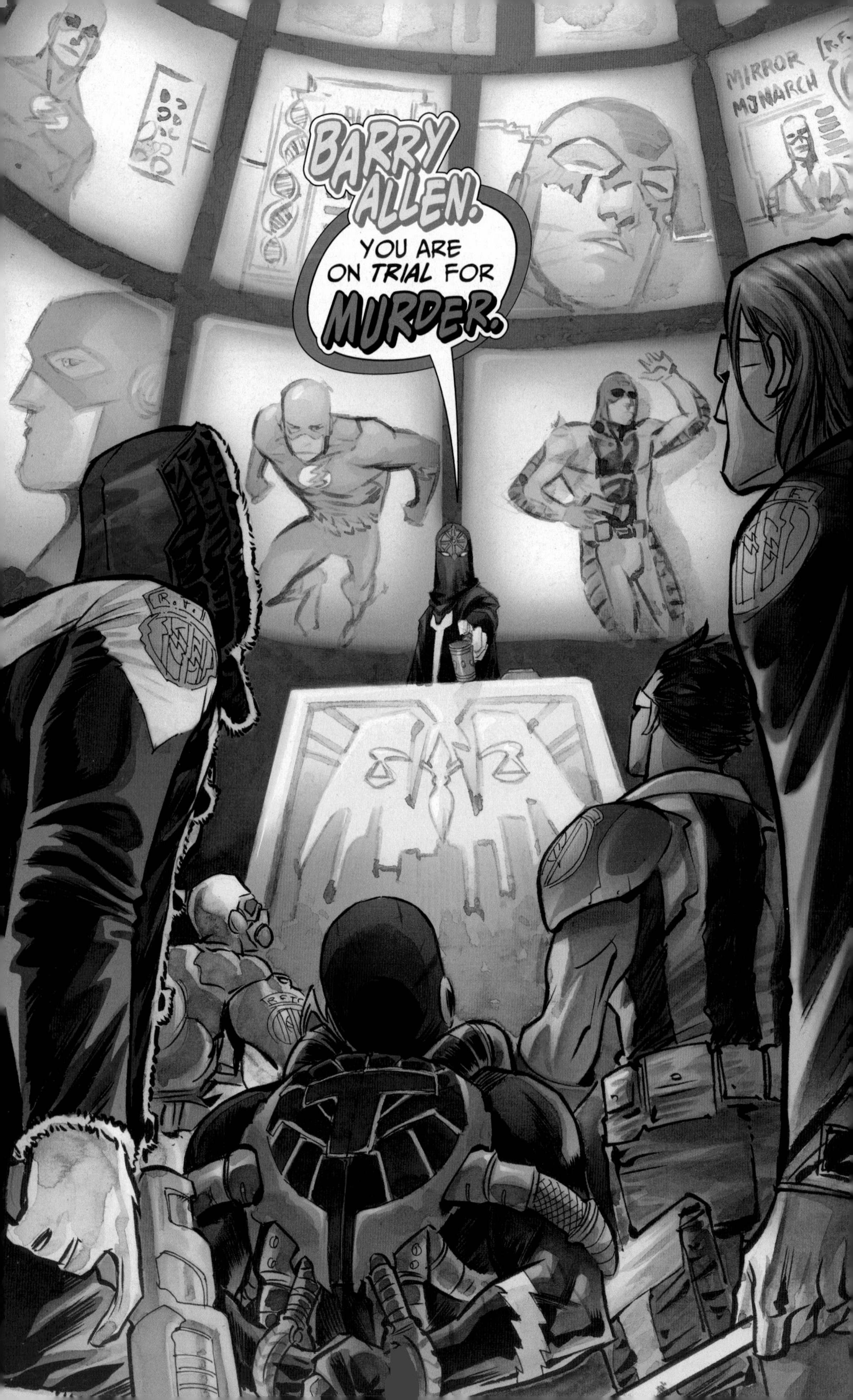
MIRROR MONARCH
BARRY ALLEN. YOU ARE ON TRIAL FOR MURDER.

THE FLASH 6

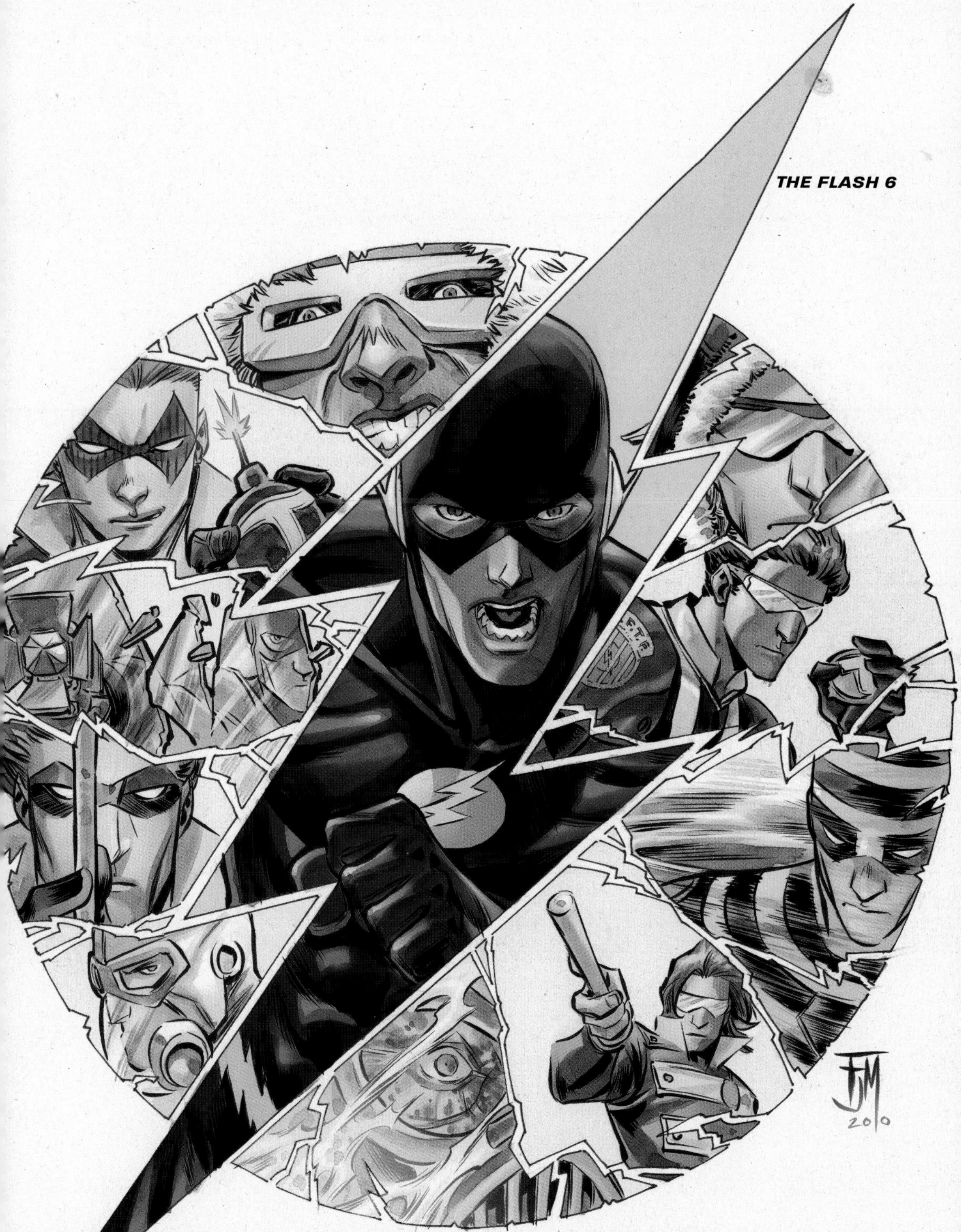

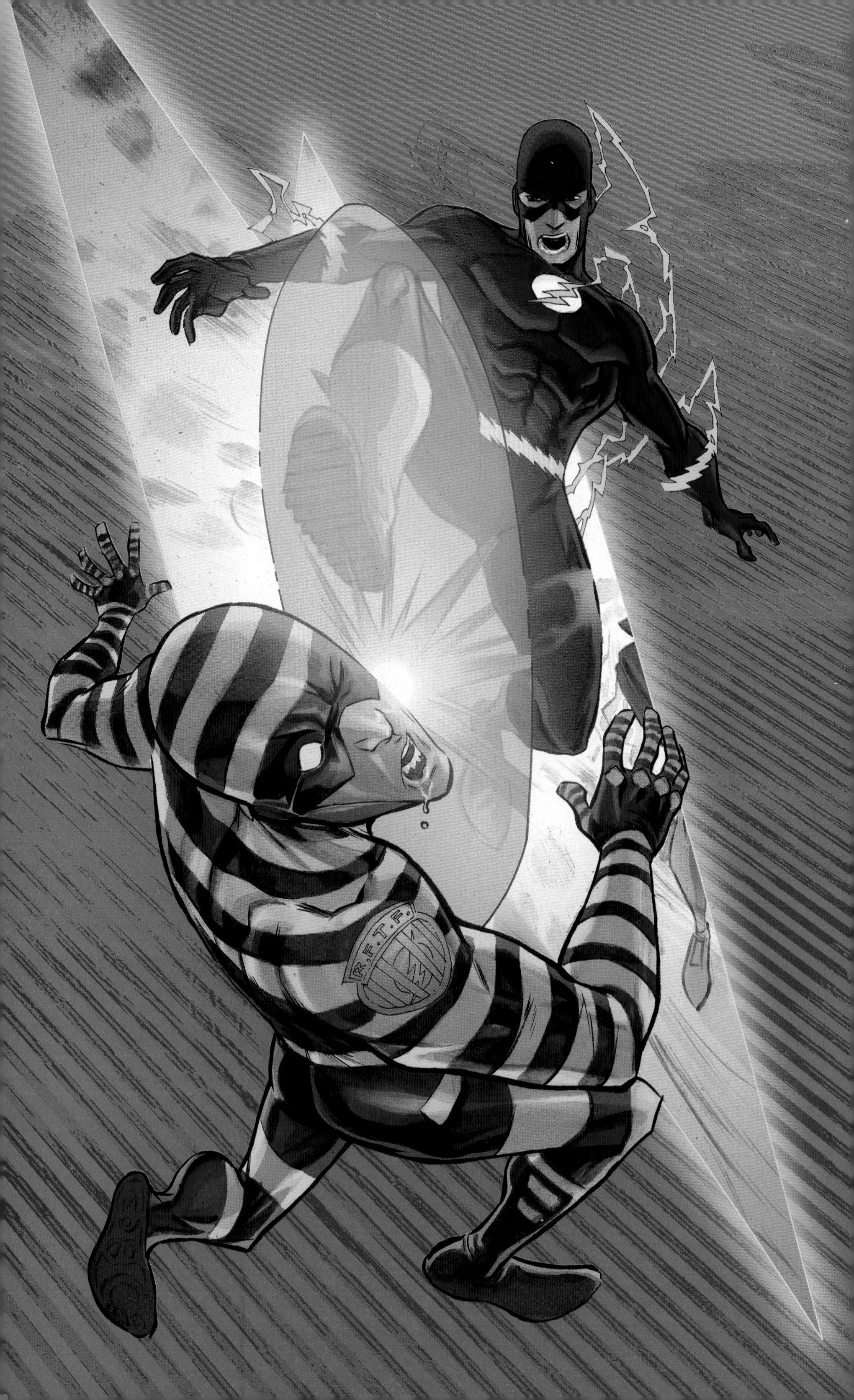
R.F.T.F.

THE 25TH CENTURY.

THE COURT OF TEMPORAL JUSTICE.

I ESTABLISHED THIS COURT TO DO ONE THING: *ERASE* CRIME FROM OUR *ERA.*

I AM TRULY SORRY IT HAS COME TO THIS FOR A HERO AS LEGENDARY AS YOURSELF, FLASH, BUT *MURDER,* EVEN IF IT WAS DUE TO *MISTAKEN IDENTITY,* IS STILL *MURDER.*

YOU ARE ON TRIAL FOR THE KILLING OF *MIRROR MONARCH:* A FOUNDING MEMBER OF THE REVERSE-FLASH TASK FORCE AND AN OFFICER OF MY COURT--

MIRROR MONARCH

WHO'S THE *TOP?!*

DON'T INTERRUPT THE JUDGE, FLASH. IT'S AGAINST THE LAW.

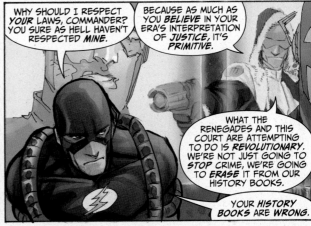

WHY SHOULD I RESPECT *YOUR* LAWS, COMMANDER? YOU SURE AS HELL HAVEN'T RESPECTED *MINE.*

BECAUSE AS MUCH AS YOU *BELIEVE* IN YOUR ERA'S INTERPRETATION OF *JUSTICE,* IT'S *PRIMITIVE.*

WHAT THE RENEGADES AND THIS COURT ARE ATTEMPTING TO DO IS *REVOLUTIONARY.* WE'RE NOT JUST GOING TO *STOP* CRIME, WE'RE GOING TO *ERASE* IT FROM OUR HISTORY BOOKS.

YOUR *HISTORY* BOOKS ARE *WRONG.*

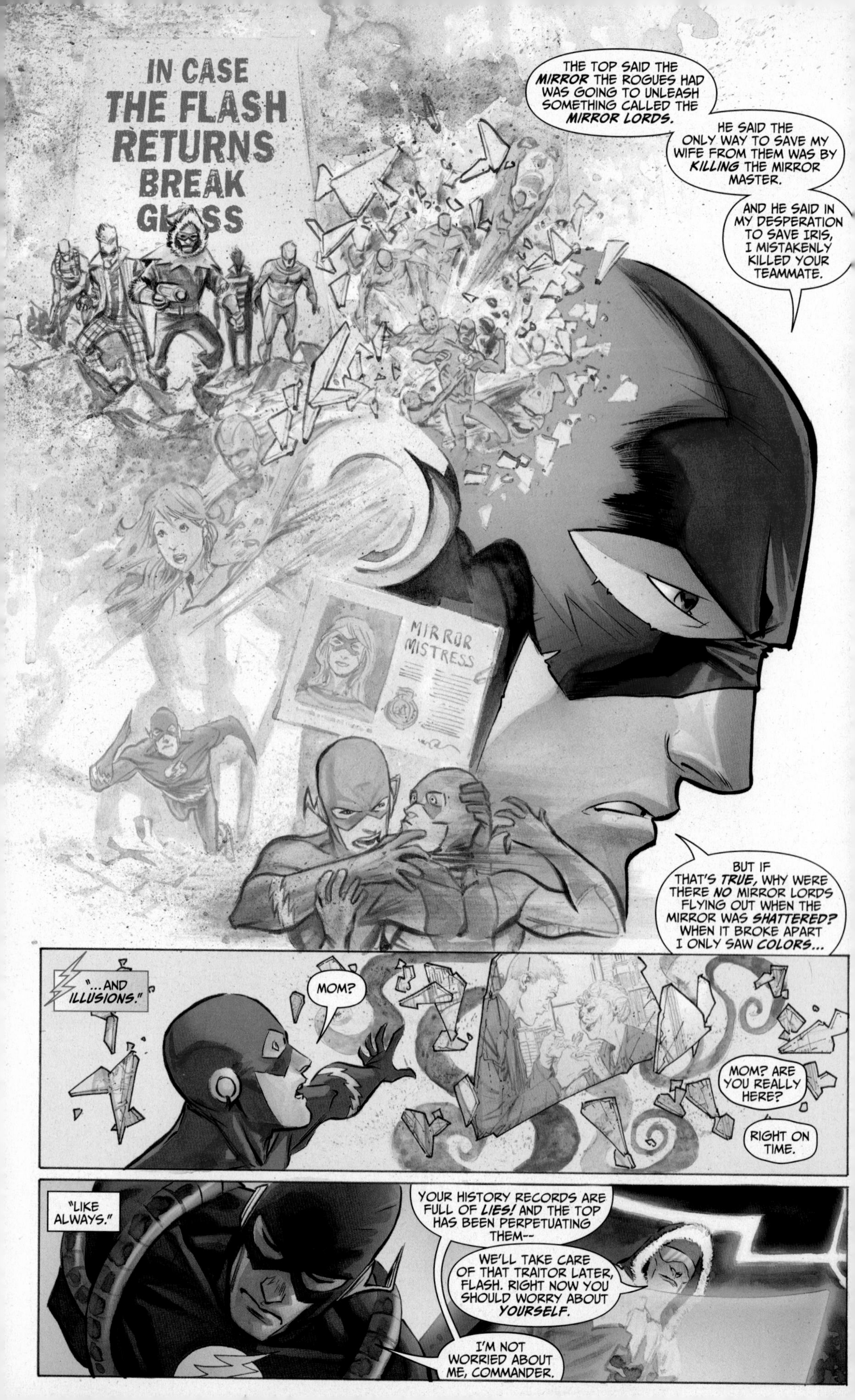
IN CASE THE FLASH RETURNS BREAK GLASS
THE TOP SAID THE MIRROR THE ROGUES HAD WAS GOING TO UNLEASH SOMETHING CALLED THE MIRROR LORDS.
HE SAID THE ONLY WAY TO SAVE MY WIFE FROM THEM WAS BY KILLING THE MIRROR MASTER.
AND HE SAID IN MY DESPERATION TO SAVE IRIS, I MISTAKENLY KILLED YOUR TEAMMATE.
MIRROR MISTRESS
BUT IF THAT'S TRUE, WHY WERE THERE NO MIRROR LORDS FLYING OUT WHEN THE MIRROR WAS SHATTERED? WHEN IT BROKE APART I ONLY SAW COLORS...
"...AND ILLUSIONS."
MOM?
MOM? ARE YOU REALLY HERE?
RIGHT ON TIME.
"LIKE ALWAYS."
YOUR HISTORY RECORDS ARE FULL OF LIES! AND THE TOP HAS BEEN PERPETUATING THEM--
WE'LL TAKE CARE OF THAT TRAITOR LATER, FLASH. RIGHT NOW YOU SHOULD WORRY ABOUT YOURSELF.
I'M NOT WORRIED ABOUT ME, COMMANDER.

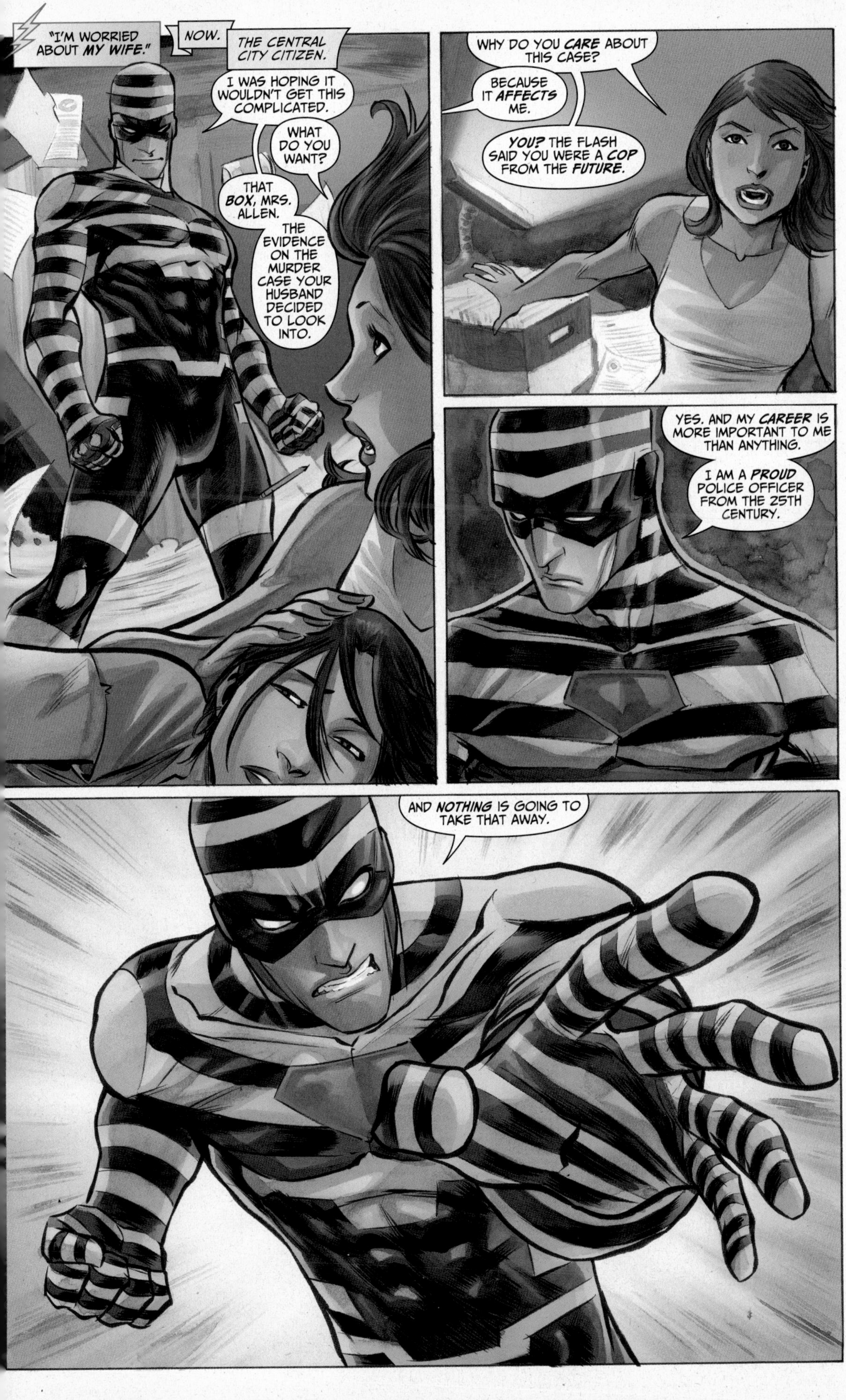
"I'M WORRIED ABOUT MY WIFE."
NOW.
THE CENTRAL CITY CITIZEN.
I WAS HOPING IT WOULDN'T GET THIS COMPLICATED.
WHAT DO YOU WANT?
THAT BOX, MRS. ALLEN.
THE EVIDENCE ON THE MURDER CASE YOUR HUSBAND DECIDED TO LOOK INTO.
WHY DO YOU CARE ABOUT THIS CASE?
BECAUSE IT AFFECTS ME.
YOU? THE FLASH SAID YOU WERE A COP FROM THE FUTURE.
YES. AND MY CAREER IS MORE IMPORTANT TO ME THAN ANYTHING.
I AM A PROUD POLICE OFFICER FROM THE 25TH CENTURY.
AND NOTHING IS GOING TO TAKE THAT AWAY.

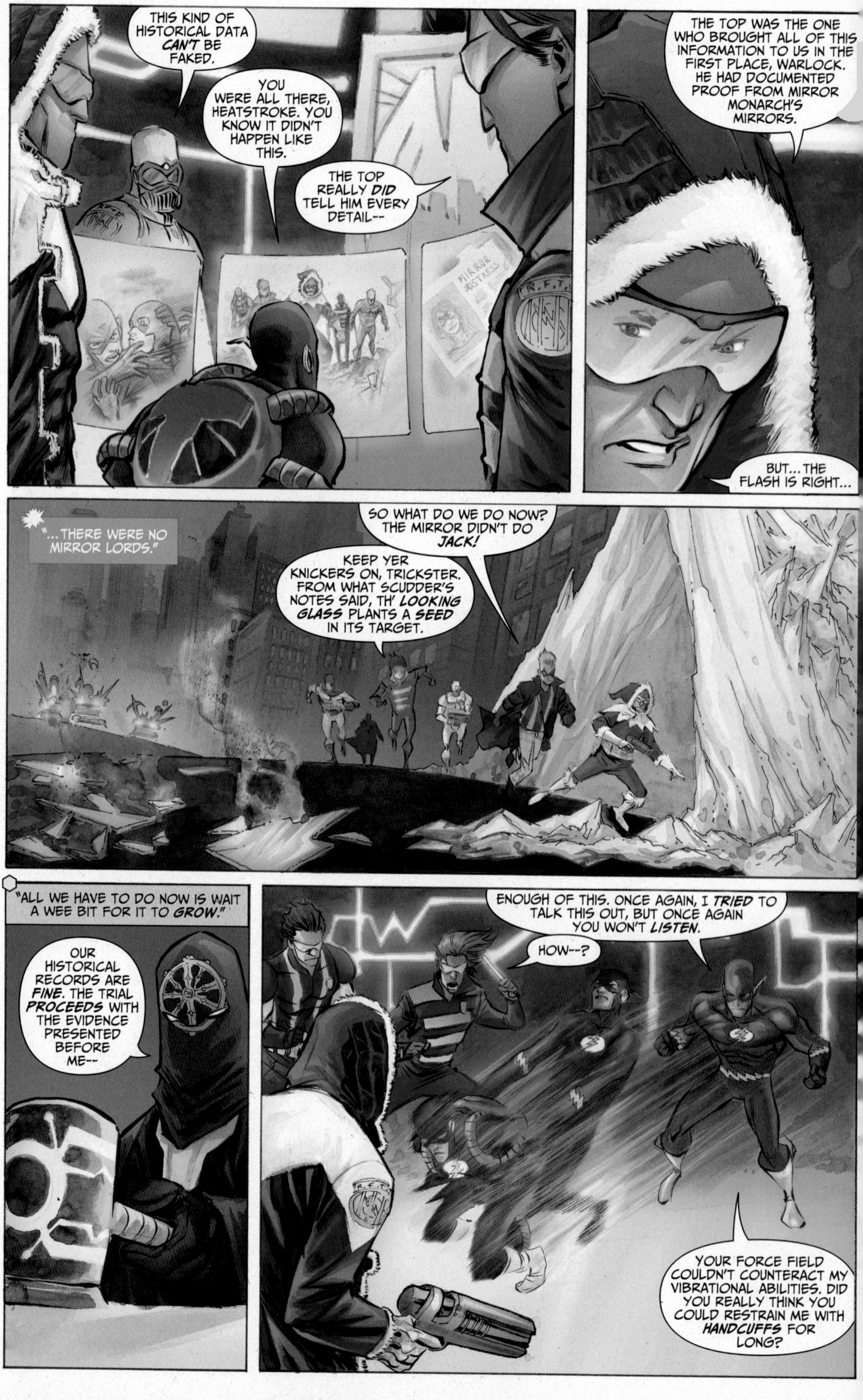
THIS KIND OF HISTORICAL DATA CAN'T BE FAKED.
YOU WERE ALL THERE, HEATSTROKE. YOU KNOW IT DIDN'T HAPPEN LIKE THIS.
THE TOP REALLY DID TELL HIM EVERY DETAIL--
THE TOP WAS THE ONE WHO BROUGHT ALL OF THIS INFORMATION TO US IN THE FIRST PLACE, WARLOCK. HE HAD DOCUMENTED PROOF FROM MIRROR MONARCH'S MIRRORS.
BUT... THE FLASH IS RIGHT...
"...THERE WERE NO MIRROR LORDS."
SO WHAT DO WE DO NOW? THE MIRROR DIDN'T DO JACK!
KEEP YER KNICKERS ON, TRICKSTER. FROM WHAT SCUDDER'S NOTES SAID, TH' LOOKING GLASS PLANTS A SEED IN ITS TARGET.
"ALL WE HAVE TO DO NOW IS WAIT A WEE BIT FOR IT TO GROW."
OUR HISTORICAL RECORDS ARE FINE. THE TRIAL PROCEEDS WITH THE EVIDENCE PRESENTED BEFORE ME--
ENOUGH OF THIS. ONCE AGAIN, I TRIED TO TALK THIS OUT, BUT ONCE AGAIN YOU WON'T LISTEN.
HOW--?
YOUR FORCE FIELD COULDN'T COUNTERACT MY VIBRATIONAL ABILITIES. DID YOU REALLY THINK YOU COULD RESTRAIN ME WITH HANDCUFFS FOR LONG?

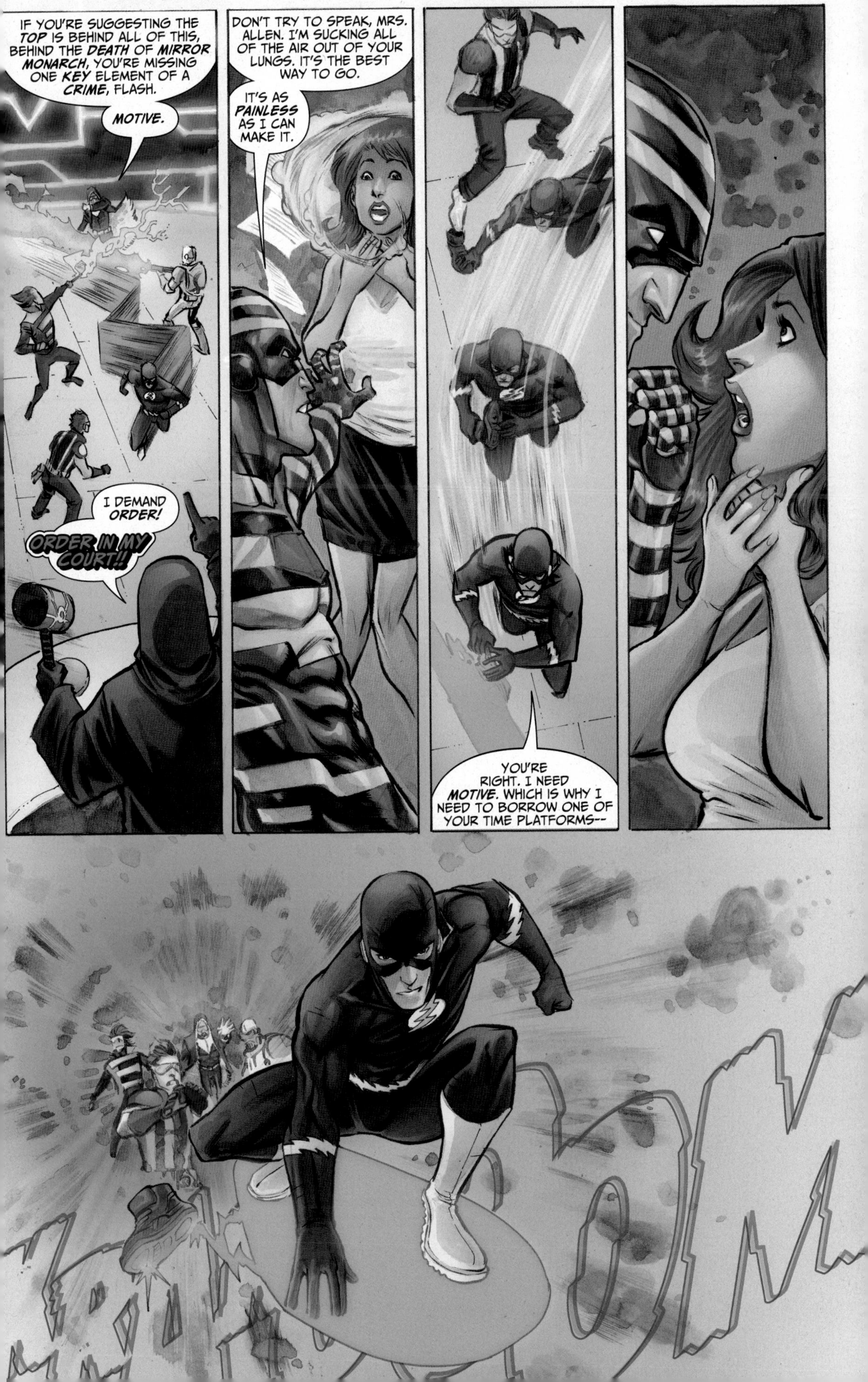
IF YOU'RE SUGGESTING THE TOP IS BEHIND ALL OF THIS, BEHIND THE DEATH OF MIRROR MONARCH, YOU'RE MISSING ONE KEY ELEMENT OF A CRIME, FLASH.
MOTIVE.
I DEMAND ORDER!
ORDER IN MY COURT!!
DON'T TRY TO SPEAK, MRS. ALLEN. I'M SUCKING ALL OF THE AIR OUT OF YOUR LUNGS. IT'S THE BEST WAY TO GO.
IT'S AS PAINLESS AS I CAN MAKE IT.
YOU'RE RIGHT. I NEED MOTIVE. WHICH IS WHY I NEED TO BORROW ONE OF YOUR TIME PLATFORMS--

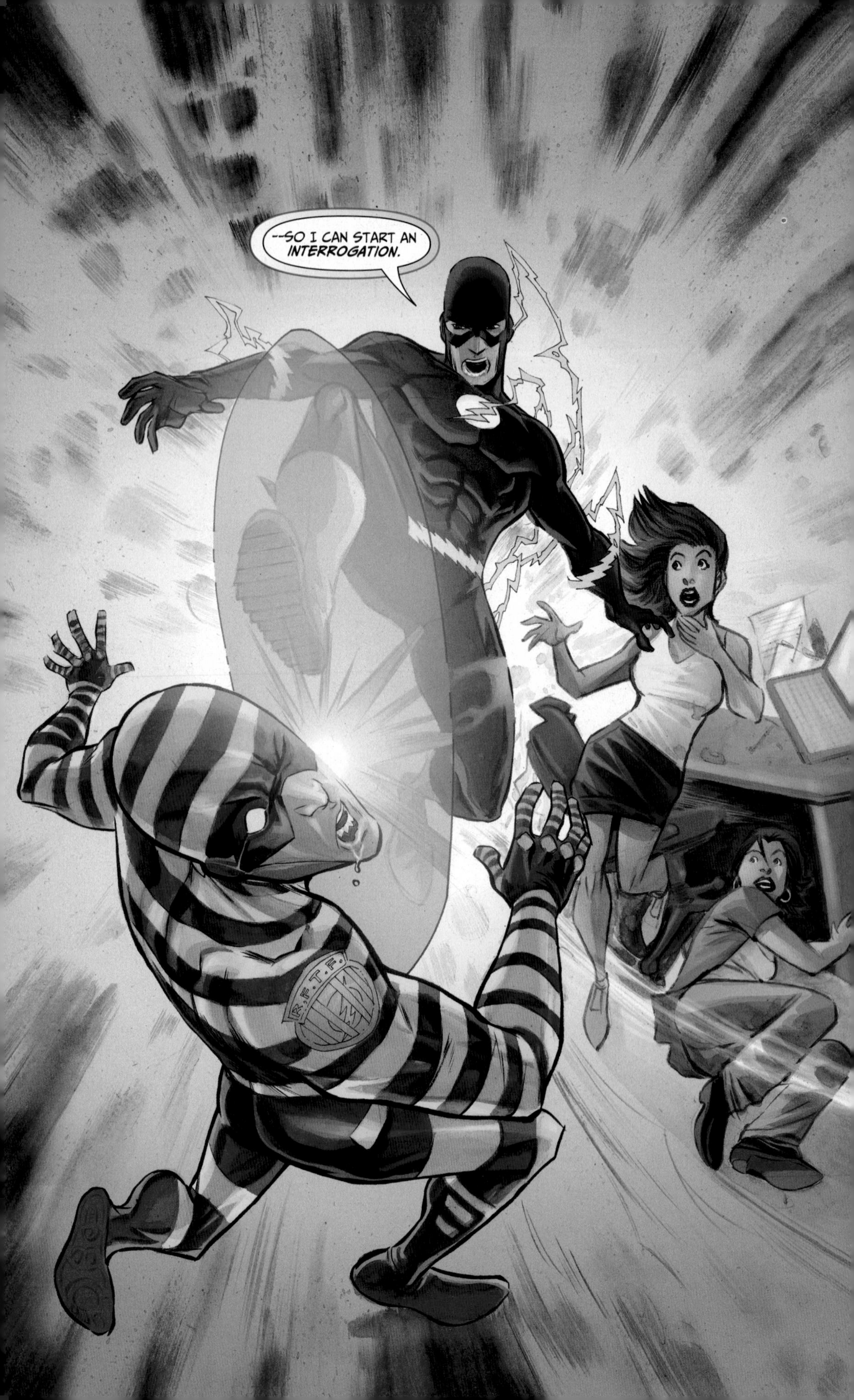
--SO I CAN START AN INTERROGATION.

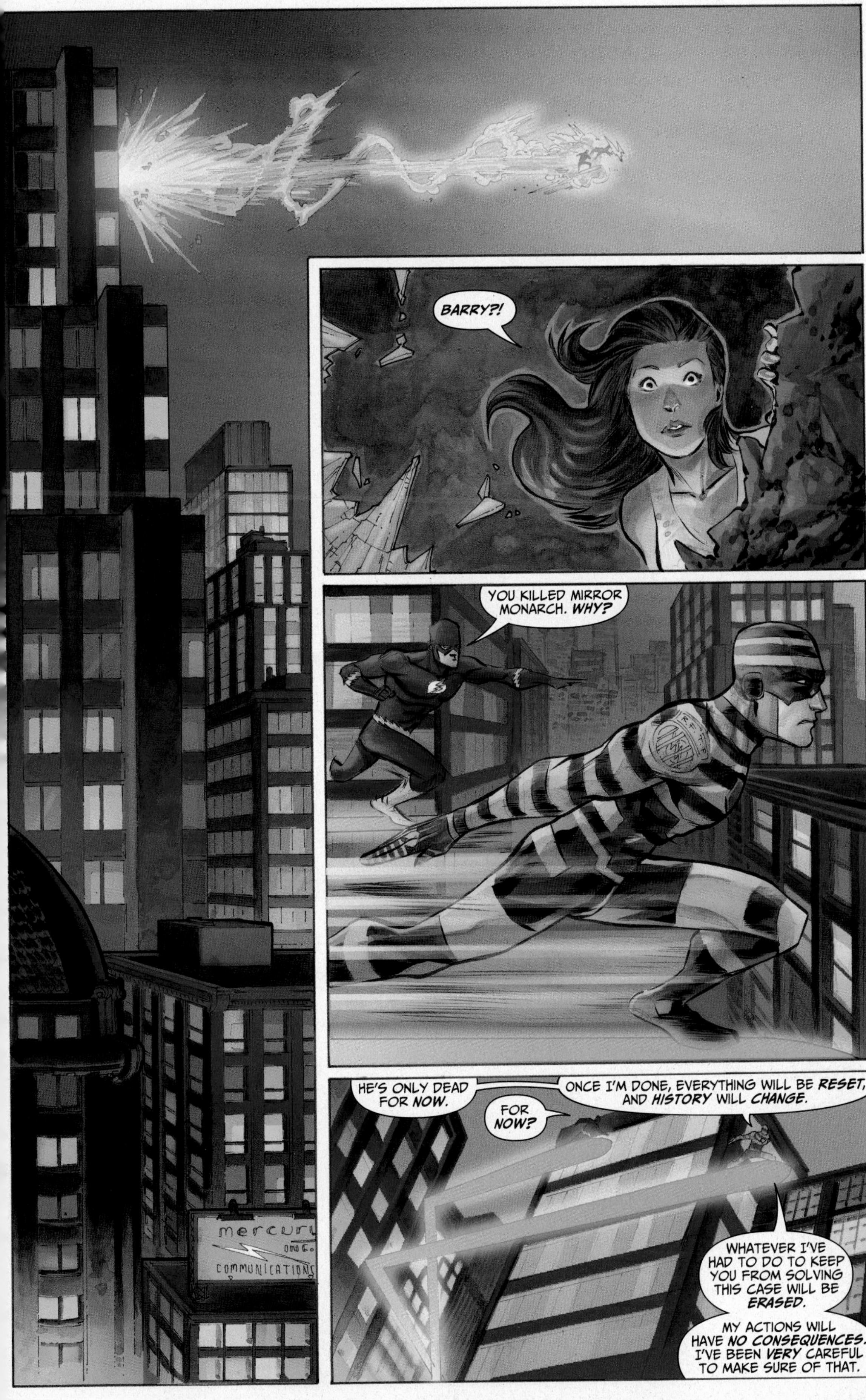
BARRY?!
YOU KILLED MIRROR MONARCH. WHY?
HE'S ONLY DEAD FOR NOW.
FOR NOW?
ONCE I'M DONE, EVERYTHING WILL BE RESET, AND HISTORY WILL CHANGE.
WHATEVER I'VE HAD TO DO TO KEEP YOU FROM SOLVING THIS CASE WILL BE ERASED.
MY ACTIONS WILL HAVE NO CONSEQUENCES. I'VE BEEN VERY CAREFUL TO MAKE SURE OF THAT.
mercury
COMMUNICATIONS

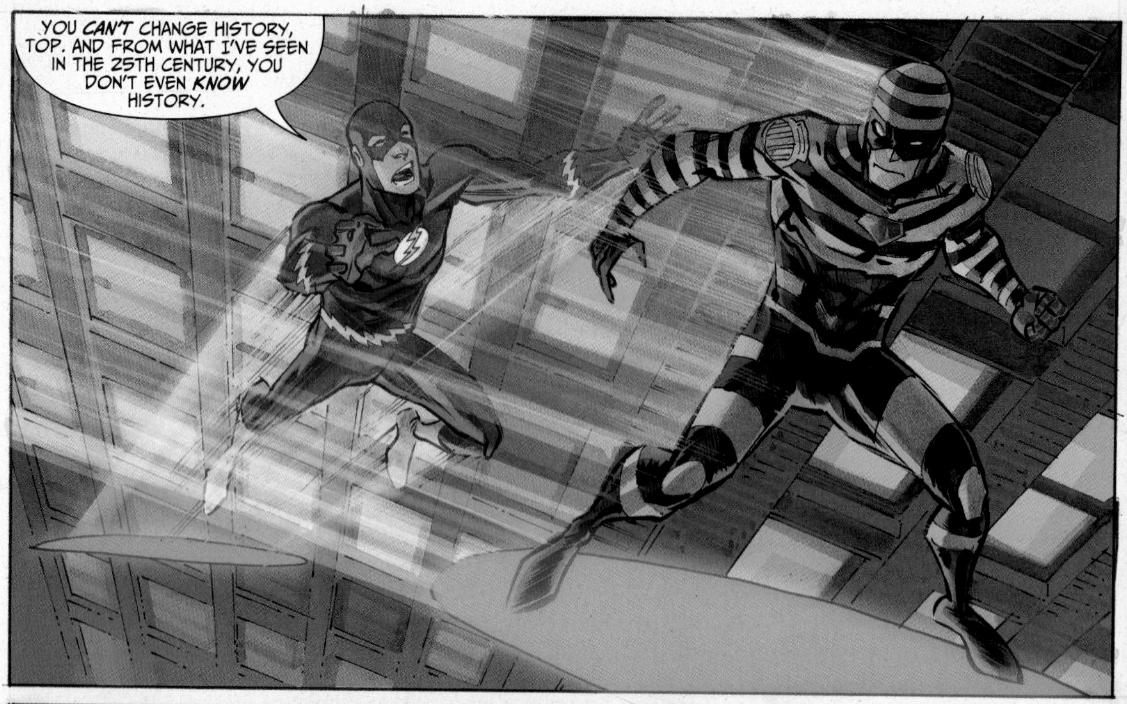

YOU CAN'T CHANGE HISTORY, TOP. AND FROM WHAT I'VE SEEN IN THE 25TH CENTURY, YOU DON'T EVEN KNOW HISTORY.

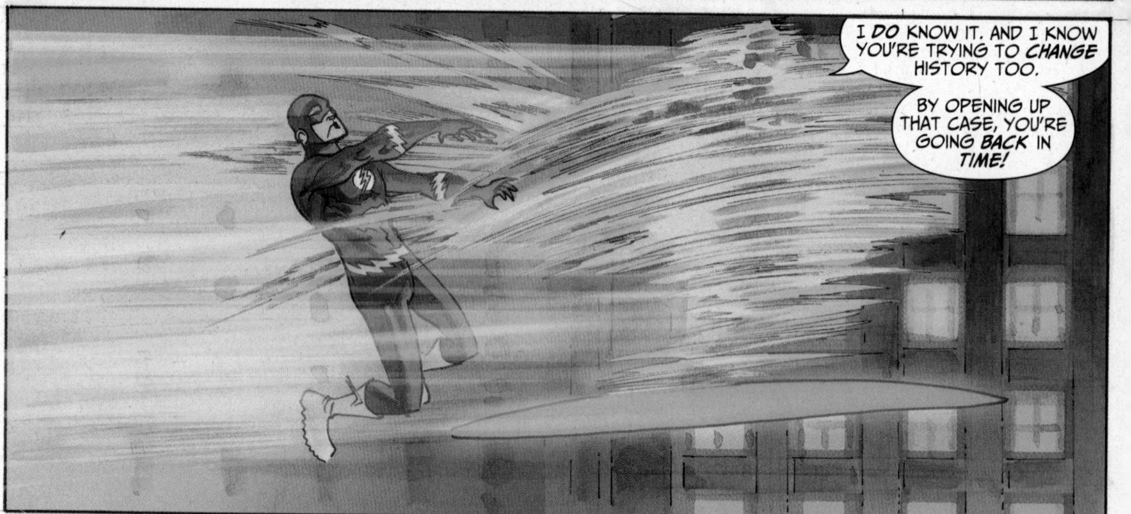

I DO KNOW IT. AND I KNOW YOU'RE TRYING TO CHANGE HISTORY TOO.
BY OPENING UP THAT CASE, YOU'RE GOING BACK IN TIME!

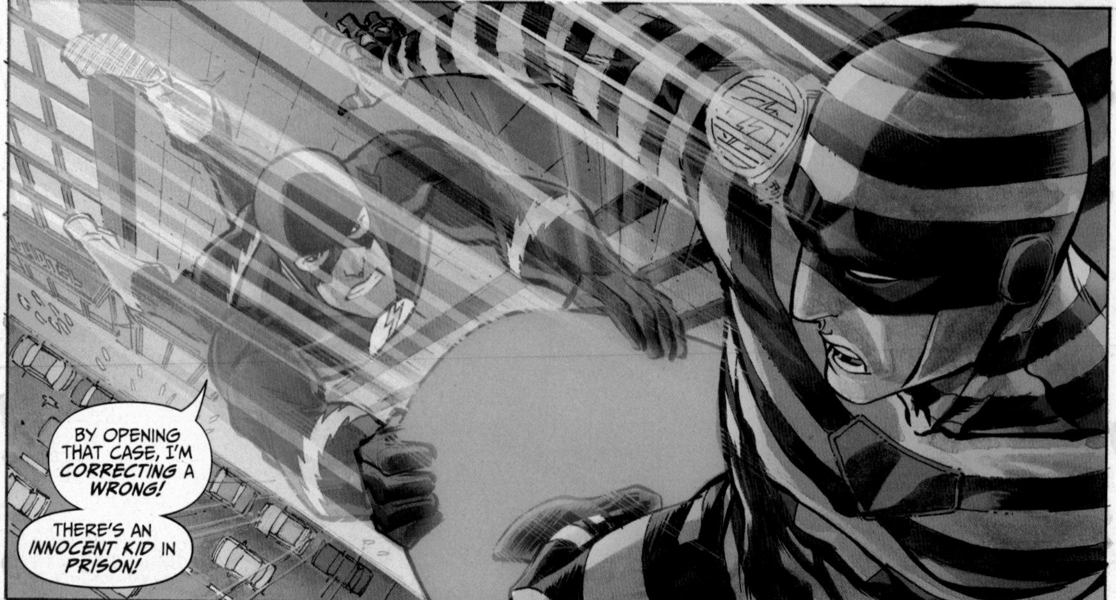

BY OPENING THAT CASE, I'M CORRECTING A WRONG!
THERE'S AN INNOCENT KID IN PRISON!

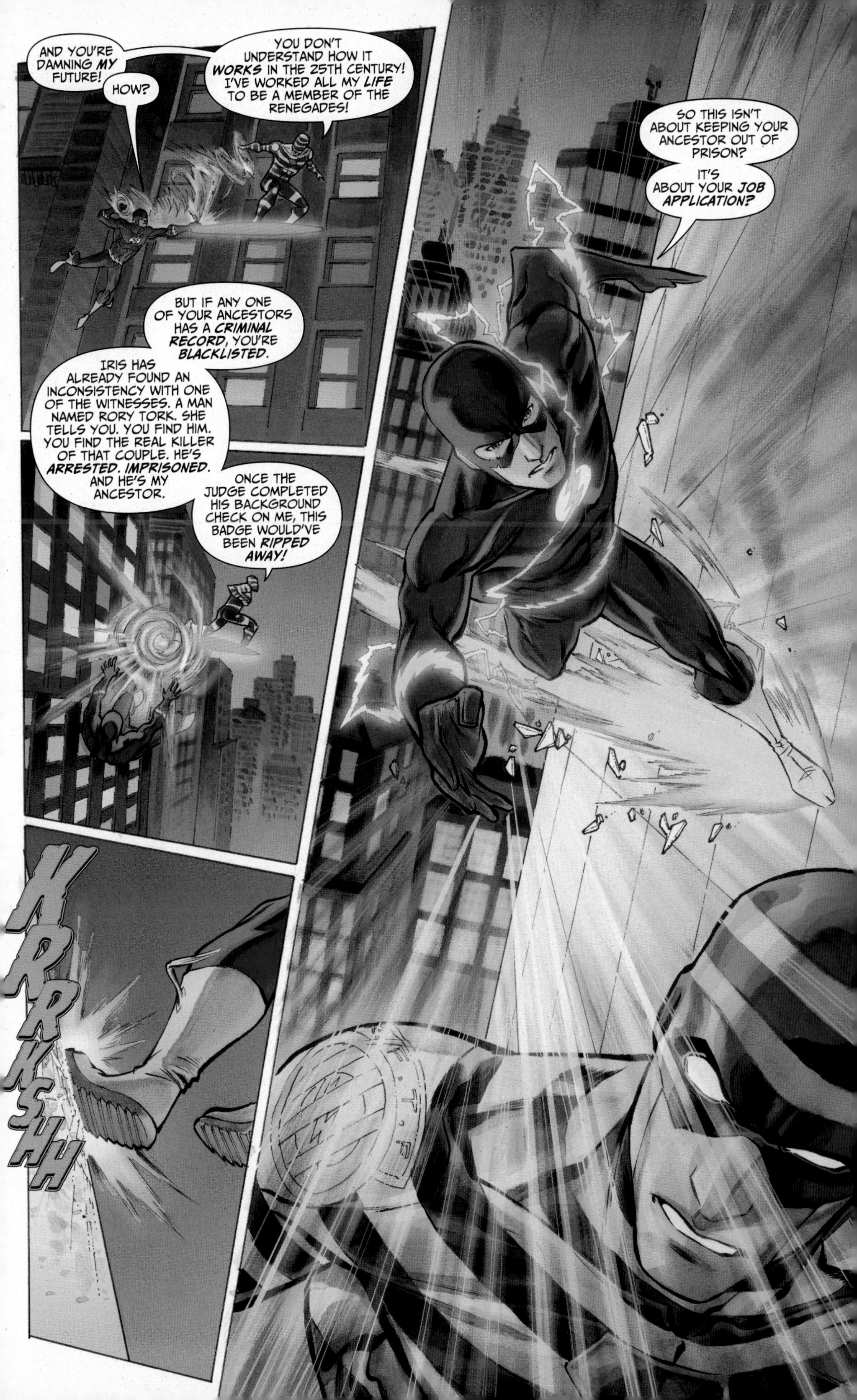
AND YOU'RE DAMNING MY FUTURE!
HOW?
YOU DON'T UNDERSTAND HOW IT WORKS IN THE 25TH CENTURY! I'VE WORKED ALL MY LIFE TO BE A MEMBER OF THE RENEGADES!
BUT IF ANY ONE OF YOUR ANCESTORS HAS A CRIMINAL RECORD, YOU'RE BLACKLISTED.
IRIS HAS ALREADY FOUND AN INCONSISTENCY WITH ONE OF THE WITNESSES. A MAN NAMED RORY TORK. SHE TELLS YOU. YOU FIND HIM. YOU FIND THE REAL KILLER OF THAT COUPLE. HE'S ARRESTED. IMPRISONED. AND HE'S MY ANCESTOR.
ONCE THE JUDGE COMPLETED HIS BACKGROUND CHECK ON ME, THIS BADGE WOULD'VE BEEN RIPPED AWAY!
SO THIS ISN'T ABOUT KEEPING YOUR ANCESTOR OUT OF PRISON?
IT'S ABOUT YOUR JOB APPLICATION?
KRRKSHH

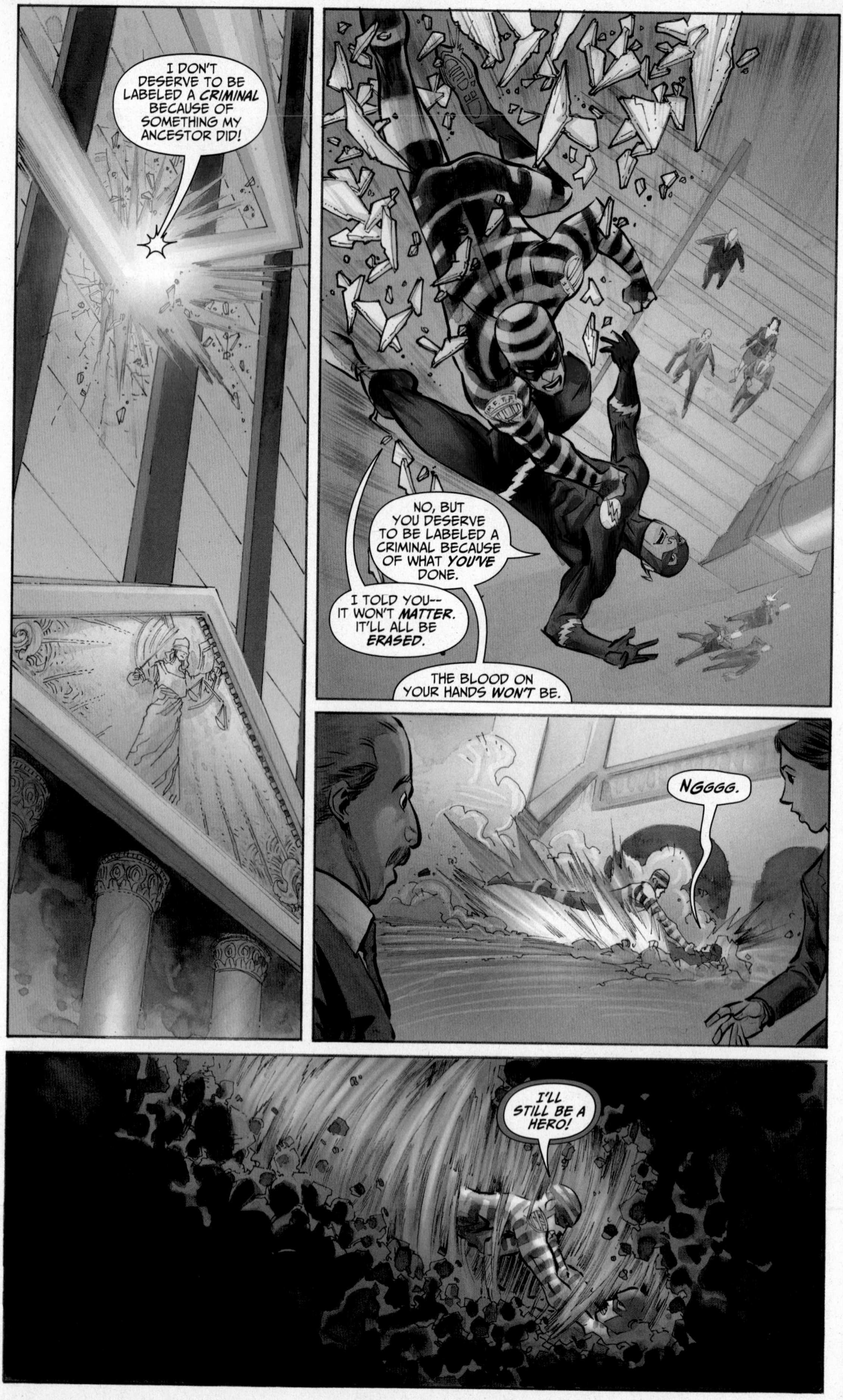
I DON'T DESERVE TO BE LABELED A CRIMINAL BECAUSE OF SOMETHING MY ANCESTOR DID!
NO, BUT YOU DESERVE TO BE LABELED A CRIMINAL BECAUSE OF WHAT YOU'VE DONE.
I TOLD YOU-- IT WON'T MATTER. IT'LL ALL BE ERASED.
THE BLOOD ON YOUR HANDS WON'T BE.
NGGGG.
I'LL STILL BE A HERO!

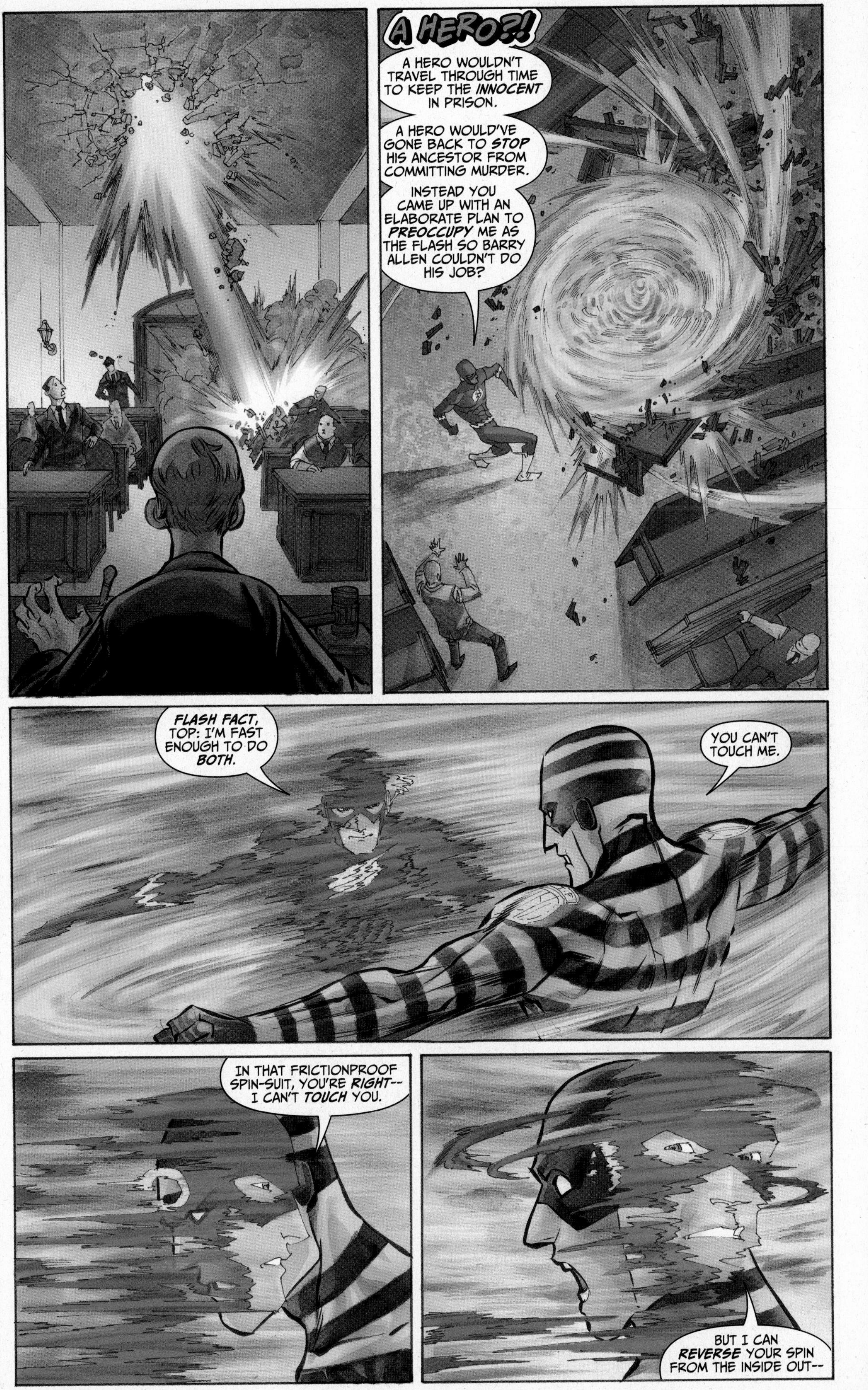
A HERO?!
A HERO WOULDN'T TRAVEL THROUGH TIME TO KEEP THE INNOCENT IN PRISON.
A HERO WOULD'VE GONE BACK TO STOP HIS ANCESTOR FROM COMMITTING MURDER.
INSTEAD YOU CAME UP WITH AN ELABORATE PLAN TO PREOCCUPY ME AS THE FLASH SO BARRY ALLEN COULDN'T DO HIS JOB?
FLASH FACT, TOP: I'M FAST ENOUGH TO DO BOTH.
YOU CAN'T TOUCH ME.
IN THAT FRICTIONPROOF SPIN-SUIT, YOU'RE RIGHT-- I CAN'T TOUCH YOU.
BUT I CAN REVERSE YOUR SPIN FROM THE INSIDE OUT--

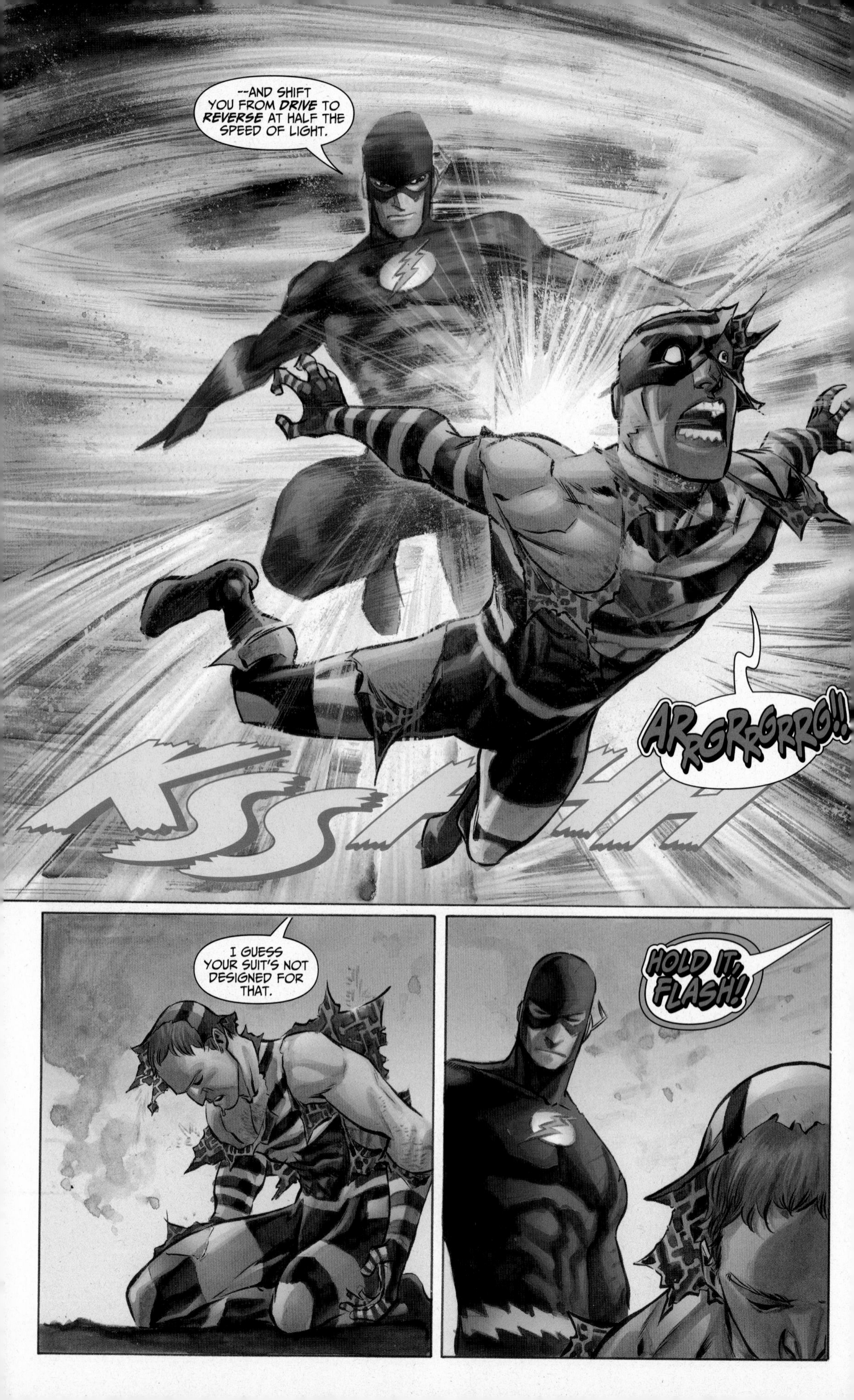
--AND SHIFT YOU FROM DRIVE TO REVERSE AT HALF THE SPEED OF LIGHT.
ARRGRRGRRG!!
KSSHH
I GUESS YOUR SUIT'S NOT DESIGNED FOR THAT.
HOLD IT, FLASH!

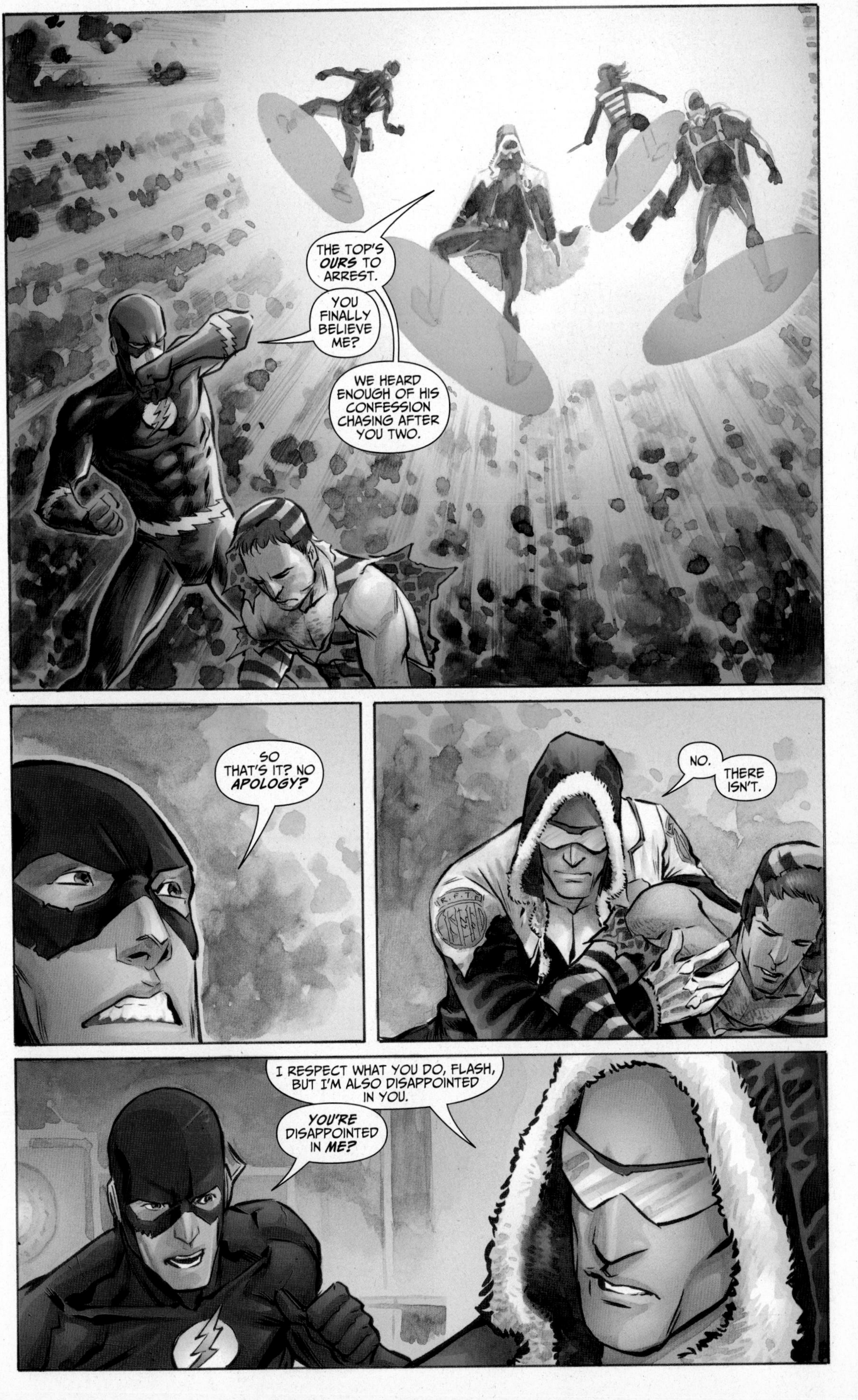
THE TOP'S *OURS* TO ARREST.
YOU FINALLY BELIEVE ME?
WE HEARD ENOUGH OF HIS CONFESSION CHASING AFTER YOU TWO.
SO THAT'S IT? NO *APOLOGY?*
NO.
THERE ISN'T.
I RESPECT WHAT YOU DO, FLASH, BUT I'M ALSO DISAPPOINTED IN YOU.
YOU'RE DISAPPOINTED IN *ME?*

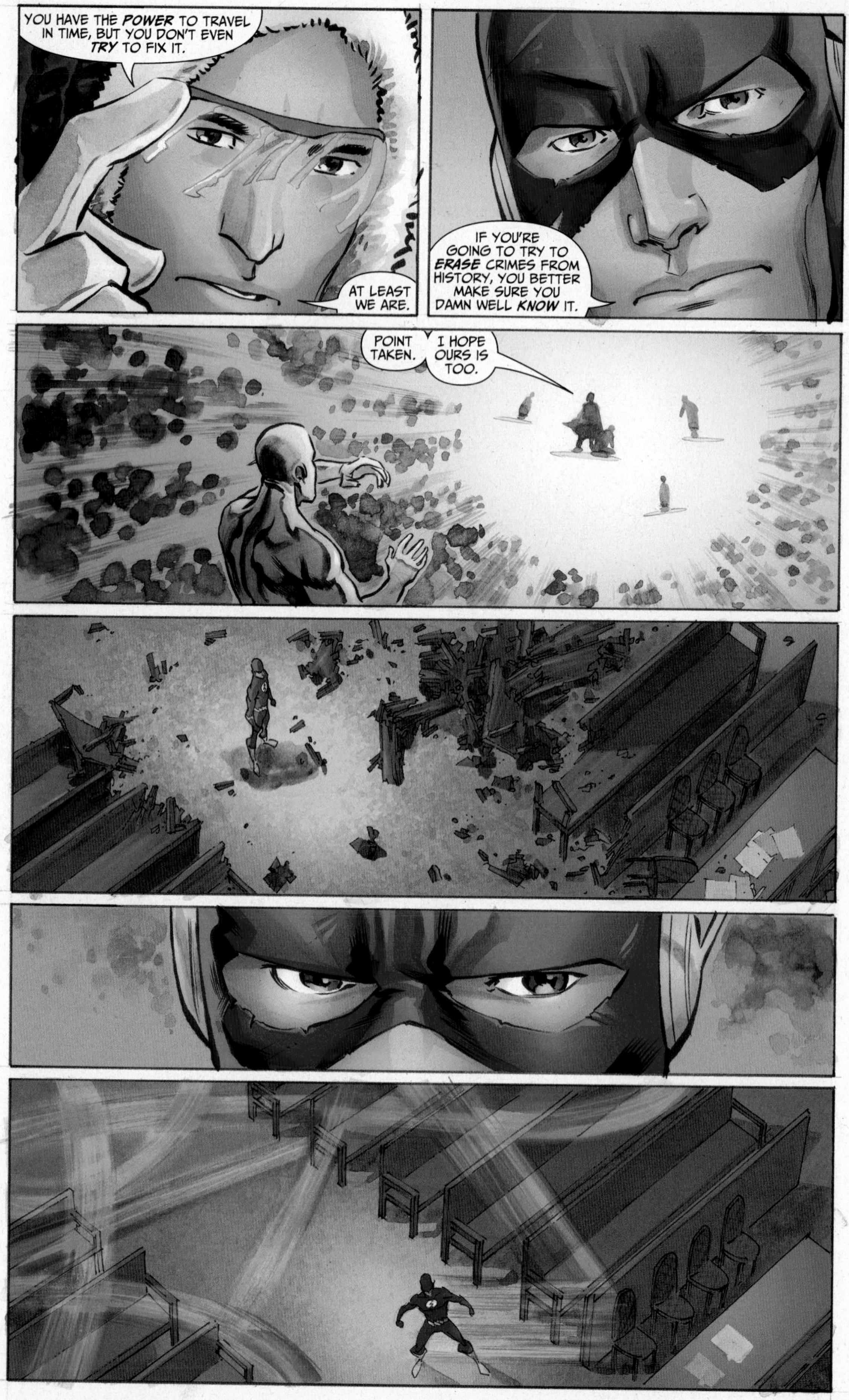
YOU HAVE THE POWER TO TRAVEL IN TIME, BUT YOU DON'T EVEN TRY TO FIX IT.
AT LEAST WE ARE.
IF YOU'RE GOING TO TRY TO ERASE CRIMES FROM HISTORY, YOU BETTER MAKE SURE YOU DAMN WELL KNOW IT.
POINT TAKEN.
I HOPE OURS IS TOO.

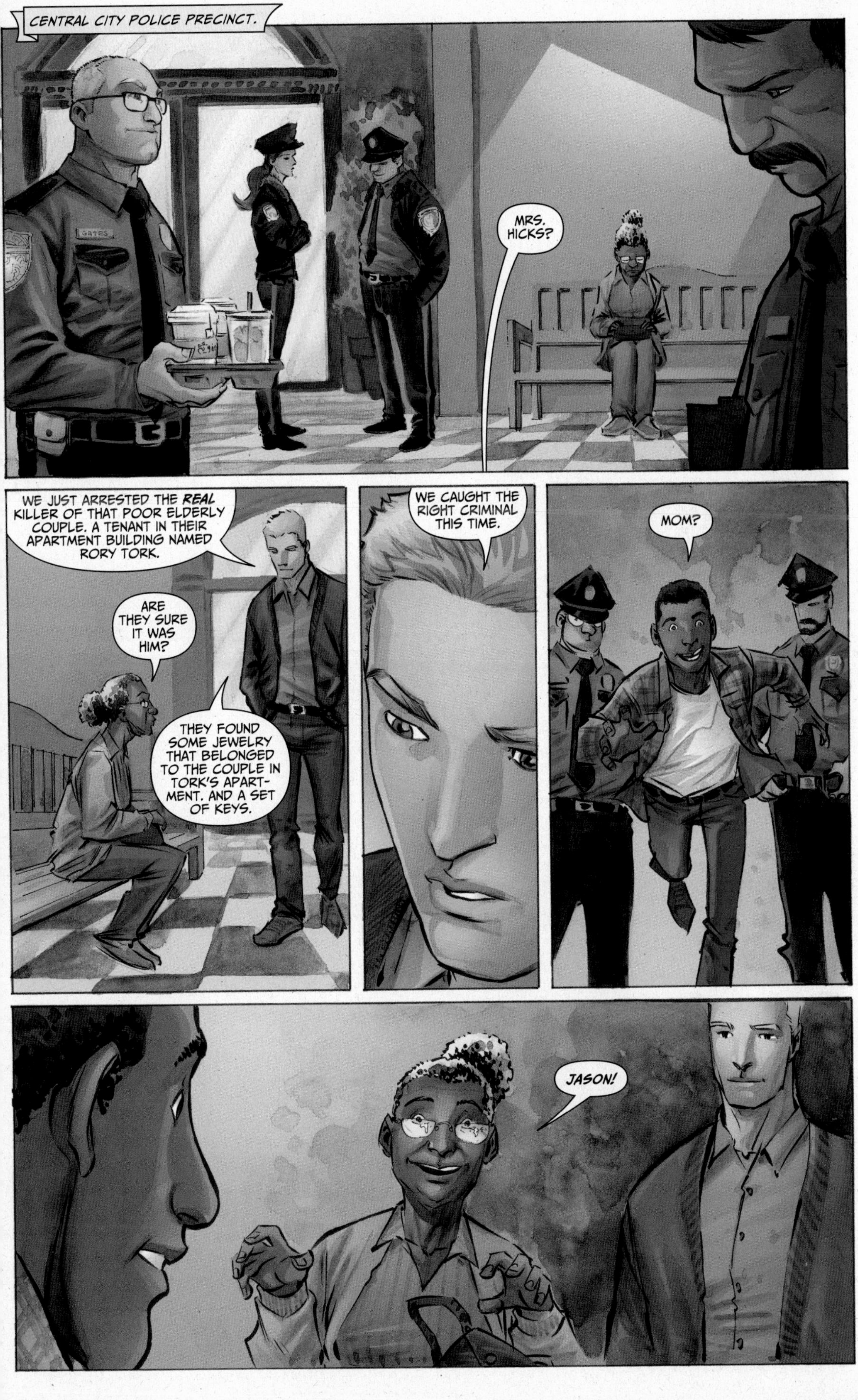
CENTRAL CITY POLICE PRECINCT.
GATES
MRS. HICKS?
WE JUST ARRESTED THE REAL KILLER OF THAT POOR ELDERLY COUPLE. A TENANT IN THEIR APARTMENT BUILDING NAMED RORY TORK.
ARE THEY SURE IT WAS HIM?
THEY FOUND SOME JEWELRY THAT BELONGED TO THE COUPLE IN TORK'S APARTMENT. AND A SET OF KEYS.
WE CAUGHT THE RIGHT CRIMINAL THIS TIME.
MOM?
JASON!

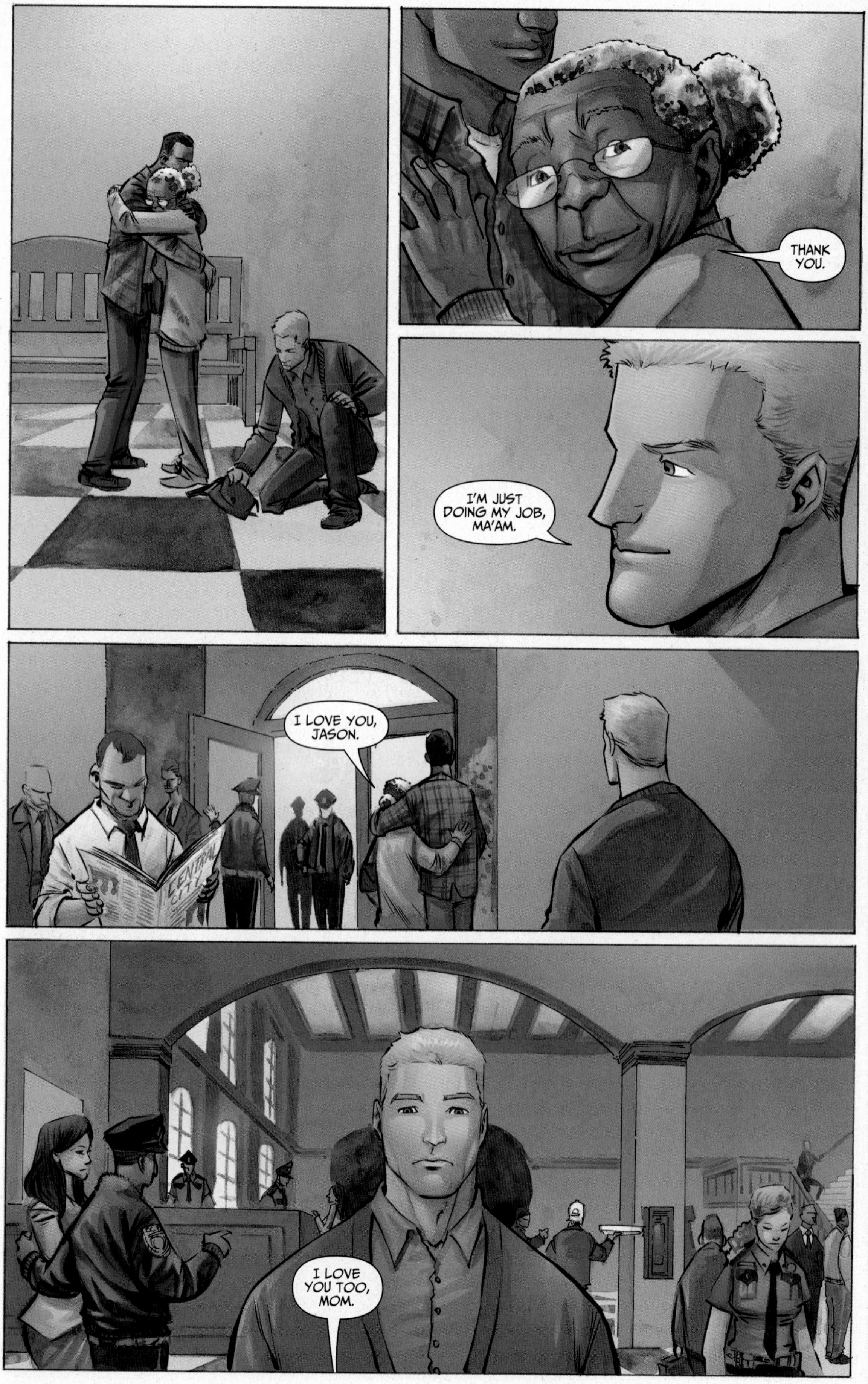
THANK YOU.
I'M JUST DOING MY JOB, MA'AM.
I LOVE YOU, JASON.
CENTRAL CITY
I LOVE YOU TOO, MOM.

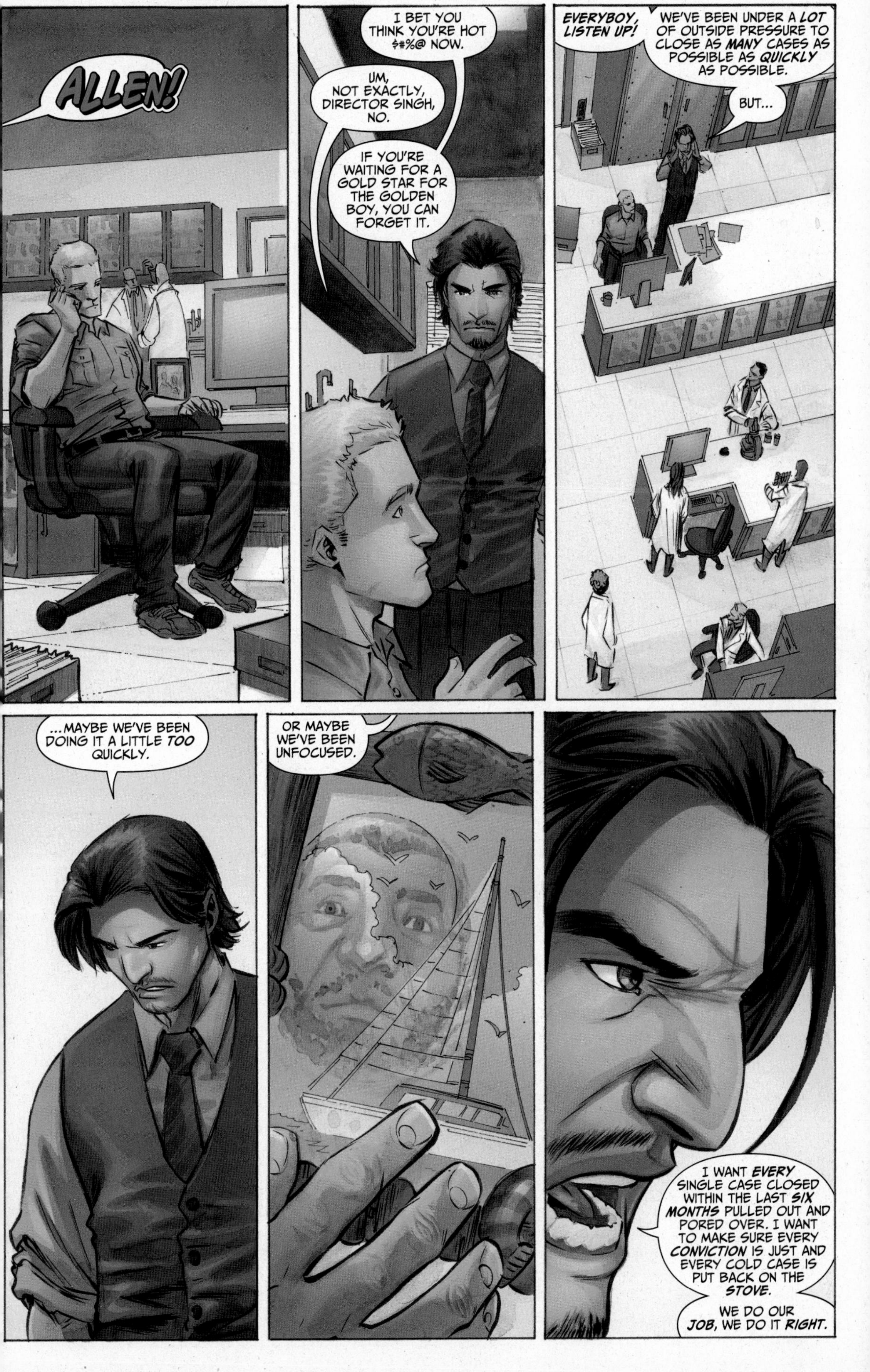
ALLEN!
I BET YOU THINK YOU'RE HOT $#%@ NOW.
UM, NOT EXACTLY, DIRECTOR SINGH, NO.
IF YOU'RE WAITING FOR A GOLD STAR FOR THE GOLDEN BOY, YOU CAN FORGET IT.
EVERYBOY, LISTEN UP!
WE'VE BEEN UNDER A LOT OF OUTSIDE PRESSURE TO CLOSE AS MANY CASES AS POSSIBLE AS QUICKLY AS POSSIBLE.
BUT...
...MAYBE WE'VE BEEN DOING IT A LITTLE TOO QUICKLY.
OR MAYBE WE'VE BEEN UNFOCUSED.
I WANT EVERY SINGLE CASE CLOSED WITHIN THE LAST SIX MONTHS PULLED OUT AND PORED OVER. I WANT TO MAKE SURE EVERY CONVICTION IS JUST AND EVERY COLD CASE IS PUT BACK ON THE STOVE.
WE DO OUR JOB, WE DO IT RIGHT.

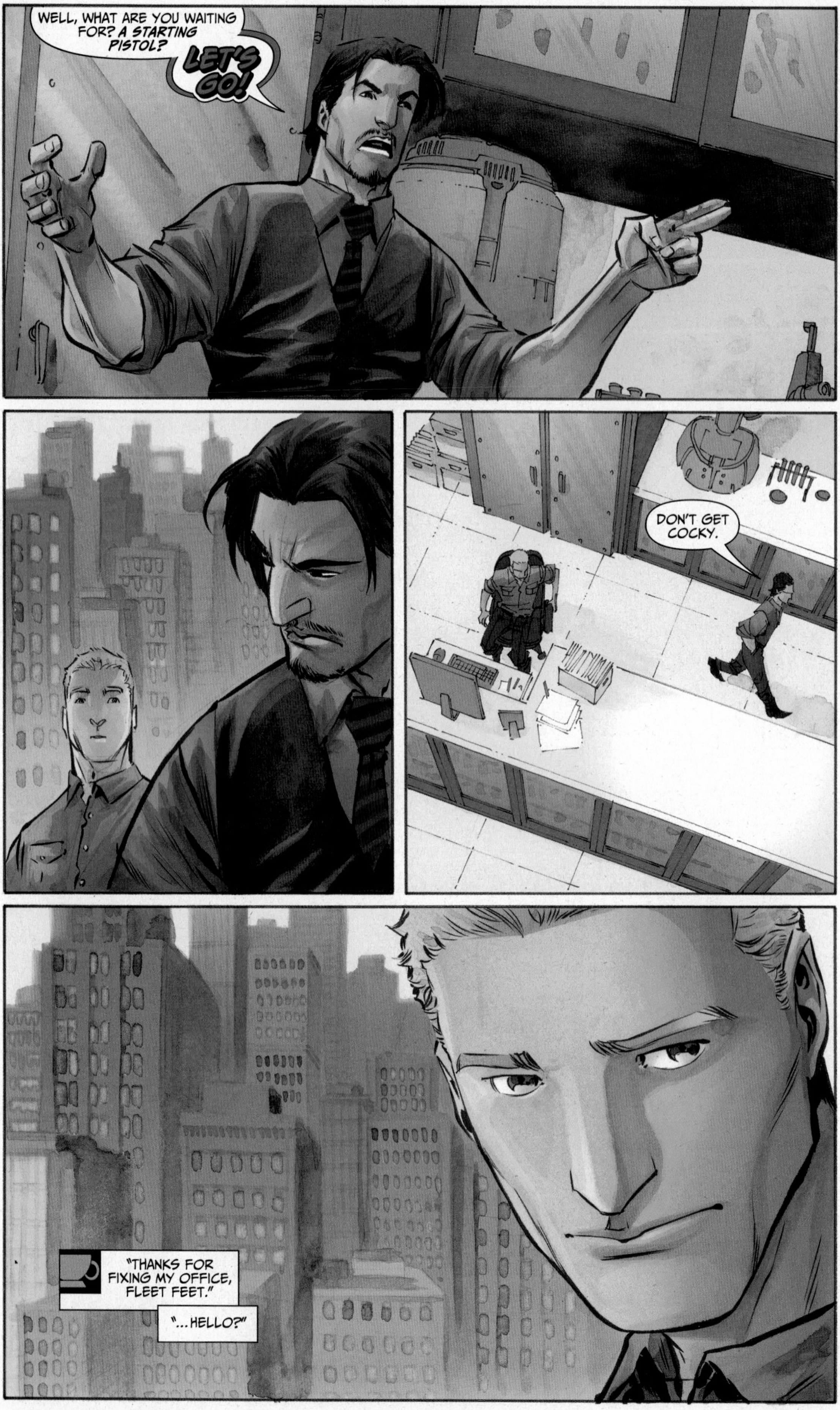

WELL, WHAT ARE YOU WAITING FOR? A STARTING PISTOL?
LET'S GO!
DON'T GET COCKY.
"THANKS FOR FIXING MY OFFICE, FLEET FEET."
"...HELLO?"

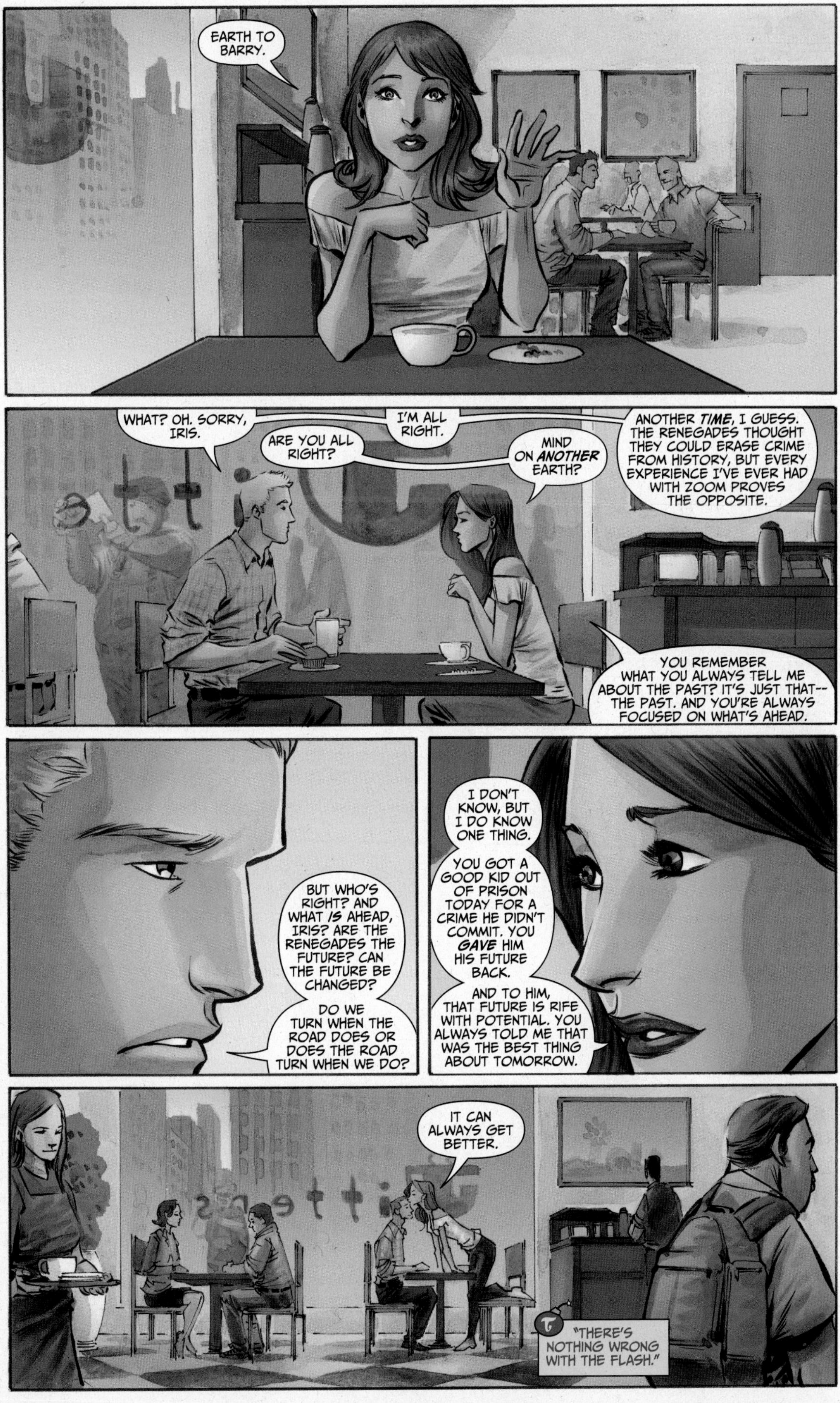
EARTH TO BARRY.
WHAT? OH. SORRY, IRIS.
ARE YOU ALL RIGHT?
I'M ALL RIGHT.
MIND ON ANOTHER EARTH?
ANOTHER TIME, I GUESS. THE RENEGADES THOUGHT THEY COULD ERASE CRIME FROM HISTORY, BUT EVERY EXPERIENCE I'VE EVER HAD WITH ZOOM PROVES THE OPPOSITE.
YOU REMEMBER WHAT YOU ALWAYS TELL ME ABOUT THE PAST? IT'S JUST THAT-- THE PAST. AND YOU'RE ALWAYS FOCUSED ON WHAT'S AHEAD.
BUT WHO'S RIGHT? AND WHAT IS AHEAD, IRIS? ARE THE RENEGADES THE FUTURE? CAN THE FUTURE BE CHANGED?
DO WE TURN WHEN THE ROAD DOES OR DOES THE ROAD TURN WHEN WE DO?
I DON'T KNOW, BUT I DO KNOW ONE THING.
YOU GOT A GOOD KID OUT OF PRISON TODAY FOR A CRIME HE DIDN'T COMMIT. YOU GAVE HIM HIS FUTURE BACK.
AND TO HIM, THAT FUTURE IS RIFE WITH POTENTIAL. YOU ALWAYS TOLD ME THAT WAS THE BEST THING ABOUT TOMORROW.
IT CAN ALWAYS GET BETTER.
"THERE'S NOTHING WRONG WITH THE FLASH."

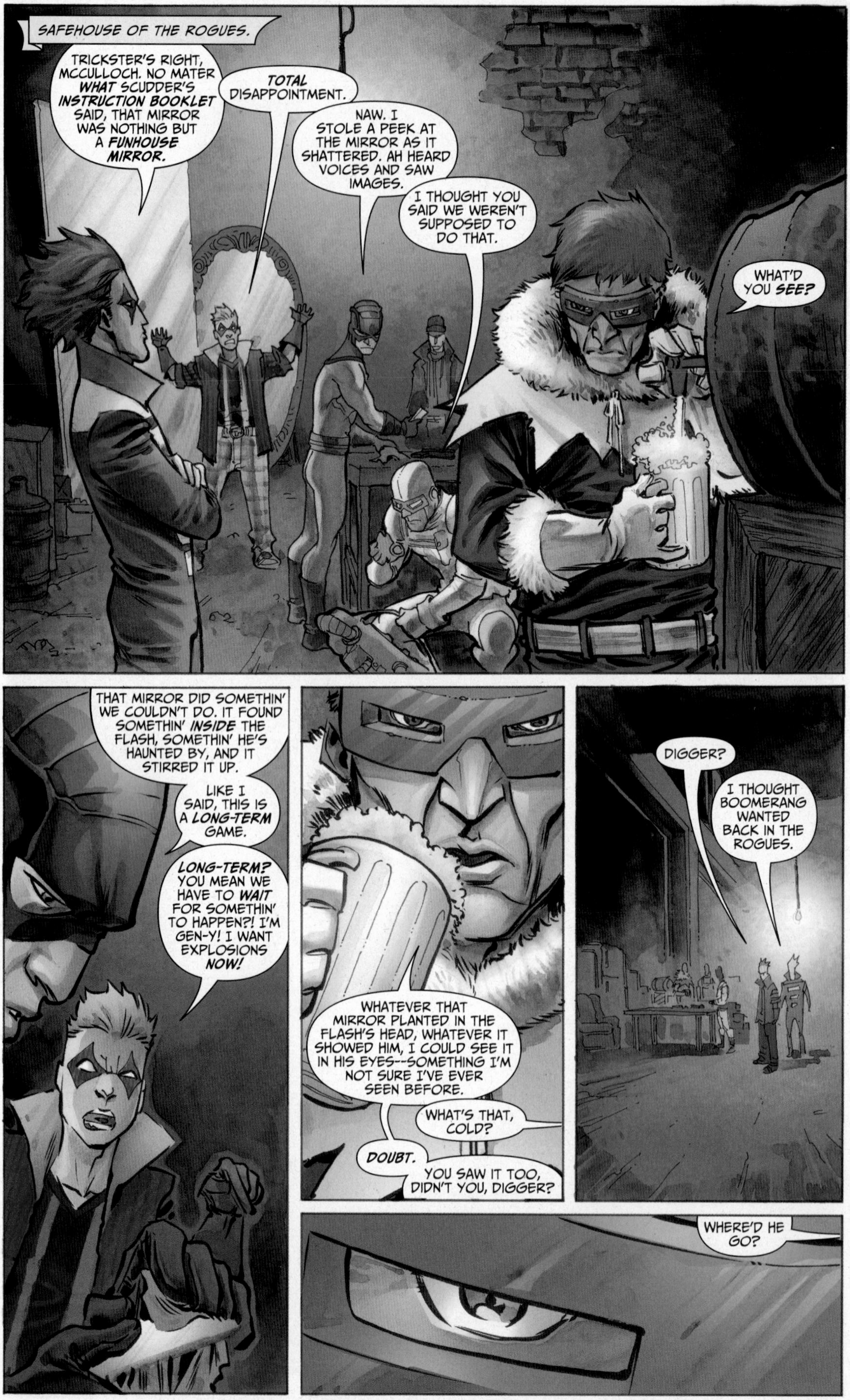
SAFEHOUSE OF THE ROGUES.
TRICKSTER'S RIGHT, MCCULLOCH. NO MATER WHAT SCUDDER'S INSTRUCTION BOOKLET SAID, THAT MIRROR WAS NOTHING BUT A FUNHOUSE MIRROR.
TOTAL DISAPPOINTMENT.
NAW. I STOLE A PEEK AT THE MIRROR AS IT SHATTERED. AH HEARD VOICES AND SAW IMAGES.
I THOUGHT YOU SAID WE WEREN'T SUPPOSED TO DO THAT.
WHAT'D YOU SEE?
THAT MIRROR DID SOMETHIN' WE COULDN'T DO. IT FOUND SOMETHIN' INSIDE THE FLASH, SOMETHIN' HE'S HAUNTED BY, AND IT STIRRED IT UP.
LIKE I SAID, THIS IS A LONG-TERM GAME.
LONG-TERM? YOU MEAN WE HAVE TO WAIT FOR SOMETHIN' TO HAPPEN?! I'M GEN-Y! I WANT EXPLOSIONS NOW!
WHATEVER THAT MIRROR PLANTED IN THE FLASH'S HEAD, WHATEVER IT SHOWED HIM, I COULD SEE IT IN HIS EYES--SOMETHING I'M NOT SURE I'VE EVER SEEN BEFORE.
WHAT'S THAT, COLD?
DOUBT.
YOU SAW IT TOO, DIDN'T YOU, DIGGER?
DIGGER?
I THOUGHT BOOMERANG WANTED BACK IN THE ROGUES.
WHERE'D HE GO?

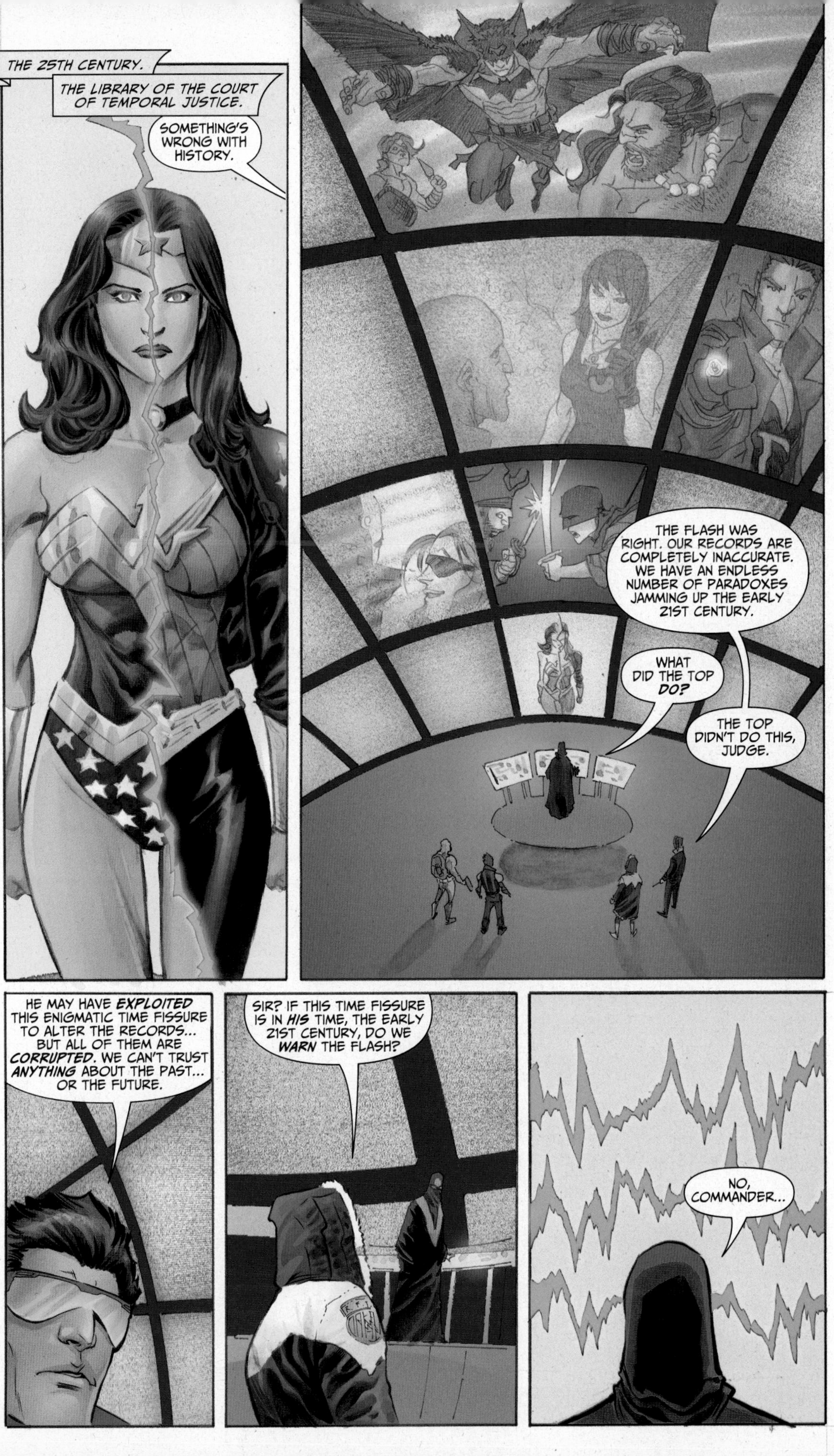
THE 25TH CENTURY.
THE LIBRARY OF THE COURT OF TEMPORAL JUSTICE.
SOMETHING'S WRONG WITH HISTORY.
THE FLASH WAS RIGHT. OUR RECORDS ARE COMPLETELY INACCURATE. WE HAVE AN ENDLESS NUMBER OF PARADOXES JAMMING UP THE EARLY 21ST CENTURY.
WHAT DID THE TOP DO?
THE TOP DIDN'T DO THIS, JUDGE.
HE MAY HAVE EXPLOITED THIS ENIGMATIC TIME FISSURE TO ALTER THE RECORDS... BUT ALL OF THEM ARE CORRUPTED. WE CAN'T TRUST ANYTHING ABOUT THE PAST... OR THE FUTURE.
SIR? IF THIS TIME FISSURE IS IN HIS TIME, THE EARLY 21ST CENTURY, DO WE WARN THE FLASH?
NO, COMMANDER...

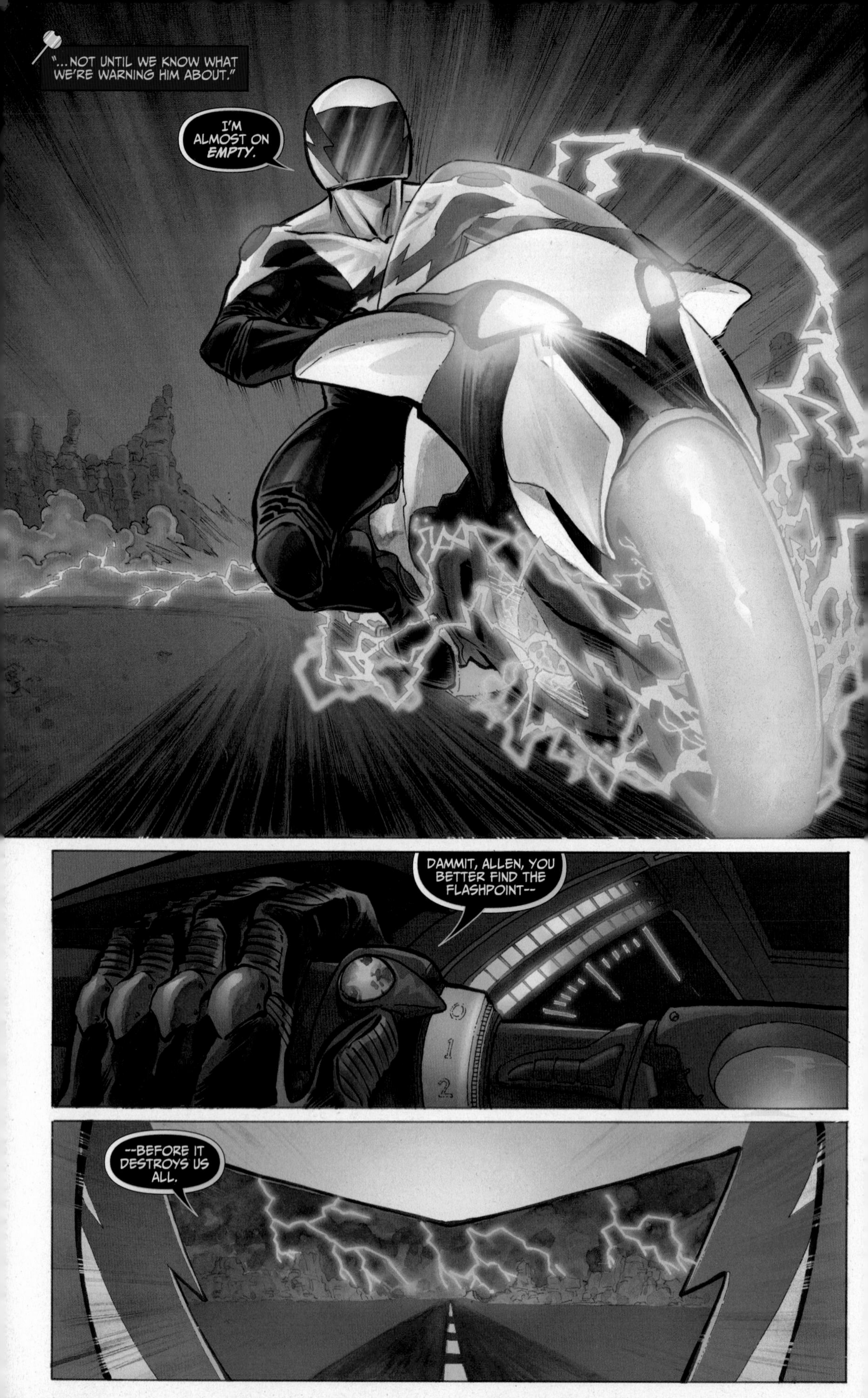
"...NOT UNTIL WE KNOW WHAT WE'RE WARNING HIM ABOUT."
I'M ALMOST ON EMPTY.
DAMMIT, ALLEN, YOU BETTER FIND THE FLASHPOINT--
--BEFORE IT DESTROYS US ALL.

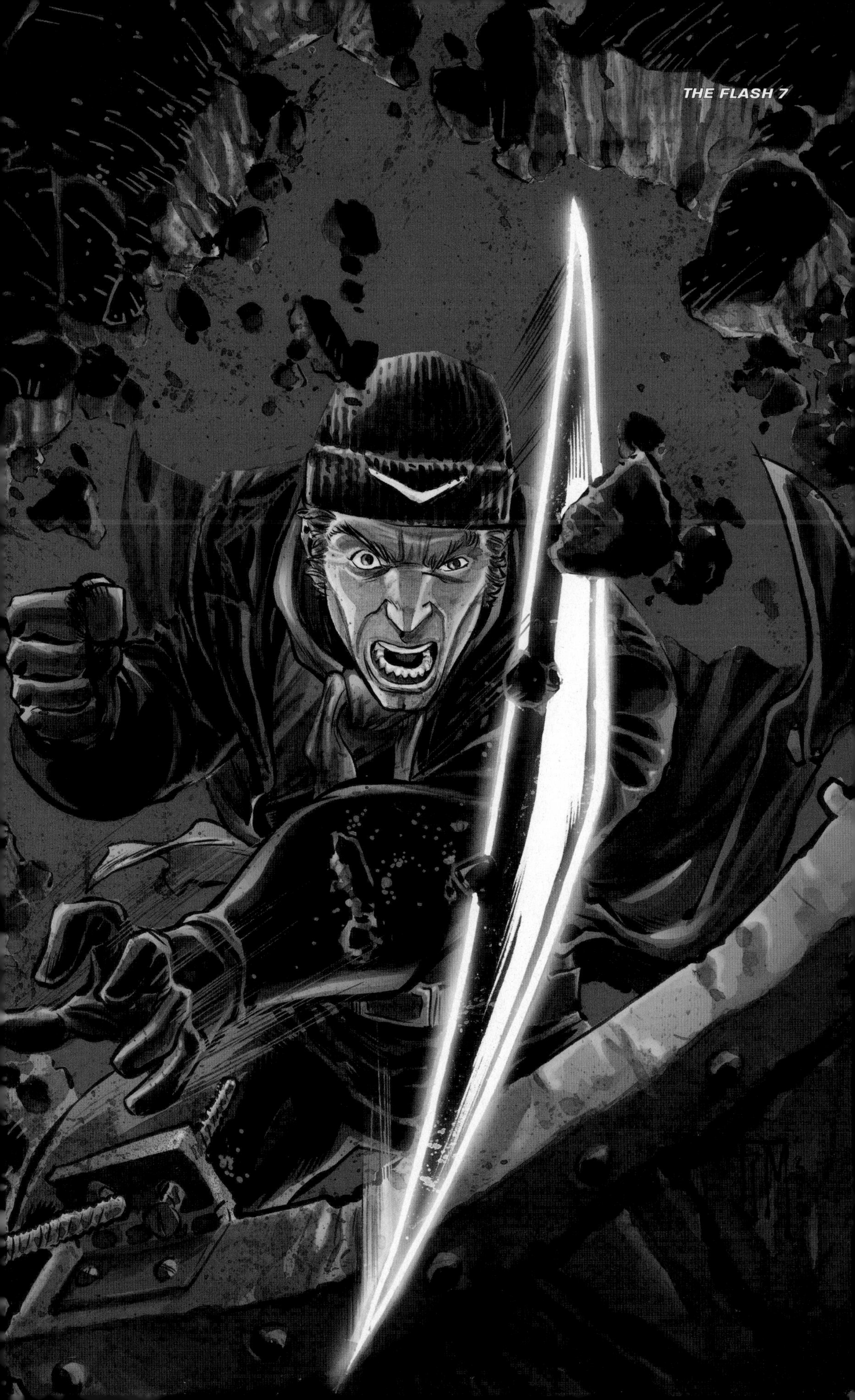
THE FLASH 7

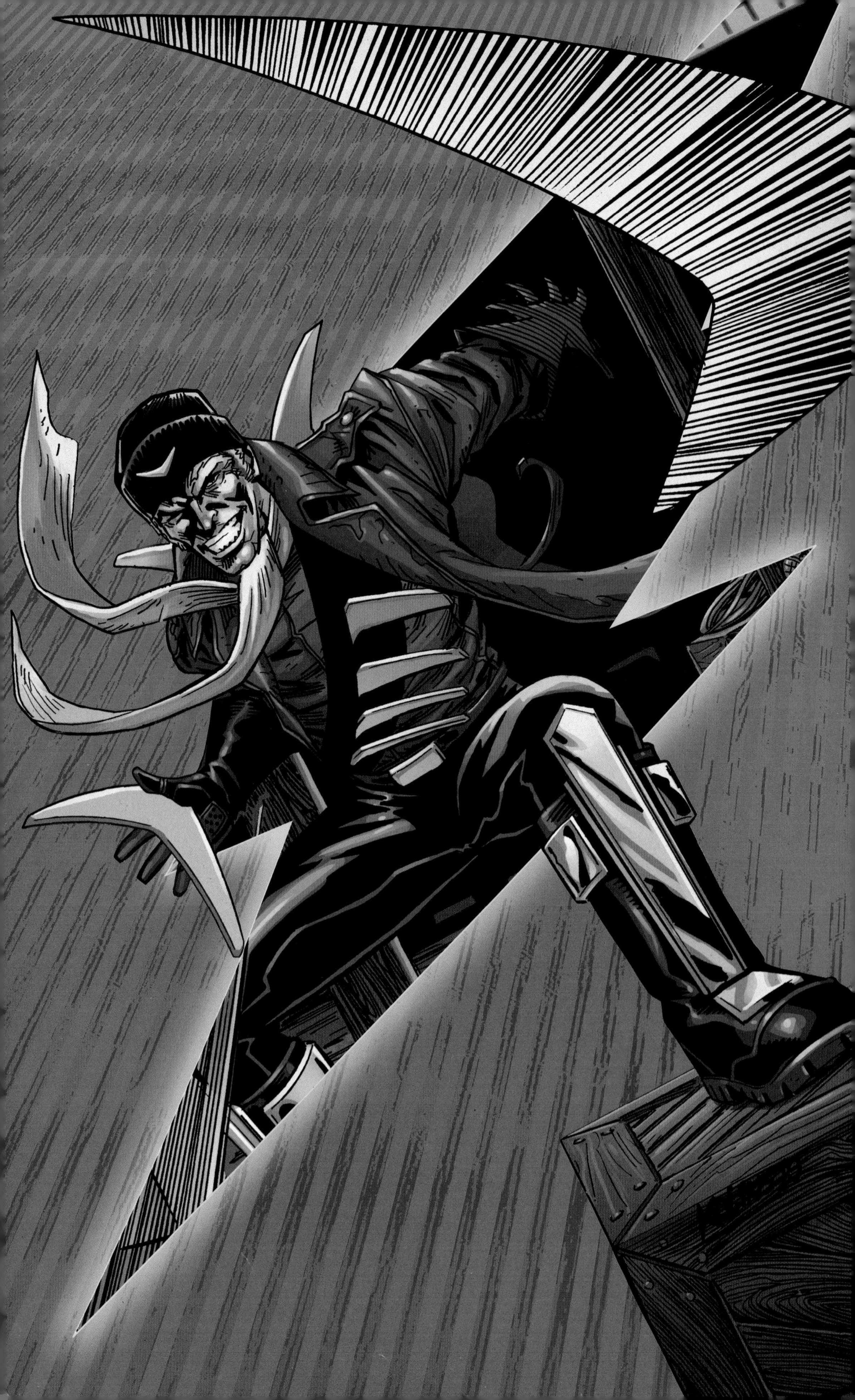

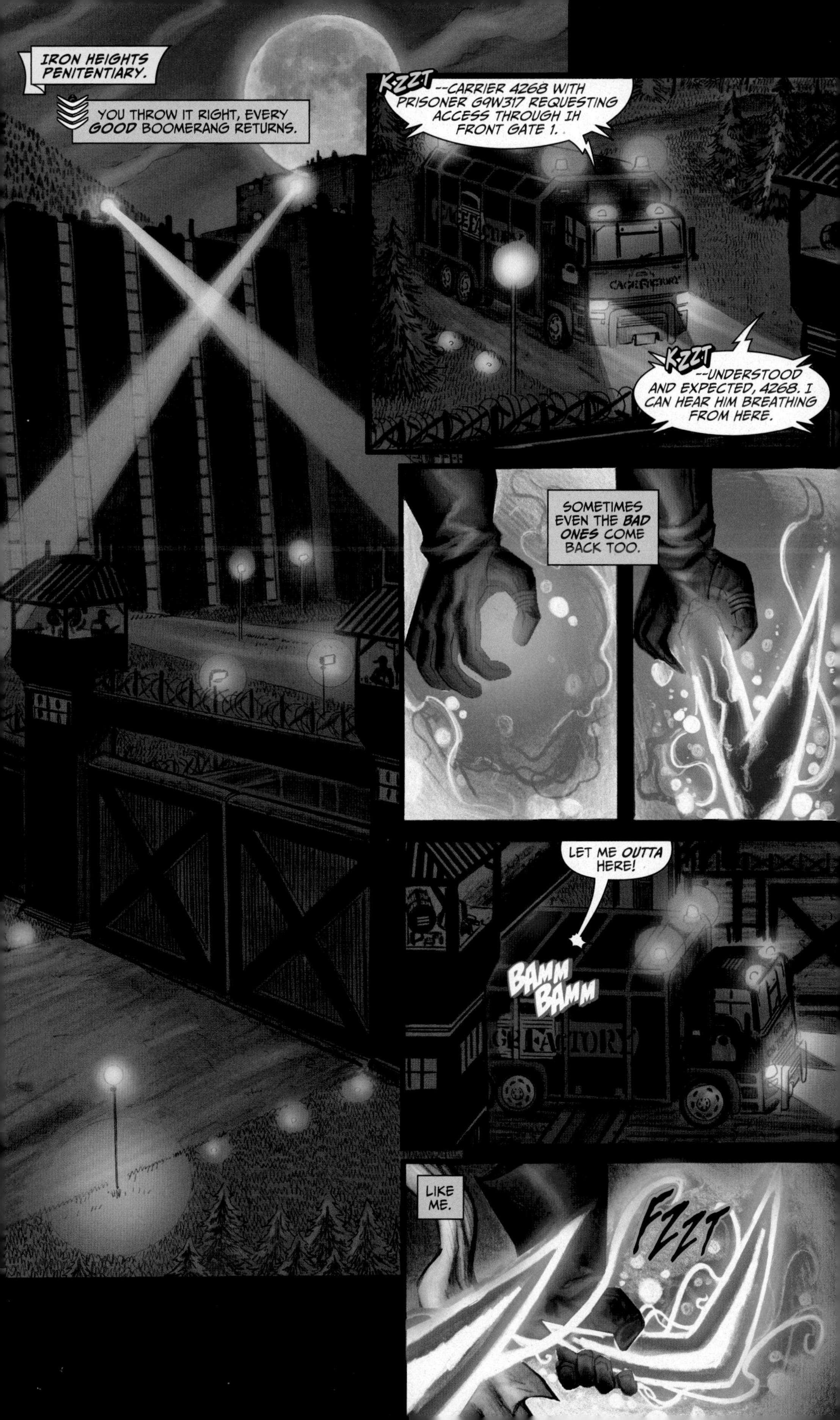
IRON HEIGHTS PENITENTIARY.
YOU THROW IT RIGHT, EVERY GOOD BOOMERANG RETURNS.
K-ZZT
--CARRIER 4268 WITH PRISONER G9W317 REQUESTING ACCESS THROUGH IH FRONT GATE 1.
K-ZZT
--UNDERSTOOD AND EXPECTED, 4268. I CAN HEAR HIM BREATHING FROM HERE.
SOMETIMES EVEN THE BAD ONES COME BACK TOO.
LET ME OUTTA HERE!
BAMM BAMM
LIKE ME.
FZZT

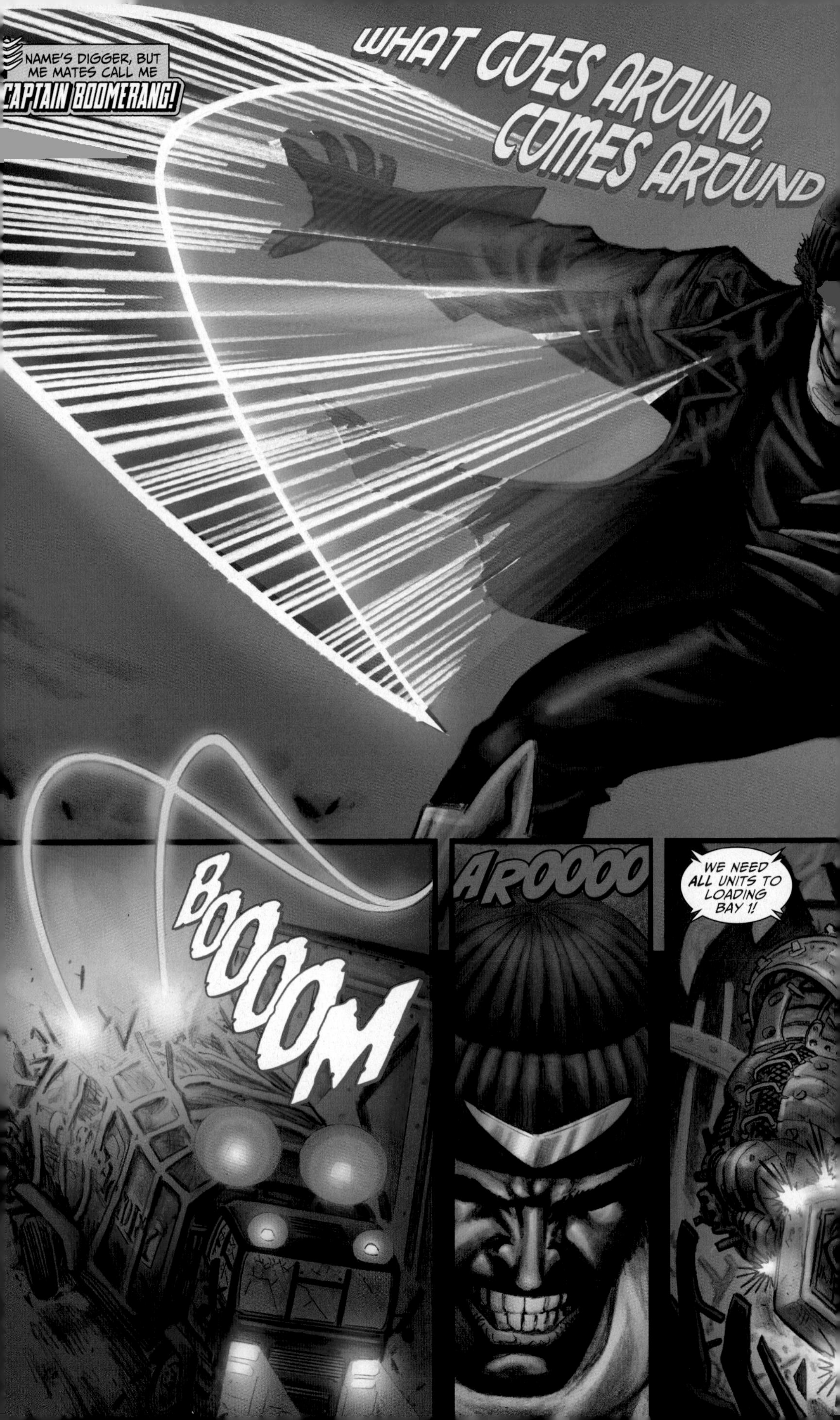
NAME'S DIGGER, BUT ME MATES CALL ME CAPTAIN BOOMERANG!
WHAT GOES AROUND, COMES AROUND
BOOOOM
AROOOO
WE NEED ALL UNITS TO LOADING BAY 1!

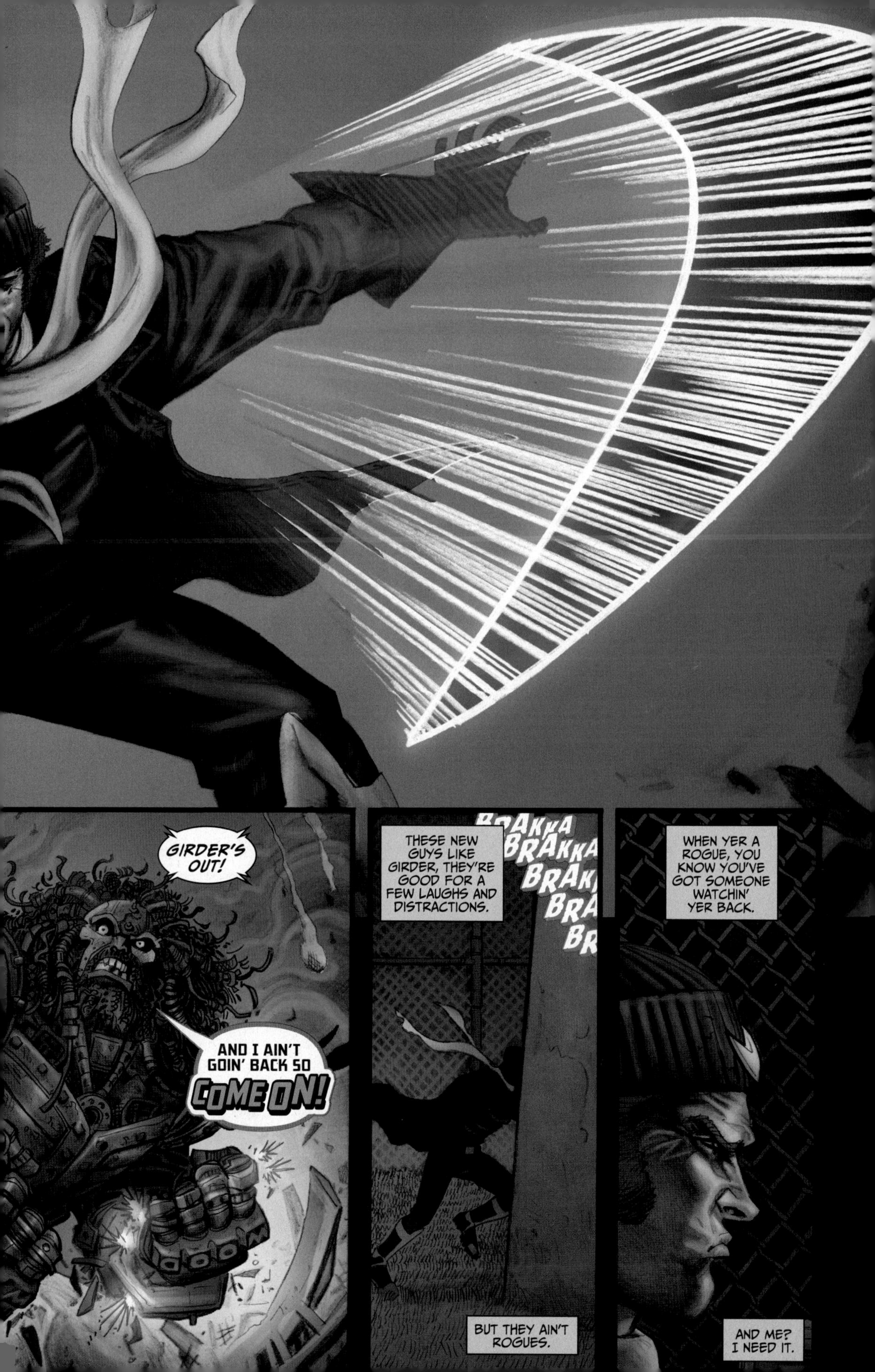
GIRDER'S OUT!
AND I AIN'T GOIN' BACK SO COME ON!
THESE NEW GUYS LIKE GIRDER, THEY'RE GOOD FOR A FEW LAUGHS AND DISTRACTIONS.
BRAKKA BRAKKA
BUT THEY AIN'T ROGUES.
WHEN YER A ROGUE, YOU KNOW YOU'VE GOT SOMEONE WATCHIN' YER BACK.
AND ME? I NEED IT.

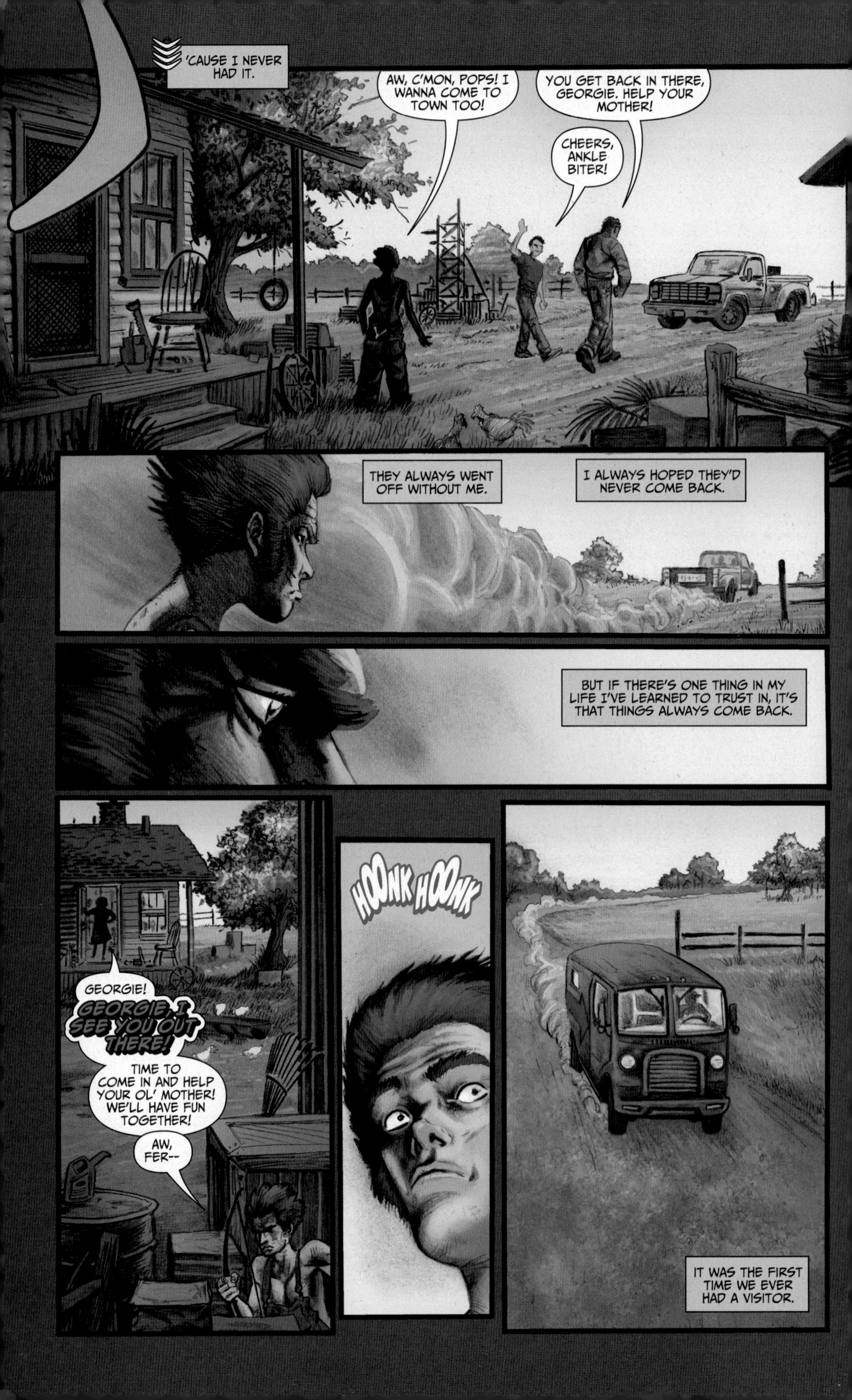
'CAUSE I NEVER HAD IT.
AW, C'MON, POPS! I WANNA COME TO TOWN TOO!
YOU GET BACK IN THERE, GEORGIE. HELP YOUR MOTHER!
CHEERS, ANKLE BITER!
THEY ALWAYS WENT OFF WITHOUT ME.
I ALWAYS HOPED THEY'D NEVER COME BACK.
BUT IF THERE'S ONE THING IN MY LIFE I'VE LEARNED TO TRUST IN, IT'S THAT THINGS ALWAYS COME BACK.
GEORGIE!
GEORGIE, I SEE YOU OUT THERE!
TIME TO COME IN AND HELP YOUR OL' MOTHER! WE'LL HAVE FUN TOGETHER!
AW, FER--
HOONK HOONK
IT WAS THE FIRST TIME WE EVER HAD A VISITOR.

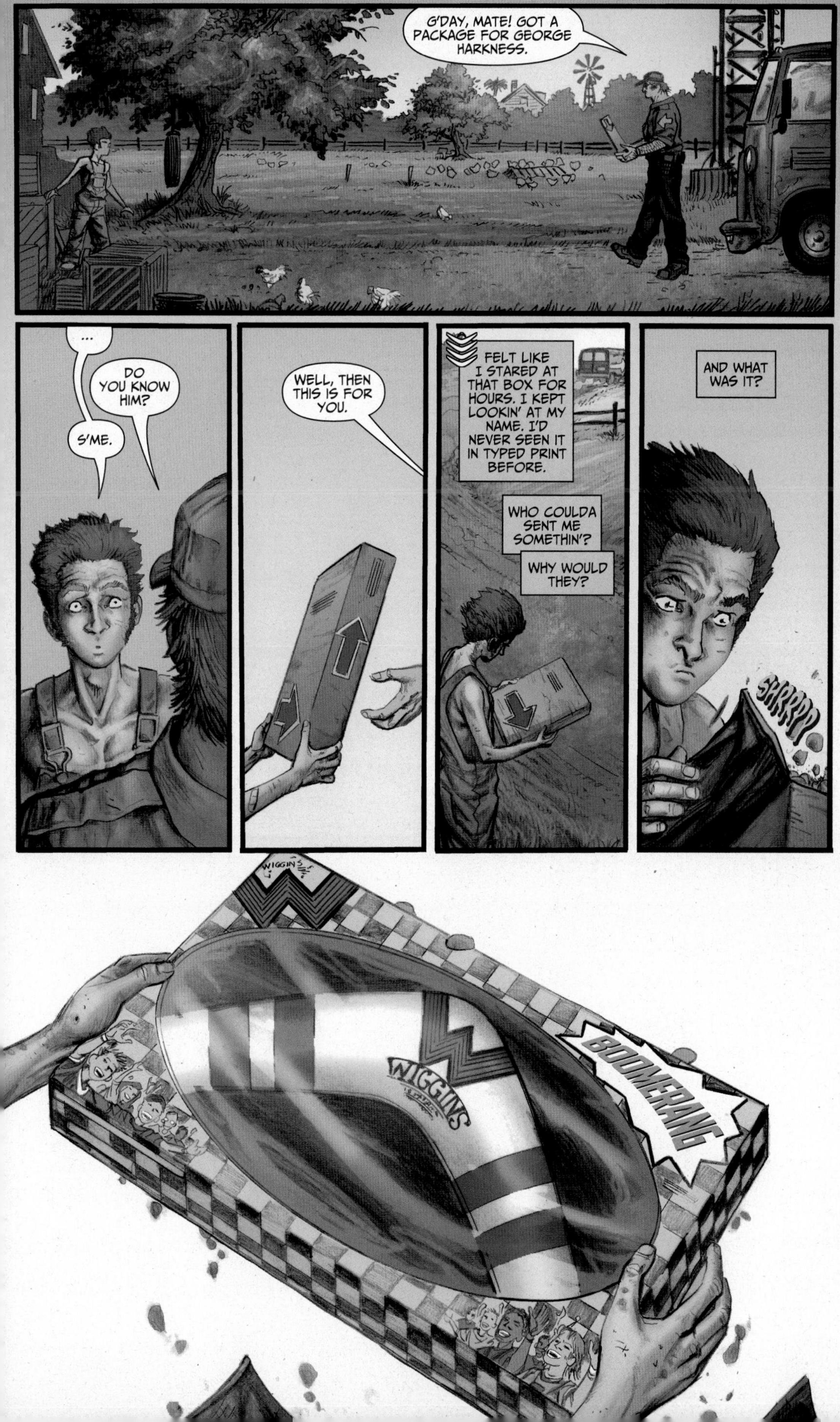
G'DAY, MATE! GOT A PACKAGE FOR GEORGE HARKNESS.
...
DO YOU KNOW HIM?
S'ME.
WELL, THEN THIS IS FOR YOU.
FELT LIKE I STARED AT THAT BOX FOR HOURS. I KEPT LOOKIN' AT MY NAME. I'D NEVER SEEN IT IN TYPED PRINT BEFORE.
WHO COULDA SENT ME SOMETHIN'?
WHY WOULD THEY?
AND WHAT WAS IT?
SKRRRP!
WIGGINS
BOOMERANG
WIGGINS

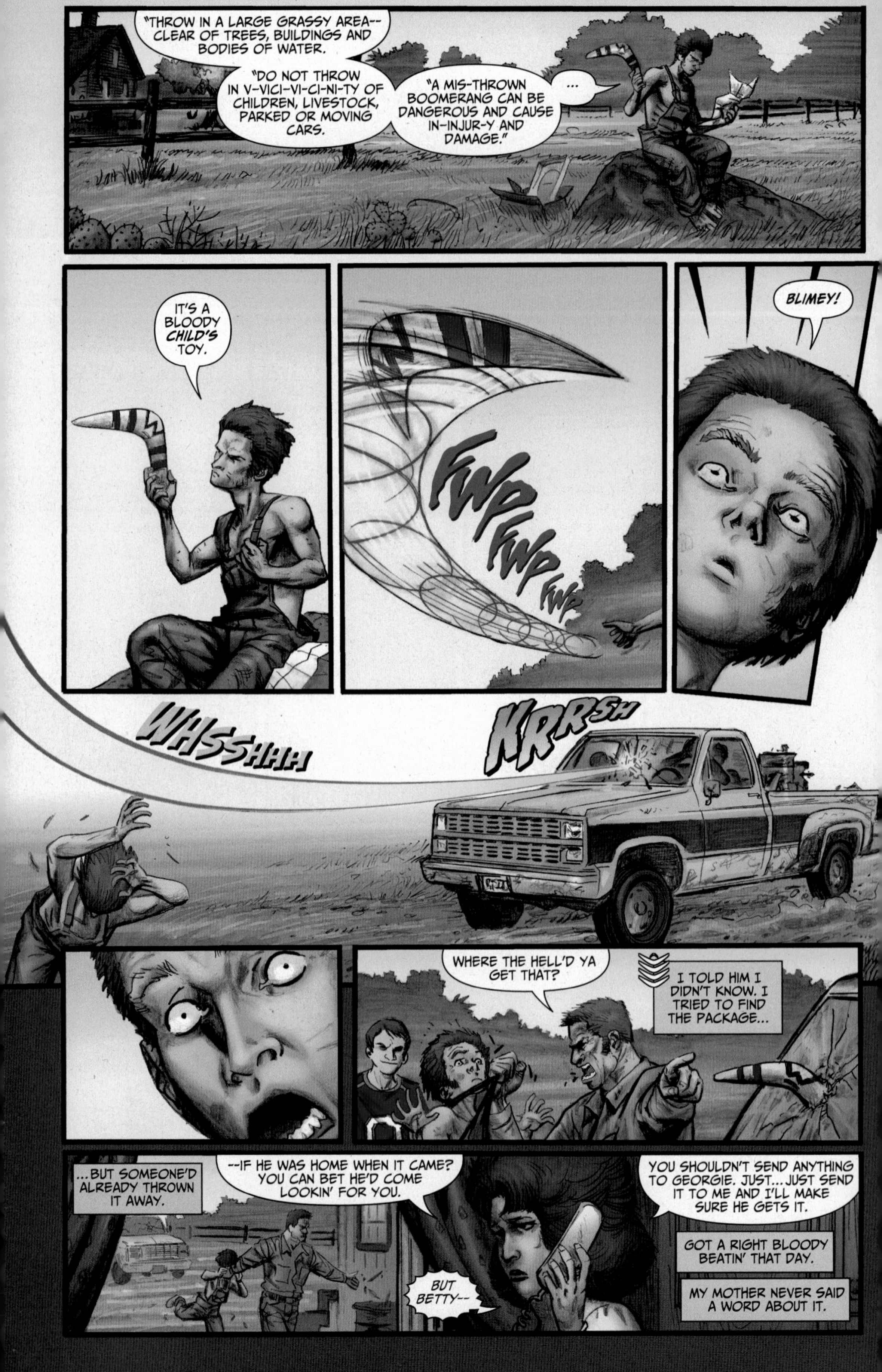

"THROW IN A LARGE GRASSY AREA-- CLEAR OF TREES, BUILDINGS AND BODIES OF WATER.
"DO NOT THROW IN V-VICI-VI-CI-NI-TY OF CHILDREN, LIVESTOCK, PARKED OR MOVING CARS.
"A MIS-THROWN BOOMERANG CAN BE DANGEROUS AND CAUSE IN-INJUR-Y AND DAMAGE."
...
IT'S A BLOODY CHILD'S TOY.
FWP FWP FWP FWP
BLIMEY!
WHSSHHH
KRRSH
WHERE THE HELL'D YA GET THAT?
I TOLD HIM I DIDN'T KNOW. I TRIED TO FIND THE PACKAGE...
...BUT SOMEONE'D ALREADY THROWN IT AWAY.
--IF HE WAS HOME WHEN IT CAME? YOU CAN BET HE'D COME LOOKIN' FOR YOU.
YOU SHOULDN'T SEND ANYTHING TO GEORGIE. JUST... JUST SEND IT TO ME AND I'LL MAKE SURE HE GETS IT.
BUT BETTY--
GOT A RIGHT BLOODY BEATIN' THAT DAY.
MY MOTHER NEVER SAID A WORD ABOUT IT.

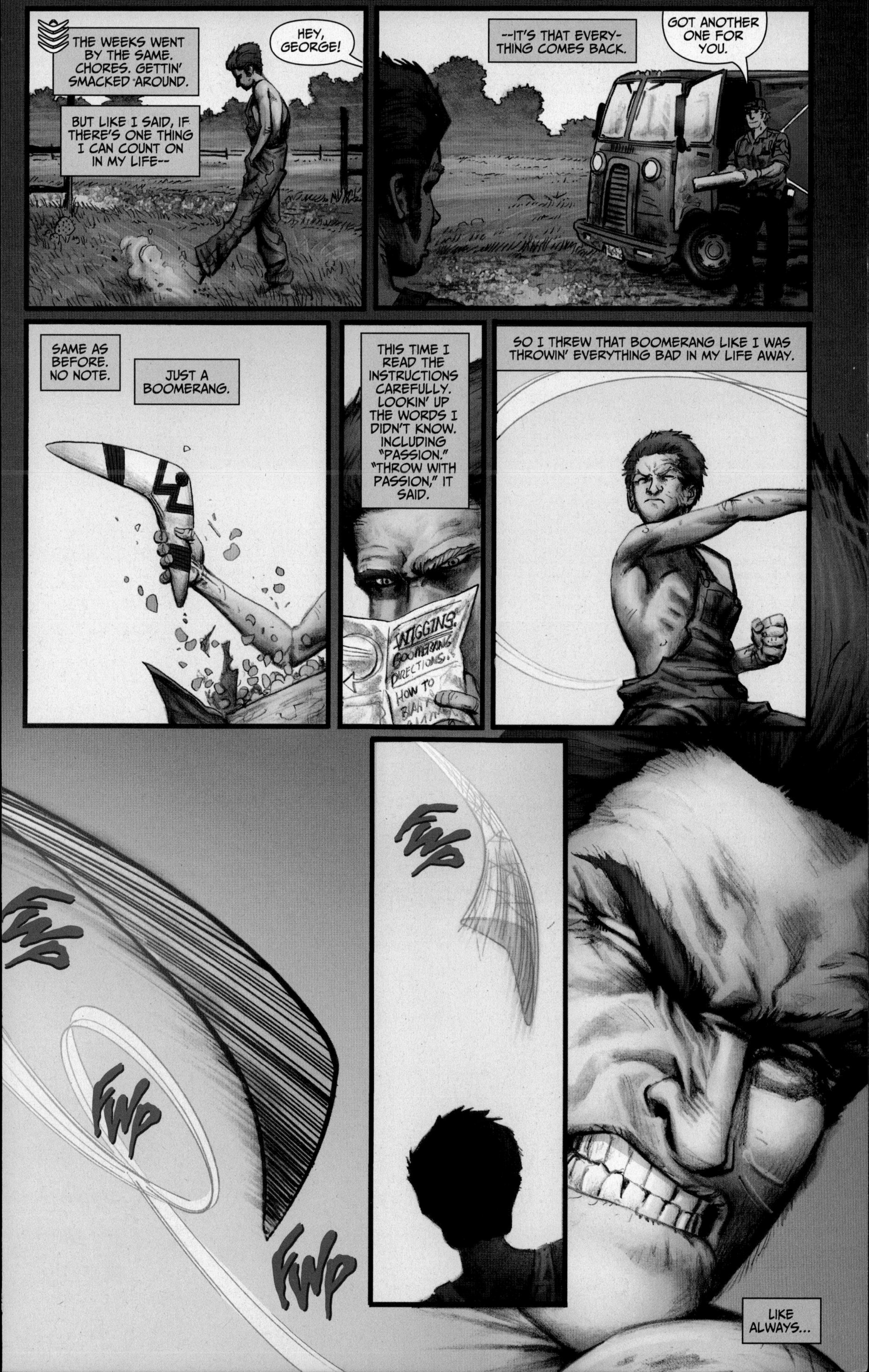
THE WEEKS WENT BY THE SAME. CHORES. GETTIN' SMACKED AROUND.
HEY, GEORGE!
BUT LIKE I SAID, IF THERE'S ONE THING I CAN COUNT ON IN MY LIFE--
--IT'S THAT EVERY-THING COMES BACK.
GOT ANOTHER ONE FOR YOU.
SAME AS BEFORE. NO NOTE.
JUST A BOOMERANG.
THIS TIME I READ THE INSTRUCTIONS CAREFULLY. LOOKIN' UP THE WORDS I DIDN'T KNOW. INCLUDING "PASSION." "THROW WITH PASSION," IT SAID.
WIGGINS BOOMERANG DIRECTIONS HOW TO
SO I THREW THAT BOOMERANG LIKE I WAS THROWIN' EVERYTHING BAD IN MY LIFE AWAY.
FWP
FWP
FWP
FWP
LIKE ALWAYS...

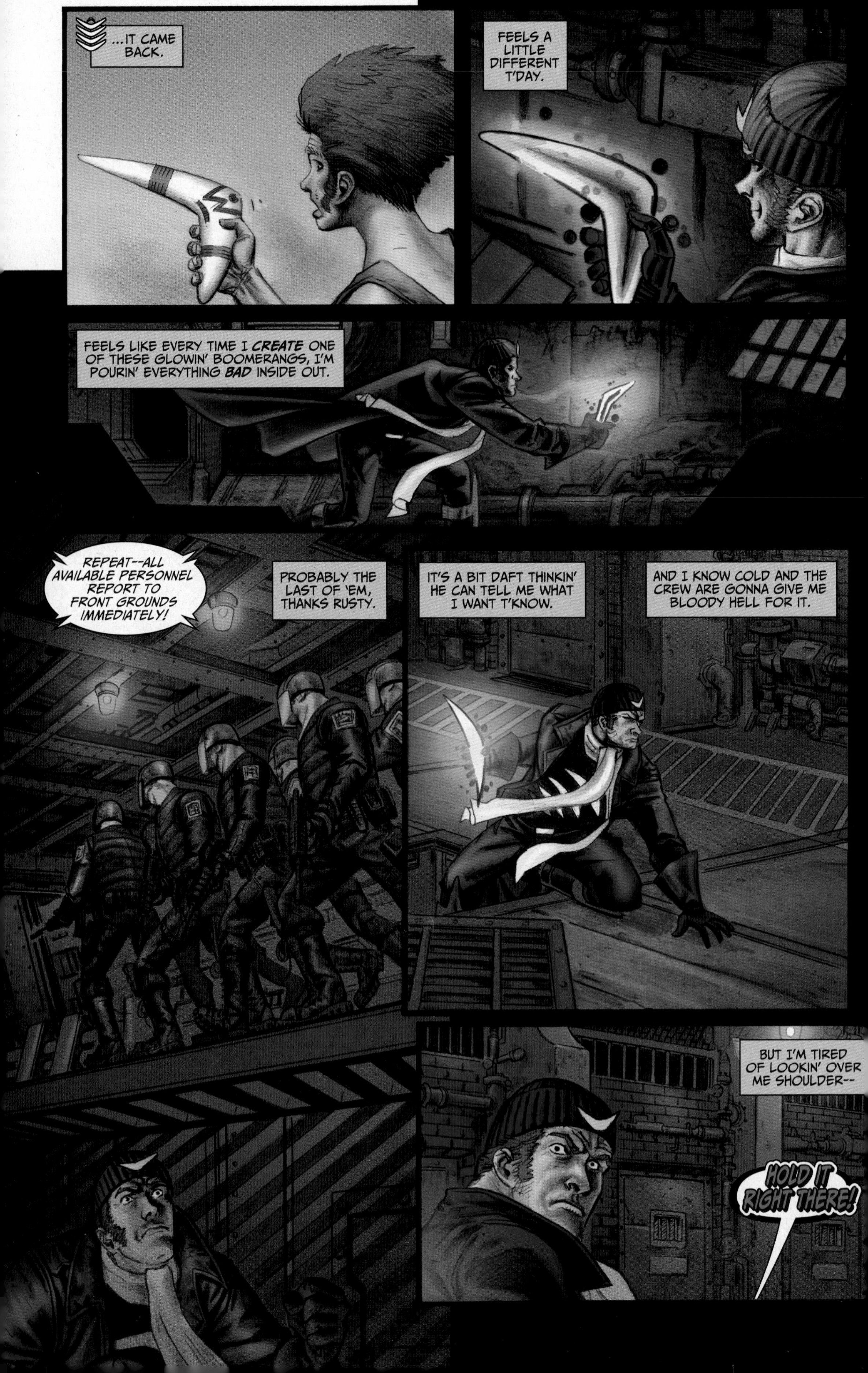
...IT CAME BACK.
FEELS A LITTLE DIFFERENT T'DAY.
FEELS LIKE EVERY TIME I CREATE ONE OF THESE GLOWIN' BOOMERANGS, I'M POURIN' EVERYTHING BAD INSIDE OUT.
REPEAT--ALL AVAILABLE PERSONNEL REPORT TO FRONT GROUNDS IMMEDIATELY!
PROBABLY THE LAST OF 'EM, THANKS RUSTY.
IT'S A BIT DAFT THINKIN' HE CAN TELL ME WHAT I WANT T'KNOW.
AND I KNOW COLD AND THE CREW ARE GONNA GIVE ME BLOODY HELL FOR IT.
BUT I'M TIRED OF LOOKIN' OVER ME SHOULDER--
HOLD IT RIGHT THERE!

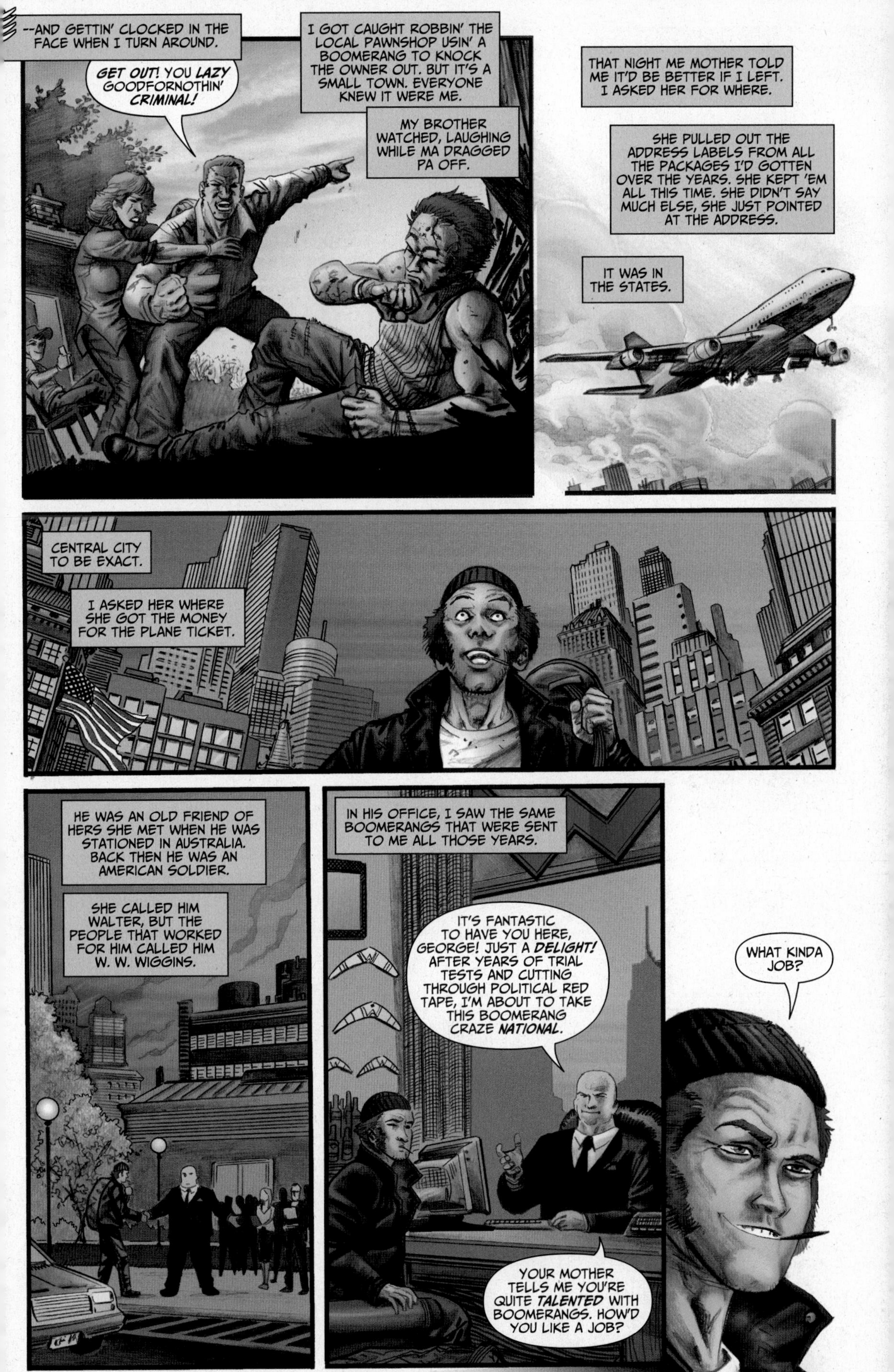
--AND GETTIN' CLOCKED IN THE FACE WHEN I TURN AROUND.
GET OUT! YOU LAZY GOODFORNOTHIN' CRIMINAL!
I GOT CAUGHT ROBBIN' THE LOCAL PAWNSHOP USIN' A BOOMERANG TO KNOCK THE OWNER OUT. BUT IT'S A SMALL TOWN. EVERYONE KNEW IT WERE ME.
MY BROTHER WATCHED, LAUGHING WHILE MA DRAGGED PA OFF.
THAT NIGHT ME MOTHER TOLD ME IT'D BE BETTER IF I LEFT. I ASKED HER FOR WHERE.
SHE PULLED OUT THE ADDRESS LABELS FROM ALL THE PACKAGES I'D GOTTEN OVER THE YEARS. SHE KEPT 'EM ALL THIS TIME. SHE DIDN'T SAY MUCH ELSE, SHE JUST POINTED AT THE ADDRESS.
IT WAS IN THE STATES.
CENTRAL CITY TO BE EXACT.
I ASKED HER WHERE SHE GOT THE MONEY FOR THE PLANE TICKET.
HE WAS AN OLD FRIEND OF HERS SHE MET WHEN HE WAS STATIONED IN AUSTRALIA. BACK THEN HE WAS AN AMERICAN SOLDIER.
SHE CALLED HIM WALTER, BUT THE PEOPLE THAT WORKED FOR HIM CALLED HIM W. W. WIGGINS.
IN HIS OFFICE, I SAW THE SAME BOOMERANGS THAT WERE SENT TO ME ALL THOSE YEARS.
IT'S FANTASTIC TO HAVE YOU HERE, GEORGE! JUST A DELIGHT! AFTER YEARS OF TRIAL TESTS AND CUTTING THROUGH POLITICAL RED TAPE, I'M ABOUT TO TAKE THIS BOOMERANG CRAZE NATIONAL.
YOUR MOTHER TELLS ME YOU'RE QUITE TALENTED WITH BOOMERANGS. HOW'D YOU LIKE A JOB?
WHAT KINDA JOB?

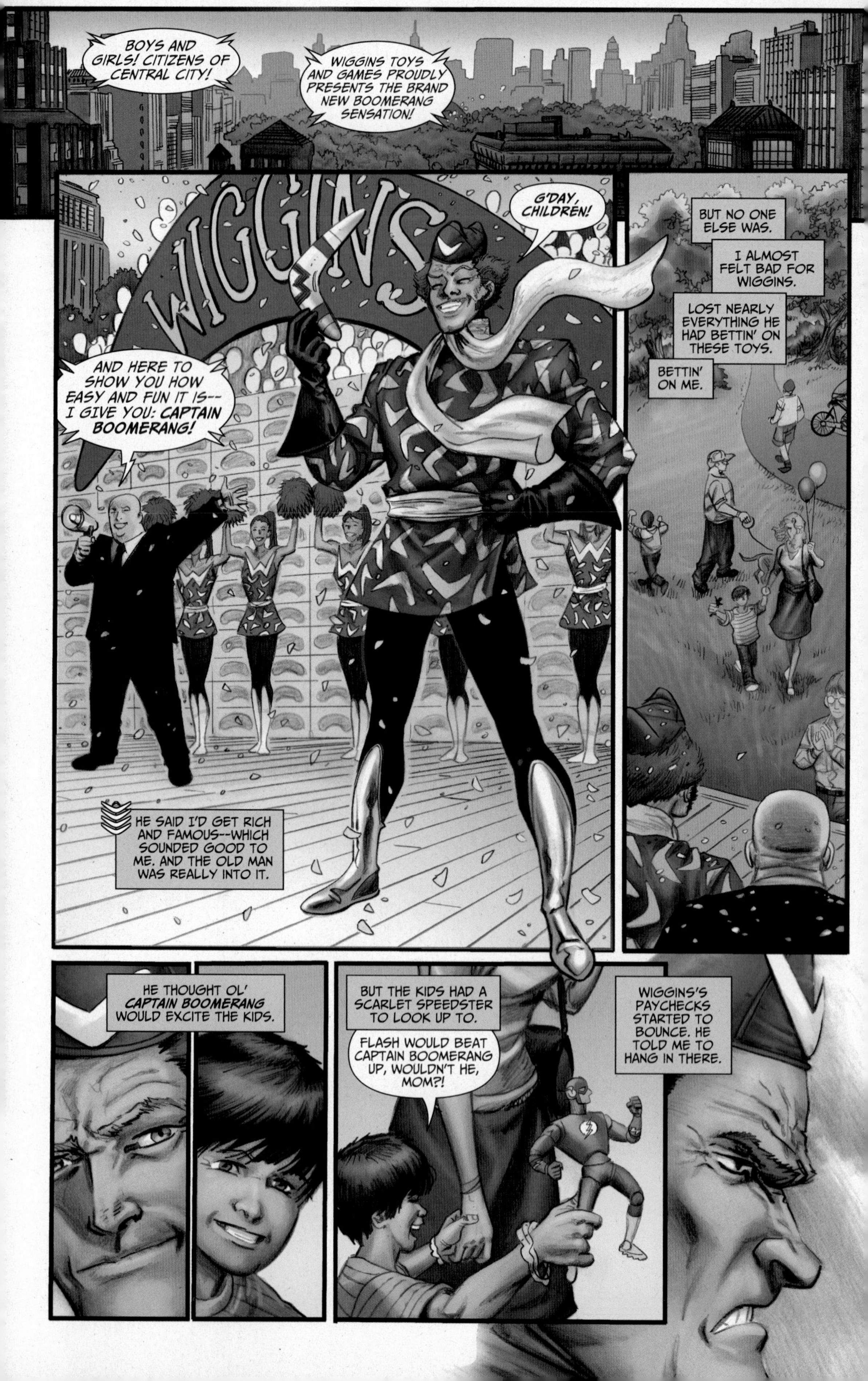
BOYS AND GIRLS! CITIZENS OF CENTRAL CITY!
WIGGINS TOYS AND GAMES PROUDLY PRESENTS THE BRAND NEW BOOMERANG SENSATION!
WIGGINS
G'DAY, CHILDREN!
AND HERE TO SHOW YOU HOW EASY AND FUN IT IS-- I GIVE YOU: CAPTAIN BOOMERANG!
HE SAID I'D GET RICH AND FAMOUS--WHICH SOUNDED GOOD TO ME. AND THE OLD MAN WAS REALLY INTO IT.
BUT NO ONE ELSE WAS.
I ALMOST FELT BAD FOR WIGGINS.
LOST NEARLY EVERYTHING HE HAD BETTIN' ON THESE TOYS.
BETTIN' ON ME.
HE THOUGHT OL' CAPTAIN BOOMERANG WOULD EXCITE THE KIDS.
BUT THE KIDS HAD A SCARLET SPEEDSTER TO LOOK UP TO.
FLASH WOULD BEAT CAPTAIN BOOMERANG UP, WOULDN'T HE, MOM?!
WIGGINS'S PAYCHECKS STARTED TO BOUNCE. HE TOLD ME TO HANG IN THERE.

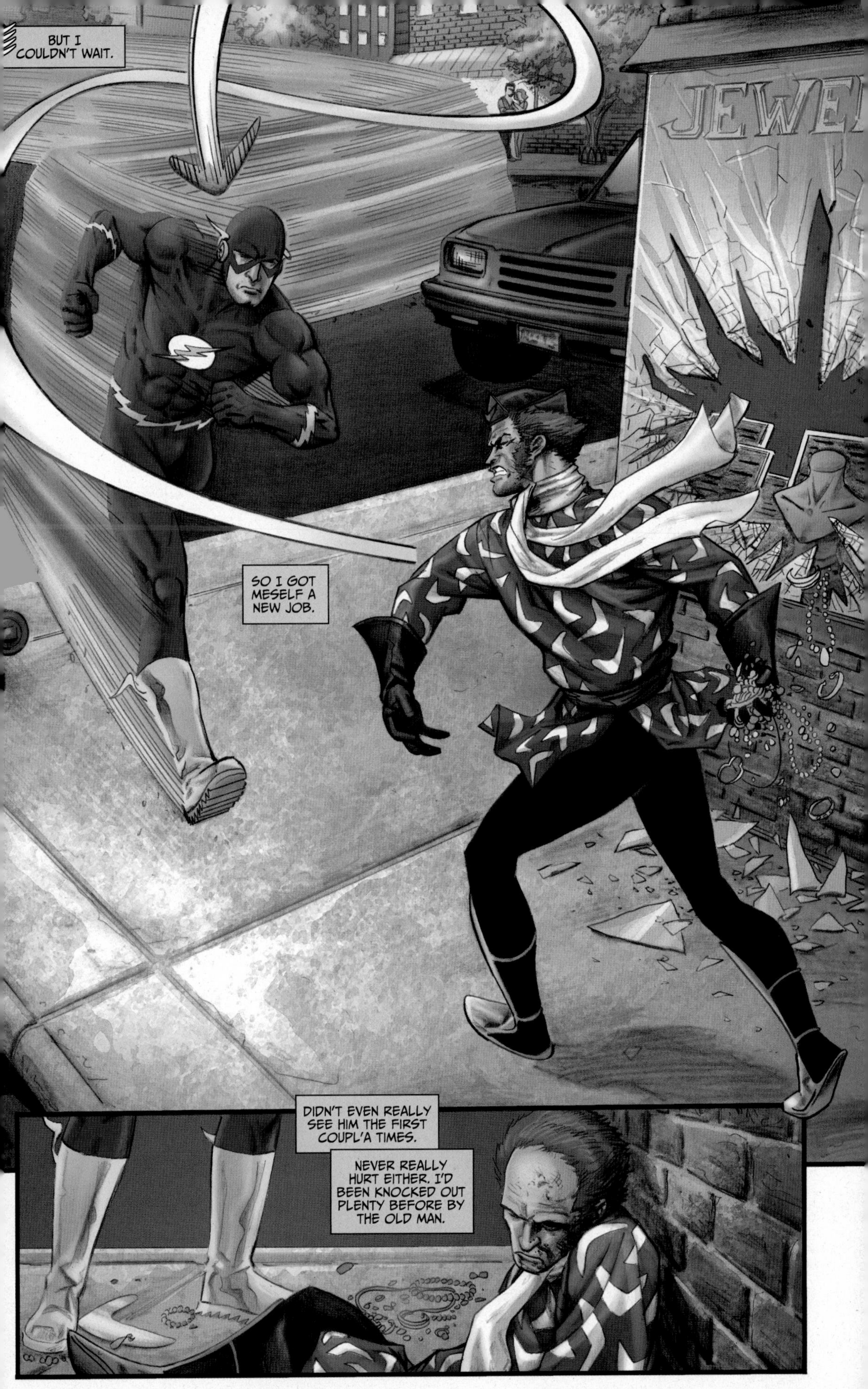
BUT I COULDN'T WAIT.
JEWE
SO I GOT MESELF A NEW JOB.
DIDN'T EVEN REALLY SEE HIM THE FIRST COUPL'A TIMES.
NEVER REALLY HURT EITHER. I'D BEEN KNOCKED OUT PLENTY BEFORE BY THE OLD MAN.

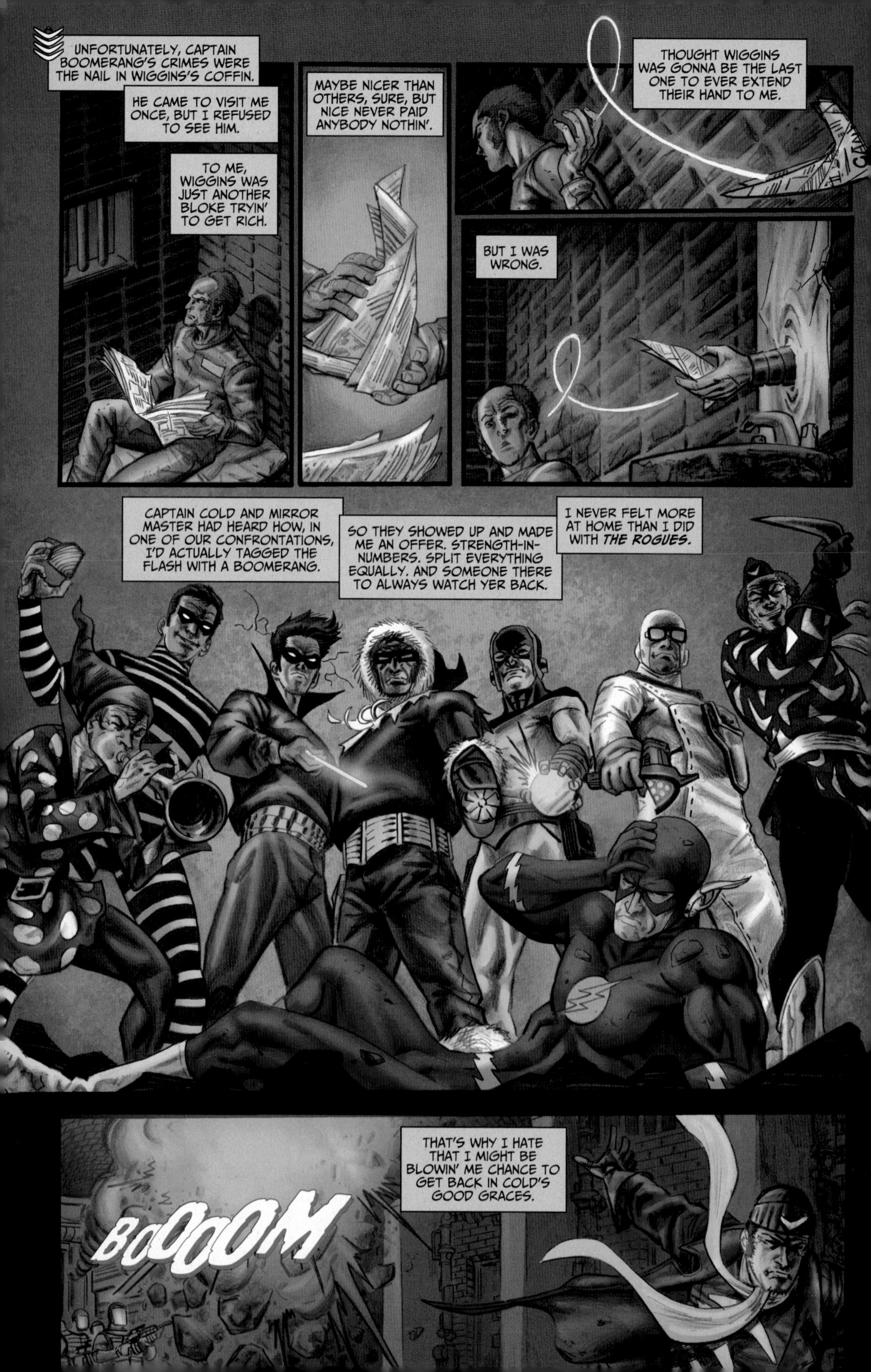
UNFORTUNATELY, CAPTAIN BOOMERANG'S CRIMES WERE THE NAIL IN WIGGINS'S COFFIN.
HE CAME TO VISIT ME ONCE, BUT I REFUSED TO SEE HIM.
TO ME, WIGGINS WAS JUST ANOTHER BLOKE TRYIN' TO GET RICH.
MAYBE NICER THAN OTHERS, SURE, BUT NICE NEVER PAID ANYBODY NOTHIN'.
THOUGHT WIGGINS WAS GONNA BE THE LAST ONE TO EVER EXTEND THEIR HAND TO ME.
BUT I WAS WRONG.
CAPTAIN COLD AND MIRROR MASTER HAD HEARD HOW, IN ONE OF OUR CONFRONTATIONS, I'D ACTUALLY TAGGED THE FLASH WITH A BOOMERANG.
SO THEY SHOWED UP AND MADE ME AN OFFER. STRENGTH-IN-NUMBERS. SPLIT EVERYTHING EQUALLY. AND SOMEONE THERE TO ALWAYS WATCH YER BACK.
I NEVER FELT MORE AT HOME THAN I DID WITH *THE ROGUES.*
THAT'S WHY I HATE THAT I MIGHT BE BLOWIN' ME CHANCE TO GET BACK IN COLD'S GOOD GRACES.
BOOOOOM

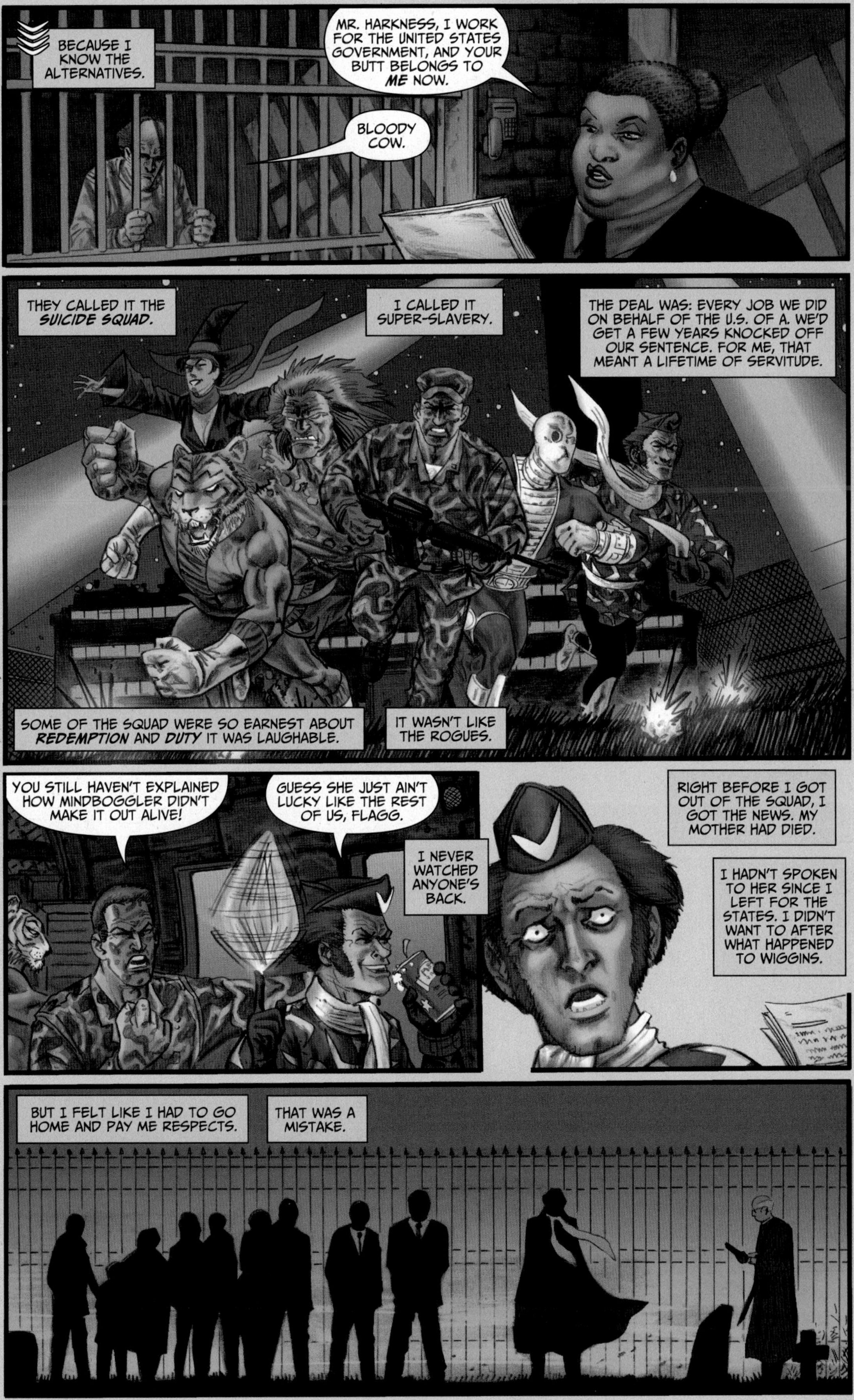
BECAUSE I KNOW THE ALTERNATIVES.
MR. HARKNESS, I WORK FOR THE UNITED STATES GOVERNMENT, AND YOUR BUTT BELONGS TO ME NOW.
BLOODY COW.
THEY CALLED IT THE SUICIDE SQUAD.
I CALLED IT SUPER-SLAVERY.
THE DEAL WAS: EVERY JOB WE DID ON BEHALF OF THE U.S. OF A. WE'D GET A FEW YEARS KNOCKED OFF OUR SENTENCE. FOR ME, THAT MEANT A LIFETIME OF SERVITUDE.
SOME OF THE SQUAD WERE SO EARNEST ABOUT REDEMPTION AND DUTY IT WAS LAUGHABLE.
IT WASN'T LIKE THE ROGUES.
YOU STILL HAVEN'T EXPLAINED HOW MINDBOGGLER DIDN'T MAKE IT OUT ALIVE!
GUESS SHE JUST AIN'T LUCKY LIKE THE REST OF US, FLAGG.
I NEVER WATCHED ANYONE'S BACK.
RIGHT BEFORE I GOT OUT OF THE SQUAD, I GOT THE NEWS. MY MOTHER HAD DIED.
I HADN'T SPOKEN TO HER SINCE I LEFT FOR THE STATES. I DIDN'T WANT TO AFTER WHAT HAPPENED TO WIGGINS.
BUT I FELT LIKE I HAD TO GO HOME AND PAY ME RESPECTS.
THAT WAS A MISTAKE.

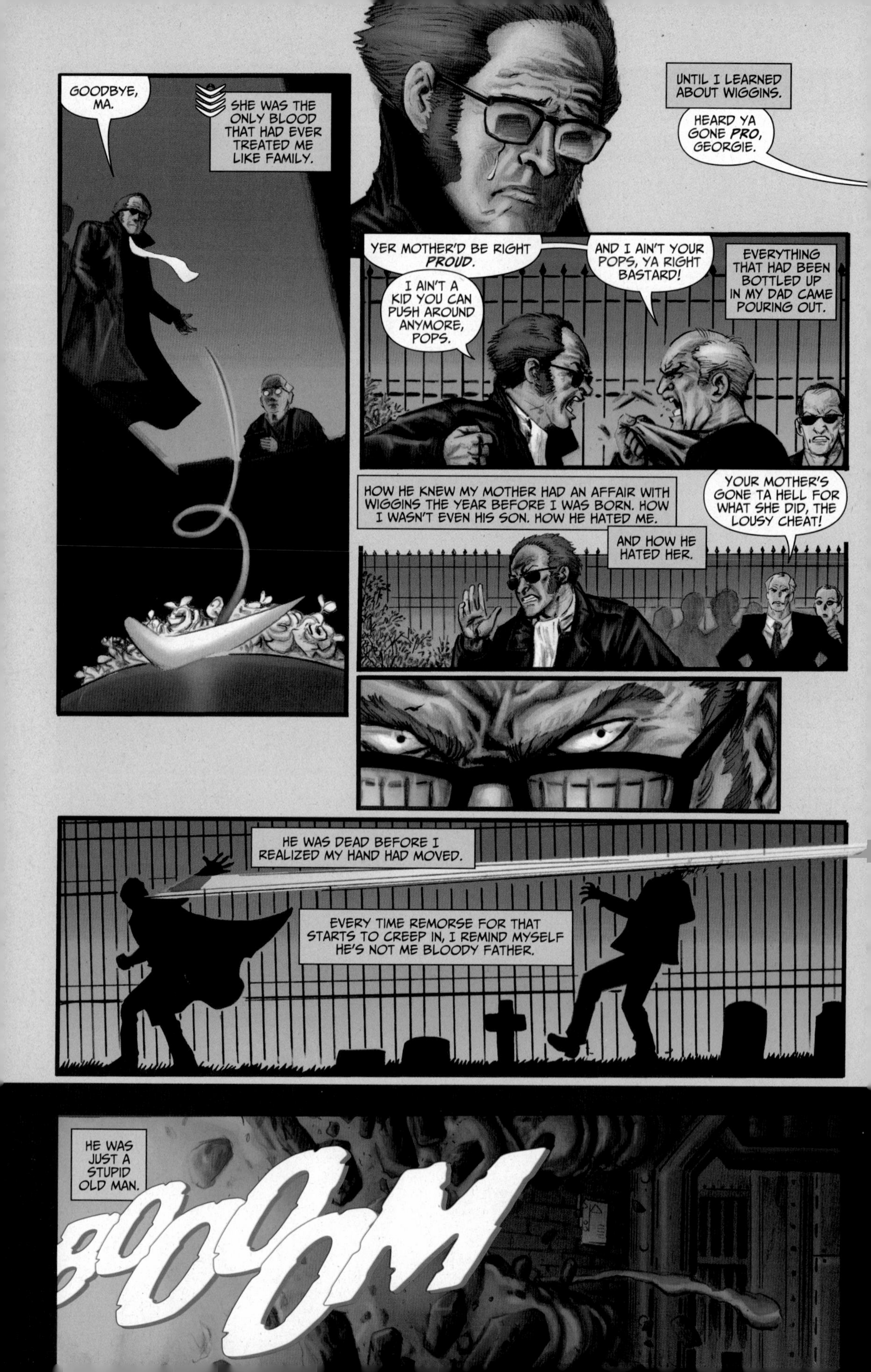
GOODBYE, MA.
SHE WAS THE ONLY BLOOD THAT HAD EVER TREATED ME LIKE FAMILY.
UNTIL I LEARNED ABOUT WIGGINS.
HEARD YA GONE PRO, GEORGIE.
YER MOTHER'D BE RIGHT PROUD.
I AIN'T A KID YOU CAN PUSH AROUND ANYMORE, POPS.
AND I AIN'T YOUR POPS, YA RIGHT BASTARD!
EVERYTHING THAT HAD BEEN BOTTLED UP IN MY DAD CAME POURING OUT.
HOW HE KNEW MY MOTHER HAD AN AFFAIR WITH WIGGINS THE YEAR BEFORE I WAS BORN. HOW I WASN'T EVEN HIS SON. HOW HE HATED ME.
AND HOW HE HATED HER.
YOUR MOTHER'S GONE TA HELL FOR WHAT SHE DID, THE LOUSY CHEAT!
HE WAS DEAD BEFORE I REALIZED MY HAND HAD MOVED.
EVERY TIME REMORSE FOR THAT STARTS TO CREEP IN, I REMIND MYSELF HE'S NOT ME BLOODY FATHER.
HE WAS JUST A STUPID OLD MAN.
BOOOOM

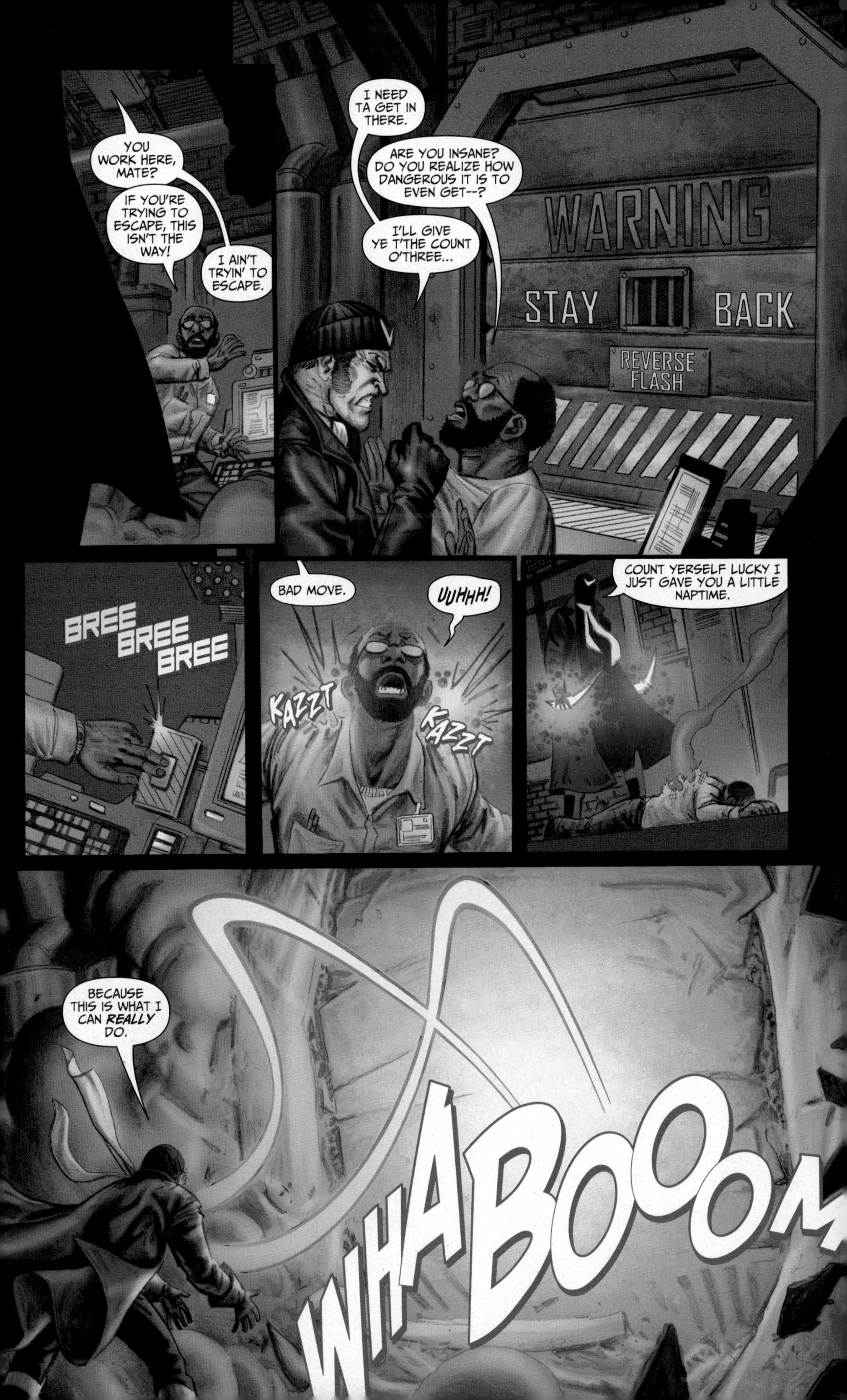
YOU WORK HERE, MATE?
IF YOU'RE TRYING TO ESCAPE, THIS ISN'T THE WAY!
I AIN'T TRYIN' TO ESCAPE.
I NEED TA GET IN THERE.
ARE YOU INSANE? DO YOU REALIZE HOW DANGEROUS IT IS TO EVEN GET--?
I'LL GIVE YE T'THE COUNT O'THREE...
WARNING
STAY BACK
REVERSE FLASH
BREE BREE BREE
BAD MOVE.
UUHHH!
KAZZT
KAZZT
COUNT YERSELF LUCKY I JUST GAVE YOU A LITTLE NAPTIME.
BECAUSE THIS IS WHAT I CAN REALLY DO.
WHABOOOOM

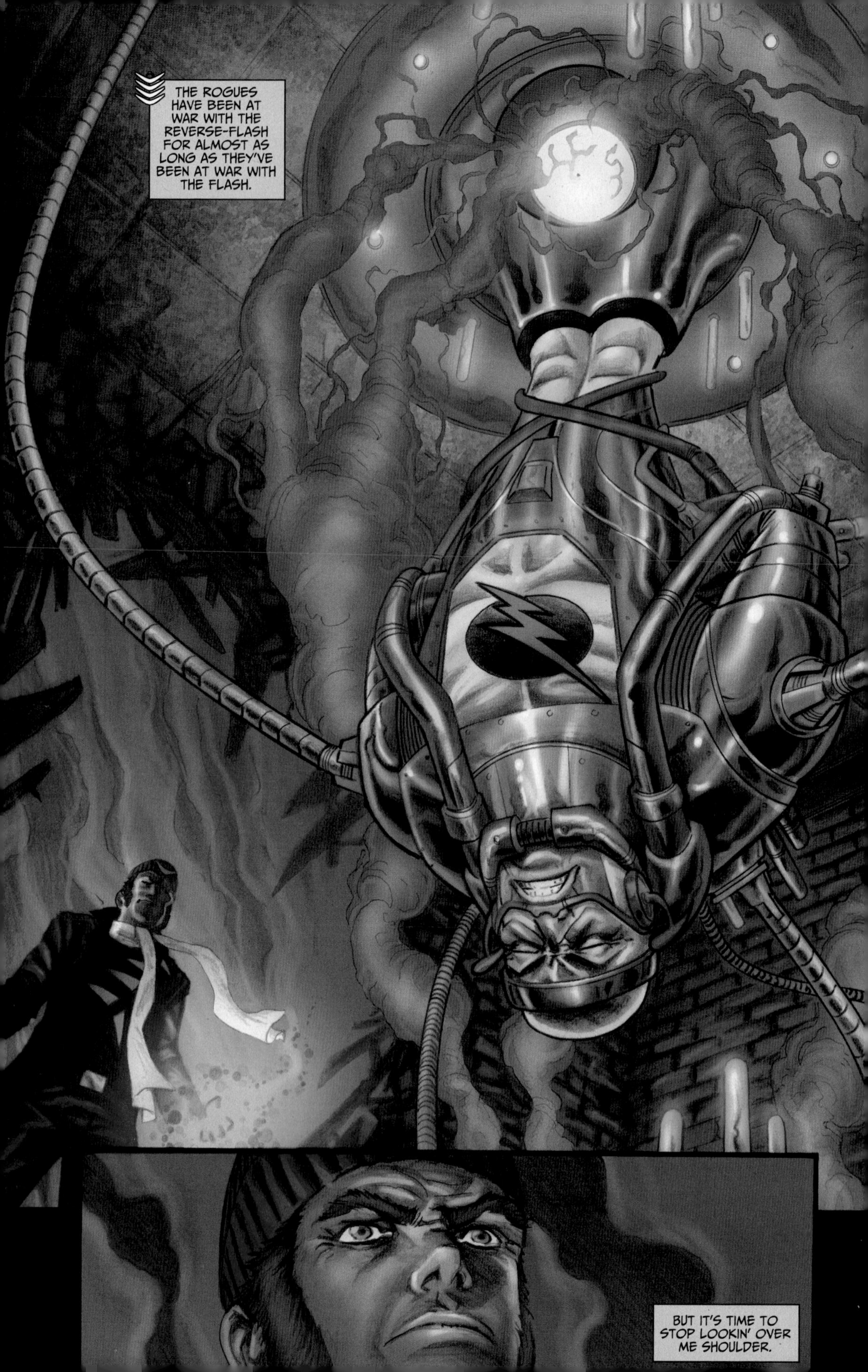
THE ROGUES HAVE BEEN AT WAR WITH THE REVERSE-FLASH FOR ALMOST AS LONG AS THEY'VE BEEN AT WAR WITH THE FLASH.
BUT IT'S TIME TO STOP LOOKIN' OVER ME SHOULDER.

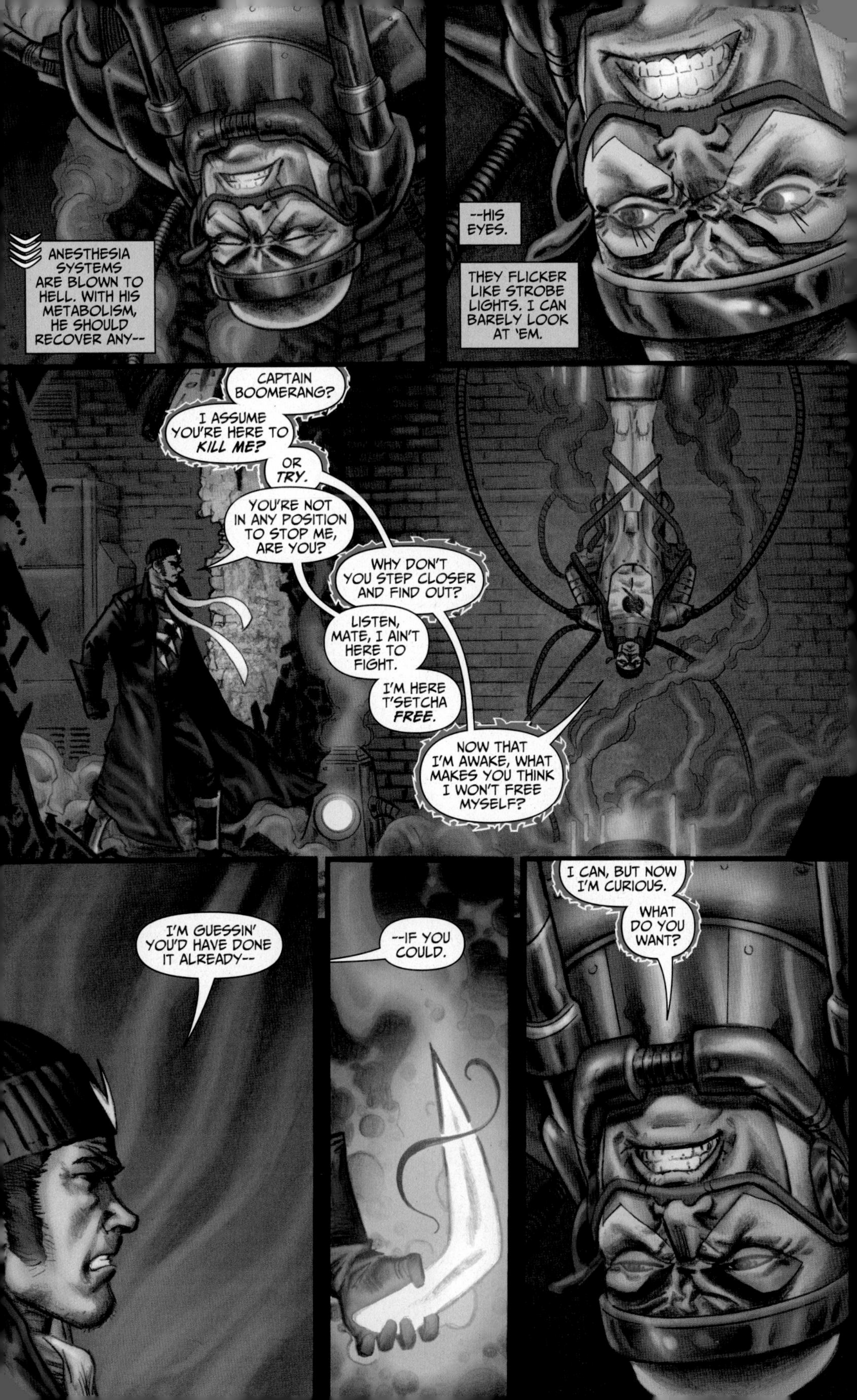
ANESTHESIA SYSTEMS ARE BLOWN TO HELL. WITH HIS METABOLISM, HE SHOULD RECOVER ANY--
--HIS EYES.
THEY FLICKER LIKE STROBE LIGHTS. I CAN BARELY LOOK AT 'EM.
CAPTAIN BOOMERANG?
I ASSUME YOU'RE HERE TO KILL ME?
OR TRY.
YOU'RE NOT IN ANY POSITION TO STOP ME, ARE YOU?
WHY DON'T YOU STEP CLOSER AND FIND OUT?
LISTEN, MATE, I AIN'T HERE TO FIGHT.
I'M HERE T'SETCHA FREE.
NOW THAT I'M AWAKE, WHAT MAKES YOU THINK I WON'T FREE MYSELF?
I'M GUESSIN' YOU'D HAVE DONE IT ALREADY--
--IF YOU COULD.
I CAN, BUT NOW I'M CURIOUS.
WHAT DO YOU WANT?

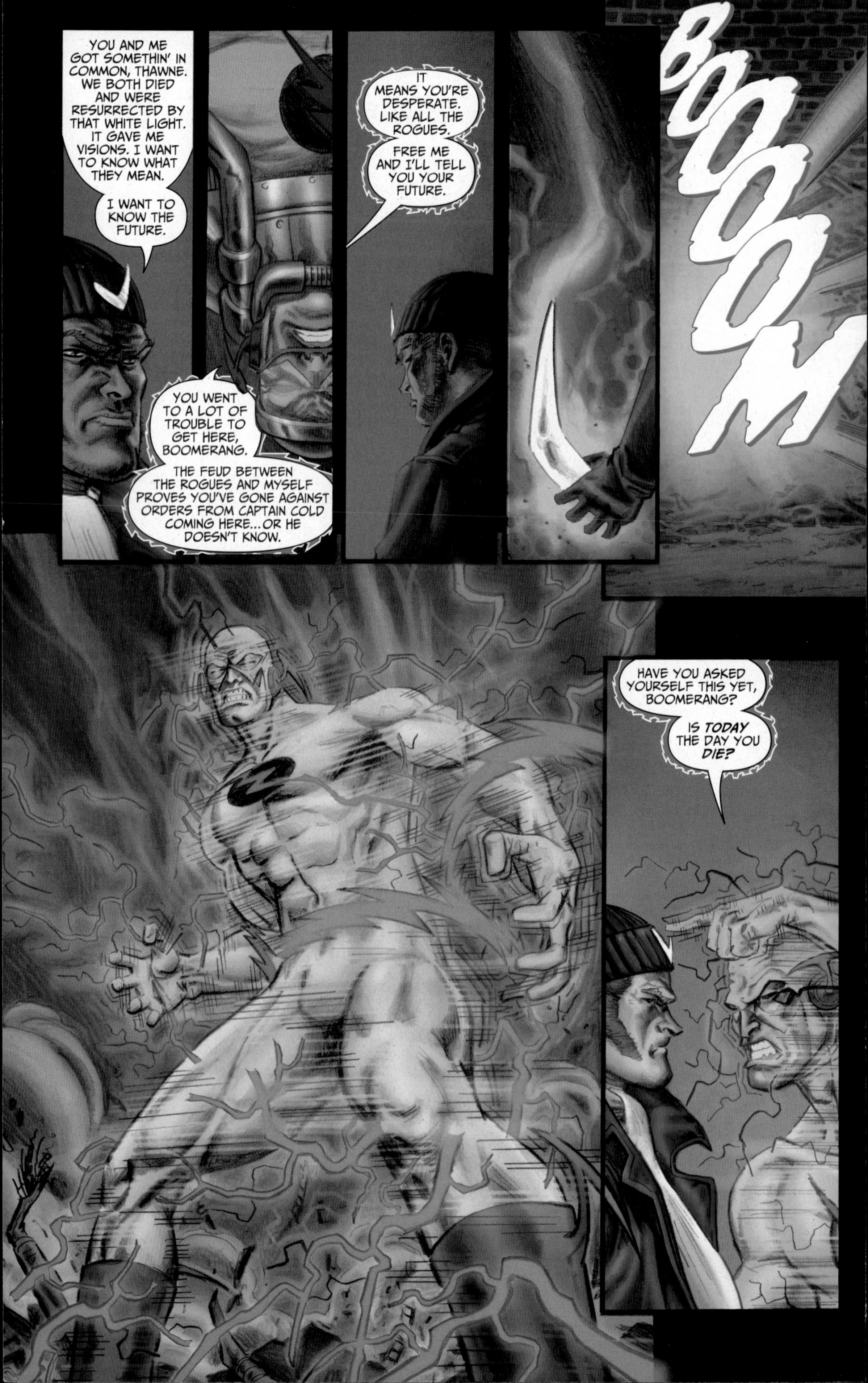
YOU AND ME GOT SOMETHIN' IN COMMON, THAWNE. WE BOTH DIED AND WERE RESURRECTED BY THAT WHITE LIGHT. IT GAVE ME VISIONS. I WANT TO KNOW WHAT THEY MEAN.
I WANT TO KNOW THE FUTURE.
YOU WENT TO A LOT OF TROUBLE TO GET HERE, BOOMERANG.
THE FEUD BETWEEN THE ROGUES AND MYSELF PROVES YOU'VE GONE AGAINST ORDERS FROM CAPTAIN COLD COMING HERE...OR HE DOESN'T KNOW.
IT MEANS YOU'RE DESPERATE. LIKE ALL THE ROGUES.
FREE ME AND I'LL TELL YOU YOUR FUTURE.
BOOOOOM
HAVE YOU ASKED YOURSELF THIS YET, BOOMERANG?
IS *TODAY* THE DAY YOU *DIE?*

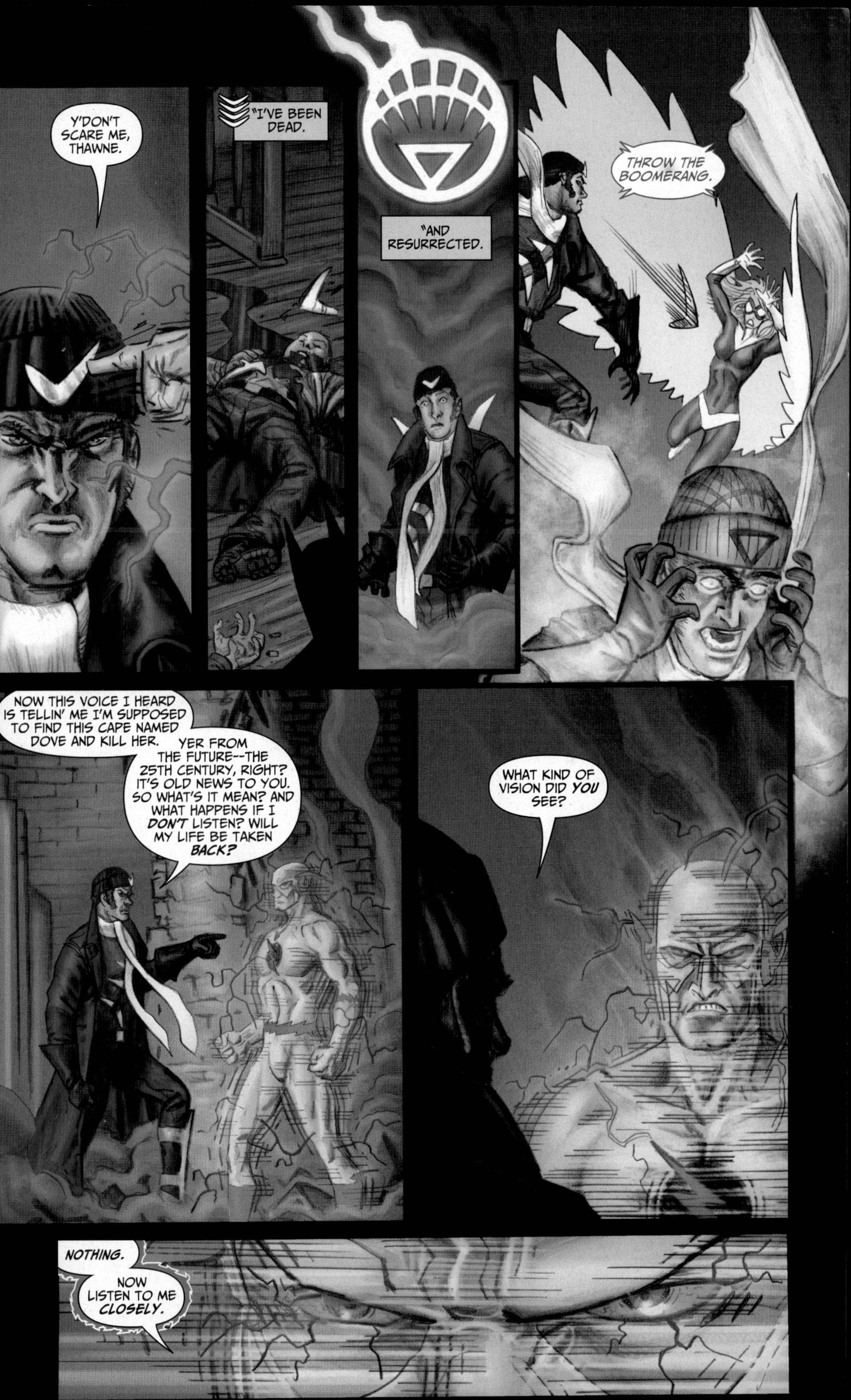
Y'DON'T SCARE ME, THAWNE.
"I'VE BEEN DEAD.
"AND RESURRECTED.
THROW THE BOOMERANG.
NOW THIS VOICE I HEARD IS TELLIN' ME I'M SUPPOSED TO FIND THIS CAPE NAMED DOVE AND KILL HER.
YER FROM THE FUTURE--THE 25TH CENTURY, RIGHT? IT'S OLD NEWS TO YOU. SO WHAT'S IT MEAN? AND WHAT HAPPENS IF I DON'T LISTEN? WILL MY LIFE BE TAKEN BACK?
WHAT KIND OF VISION DID YOU SEE?
NOTHING.
NOW LISTEN TO ME CLOSELY.

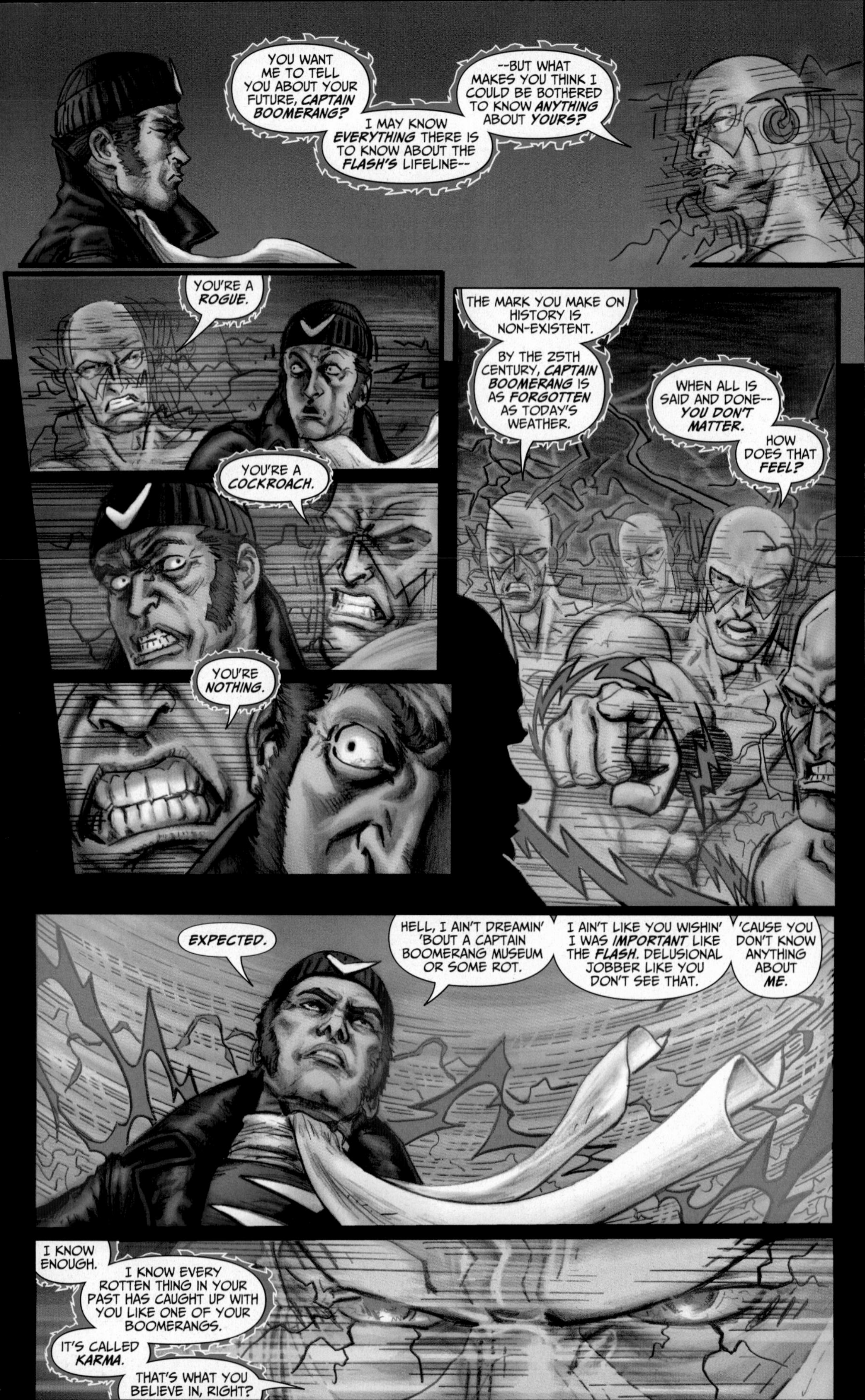
YOU WANT ME TO TELL YOU ABOUT YOUR FUTURE, CAPTAIN BOOMERANG?
I MAY KNOW EVERYTHING THERE IS TO KNOW ABOUT THE FLASH'S LIFELINE--
--BUT WHAT MAKES YOU THINK I COULD BE BOTHERED TO KNOW ANYTHING ABOUT YOURS?
YOU'RE A ROGUE.
YOU'RE A COCKROACH.
YOU'RE NOTHING.
THE MARK YOU MAKE ON HISTORY IS NON-EXISTENT.
BY THE 25TH CENTURY, CAPTAIN BOOMERANG IS AS FORGOTTEN AS TODAY'S WEATHER.
WHEN ALL IS SAID AND DONE-- YOU DON'T MATTER.
HOW DOES THAT FEEL?
EXPECTED.
HELL, I AIN'T DREAMIN' 'BOUT A CAPTAIN BOOMERANG MUSEUM OR SOME ROT.
I AIN'T LIKE YOU WISHIN' I WAS IMPORTANT LIKE THE FLASH. DELUSIONAL JOBBER LIKE YOU DON'T SEE THAT.
'CAUSE YOU DON'T KNOW ANYTHING ABOUT ME.
I KNOW ENOUGH.
I KNOW EVERY ROTTEN THING IN YOUR PAST HAS CAUGHT UP WITH YOU LIKE ONE OF YOUR BOOMERANGS.
IT'S CALLED KARMA.
THAT'S WHAT YOU BELIEVE IN, RIGHT?

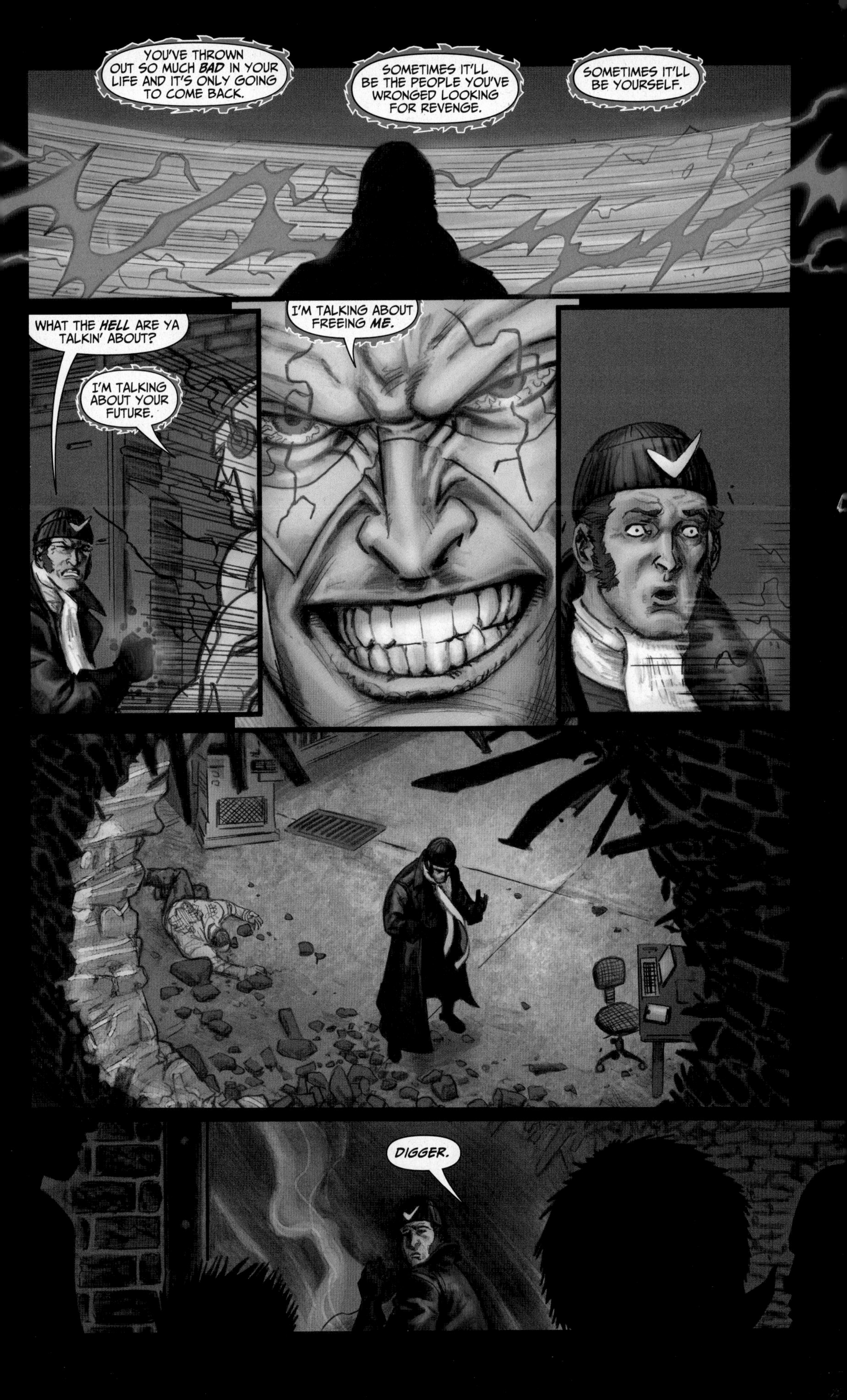
YOU'VE THROWN OUT SO MUCH BAD IN YOUR LIFE AND IT'S ONLY GOING TO COME BACK.
SOMETIMES IT'LL BE THE PEOPLE YOU'VE WRONGED LOOKING FOR REVENGE.
SOMETIMES IT'LL BE YOURSELF.
WHAT THE HELL ARE YA TALKIN' ABOUT?
I'M TALKING ABOUT YOUR FUTURE.
I'M TALKING ABOUT FREEING ME.
DIGGER.

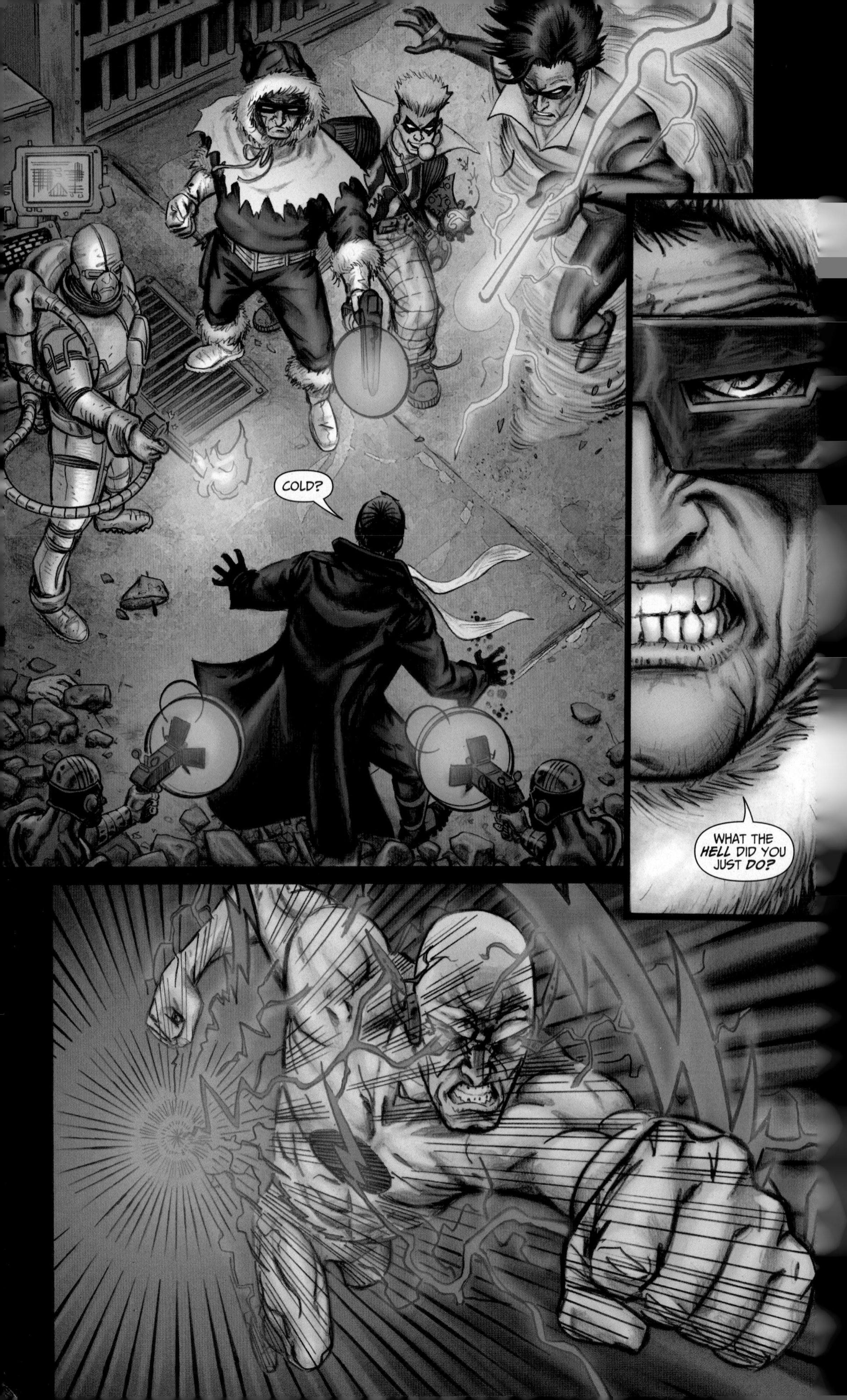
COLD?
WHAT THE HELL DID YOU JUST DO?

THE FLASH
Secret Files & Origins 2010

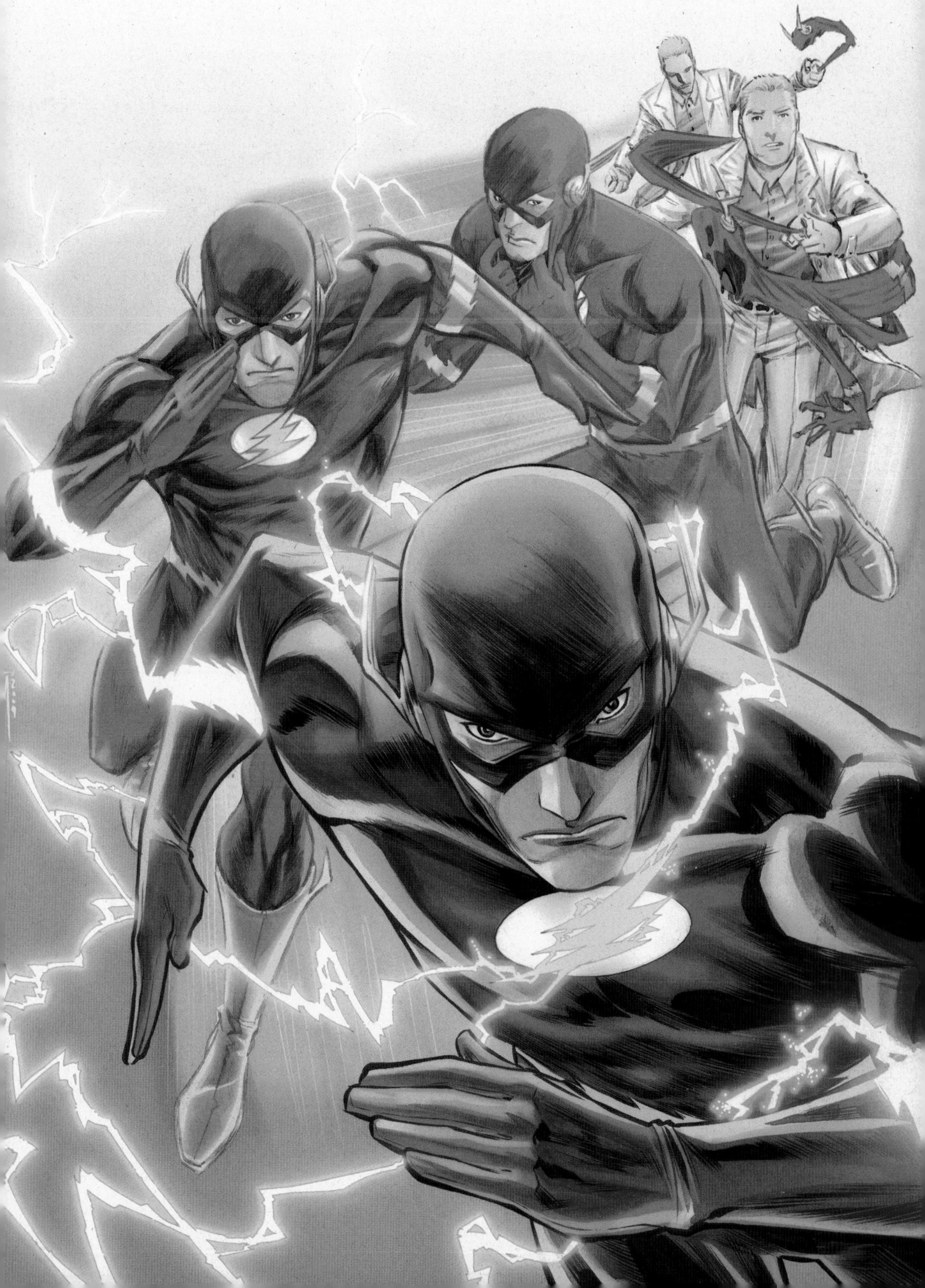

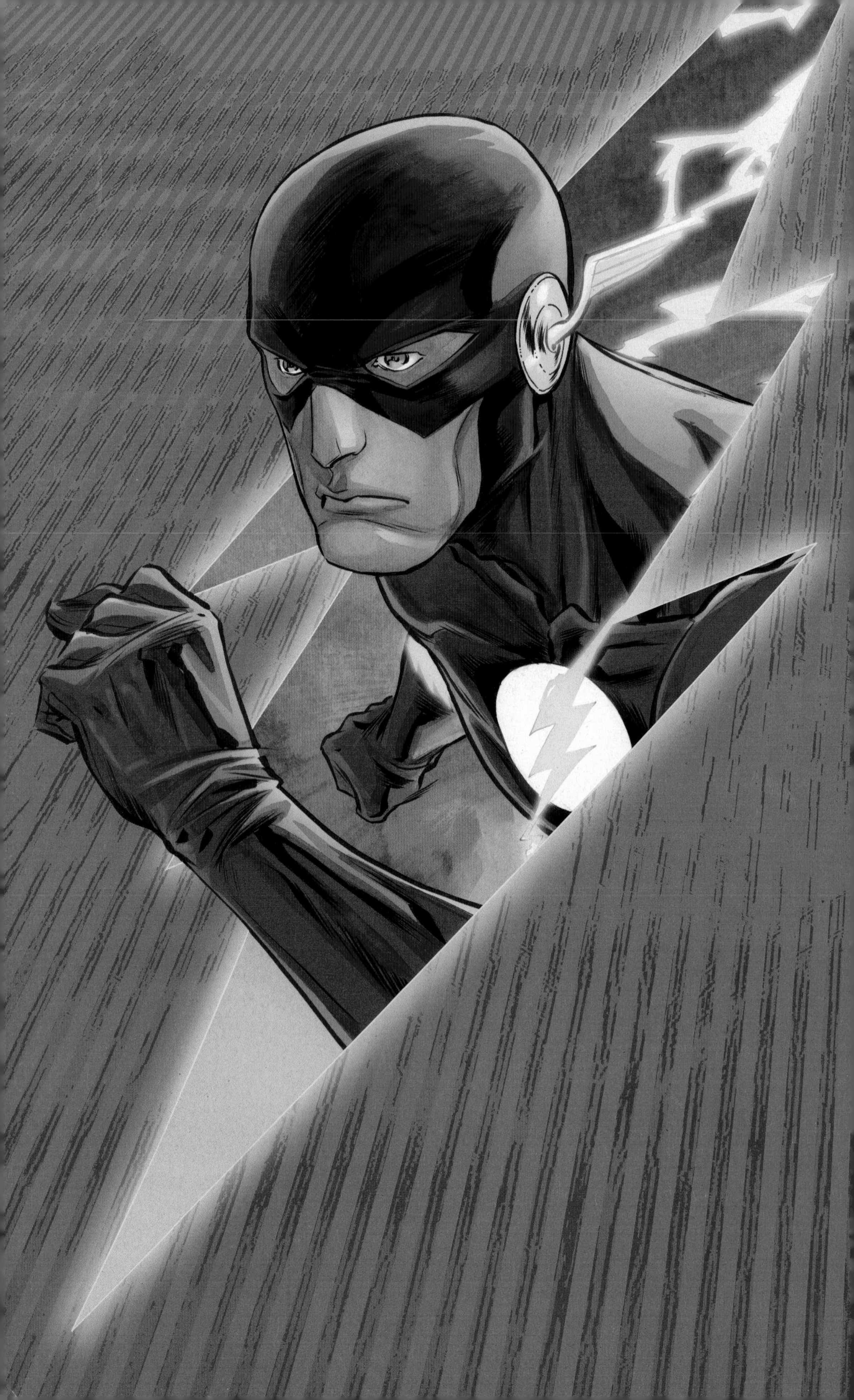

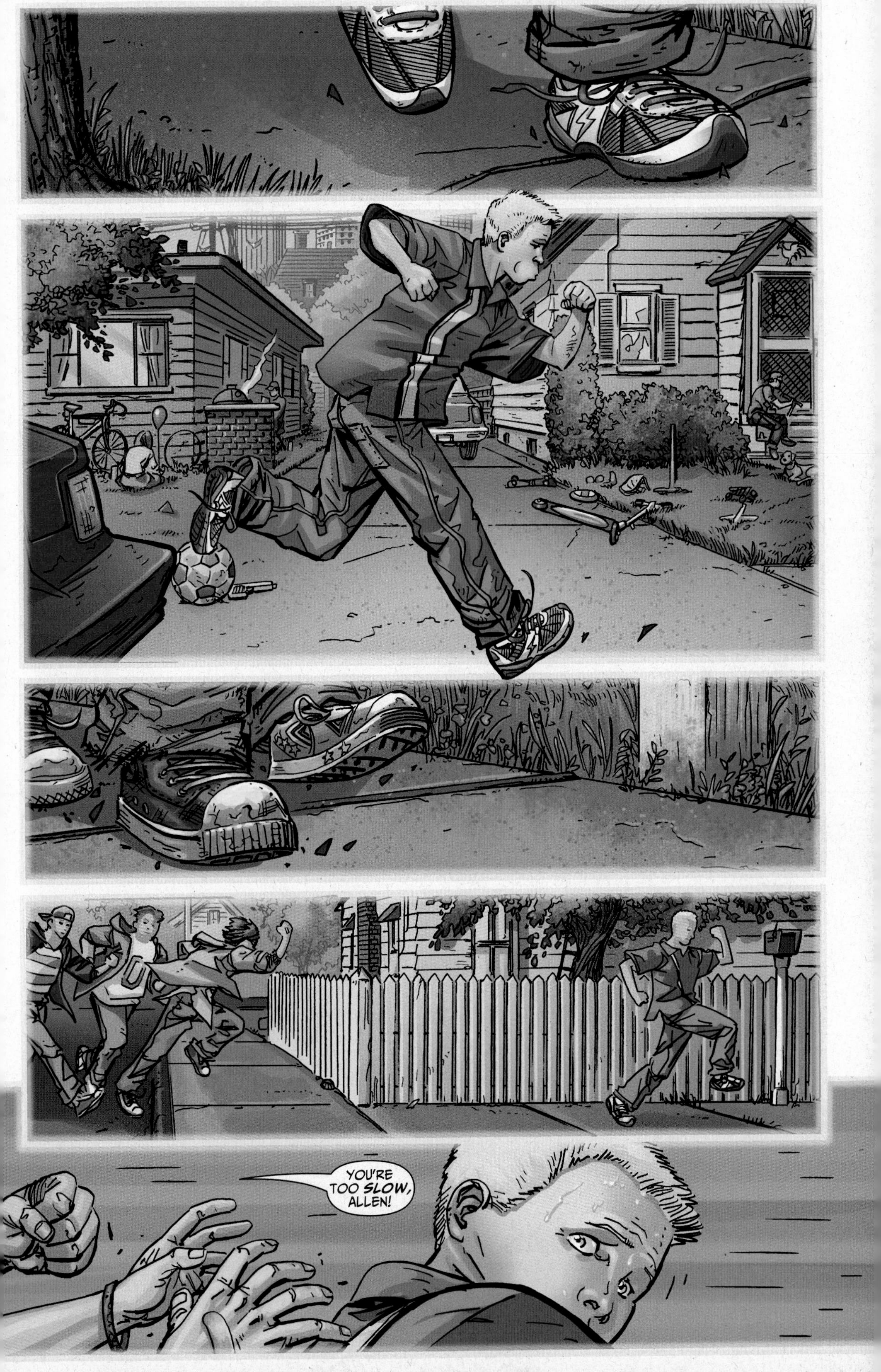
YOU'RE TOO SLOW, ALLEN!

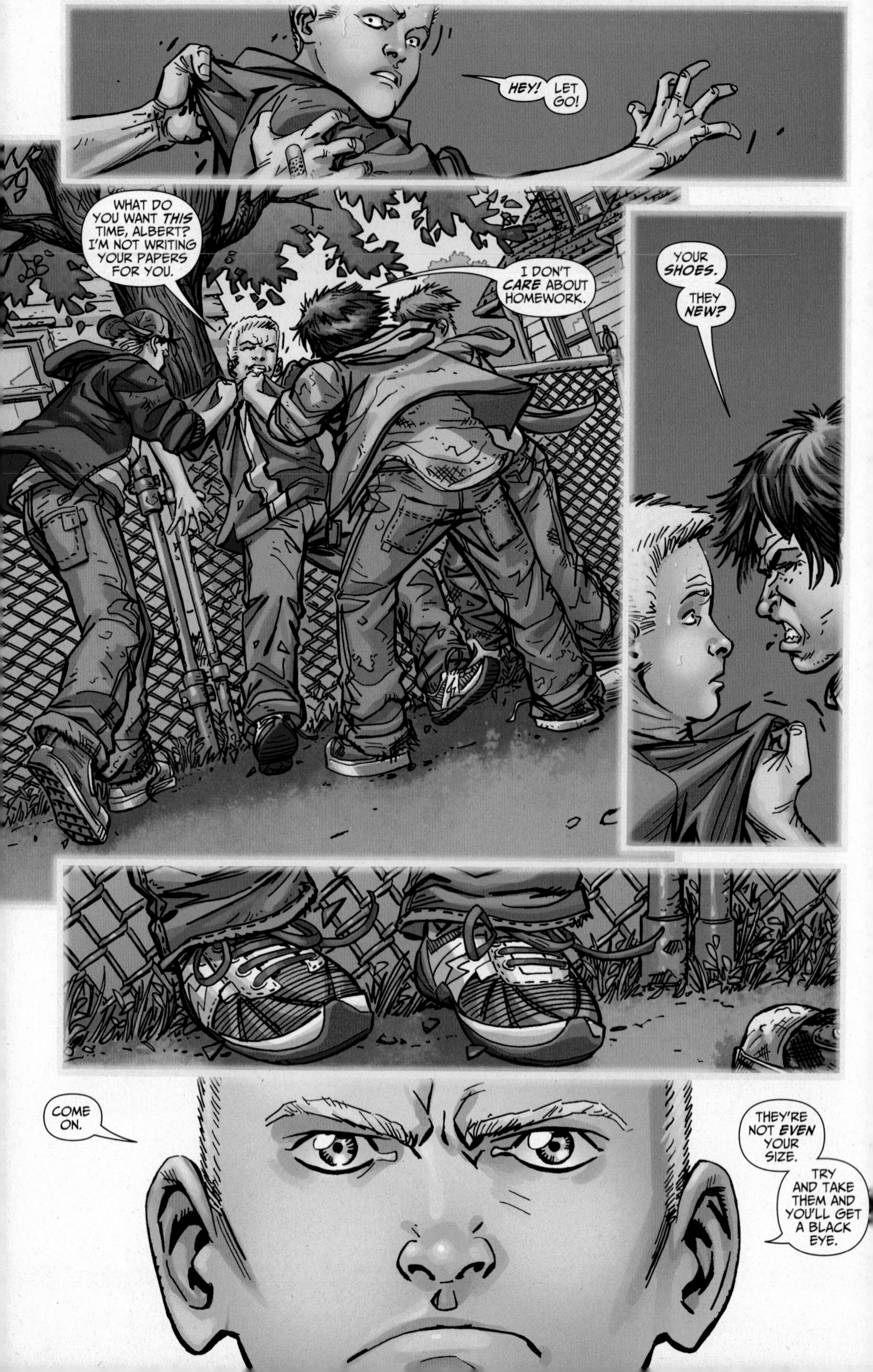
HEY! LET GO!
WHAT DO YOU WANT THIS TIME, ALBERT? I'M NOT WRITING YOUR PAPERS FOR YOU.
I DON'T CARE ABOUT HOMEWORK.
YOUR SHOES.
THEY NEW?
COME ON.
THEY'RE NOT EVEN YOUR SIZE.
TRY AND TAKE THEM AND YOU'LL GET A BLACK EYE.

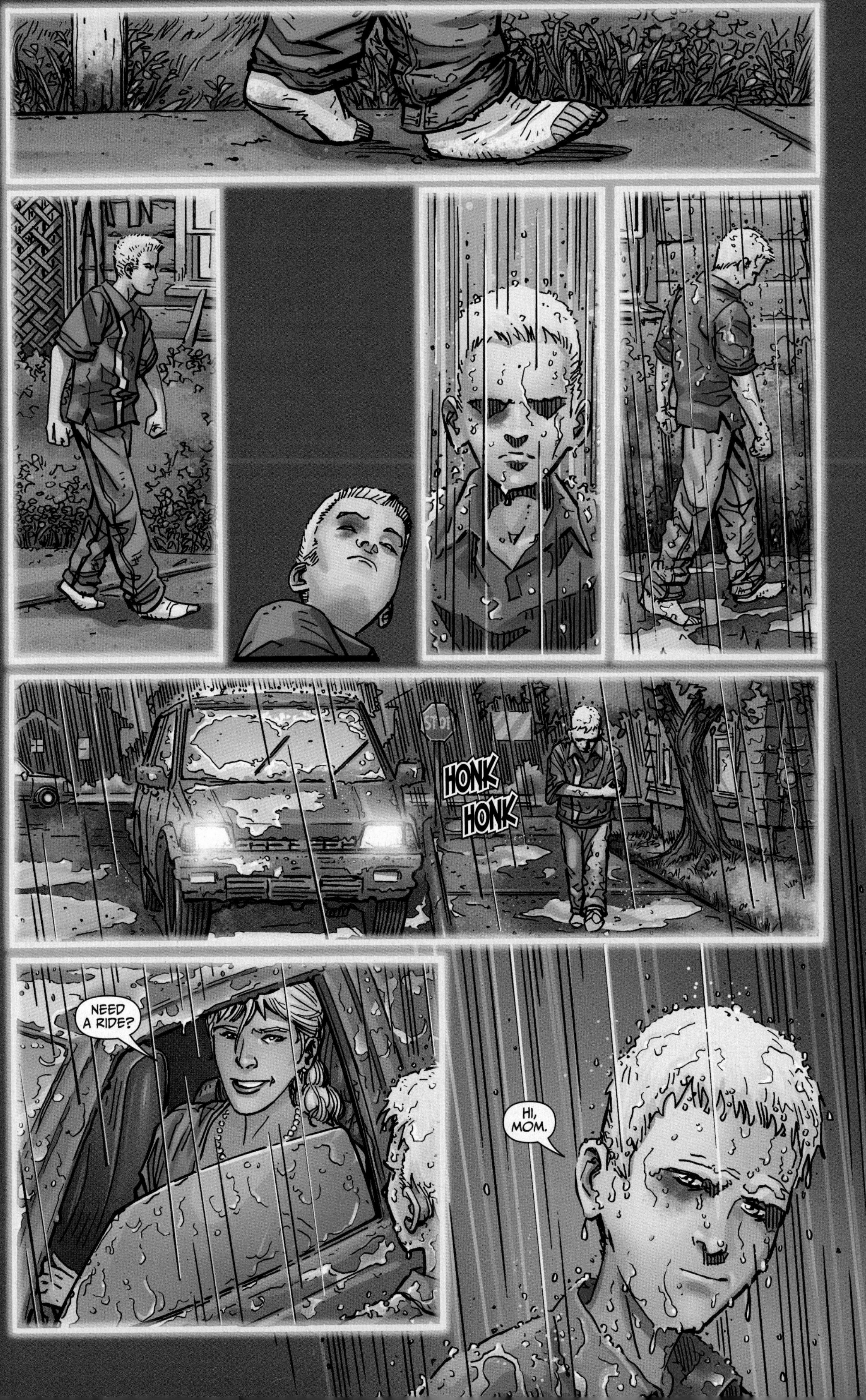

ST OP
HONK
HONK
NEED A RIDE?
HI, MOM.

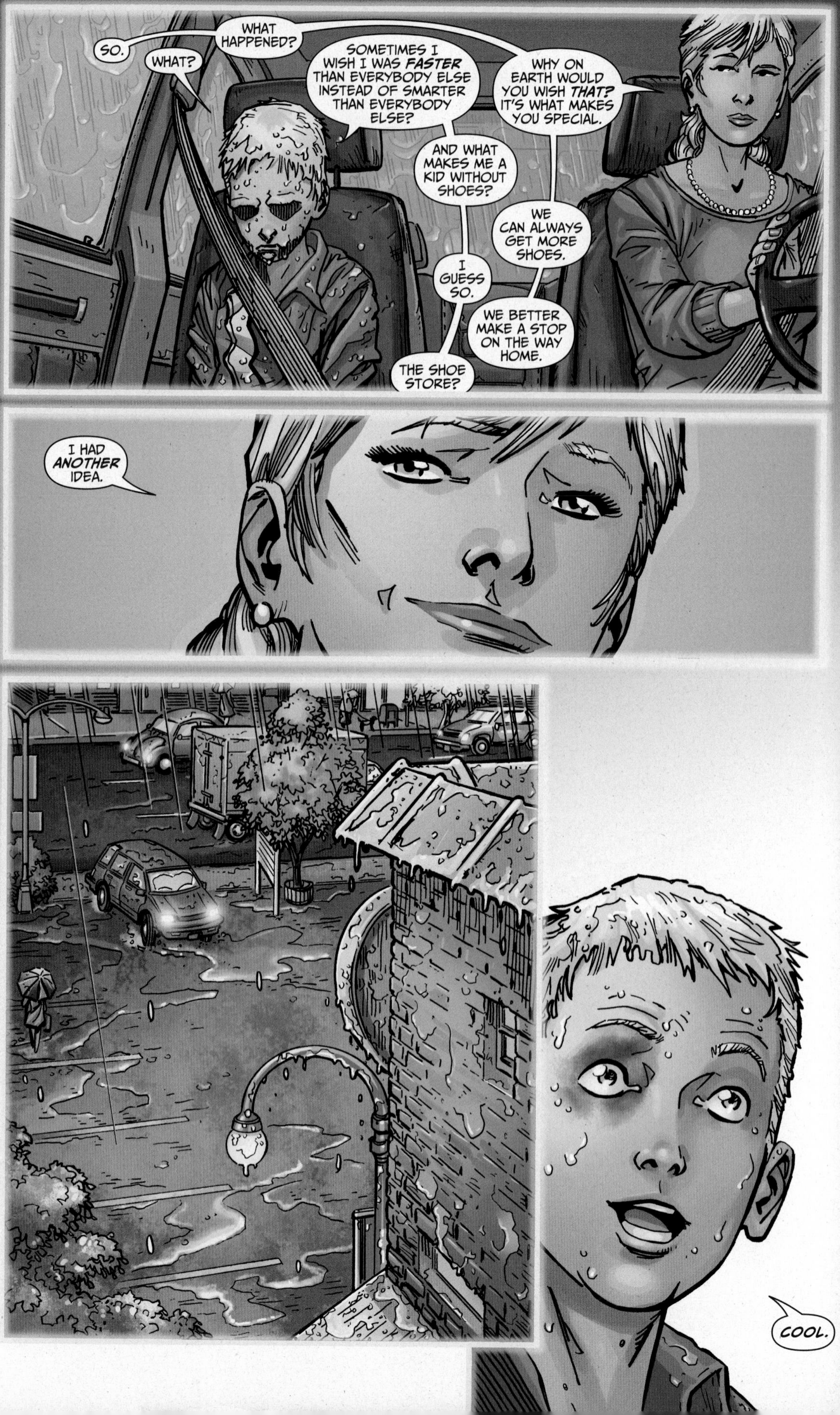
SO.
WHAT HAPPENED?
WHAT?
SOMETIMES I WISH I WAS FASTER THAN EVERYBODY ELSE INSTEAD OF SMARTER THAN EVERYBODY ELSE?
WHY ON EARTH WOULD YOU WISH THAT? IT'S WHAT MAKES YOU SPECIAL.
AND WHAT MAKES ME A KID WITHOUT SHOES?
WE CAN ALWAYS GET MORE SHOES.
I GUESS SO.
WE BETTER MAKE A STOP ON THE WAY HOME.
THE SHOE STORE?
I HAD ANOTHER IDEA.
COOL.

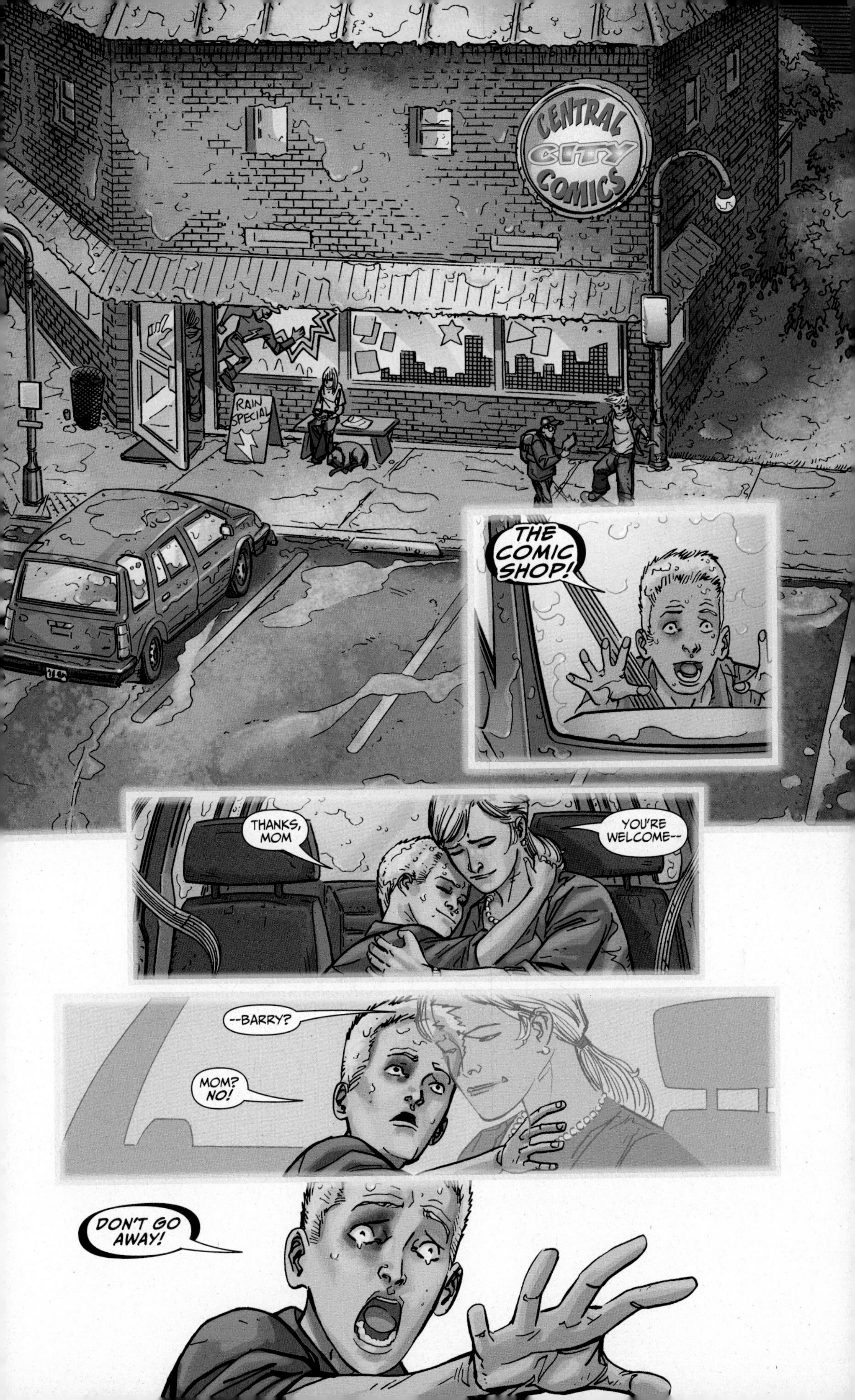
CENTRAL CITY COMICS
RAIN SPECIAL
THE COMIC SHOP!
THANKS, MOM
YOU'RE WELCOME--
--BARRY?
MOM? NO!
DON'T GO AWAY!

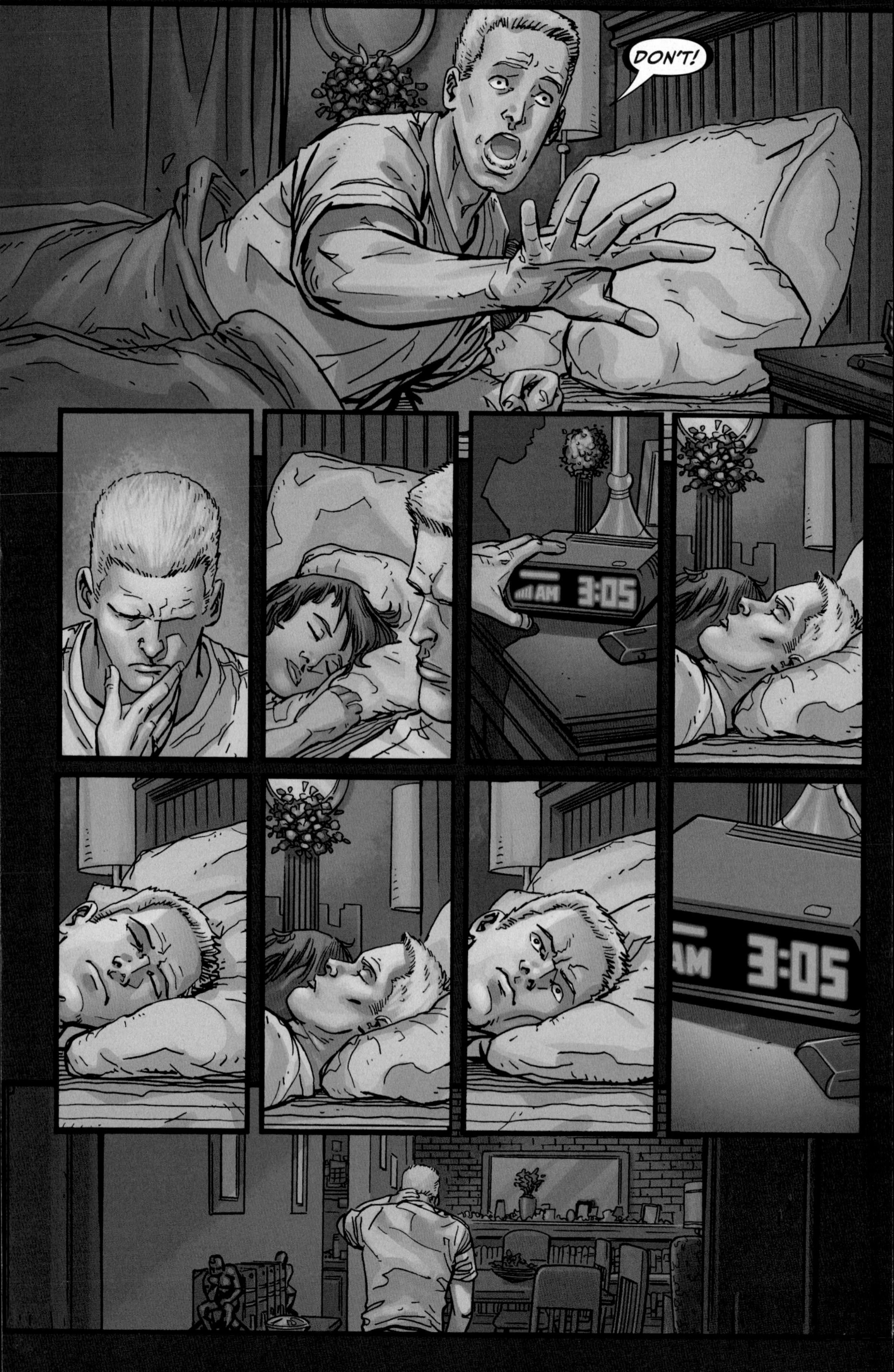
DON'T!
AM 3:05
AM 3:05

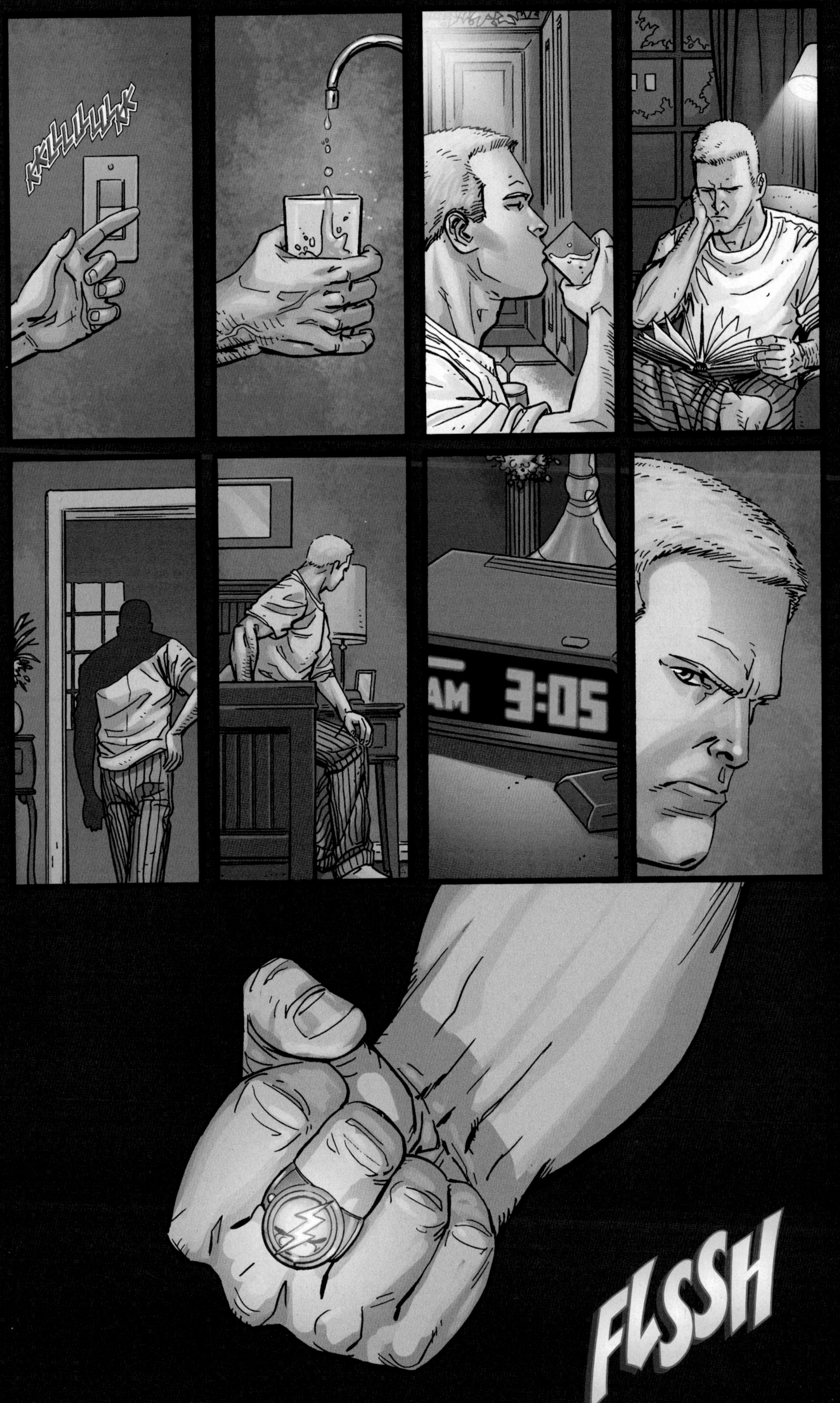
KLLLLLK
AM 3:05
FLSH

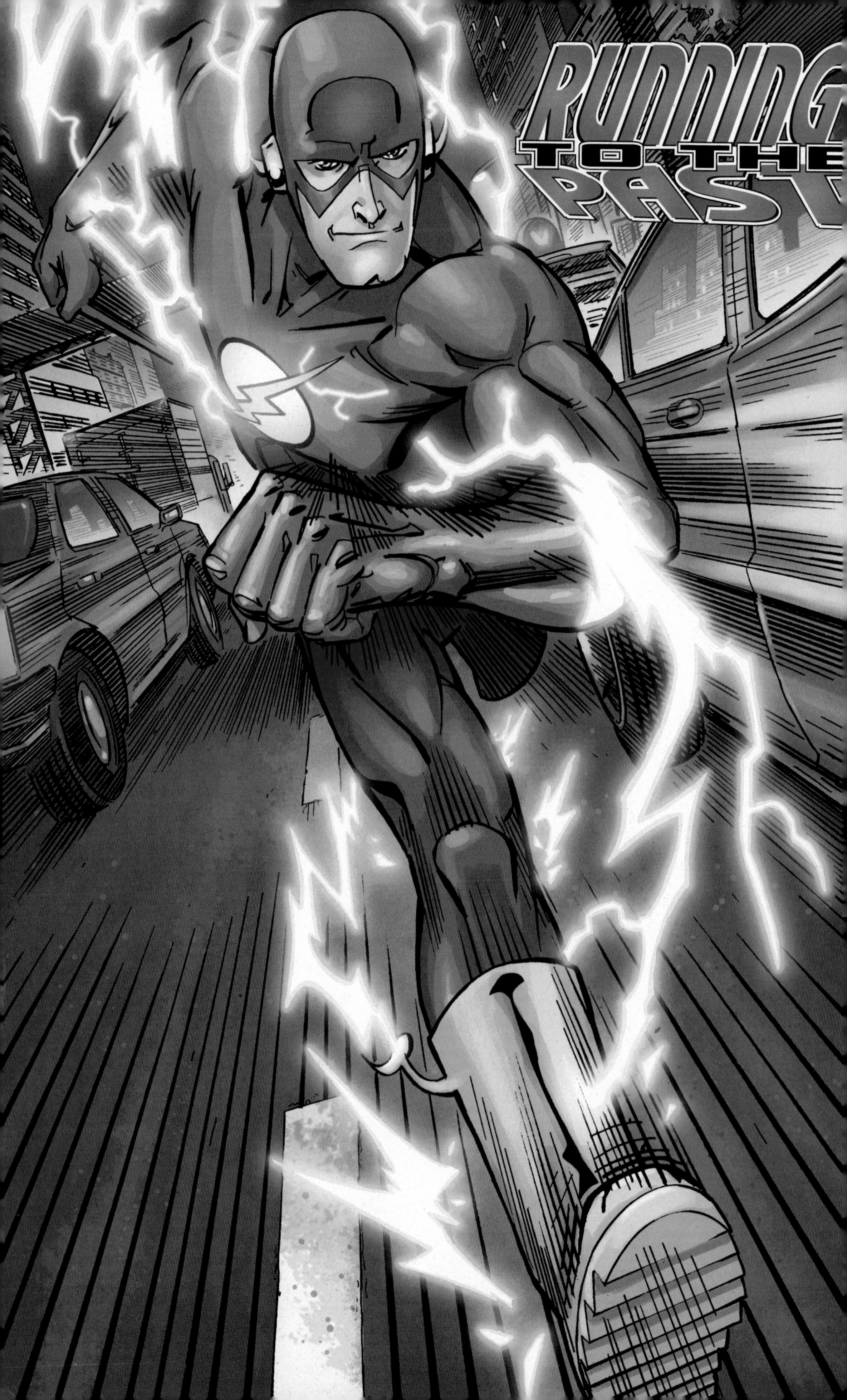
RUNNING
TO THE
PAST

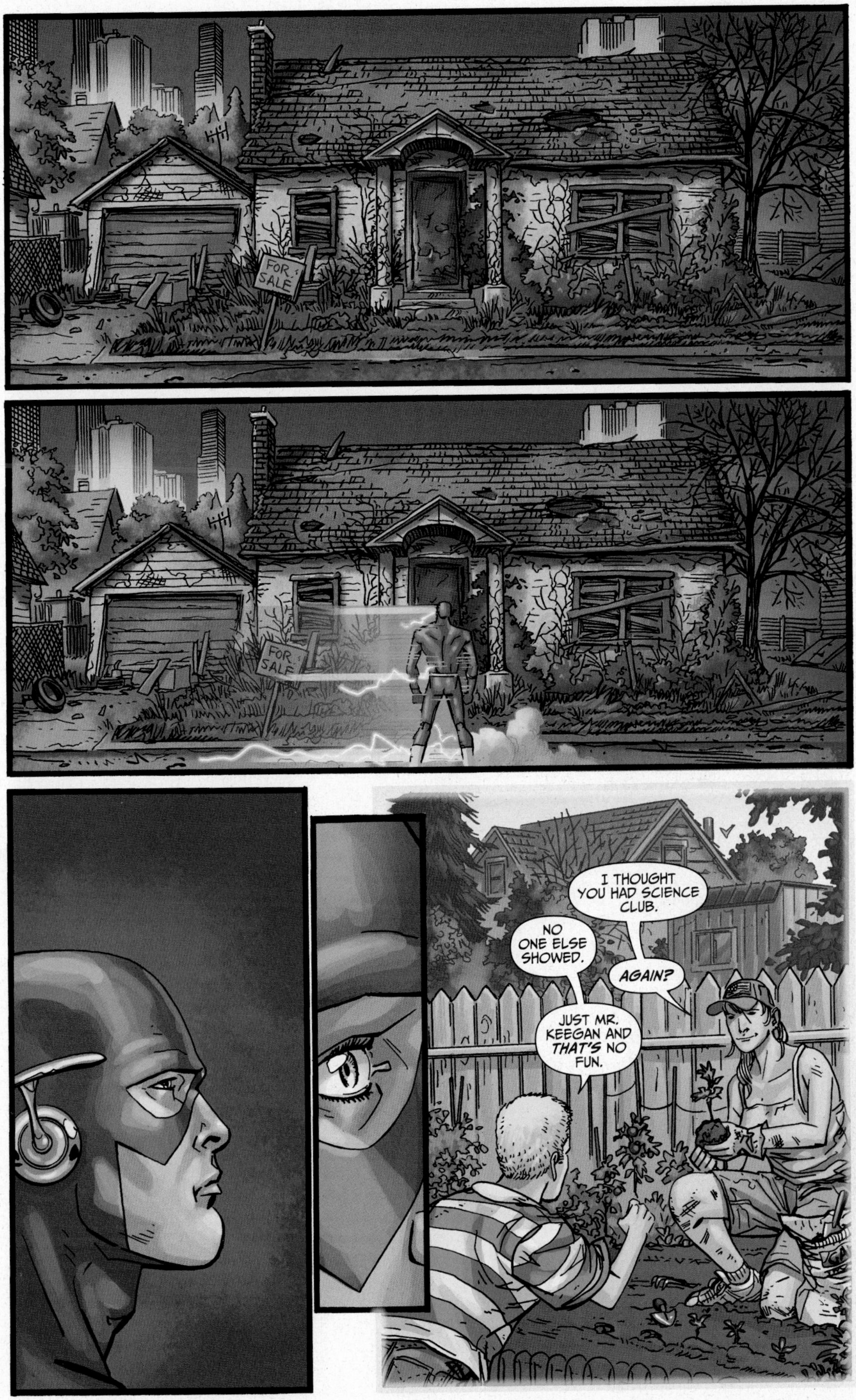
I THOUGHT YOU HAD SCIENCE CLUB.
NO ONE ELSE SHOWED.
AGAIN?
JUST MR. KEEGAN AND THAT'S NO FUN.
FOR SALE

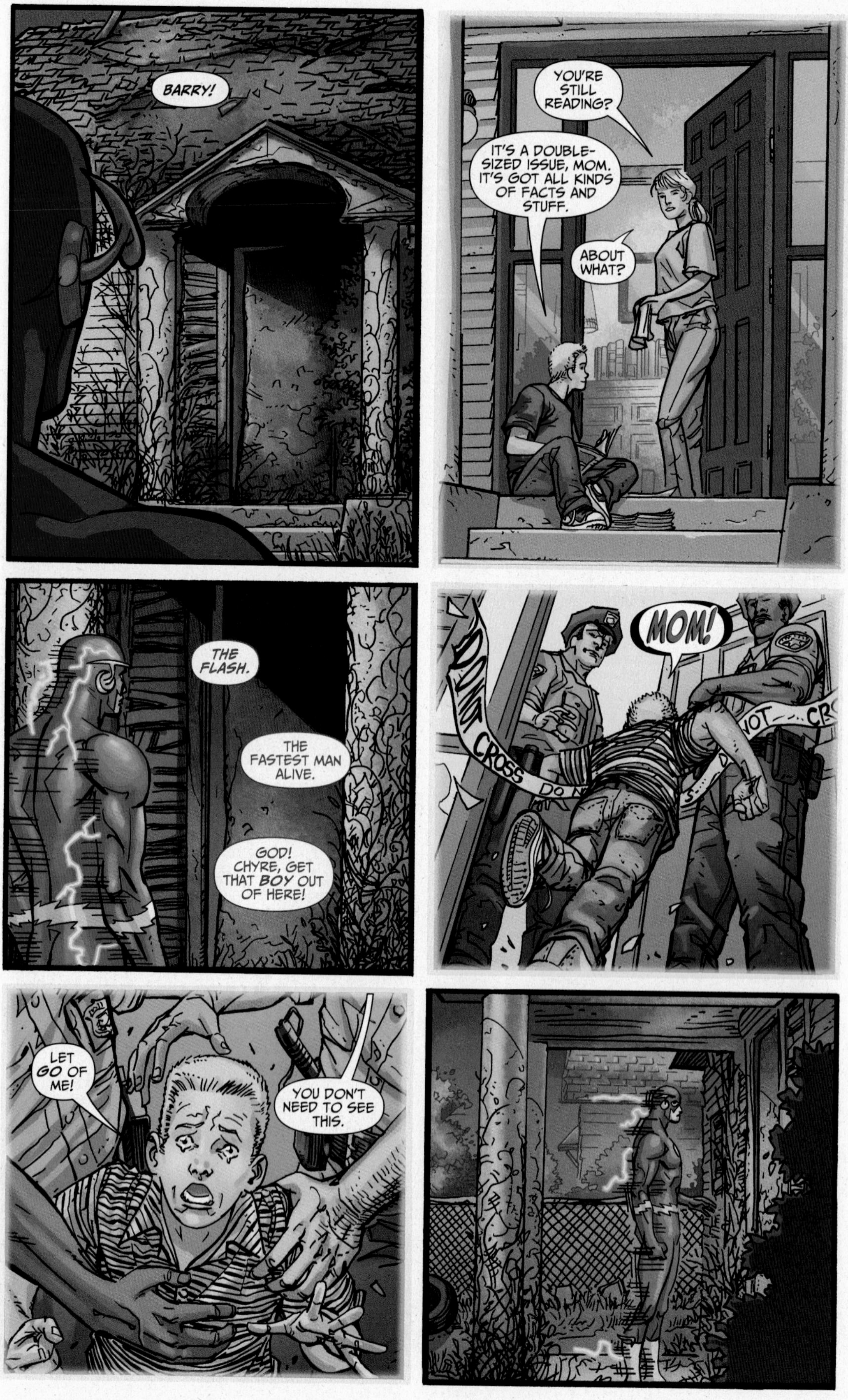
BARRY!
YOU'RE STILL READING?
IT'S A DOUBLE-SIZED ISSUE, MOM. IT'S GOT ALL KINDS OF FACTS AND STUFF.
ABOUT WHAT?
THE FLASH.
THE FASTEST MAN ALIVE.
GOD! CHYRE, GET THAT BOY OUT OF HERE!
MOM!
DO NOT CROSS
LET GO OF ME!
YOU DON'T NEED TO SEE THIS.

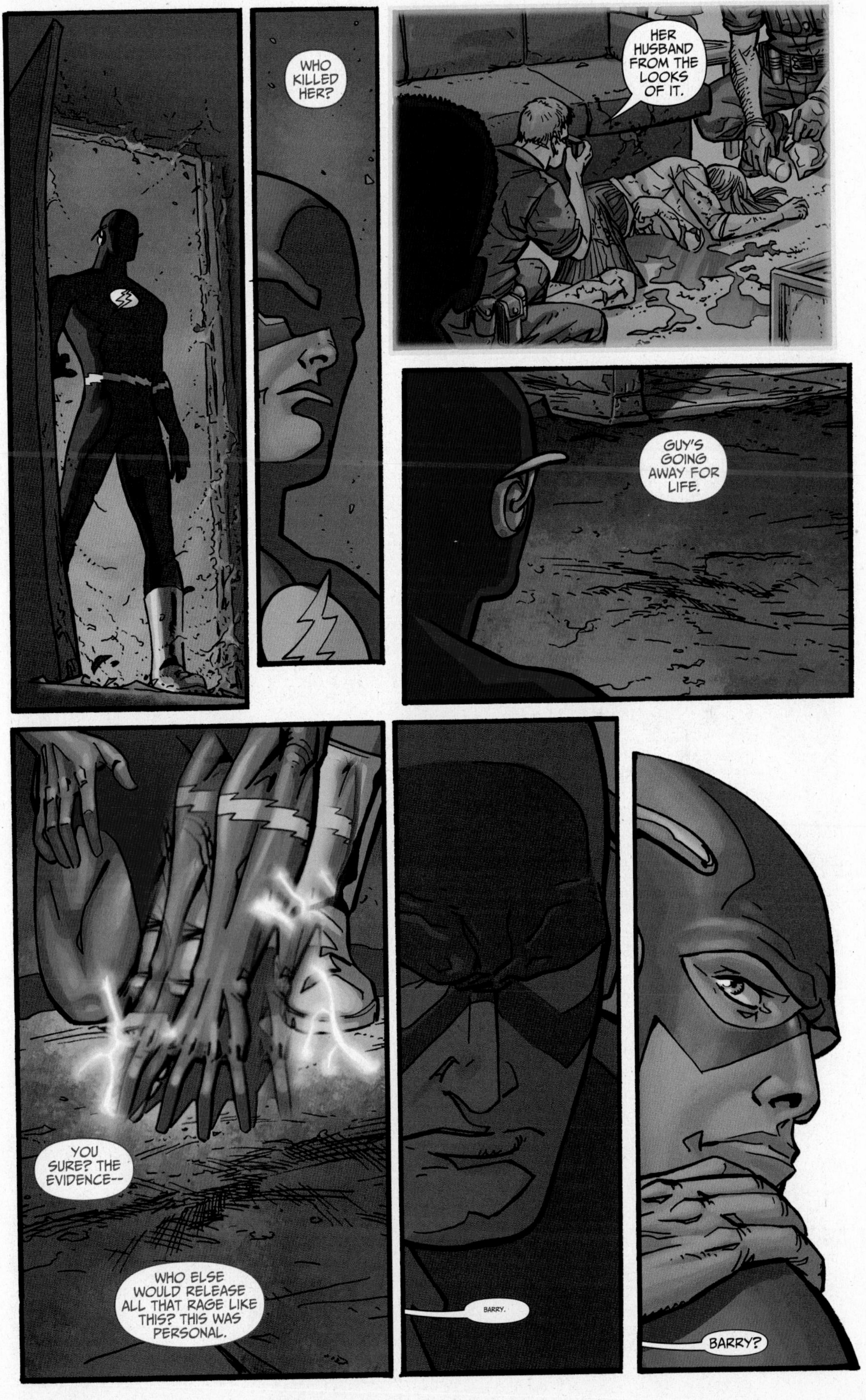
WHO KILLED HER?
HER HUSBAND FROM THE LOOKS OF IT.
GUY'S GOING AWAY FOR LIFE.
YOU SURE? THE EVIDENCE--
WHO ELSE WOULD RELEASE ALL THAT RAGE LIKE THIS? THIS WAS PERSONAL.
BARRY.
BARRY?

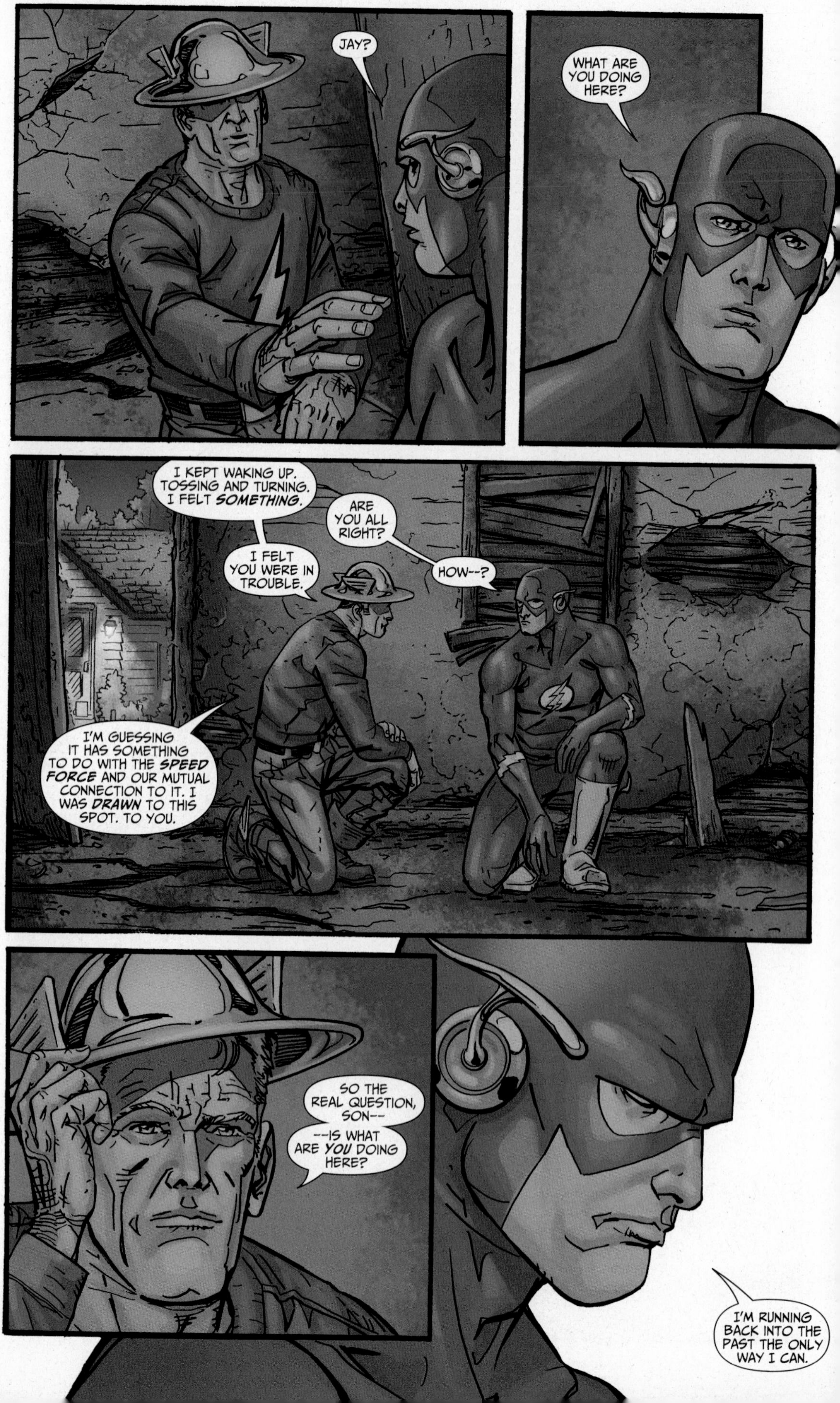

JAY?
WHAT ARE YOU DOING HERE?
I KEPT WAKING UP. TOSSING AND TURNING. I FELT SOMETHING.
I FELT YOU WERE IN TROUBLE.
ARE YOU ALL RIGHT?
HOW--?
I'M GUESSING IT HAS SOMETHING TO DO WITH THE SPEED FORCE AND OUR MUTUAL CONNECTION TO IT. I WAS DRAWN TO THIS SPOT. TO YOU.
SO THE REAL QUESTION, SON--
--IS WHAT ARE YOU DOING HERE?
I'M RUNNING BACK INTO THE PAST THE ONLY WAY I CAN.

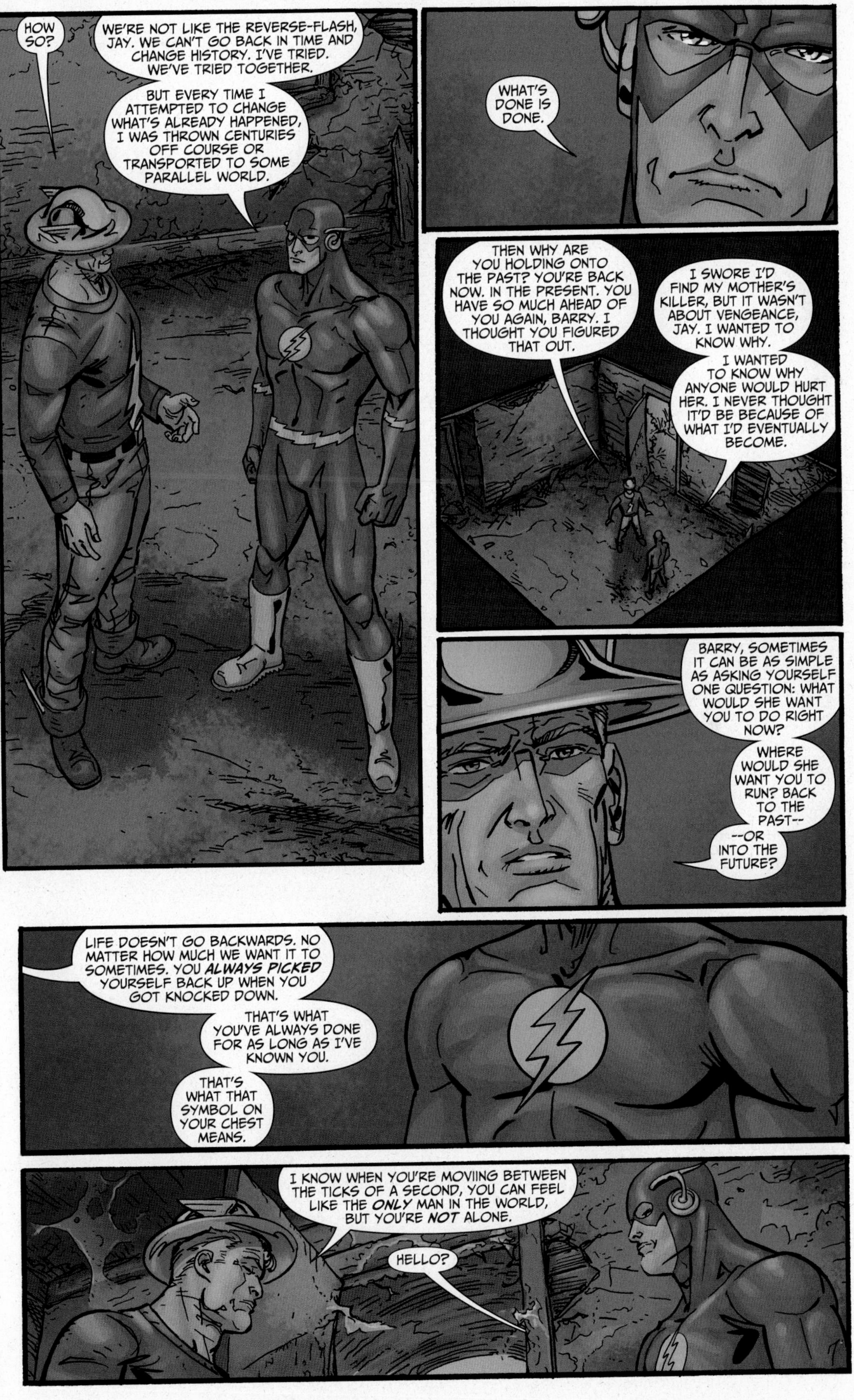
HOW SO?
WE'RE NOT LIKE THE REVERSE-FLASH, JAY. WE CAN'T GO BACK IN TIME AND CHANGE HISTORY. I'VE TRIED. WE'VE TRIED TOGETHER.
BUT EVERY TIME I ATTEMPTED TO CHANGE WHAT'S ALREADY HAPPENED, I WAS THROWN CENTURIES OFF COURSE OR TRANSPORTED TO SOME PARALLEL WORLD.
WHAT'S DONE IS DONE.
THEN WHY ARE YOU HOLDING ONTO THE PAST? YOU'RE BACK NOW. IN THE PRESENT. YOU HAVE SO MUCH AHEAD OF YOU AGAIN, BARRY. I THOUGHT YOU FIGURED THAT OUT.
I SWORE I'D FIND MY MOTHER'S KILLER, BUT IT WASN'T ABOUT VENGEANCE, JAY. I WANTED TO KNOW WHY.
I WANTED TO KNOW WHY ANYONE WOULD HURT HER. I NEVER THOUGHT IT'D BE BECAUSE OF WHAT I'D EVENTUALLY BECOME.
BARRY, SOMETIMES IT CAN BE AS SIMPLE AS ASKING YOURSELF ONE QUESTION: WHAT WOULD SHE WANT YOU TO DO RIGHT NOW?
WHERE WOULD SHE WANT YOU TO RUN? BACK TO THE PAST--
--OR INTO THE FUTURE?
LIFE DOESN'T GO BACKWARDS. NO MATTER HOW MUCH WE WANT IT TO SOMETIMES. YOU ALWAYS PICKED YOURSELF BACK UP WHEN YOU GOT KNOCKED DOWN.
THAT'S WHAT YOU'VE ALWAYS DONE FOR AS LONG AS I'VE KNOWN YOU.
THAT'S WHAT THAT SYMBOL ON YOUR CHEST MEANS.
I KNOW WHEN YOU'RE MOVIING BETWEEN THE TICKS OF A SECOND, YOU CAN FEEL LIKE THE ONLY MAN IN THE WORLD, BUT YOU'RE NOT ALONE.
HELLO?

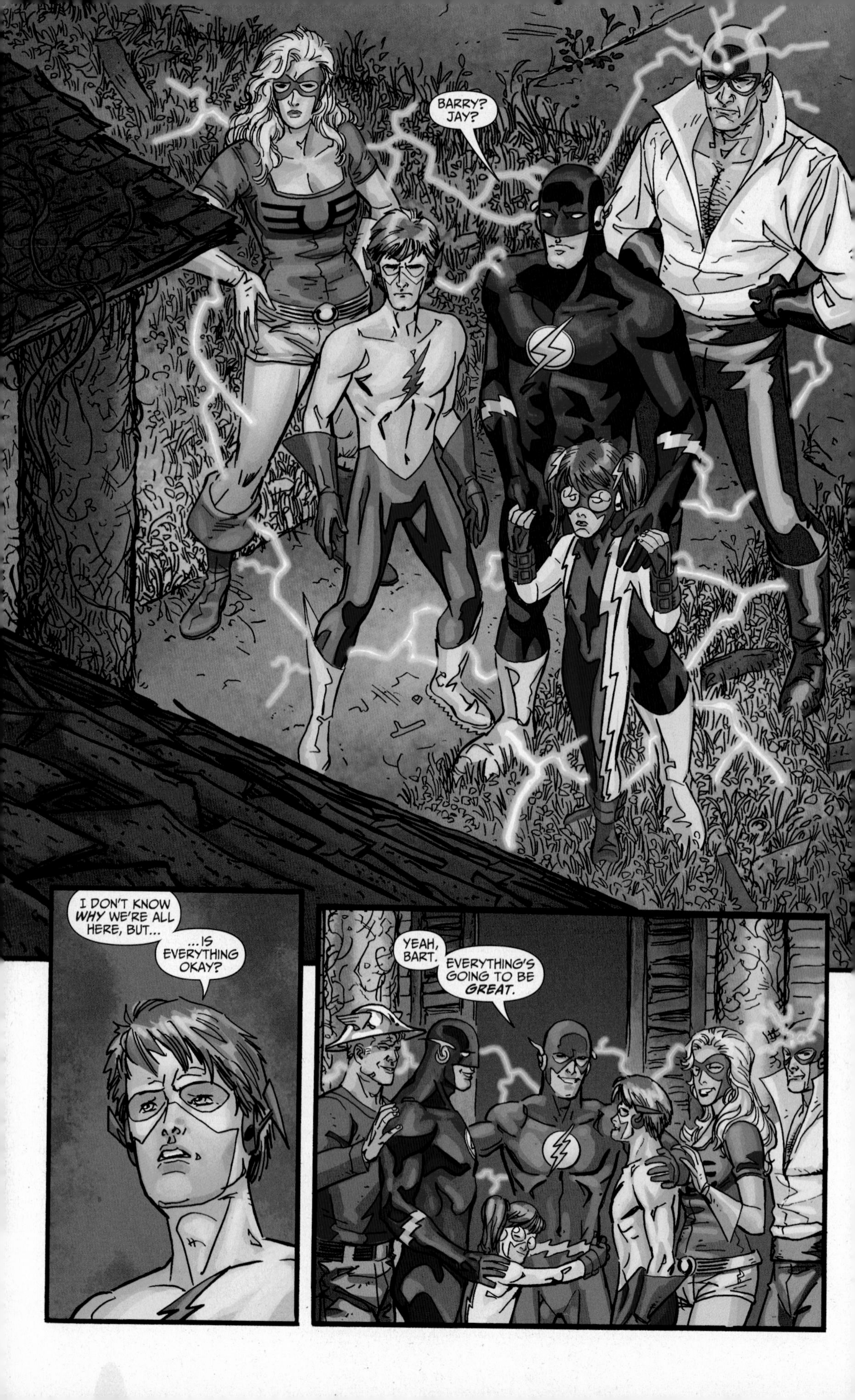
BARRY? JAY?
I DON'T KNOW *WHY* WE'RE ALL HERE, BUT...
...IS EVERYTHING OKAY?
YEAH, BART.
EVERYTHING'S GOING TO BE *GREAT*.

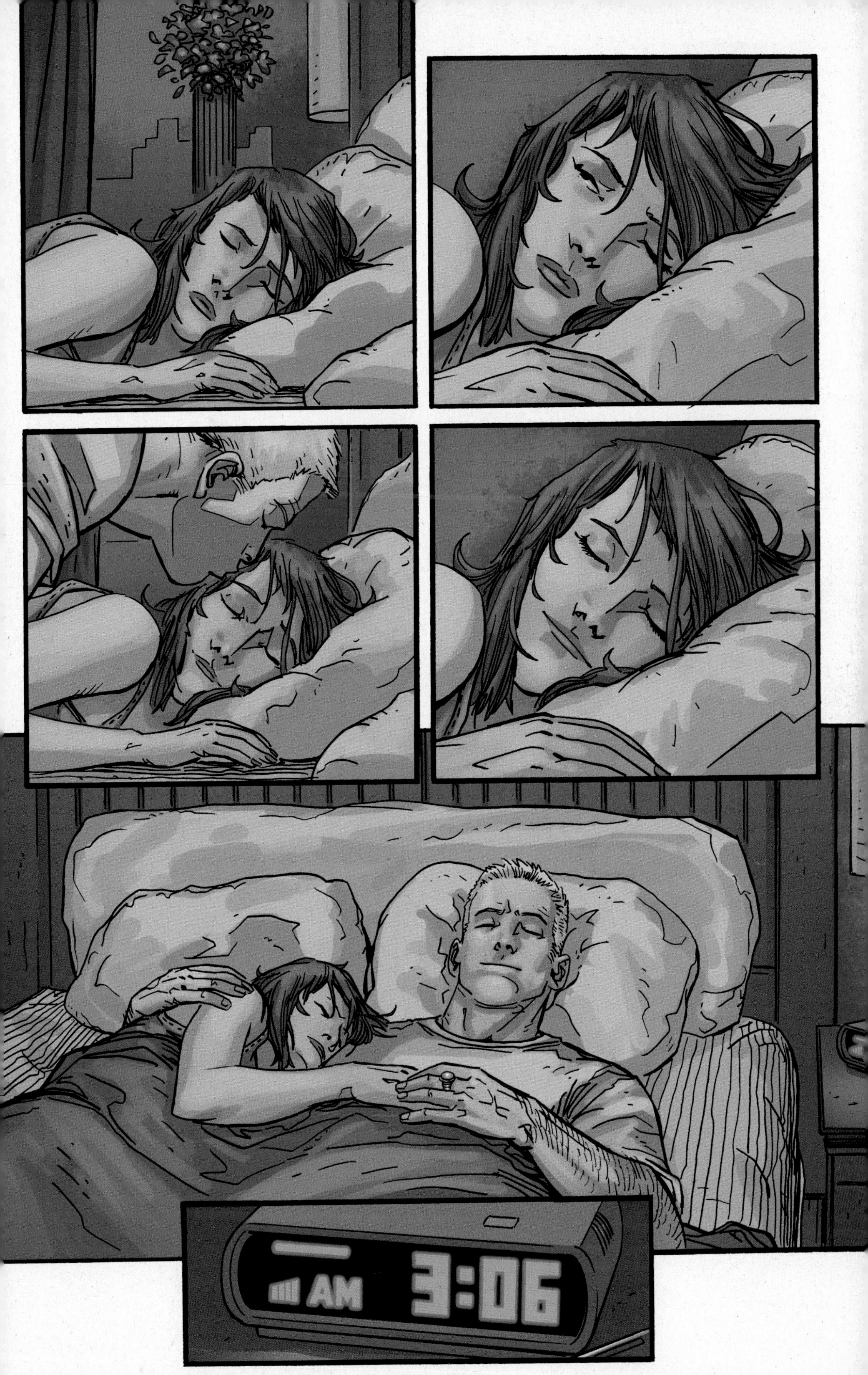
AM 3:06

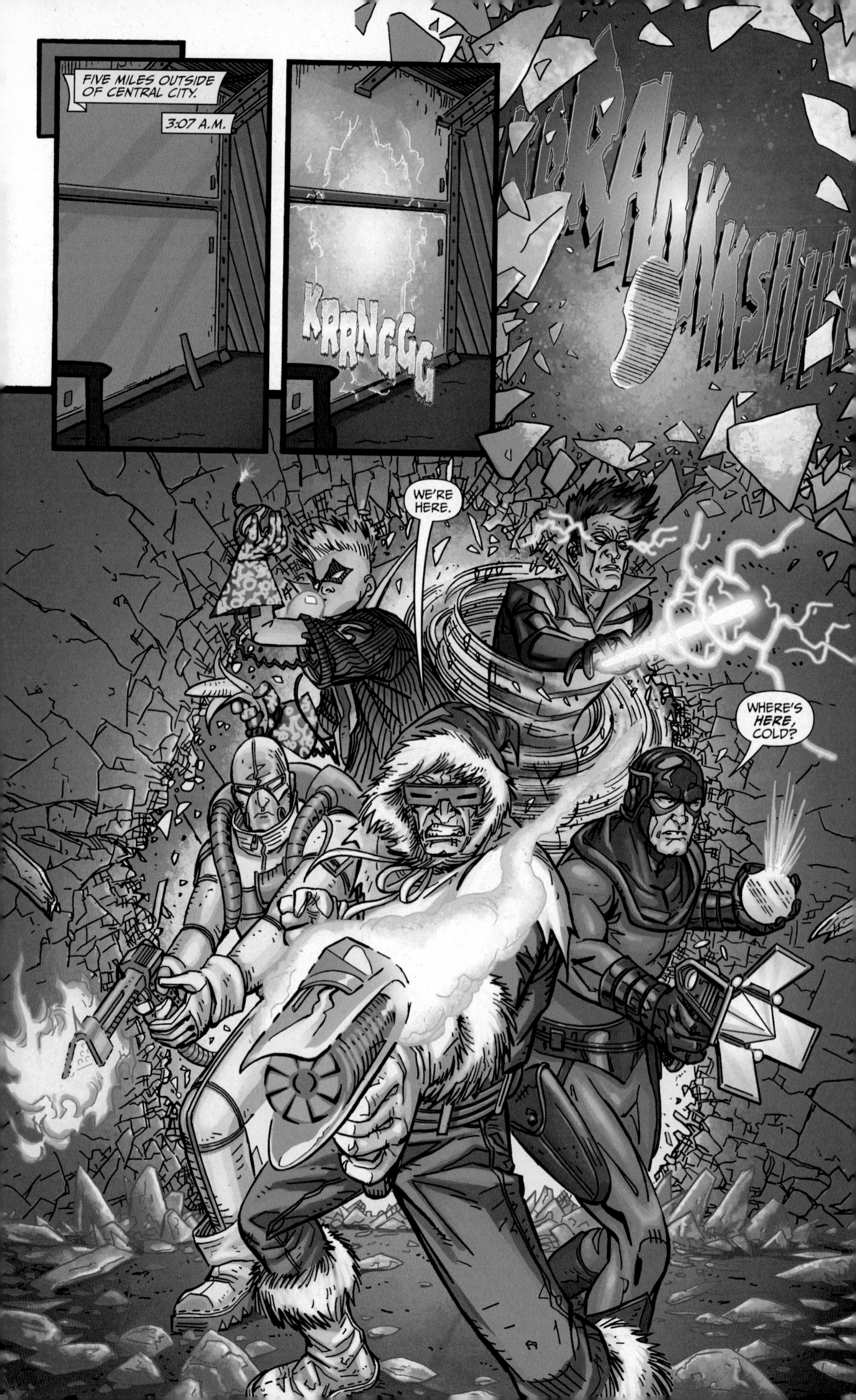
FIVE MILES OUTSIDE OF CENTRAL CITY.
3:07 A.M.
KRRNGGG
WE'RE HERE.
WHERE'S HERE, COLD?

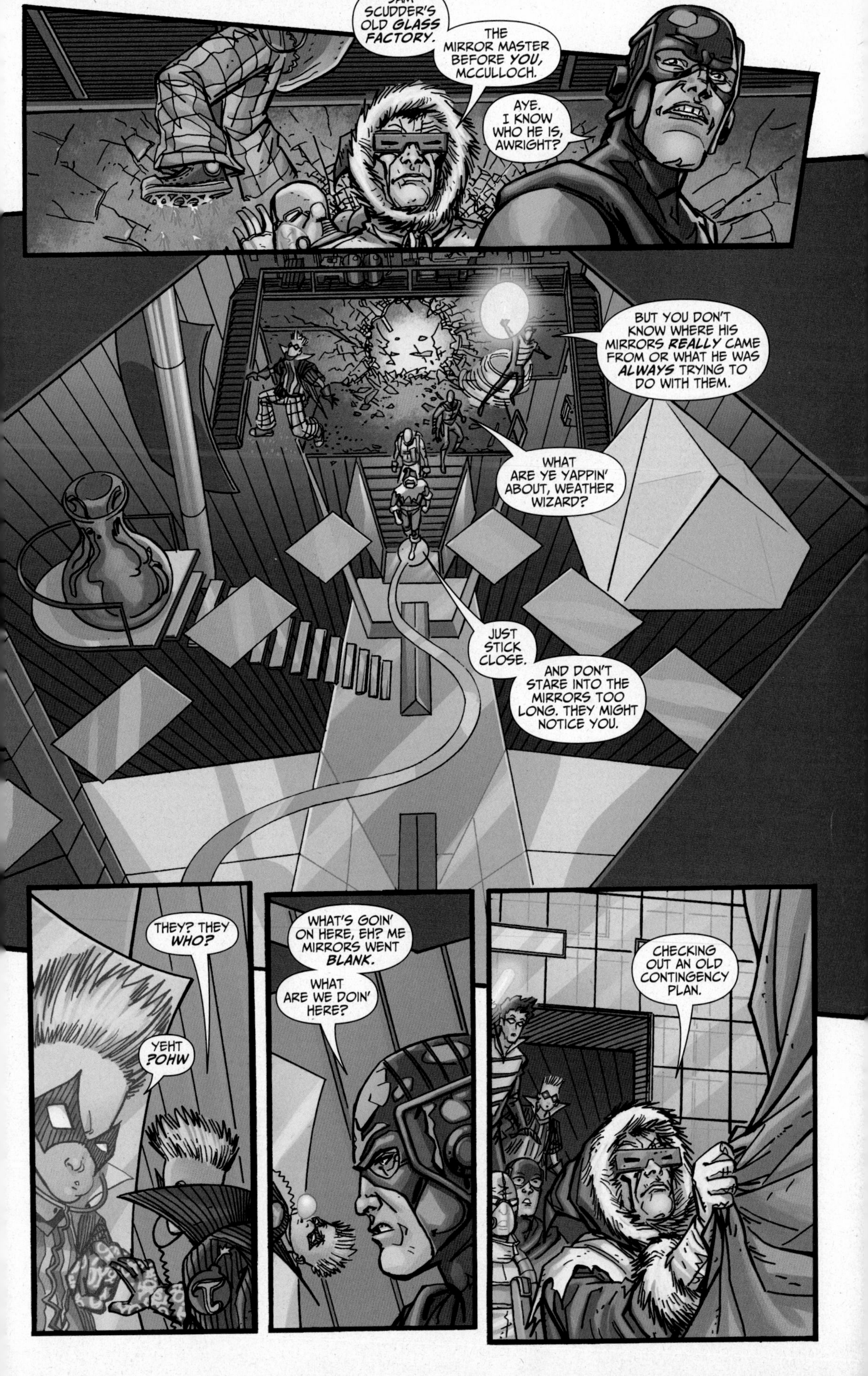
SAM SCUDDER'S OLD GLASS FACTORY.
THE MIRROR MASTER BEFORE YOU, MCCULLOCH.
AYE. I KNOW WHO HE IS, AWRIGHT?
BUT YOU DON'T KNOW WHERE HIS MIRRORS REALLY CAME FROM OR WHAT HE WAS ALWAYS TRYING TO DO WITH THEM.
WHAT ARE YE YAPPIN' ABOUT, WEATHER WIZARD?
JUST STICK CLOSE.
AND DON'T STARE INTO THE MIRRORS TOO LONG. THEY MIGHT NOTICE YOU.
THEY? THEY WHO?
YEHT ?OHW
WHAT'S GOIN' ON HERE, EH? ME MIRRORS WENT BLANK.
WHAT ARE WE DOIN' HERE?
CHECKING OUT AN OLD CONTINGENCY PLAN.

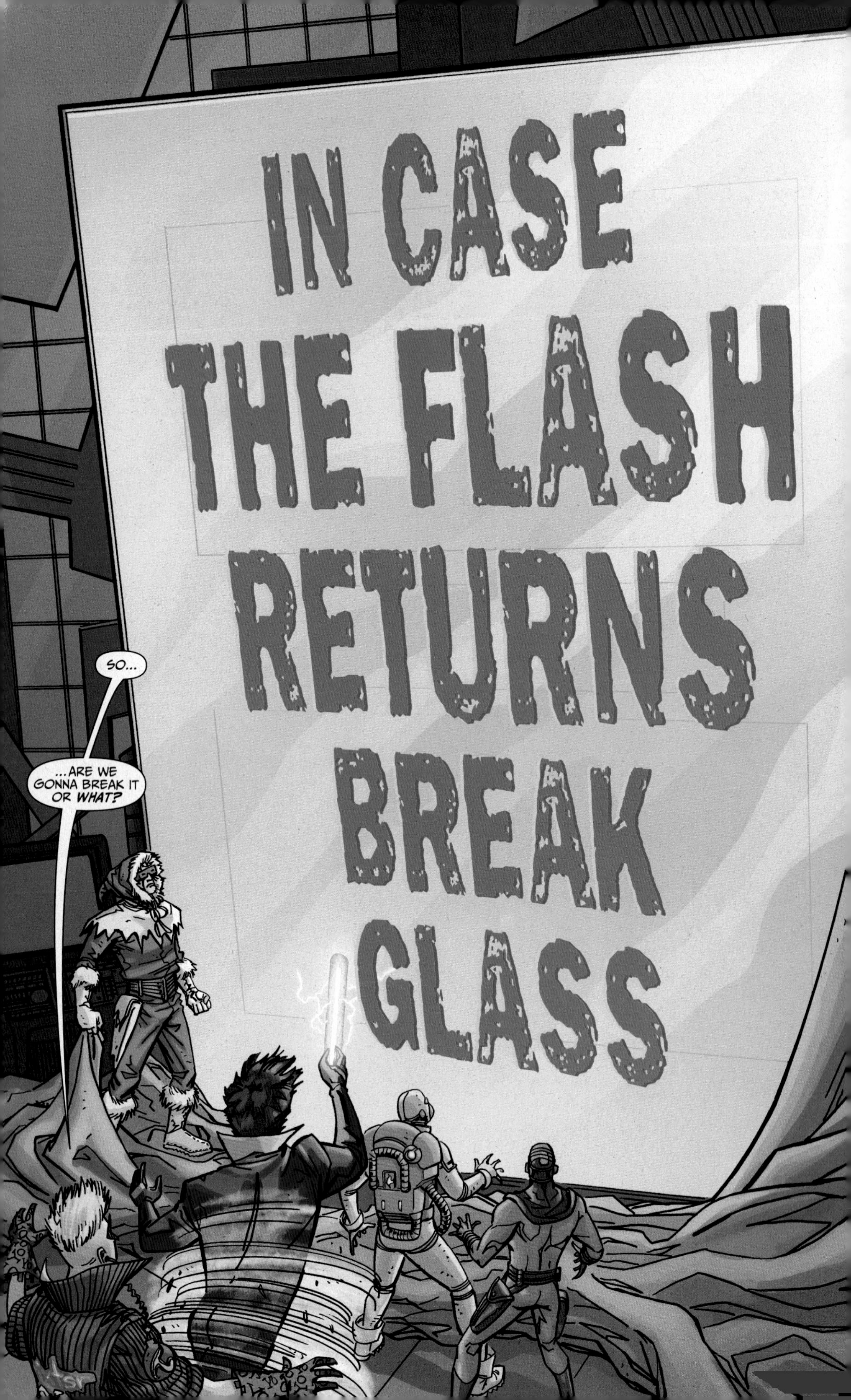
IN CASE THE FLASH RETURNS BREAK GLASS
SO...
...ARE WE GONNA BREAK IT OR WHAT?

INKS: PAUL NEARY

COLORS: ALEX SINCLAIR

EVEN THE FASTEST MAN ALIVE

WILL RUN OUT OF TIME.

NOW.

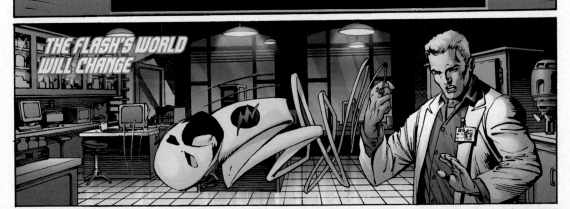

THE FLASH'S WORLD WILL CHANGE

AND THEIR WORLD WILL CHANGE WITH IT.

IF THERE IS TO BE ANYTHING LEFT OF THE PAST, PRESENT AND FUTURE

THEY MUST LEARN THE SECRET OF...

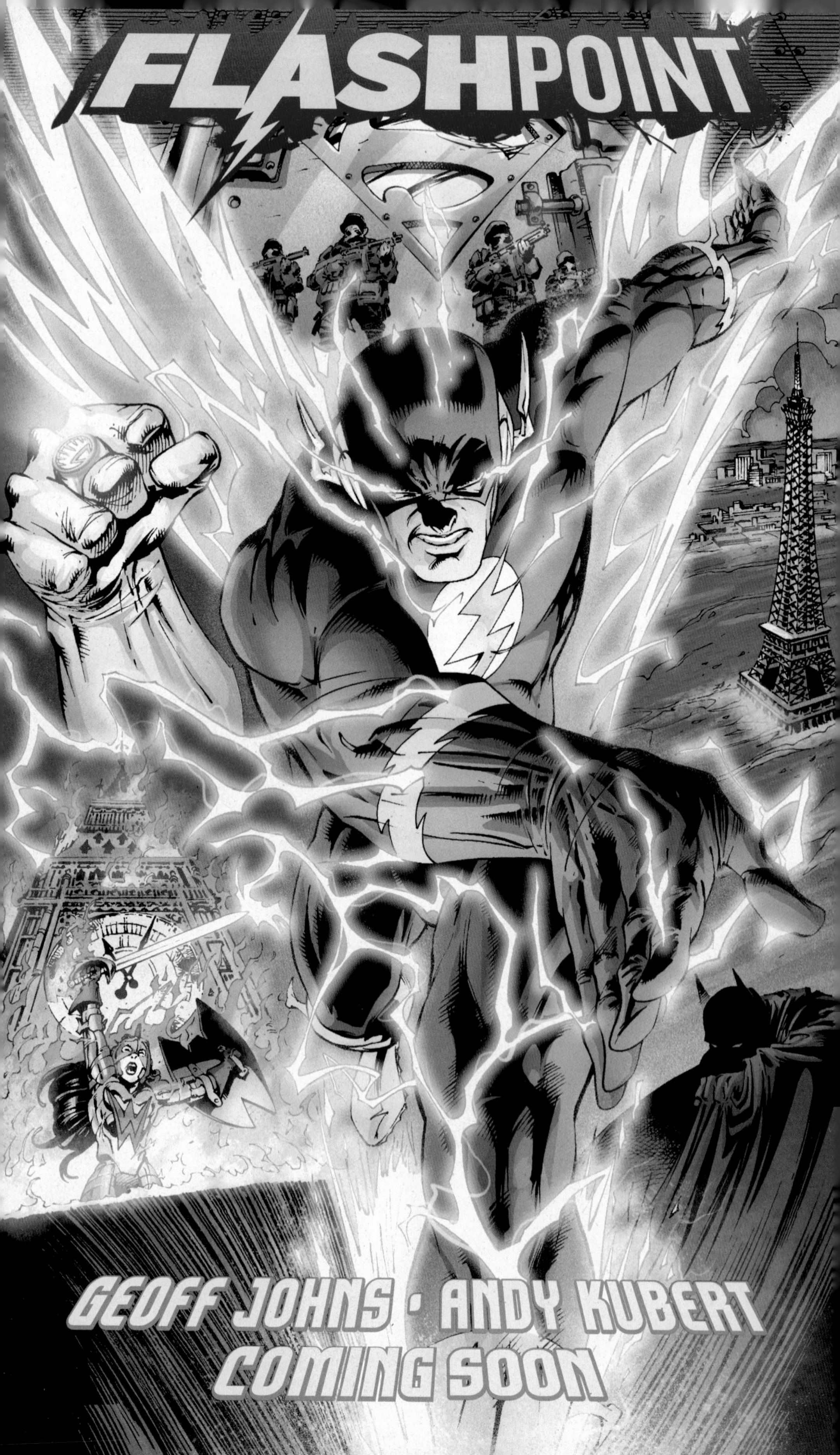
FLASHPOINT
GEOFF JOHNS · ANDY KUBERT
COMING SOON

FLASH FACTS: BOOMERANGS PART ONE!
HOW DOES A BOOMERANG WORK?

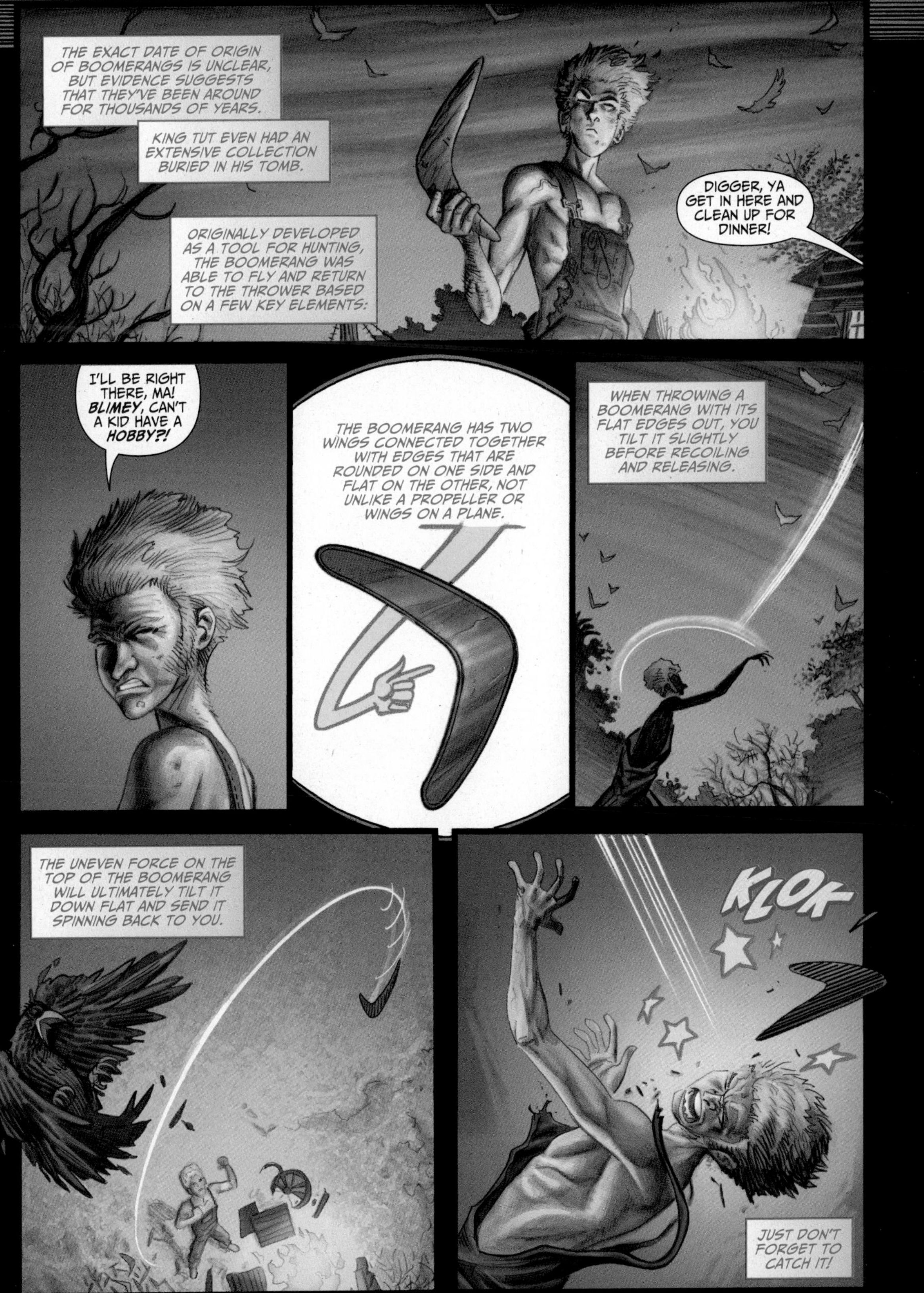
THE EXACT DATE OF ORIGIN OF BOOMERANGS IS UNCLEAR, BUT EVIDENCE SUGGESTS THAT THEY'VE BEEN AROUND FOR THOUSANDS OF YEARS.
KING TUT EVEN HAD AN EXTENSIVE COLLECTION BURIED IN HIS TOMB.
ORIGINALLY DEVELOPED AS A TOOL FOR HUNTING, THE BOOMERANG WAS ABLE TO FLY AND RETURN TO THE THROWER BASED ON A FEW KEY ELEMENTS:
DIGGER, YA GET IN HERE AND CLEAN UP FOR DINNER!
I'LL BE RIGHT THERE, MA! BLIMEY, CAN'T A KID HAVE A HOBBY?!
THE BOOMERANG HAS TWO WINGS CONNECTED TOGETHER WITH EDGES THAT ARE ROUNDED ON ONE SIDE AND FLAT ON THE OTHER, NOT UNLIKE A PROPELLER OR WINGS ON A PLANE.
WHEN THROWING A BOOMERANG WITH ITS FLAT EDGES OUT, YOU TILT IT SLIGHTLY BEFORE RECOILING AND RELEASING.
THE UNEVEN FORCE ON THE TOP OF THE BOOMERANG WILL ULTIMATELY TILT IT DOWN FLAT AND SEND IT SPINNING BACK TO YOU.
KLOK
JUST DON'T FORGET TO CATCH IT!

FLASH FACTS: BOOMERANGS PART TWO:
HOW DO CAPTAIN BOOMERANG'S BOOMERANGS WORK?

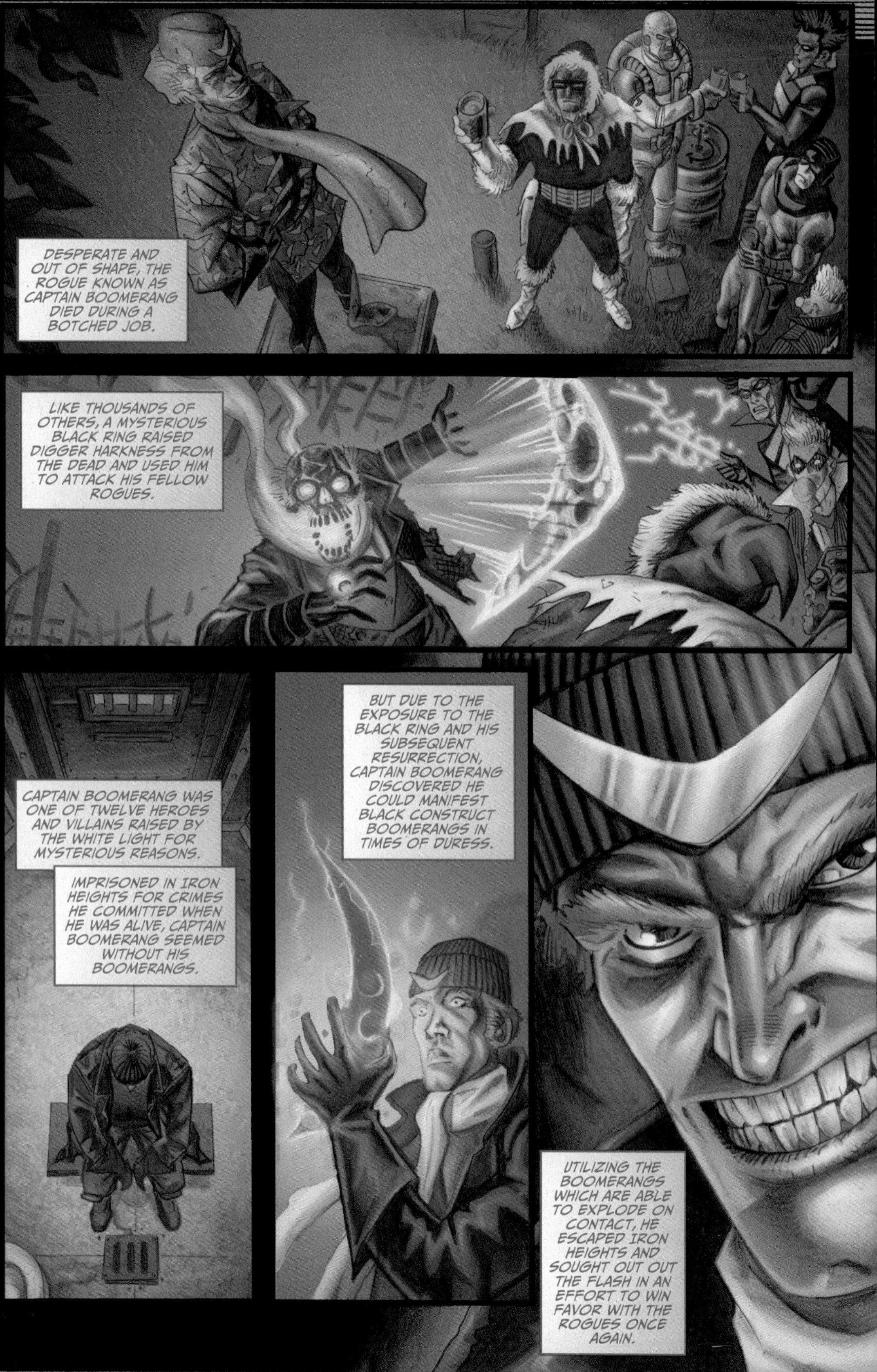
DESPERATE AND OUT OF SHAPE, THE ROGUE KNOWN AS CAPTAIN BOOMERANG DIED DURING A BOTCHED JOB.
LIKE THOUSANDS OF OTHERS, A MYSTERIOUS BLACK RING RAISED DIGGER HARKNESS FROM THE DEAD AND USED HIM TO ATTACK HIS FELLOW ROGUES.
CAPTAIN BOOMERANG WAS ONE OF TWELVE HEROES AND VILLAINS RAISED BY THE WHITE LIGHT FOR MYSTERIOUS REASONS.
IMPRISONED IN IRON HEIGHTS FOR CRIMES HE COMMITTED WHEN HE WAS ALIVE, CAPTAIN BOOMERANG SEEMED WITHOUT HIS BOOMERANGS.
BUT DUE TO THE EXPOSURE TO THE BLACK RING AND HIS SUBSEQUENT RESURRECTION, CAPTAIN BOOMERANG DISCOVERED HE COULD MANIFEST BLACK CONSTRUCT BOOMERANGS IN TIMES OF DURESS.
UTILIZING THE BOOMERANGS WHICH ARE ABLE TO EXPLODE ON CONTACT, HE ESCAPED IRON HEIGHTS AND SOUGHT OUT OUT THE FLASH IN AN EFFORT TO WIN FAVOR WITH THE ROGUES ONCE AGAIN.

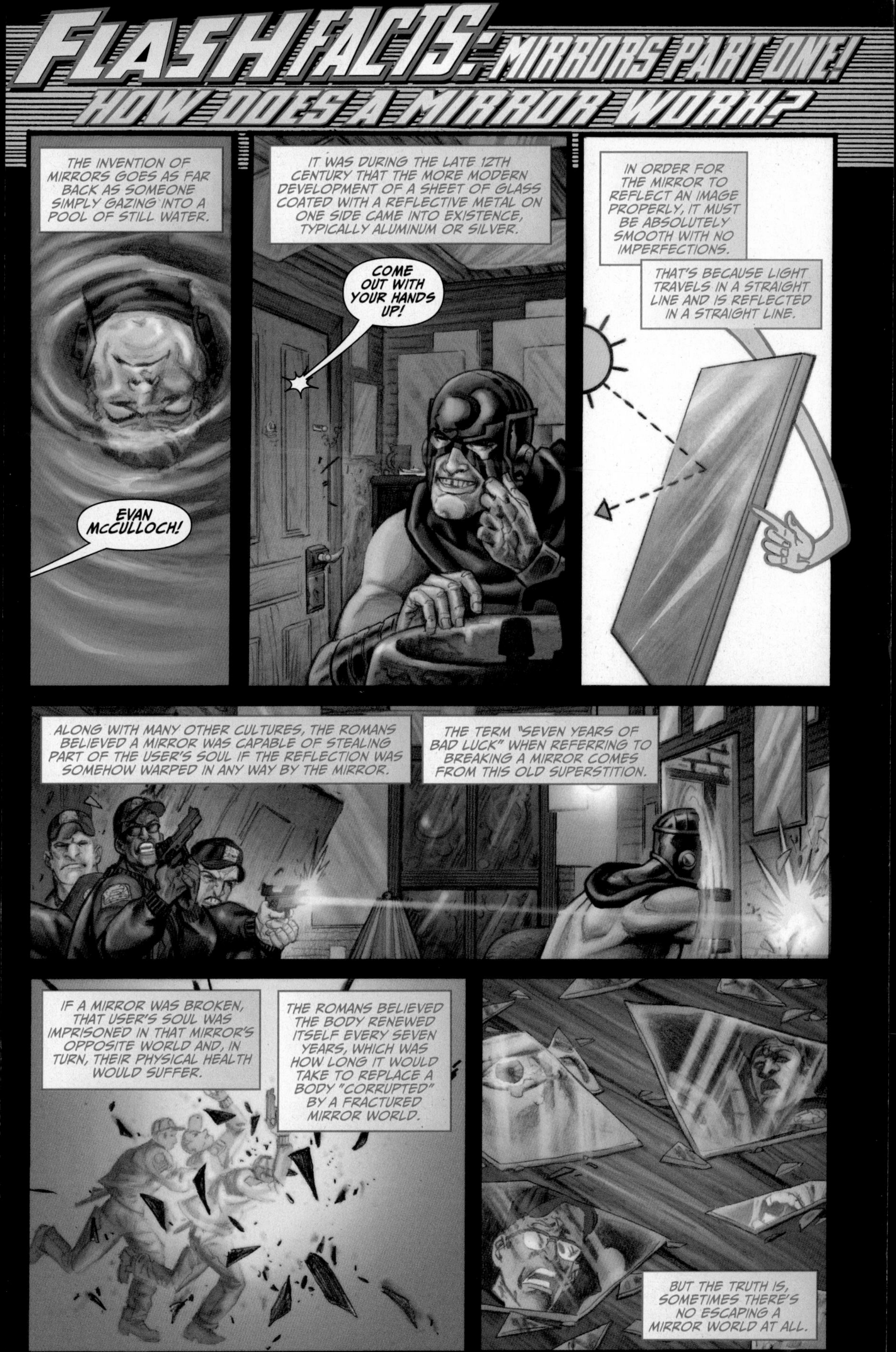
FLASH FACTS: MIRRORS PART ONE! HOW DOES A MIRROR WORK?
THE INVENTION OF MIRRORS GOES AS FAR BACK AS SOMEONE SIMPLY GAZING INTO A POOL OF STILL WATER.
EVAN McCULLOCH!
IT WAS DURING THE LATE 12TH CENTURY THAT THE MORE MODERN DEVELOPMENT OF A SHEET OF GLASS COATED WITH A REFLECTIVE METAL ON ONE SIDE CAME INTO EXISTENCE, TYPICALLY ALUMINUM OR SILVER.
COME OUT WITH YOUR HANDS UP!
IN ORDER FOR THE MIRROR TO REFLECT AN IMAGE PROPERLY, IT MUST BE ABSOLUTELY SMOOTH WITH NO IMPERFECTIONS.
THAT'S BECAUSE LIGHT TRAVELS IN A STRAIGHT LINE AND IS REFLECTED IN A STRAIGHT LINE.
ALONG WITH MANY OTHER CULTURES, THE ROMANS BELIEVED A MIRROR WAS CAPABLE OF STEALING PART OF THE USER'S SOUL IF THE REFLECTION WAS SOMEHOW WARPED IN ANY WAY BY THE MIRROR.
THE TERM "SEVEN YEARS OF BAD LUCK" WHEN REFERRING TO BREAKING A MIRROR COMES FROM THIS OLD SUPERSTITION.
IF A MIRROR WAS BROKEN, THAT USER'S SOUL WAS IMPRISONED IN THAT MIRROR'S OPPOSITE WORLD AND, IN TURN, THEIR PHYSICAL HEALTH WOULD SUFFER.
THE ROMANS BELIEVED THE BODY RENEWED ITSELF EVERY SEVEN YEARS, WHICH WAS HOW LONG IT WOULD TAKE TO REPLACE A BODY "CORRUPTED" BY A FRACTURED MIRROR WORLD.
BUT THE TRUTH IS, SOMETIMES THERE'S NO ESCAPING A MIRROR WORLD AT ALL.

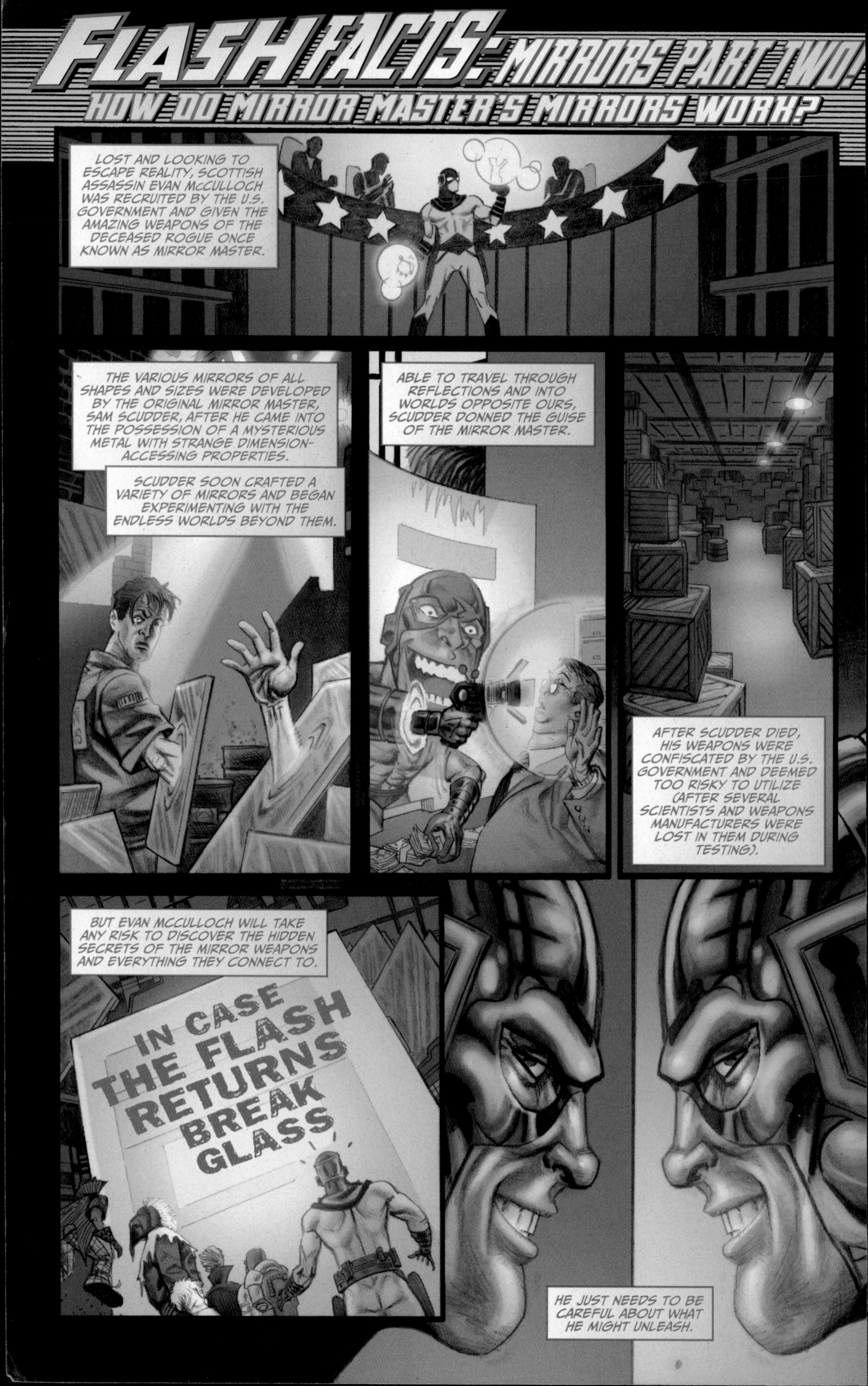

FLASH FACTS: MIRRORS PART TWO!
HOW DO MIRROR MASTER'S MIRRORS WORK?
LOST AND LOOKING TO ESCAPE REALITY, SCOTTISH ASSASSIN EVAN McCULLOCH WAS RECRUITED BY THE U.S. GOVERNMENT AND GIVEN THE AMAZING WEAPONS OF THE DECEASED ROGUE ONCE KNOWN AS MIRROR MASTER.
THE VARIOUS MIRRORS OF ALL SHAPES AND SIZES WERE DEVELOPED BY THE ORIGINAL MIRROR MASTER, SAM SCUDDER, AFTER HE CAME INTO THE POSSESSION OF A MYSTERIOUS METAL WITH STRANGE DIMENSION-ACCESSING PROPERTIES.
SCUDDER SOON CRAFTED A VARIETY OF MIRRORS AND BEGAN EXPERIMENTING WITH THE ENDLESS WORLDS BEYOND THEM.
ABLE TO TRAVEL THROUGH REFLECTIONS AND INTO WORLDS OPPOSITE OURS, SCUDDER DONNED THE GUISE OF THE MIRROR MASTER.
AFTER SCUDDER DIED, HIS WEAPONS WERE CONFISCATED BY THE U.S. GOVERNMENT AND DEEMED TOO RISKY TO UTILIZE (AFTER SEVERAL SCIENTISTS AND WEAPONS MANUFACTURERS WERE LOST IN THEM DURING TESTING).
BUT EVAN McCULLOCH WILL TAKE ANY RISK TO DISCOVER THE HIDDEN SECRETS OF THE MIRROR WEAPONS AND EVERYTHING THEY CONNECT TO.
IN CASE THE FLASH RETURNS BREAK GLASS
HE JUST NEEDS TO BE CAREFUL ABOUT WHAT HE MIGHT UNLEASH.

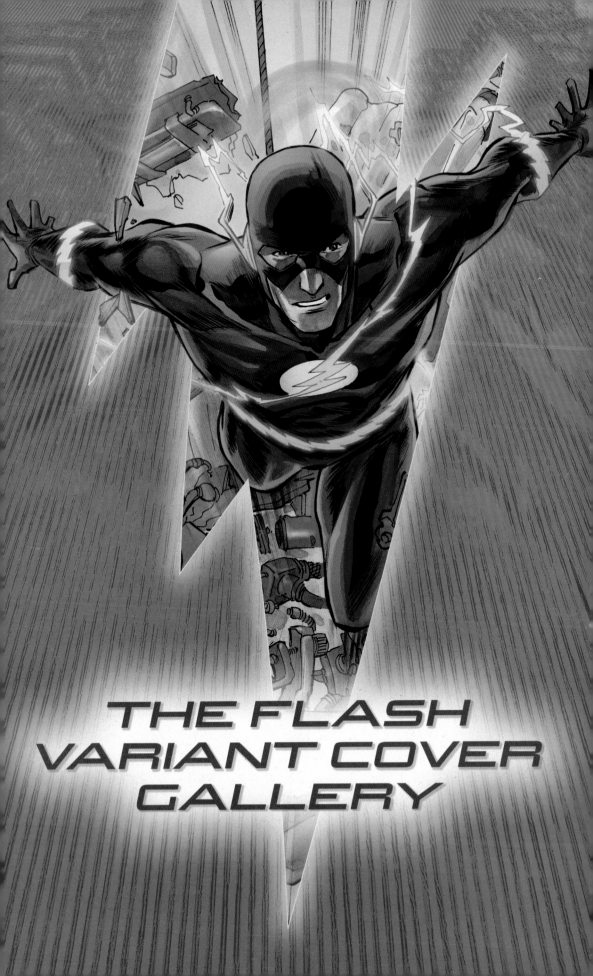

THE FLASH
VARIANT COVER
GALLERY

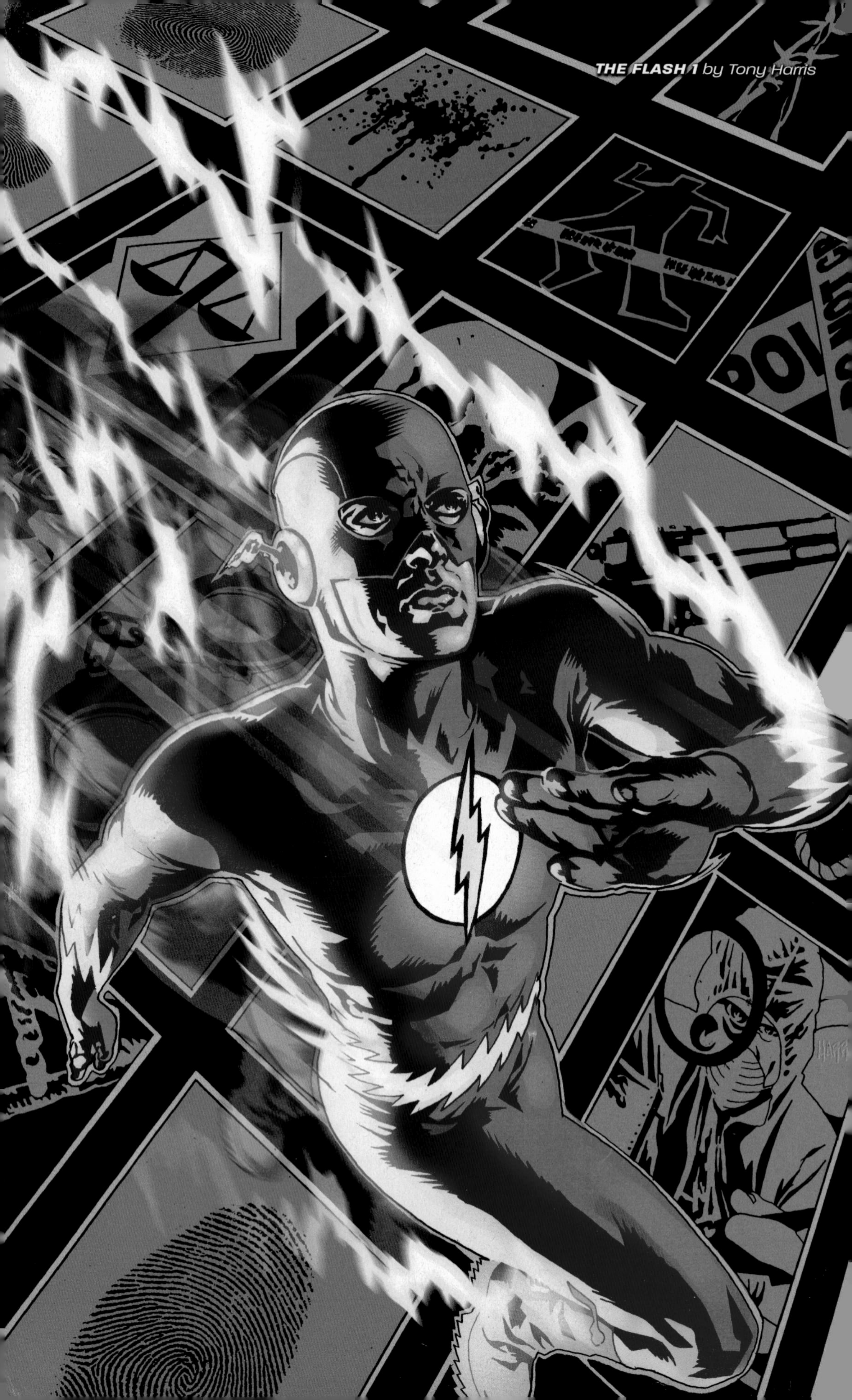

THE FLASH 1 by Tony Harris

THE FLASH 2 by Ryan Sook

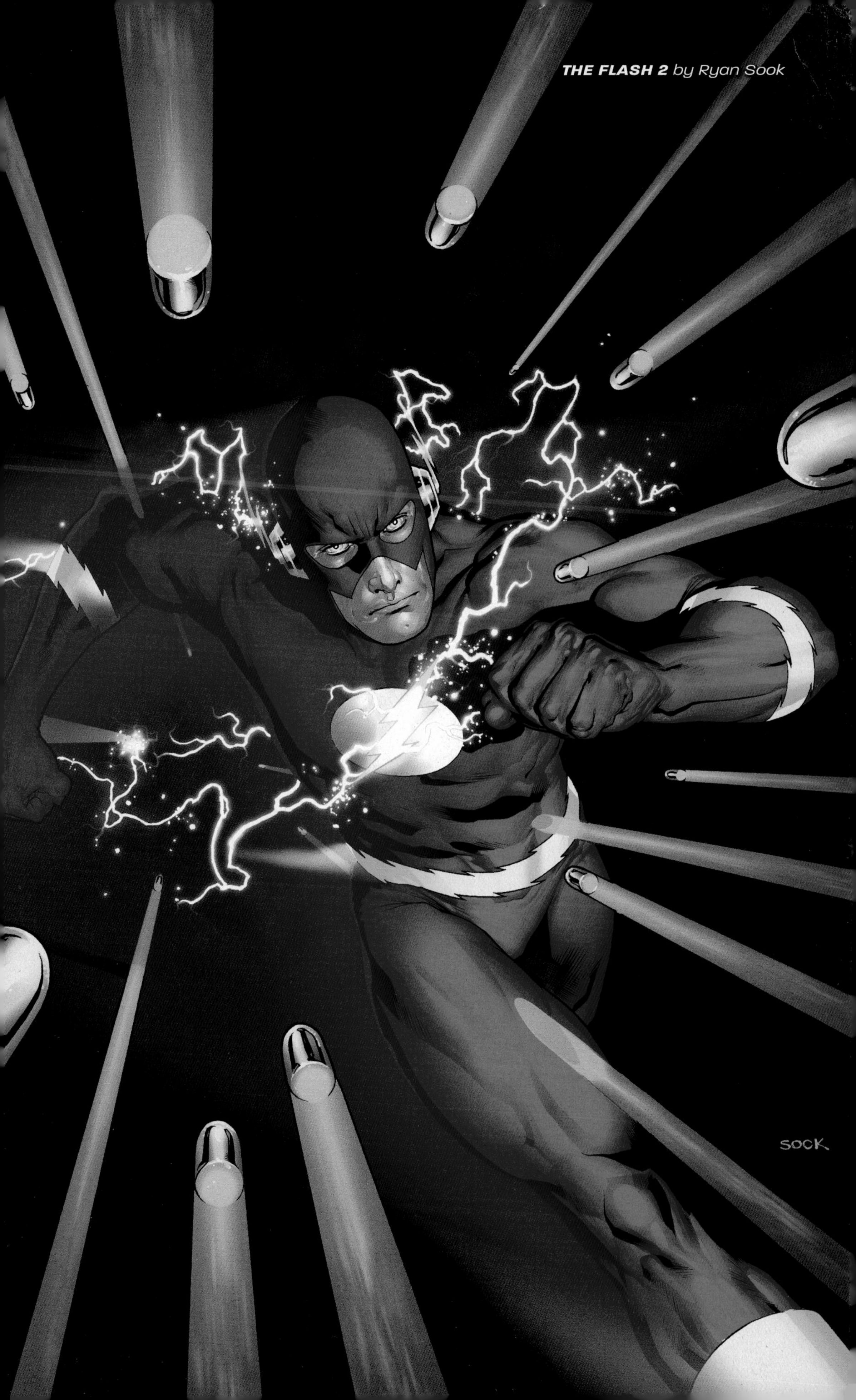
SOOK

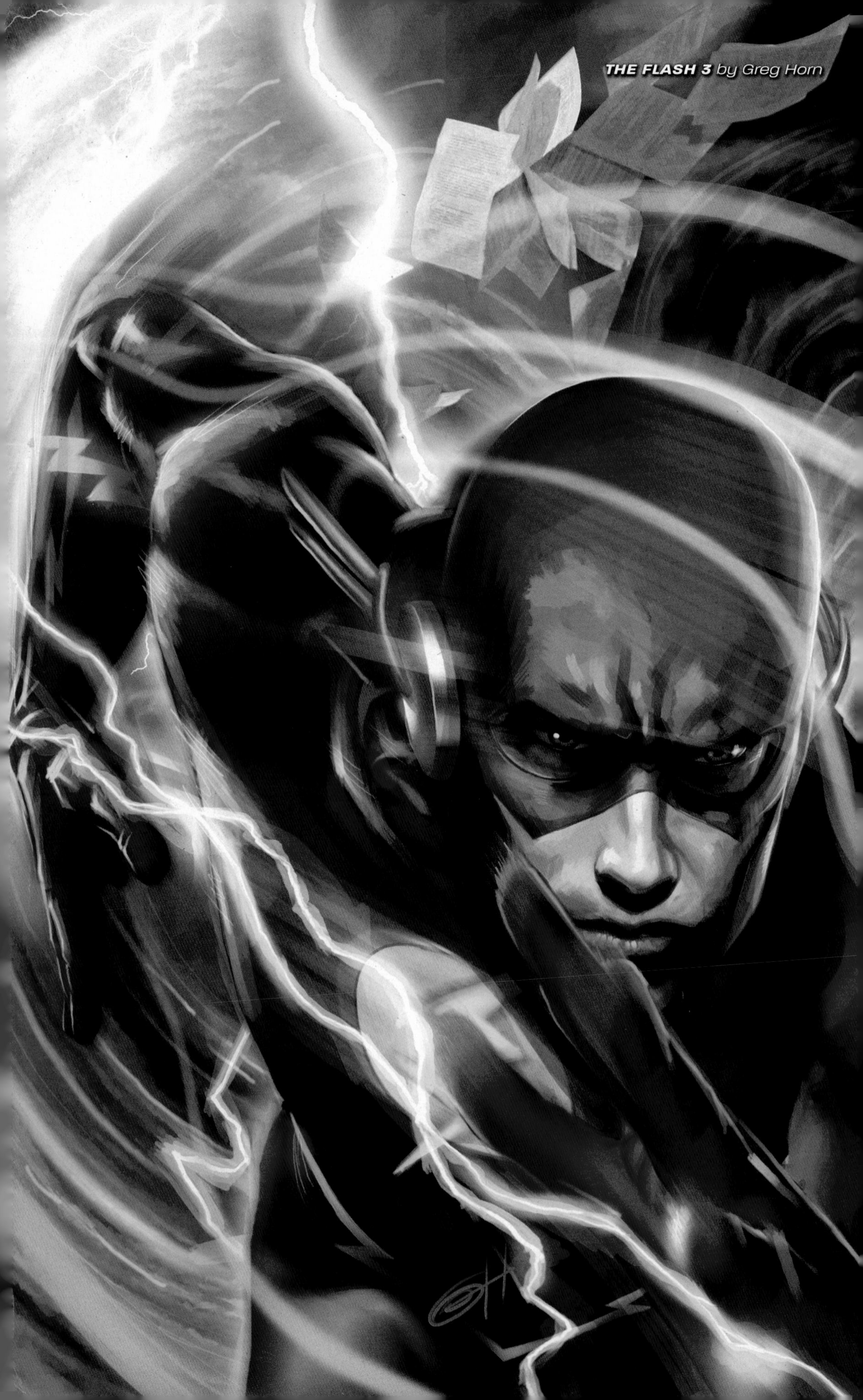

THE FLASH 3 by Greg Horn

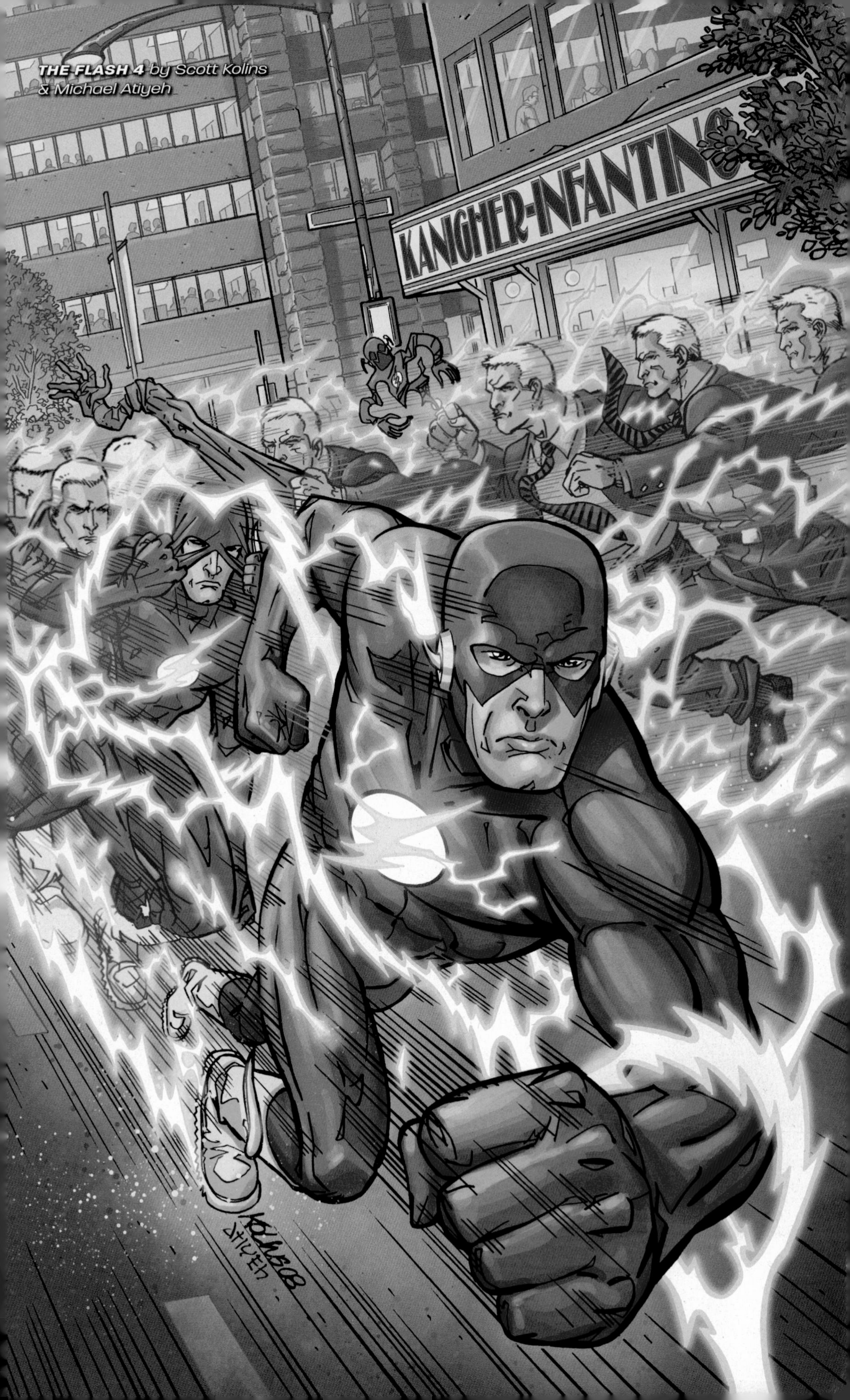
THE FLASH 4 by Scott Kolins
& Michael Atiyeh
KANIGHER-INFANTINO

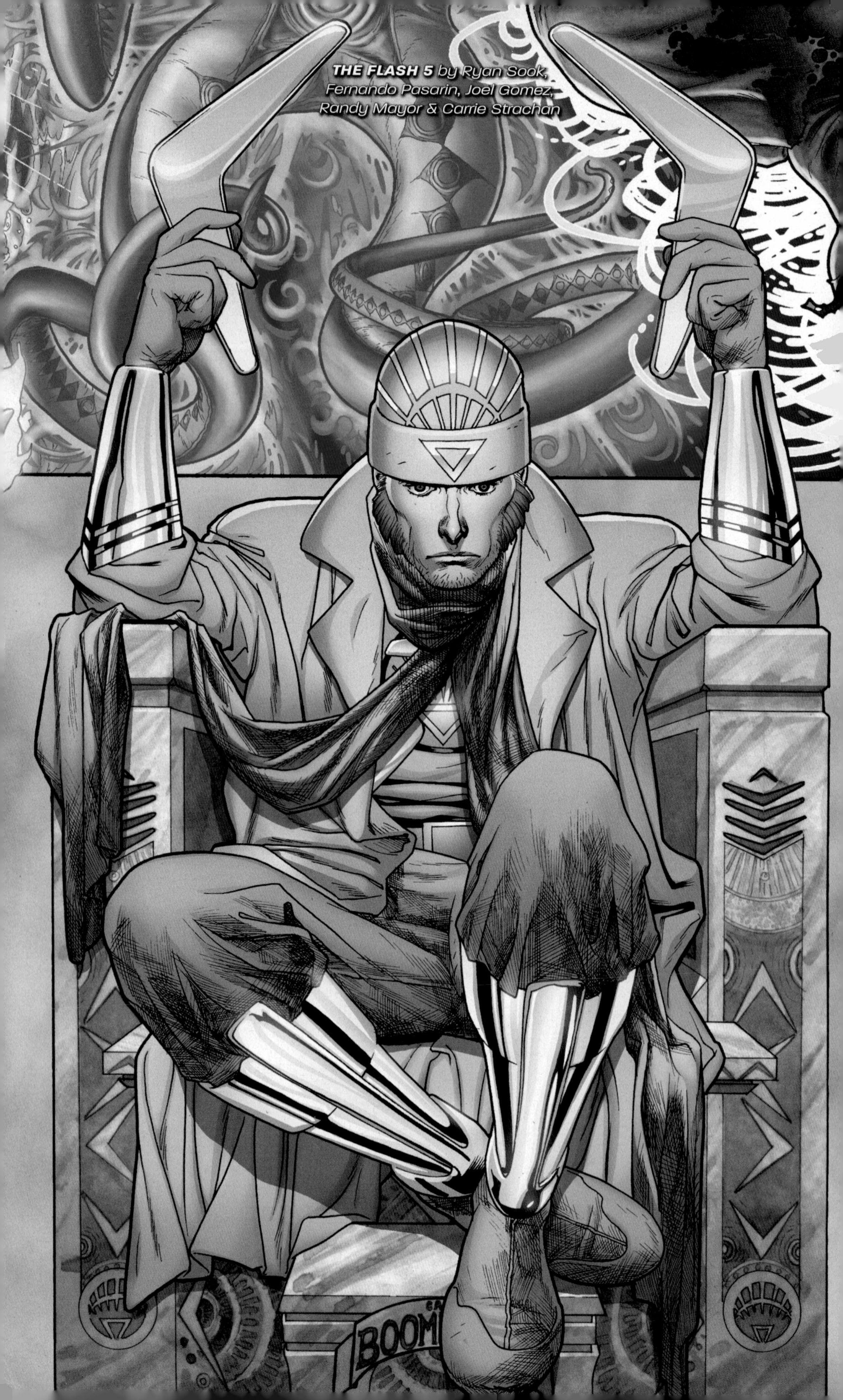
BOOM

THE FLASH 5 by Ryan Sook, Fernando Pasarin, Joel Gomez, Randy Mayor & Carrie Strachan

***THE FLASH 6** by Alē Garza,*
Sandra Hope & Alex Sinclair

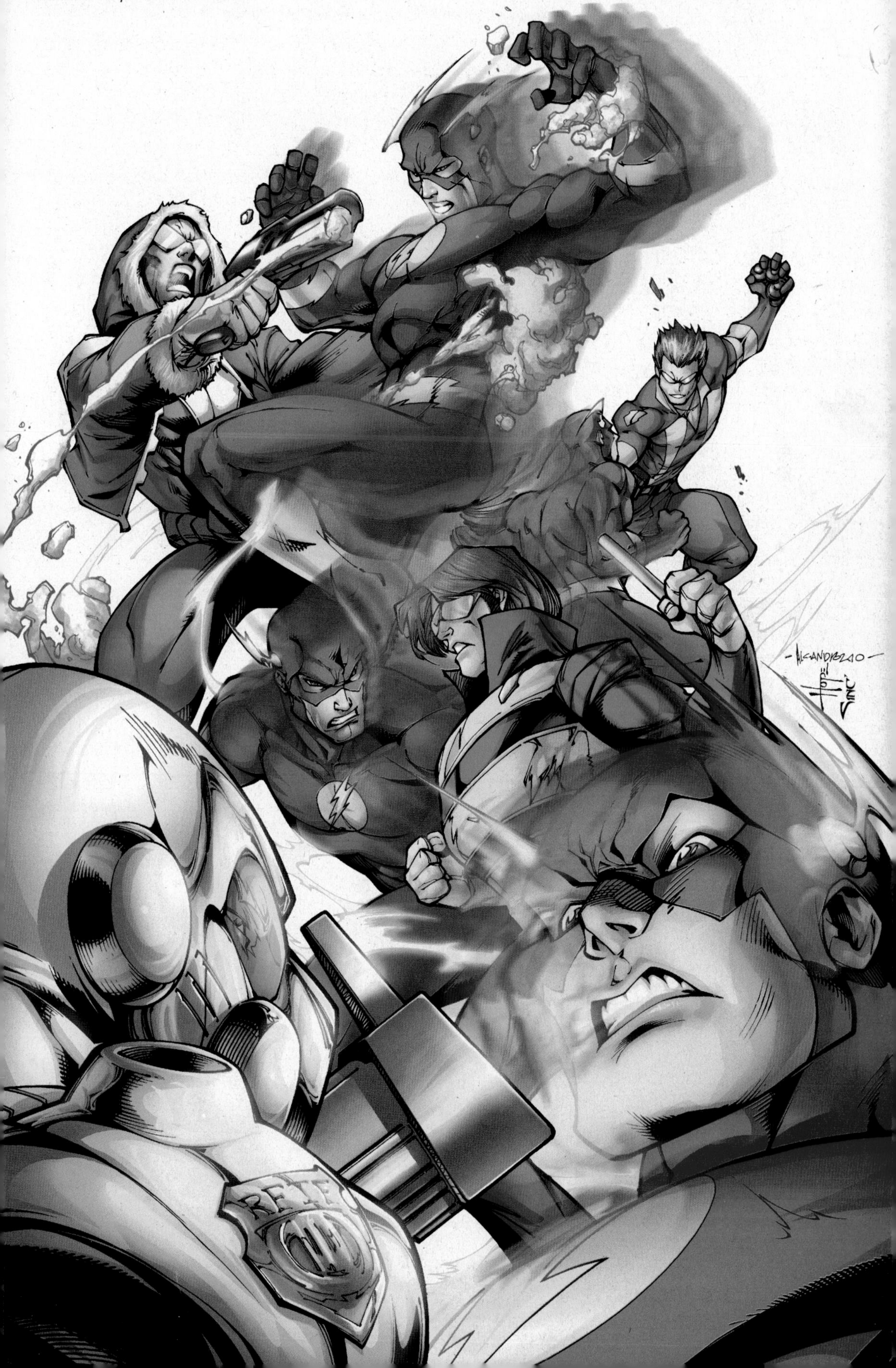

THE FLASH 7 by Darwyn Cooke

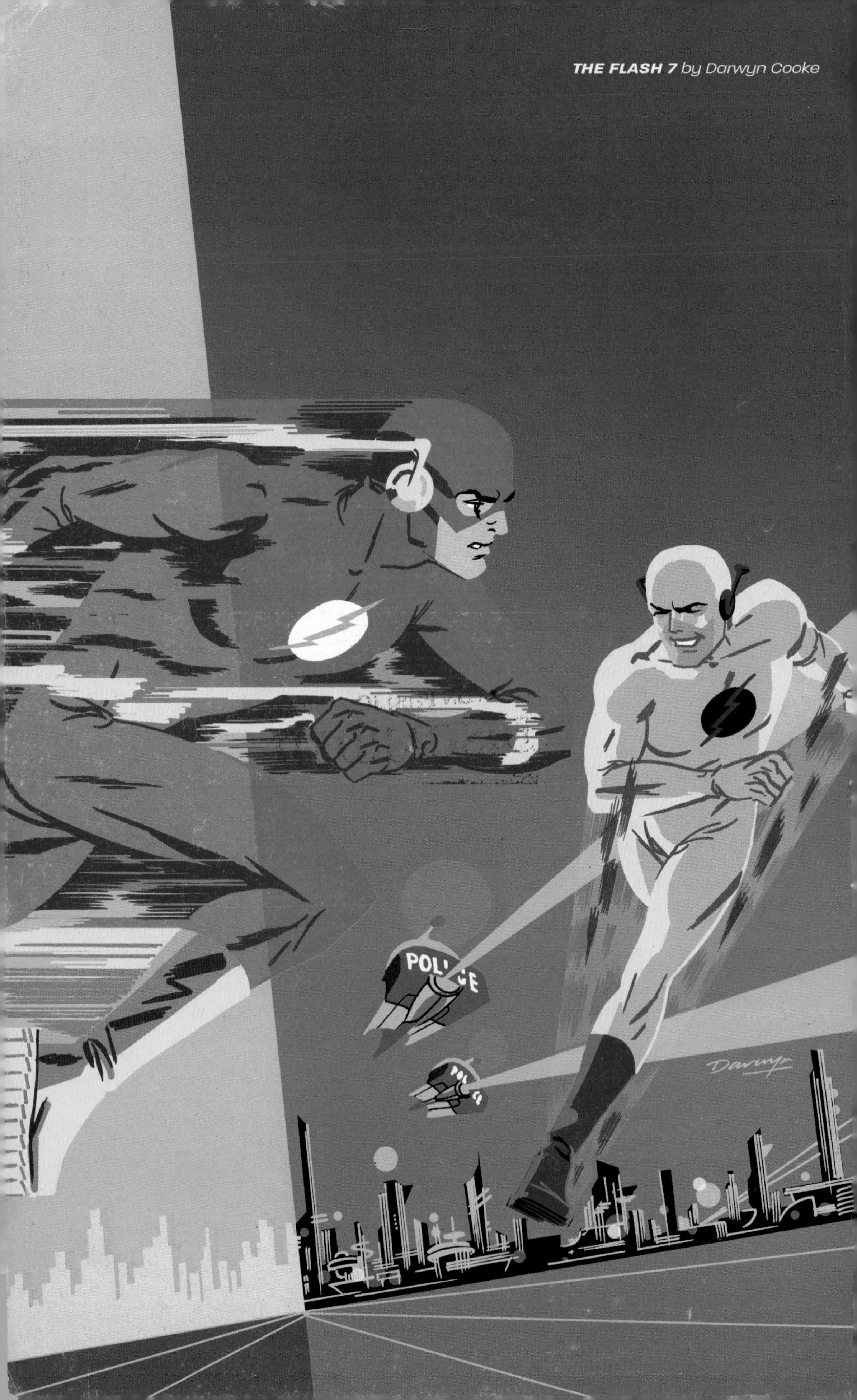

POLICE
Darwyn